SECURITY WITHOUT NUCLEAR DETERRENCE

ALSO BY
COMMANDER ROBERT GREEN,
ROYAL NAVY (Ret'd)

The Naked Nuclear Emperor:
Debunking Nuclear Deterrence

Fast Track to Zero Nuclear Weapons

A Thorn in Their Side:
The Hilda Murrell Murder

SECURITY WITHOUT NUCLEAR DETERRENCE

COMMANDER ROBERT GREEN,
ROYAL NAVY (Ret'd)

FOREWORD BY
VICE ADMIRAL SIR JEREMY BLACKHAM KCB MA

SPOKESMAN
NOTTINGHAM

DEDICATION

For Oscar, Nellie, Maia, and Louis, that they will witness and rejoice in a nuclear weapon-free world.

Published in 2018 by
Spokesman
Russell House, Bulwell Lane,
Nottingham, NG6 0BT, United Kingdom.
www.spokesmanbooks.com
with support of the Atlantic Peace Foundation

First published in 2010 by
Astron Media and
Disarmament & Security Centre
Christchurch, New Zealand

Copyright © Robert D. Green, © Jeremy Blackham, Foreword

All rights reserved. Except for brief quotations in a review, this book, or any part thereof, may not be reproduced, stored in or introduced into a retrieval system, or transmitted, in any form or by any means, electronic, mechanical, photocopying, recording or otherwise, without the prior written permission of the publisher.

ISBN 9780 85214 8721

A cataloguing-in-publication (CIP) record is available from the British Library.

CONTENTS

Author's Note   9
Foreword by Vice Admiral Sir Jeremy
          Blackham KCB MA   13

Chapter One: Why I Rejected Nuclear Deterrence   27

Chapter Two: A Brief History   37
From Monopoly to Massive Retaliation   37
The British Debate   38
UK Dependence on the US   40
UK Pay-back   43
The US: From Massive Retaliation to Controlled Response   47
From Controlled Response to MAD   49
Counter-value versus Counter-Force   51
First Use   51
Post-Cold War US Nuclear War Plan Changes   52
US Nuclear Posture Review 1993-97   53
NATO's Post-Cold War Nuclear Posture   54
US Doubts about Nuclear Deterrence   58
The 2002 US Nuclear Posture Review   60
Implications for US Nuclear Deterrence Doctrine   62
The Bush Doctrine of Pre-emption   63

Pentagon Confirms Plan for Pre-emptive Use of Nuclear Weapons	65
France's *Force de Frappe*	69
The Anglo-French *Entente Nucléaire*	72
Has Reality Begun to Prevail over Vested Interest?	74
The Impact of Presidents Obama and Trump	75
Summary	77

Chapter Three: Nuclear Deterrence in the Real World	**85**
The Cuban Missile Crisis	85
A Question of Credibility	87
Nuclear Deterrence and the Absence of War Between the Major Powers	89
The 1986 Reykjavik Summit	92
The Experience of India and Pakistan	95
Self-Deterrence	97
'Sub-Strategic' Nuclear Deterrence	98
Extended Nuclear Deterrence	101
Escalation is Inevitable	101
Nuclear Deterrence against Chemical and Biological Weapon Attacks	102
Nuclear Deterrence is a Two-Way Street	104
Was Iraq Deterred in the First Gulf War?	106
Terrorists are Undeterrable with Nuclear Weapons	107
Nuclear Deterrence Undermines Security	108
Nuclear Deterrence Creates Instability	109
Nuclear Deterrence Provokes Proliferation	111
Nuclear Deterrence Threatens Democracy	111
Launch on Warning	112
Summary	115

Chapter Four: Nuclear Deterrence and Proliferation: Israel, India and Pakistan	**121**
Israel and the 'Samson Option'	122
India and Pakistan	133
Summary	161

Chapter Five: Morality and Legality	**175**
The Nub of the Moral Argument	178
Nuclear Deterrence and the 'Just War' Doctrine	179
Nuclear Weapons and Slavery	183
Stigmatising Nuclear Weapons	183
Legal Challenges to Nuclear Deterrence	184
The 1996 World Court Advisory Opinion	186

NATO's Nuclear Trio Respond	190
US Military Legal Assessments	192
UK Trident, Nuremburg and Prime Minister Blair	193
Sir Michael Quinlan's Critique of the ICJ Opinion	195
Trident Ploughshares v Scottish High Court	198
Errors in the Scottish High Court's Findings	200
A Treaty on the Prohibition of Nuclear Weapons	202
Legal Impact of Trump's Interventions on North Korea	203
Summary	203

Chapter Six: Safer Security Strategies — 209

Incentives to Find Alternatives	210
Shifting the Mindset	214
Terrorists and Nuclear Blackmail	217
Security Does Not Need Nuclear Deterrence	218
Strengthening Self-Deterrence	219
Stand Down Nuclear Forces from High Alert	219
Start Negotiating a Nuclear Weapons Convention	221
Promote Nuclear Weapon Free Zones	225
De-Couple Nuclear Weapons from Permanent UN Security Council Membership	228
From Nuclear Deterrence to Non-Provocative Defence	229
A Non-Nuclear Strategy for NATO	230
Safeguards Against Cheating	233
Securing a Durable Nuclear Weapon Free World	234
Summary	238

Chapter Seven: Conclusions — 243

Glossary	251
Selected Bibliography	262
Index	265
About the Foreword's Author	271
About the Author	272

AUTHOR'S NOTE AND ACKNOWLEDGEMENTS

Eight years on from first publishing this book, I have updated it, and corrected a few errors.

Sadly but unsurprisingly, President Obama found the US military-industrial complex's vested interest in sustaining its vast nuclear arsenal too powerfully embedded to restrain. In his famous 2009 Prague speech, Obama's correct assessment that a nuclear weapon-free world would be more secure was undermined when he then declared that, nevertheless, 'as long as these weapons exist, we will maintain a safe, secure and effective arsenal to deter any adversary, and guarantee that defense to our allies...'. This showed that he dared not challenge the enduring, unquestioned (but unprovable) consensus among the five recognised nuclear weapon states and their allies that nuclear deterrence has prevented major war among them, and provides an indispensable 'insurance policy' as the ultimate guarantor of national security in an unpredictable world.

This dogma, with its contradictions and fallacies, is now under fresh challenge. A new, determined citizen-driven initiative to apply a humanitarian approach to nuclear disarmament, the International Campaign to Abolish Nuclear Weapons, bore fruit on 7 July 2017 when 122 member states of the UN General Assembly adopted a Treaty on the Prohibition of Nuclear Weapons. This was the culmination of a fast-track process, successfully trialled by the World Court Project resulting in the 1996 Advisory Opinion of the International Court of Justice on the threat or use of nuclear weapons, and adapted by the campaigns for treaties banning anti-personnel landmines (1997) and cluster munitions (2008). Though boycotted by the nuclear weapon states and almost all their allies, this has strengthened the stigmatization of nuclear deterrence and provided a new tool to mobilise public awareness and opposition to the current modernization of nuclear arsenals.

These developments will inevitably impact upon Britain's 'main gate' decision on 18 July 2016 to renew its Trident nuclear-armed ballistic missile submarine force, with its huge implications for the future effectiveness, image and ethos of the Royal Navy. It is especially appropriate, therefore, that Vice Admiral Sir Jeremy Blackham courageously agreed to contribute a major new Foreword. I am deeply indebted to him, as one of the leading British authorities on the thorny theology of deterrence, for giving me his moral and intellectual support on this, the most sensitive and contentious issue for British defence policy.

My gratitude also goes to Tony Simpson, co-director of the Bertrand Russell Peace Foundation and editor of its publishing arm Spokesman Books, for offering to produce this updated edition. Ironically, he became convinced of the need for this by the sudden revival of global awareness of the nuclear threat following US President Donald Trump's alarmingly simplistic and belligerent exchanges with North Korea's leader Kim Jong-un.

During over 25 years of opposing nuclear deterrence, I have felt supremely vindicated by General Lee Butler US Air Force (Ret). In 2016, I helped proof-read his memoirs, *Uncommon Cause*, Volume II of which chronicles his transformation from top US nuclear warrior to uniquely authoritative advocate for a nuclear weapon-free world. In his final appointment from 1992-94 as Commander in Chief Strategic Command running the entire US strategic nuclear war machine, Butler was horrified to discover the incoherent madness of nuclear deterrence thinking. After retirement, he made a prodigious personal effort to bring some wisdom to the nuclear weapon debate; but he could not prevail against years of pro-nuclear hubris, indoctrination and outmoded thinking.

Permission to reproduce photographs, a cartoon and other graphics has been generously given by the late Murray Ball, Martin Dunkerton, Thomas Green, Gil Hanly, Robert S. Norris, and Robert Del Tredici.

Finally, this book would not have happened without advice and encouragement from Robin Collins, Dr Rebecca Johnson, David Krieger, the late Commander Michael MccGwire RN (Ret'd), Randy Rydell, Alyn Ware, and my wife Dr Kate Dewes. With the death in 2016 of Cdr MccGwire at the age of 91, I wish to pay special tribute to his penetrating insight into the realities of nuclear deterrence, and for his invaluable support. As this new edition constitutes a specifically ex-Royal Navy contribution to the debate, I feel it is fitting to end with these closing words from his unrivalled rebuttal in 1994 of the late Sir Michael Quinlan's justifications for sustaining Western nuclear arsenals:

AUTHOR'S NOTE

...[W]hat is unique about this particular threat to human survival is that we have ready to hand the certain means of avoiding it, if we can only change our habits of mind. Britain should, therefore, relinquish its self-appointed role of intellectual and policy bag-carrier for the American nuclear weapons establishment, and focus on how that change can be brought about.[1]

Almost a quarter of a century on, far from losing its force this advice has gained in urgency.

Robert Green
Christchurch, New Zealand
March 2018

Note

[1] Michael MccGwire, 'Is there a future for nuclear weapons?', *International Affairs*, Volume 70, Issue 2, 1 April 1994, pp211-228, https://doi.org/10.2307/2625231.

FOREWORD

by
Vice Admiral Sir Jeremy Blackham KCB MA

Humanity faces three largely man-made existential challenges. The first is over-population, with its consequent excessive demand on natural resources, especially on food and water supplies, and its huge increase in energy consumption and pollution which is in the long term life-threatening, and is arguably the underlying cause of the other two. The second is climate change, whether man-made or cyclical (or even both), with its probable consequences of massive migration, destruction of habitat and fauna, famine and disease. These two are already under way; but the third, the threat of nuclear war, is almost certainly the most devastating in the short term, the most directly susceptible to human agency, and the most immediately destructive of human and other life on a global scale. The massive scale and duration of death and destruction caused by the relatively small yield weapons detonated over Japan in 1945 show just how catastrophic a modern nuclear exchange would be.

There can be no greater priority or urgency for political leaders and governments today than the prevention of nuclear war and the removal of the threat of it altogether. Faced with these challenges, and perhaps even because of them, we also find ourselves at one of history's 'hinge points'. The Western liberal consensus is fragmenting, and governance is breaking down in many areas of the world whilst global power, wealth and influence are shifting markedly. It is an environment of greater instability than for some time, with many violent but non-state groups, spurred on by extreme ideologies, also on the stage. Our political leaders and populations often seem either to be in denial of, or unsurprisingly paralysed by, the scale of the problems and seek refuge in dealing with rather more trivial and selfish issues.

Of course, there are few dissenters – although there are some important ones – from the proposition that the avoidance of nuclear war is the principal immediate task of international leaders. One is tempted to think that those dissenters cannot have thought very clearly about the probable consequences of such a war, fought with weapons very much more destructive than the Hiroshima bomb. There is, however, much less agreement as to how its prevention is best achieved and whether it must be avoided 'at all costs' – whatever that means, or whether it could be justified in some circumstances. On the whole, and perhaps rather simplistically, there seem to be two main schools of thought. The first tends to the view that unilateral nuclear disarmament, perhaps as an example to others, and anyway as a clear moral imperative, is the correct and most effective route. The other is that a massively large number of these weapons still exist and so, for the present at least, mutual deterrence and such legal controls as, for example, the Comprehensive Nuclear Test Ban Treaty, and the Nuclear Non-Proliferation Treaty (of which more anon) as means of limiting the risks, are the more practical route to achieving the same eventual goal.

Between these two positions lies the uncomfortable fact that whilst no nuclear weapon has been detonated in anger for almost 73 years, it is not possible to explain why with any real conviction. Whilst the failure of nuclear deterrence would be an incontrovertible fact for anyone who survived a nuclear exchange, the success of such deterrence is always an assertion rather than a provable fact. If one were to attempt to construct a logical syllogism on the lines of:

1. The USA and Russia have both had substantial strategic nuclear arsenals for the last 70 years
2. The USA and Russia have not been to war with each other for 70 years
3. Therefore the ownership of such weapons prevents war between two nuclear armed states,

the argument would immediately be seen to be logically invalid. It is at least as likely to be false as it is to be true and cannot be proved to be either.

Before going further, I should confess that, while the author of this book and I are committed to the same goals, the prevention of nuclear war and the removal of the threat of it, we have not always been on the same side of this intellectual divide, but I nevertheless welcome the new edition of *Security Without Nuclear Deterrence*.

I want to discuss these two approaches more fully, but first I think it will be useful to remind ourselves of some of the basic facts about deterrence theory in general. It is important to understand that it is a concept of considerable antiquity, which goes far wider than simply nuclear deterrence.

A brief history of nuclear deterrence

The Hiroshima and Nagasaki nuclear bombs demonstrated the appalling and lasting damage that even relatively low yield nuclear weapons can cause. Following this, the development of a nuclear weapon by the then USSR and the invention of the so-called hydrogen bomb, made very clear the overwhelming importance of preventing the further use of nuclear weapons. In a world initially of only two nuclear powers, the answer was seen to be mutual nuclear deterrence of which the principal deterrent factor was the survivability, following a first strike, of sufficient capacity still to inflict unacceptable damage on the first striker; there was to be no risk-free option. The deterrence lay in the idea that a successful disarming strike would not be possible. This tended to put great emphasis on nuclear superiority, and led to a rapid growth of nuclear weapons, a nuclear arms race in fact, between the USA and the then USSR, to try to guarantee the survivability of a sufficient retaliatory force. Eventually, both sides concluded that it might make more sense if they both agreed to be vulnerable to each other and that this might make for more effective deterrence. By this time six, or almost certainly seven, other nations had followed the two main protagonists into building nuclear arsenals. In the words of Ban Ki-moon, quoted here by the author in Chapter 4, '...the doctrine of nuclear deterrence has proven to be contagious'.

Following the ending of the Cold War, there was a natural reaction in the gradual running down of conventional forces, particularly in Europe, although the two European nuclear powers, Britain and France, retained their nuclear deterrents. Indeed, the UK recently decided to replace hers, despite simultaneously running down her conventional forces to the lowest effective levels of modern times.

Now, there are those who believe that the days of force-on-force conventional kinetic engagements are over, and that intervention and military action of the future will be limited and more concerned with nation building, general stability and anti-terrorism support for allies and friends. Despite the lamentable record of history, they may be right, but our ability accurately to forecast events in the last couple of centuries has also been lamentable and there is no real evidence that it will get better. Moreover, those who hold this view must surely acknowledge that deterring all war and conflict is the goal, and the best way to avoid escalation to nuclear warfare. We are not debating ends, but ways and means and I believe strongly that for this a credible conventional capability must underpin all other deterrent tools, soft or hard. We need therefore to understand the relationship between conventional and nuclear capabilities in the pursuit of a credible overall deterrent strategy. I shall use the example of the UK.

How does general deterrence work?

In April 2013, UK Prime Minister David Cameron made an important speech, firstly reaffirming his strong commitment to the full replacement of the UK's strategic nuclear deterrent as the ultimate guarantee of the nation's security. Secondly, he said that the Armed Services were receiving the best conventional equipment. But he ignored some highly significant conventional capability gaps created by his government's 2010 Strategic Defence and Security Review (SDSR). Together with depleted equipment numbers and delays and reductions in new equipment, further exacerbated by his 2015 SDSR and subsequently, these have seriously unbalanced the UK's force structure. No solutions to this problem are yet fully identified, let alone funded. These weaknesses seriously, possibly even fatally, undermine his major premise.

There is a dangerous and potentially misleading paradox here. The replacement nuclear deterrent is likely to pose a far more severe challenge to a shrinking UK defence industry than did either Polaris or Trident; and it is very difficult to believe that the full costs, infrastructure and timescales have yet been firmly identified: moreover, most of the costs still lie outside the current financial planning period. So, without new money the risks to the much-reduced remaining conventional programme appear to be considerable. Consequentially, conventional force levels are almost certainly facing yet further reductions and so therefore is the credibility both of the nuclear deterrent and of deterrence more generally, as I shall now explain.

The highly dangerous, and surely incredible, doctrine of 'Nuclear Tripwire' of the early days of nuclear deterrence, which envisaged rapid and possibly massive use of nuclear weapons in the event of any Soviet aggression, was abandoned in the 1960s. The more persuasive, although still dangerous, 'Flexible Response' which followed, and importantly included a variety of both conventional and nuclear escalation options, assumed that use of nuclear weapons was a last resort. NATO members signed up to this strategy and its consequences for defence spending. It has been UK policy that nuclear weapons would never be used against non-nuclear states party to the Nuclear Non-Proliferation Treaty (NPT), although the UK has never ruled out first nuclear use. This policy was perhaps inevitable during the Cold

War when the country possessed so-called 'tactical' nuclear weapons to bridge the gap between conventional and strategic nuclear forces, but was surprisingly maintained during the 2017 election campaign.

By the 1980s the Anti-Ballistic Missile (ABM) Treaty of 1972 had been followed by Strategic Arms Limitation (SALT) talks, the Intermediate Nuclear Forces (INF) Treaty of 1987, and then the two Strategic Arms Reduction Treaties (1991 and 1994), which in turn were superseded by the 2002 Strategic Offensive Reductions Treaty (SORT). Some of these have now effectively been overtaken by the 2010 New Strategic Arms Reduction Treaty (New START), and Russia and the USA have very recently reached the missile launcher levels required by that treaty. However, it did not further limit weapon stockpiles and a huge number of nuclear warheads still remain.

The ABM Treaty of 1972 added what was perhaps the most sophisticated twist to the theory of nuclear deterrence. In effect, both sides agreed to limit their missile defence capability, thus deliberately leaving themselves vulnerable to a retaliatory attack, following a first nuclear strike. This was the so-called Mutual Assured Destruction, with its ironic acronym MAD. Counter-intuitively perhaps this was actually, in the circumstances, a stabilising measure because it greatly reduced the prospects of surviving a retaliatory attack, thus reducing the incentive to engage in a first strike. I shall return to this point later.

But the cardinal point is that the nuclear deterrent is not, and cannot be, a substitute for conventional capabilities. The credibility of flexible response depends upon deferring any decision to use nuclear weapons until the very existence of the nation is at stake. This requirement means that the conventional forces must be of sufficient capability to deal with any lesser threat; and that one's potential enemy must believe this to be so. The matter at issue must be of such severity that the risk of nuclear obliteration, possibly on a global scale, is worth even considering; one's opponent must believe that too. Self-evidently there are very few such issues; most people would probably argue that there are none. Some will argue that an opponent might never believe the threat is credible anyway, but the deterrent effect may in fact rest on a deliberate ambiguity – 'you may not be sure I have nuclear weapons or would use them, but can you afford to take the risk?' This ambiguity is something Israel has exploited in her policy of neither confirming nor denying her possession of nuclear weapons.

If the conventional means at our disposal are weak, the point of transition to nuclear use may be lowered to levels at which the threat of nuclear obliteration is self-evidently wholly disproportionate to the issue at stake. At that point, it is likely that deterrence through the threat of nuclear use becomes overtly incredible and can be so perceived by an opponent – a bluff waiting to be called. Thus, through *conventional* weakness, the nuclear deterrent is compromised, whether it is a rogue state or a major power that is involved. To be credible, it must be underpinned by strong conventional deterrence. The idea that nuclear deterrence is synonymous with strong defence is to assume that 'big bang' is 'big defence'. It isn't; it may even be quite the reverse.

Moreover, there is little evidence from the past 50 years that a nuclear deterrent is particularly effective at deterring non-nuclear nations', or non-state groups', actions for precisely the same set of reasons. It is not credible to suppose that nuclear weapons would be used against such nations or groups. Indeed, the UK has specifically ruled that out and it is clear that in 1982, Argentina (a non-nuclear nation) was not deterred from invading the Falkland Islands by the fact that the UK possessed both strategic and 'tactical' nuclear weapons at the time.

But conventional military action must also be deterred if we are to reduce the risk of escalation. The key here is that deterrence is a broad continuum; conventional deterrence also deters. The threatened use of conventional force, at a lower level of intensity, is genuinely credible because it is plainly *usable*. Any potential adversary is likely to believe in the possibility of its use, but only provided that it is also clearly sufficient for the particular purpose or operation to hand. And in so doing it can snuff out dangers before they escalate, thus preventing bad things happening and getting worse, so that escalation towards 'nuclear territory' does not occur. Some people may believe that bad things are never going to happen, but this demands a very eccentric view of both human nature and human history. When bad things don't happen, it is probably because they have been deterred. Nuclear deterrence is simply the most extreme example of this.

That was the missing link in Mr Cameron's speech – recognition of the link between conventional deterrence and nuclear deterrence. This continuum of deterrence should set out wherever possible to deter action at the earliest and least violent point and postpone or prevent arrival at the point of nuclear decision, allowing time to be bought for resolution of whatever may be the cause of conflict.

'New ways of warfare' and asymmetric warfare

Unfortunately, the situation has become further complicated by the development of so-called 'new ways of warfare', of which the best known, but not the only, example is cyber warfare. This phenomenon has become categorised, perhaps rather lazily, as 'asymmetric warfare' and is held by some to signal the decline of kinetic warfare and to justify an assumption that future wars will not be of the kinetic variety and thus to smuggle in an assumption that they may also replace nuclear warfare and the risk of it.

This is surely to misunderstand the nature of asymmetric warfare, which is not warfare of any particular kind. Rather it is an attempt to fight the war on a battlefield where the enemy is not significantly present – to find his greatest vulnerability, his 'weakest link'. The unfortunate consequence of this is that, whenever a new way of war fighting is developed, it does not mean *ipso facto* that an existing form is rendered obsolete and unnecessary. It means rather that there is a new vulnerability, a new base to be covered. But if the old base is stripped of cover in order to fortify the new one, then the old base may become a new vulnerability, and more attractive for an enemy to target. This leads to the very uncomfortable consequence that kinetic warfare is not dead (as a brief glance round the world will confirm) but rather that it is only one of the forms of warfare. The invention of new forms almost certainly means that a nation's defence becomes more complex and more expensive as new threats open. This was probably best put by the late Sir Michael Quinlan:

> In matters of military contingency, the expected, precisely because it is expected, is not to be expected ... What we expect we plan and provide for; what we plan and provide for, we thereby deter; what we deter does not happen. What does happen is what we did not deter, because we did not plan and provide for it, because we did not expect it.[1]

The greater the risk of defeat in any of these varying forms of warfare, the closer becomes the decision point for a nuclear nation of the choice between capitulation and escalation to nuclear use, which the whole concept of deterrence is designed to avoid. From a rational strategic viewpoint therefore, and for as long as nuclear weapons exist, I would argue that it is not possible to separate nuclear doctrine, force structure and strength from conventional force structure and strength, across an increasingly wide range of non-nuclear war making capabilities. Moreover, this is of particular relevance to the second-rank nuclear powers, such as Britain and France, which have tended to sacrifice substantial conventional and other non-nuclear capabilities in order to finance their strategic nuclear forces, thus undermining the credibility of those very forces.

Tactical nuclear weapons and Ballistic Missile Defence

The situation is further complicated by two other recent developments. Firstly, by recent American proposals to solve the problem of the conventional/nuclear gap by re-introducing so-called battlefield, 'tactical' or theatre nuclear weapons and increasing the temptation of first nuclear use. This may be a response to Russia's apparent breach of the INF Treaty by deploying Iskander short range ballistic missiles in Kaliningrad. Both are dangerous developments. The second complication is the planned deployment of Theatre Ballistic Missile Defence (TBMD) systems. Whilst the supporters of both are able to advance rational and logical arguments for their plans, there are good reasons for concern, which I examine next. There is a considerable irony in the fact that some of the reactions to the end of the Cold War may have made nuclear war more likely.

In the first case, that of 'tactical' nuclear weapons, there is a legitimate philosophical debate about this additional, but qualitatively distinct, 'step' on the escalation ladder. Does it provide additional space for consideration and negotiation, or does it smooth the path to further nuclear use, effectively removing an important taboo? Is there in reality, as opposed to in nuclear 'theology', such a thing as a 'sub-strategic' nuclear weapon, given the substantial and potentially long-lasting consequences of any such use? Does the breaking of the taboo represent a greater threat than the strengthening of the escalation ladder represents a stronger deterrent to strategic use? And does the development and deployment of a 'sub-strategic' capability, and the way it might be perceived by potential opponents, contravene the spirit if not the letter of the NPT and the INF, and open the way to other even more dangerous breaches? In a nutshell, does it improve or reduce stability? These are not readily answerable questions, but they certainly cannot be answered by simple appeal to perceived military necessities. One thing can, however, be said with reasonable certainty: it can never be wise to increase the number of nuclear weapons in a world which already has the capacity to destroy almost every living creature on the planet.

The potential deployment of widespread TBMD systems following the Bush Jr administration's unilateral withdrawal from the ABM Treaty in 2002 and its impact on nuclear deterrence is much more difficult to assess. On the face of it, gaining the ability to defend one's deployed forces against ballistic missile attack (whether with conventional or nuclear warheads) is a reasonable, if very expensive ambition. Moreover, it is significantly less grandiose than President Ronald Reagan's Strategic Defence Initiative, which sought to provide complete protection to the USA and her allies against strategic nuclear attack and which was, in the mid-1980s, seen as a potentially deeply destabilising concept. This was because it would have overturned the mutual vulnerability described earlier and made a first disarming strike more feasible. Similar concerns seem to surround the potential deployment of TBMD; and at least one significant research project is under way with an international cast of participants to investigate the impact of these weapons on deterrence.

All this demonstrates the considerable difficulty and complexity of the whole subject of deterrence, whether conventional or nuclear. And deterrence is surely the central issue of the nuclear debate in a world in which war seems very unlikely to disappear as long as human beings remain competitive, and the resources for which they compete become increasingly scarce. The sad fact is that, over the period of recorded history – perhaps about 6,000 years – human nature shows very little sign of having changed very much. If deterrence, and specifically nuclear deterrence, could be relied upon to hold in all circumstances, then the problem might perhaps be contained. If it cannot be so relied upon, then we have to consider other ways in which the goal can be achieved. This returns us to the two different approaches to which I referred earlier.

Approach 1 – general nuclear disarmament

Nuclear weapons obviously cannot be uninvented and the knowledge of how to make them somehow lost, nor is ownership of them incontrovertibly *per se* illegal, as the NPT clearly implies. So the first approach is of course the voluntary abandonment of nuclear weapons by those nations which own them and those which aspire to do so. This has long been the dream of many nuclear disarmers, and is entirely understandable, worthy and moral. The difficulty of course lies in the practicalities and durability of such a decision – which in turn hinge on a paradigm shift in the mindset from indispensable security and prestige assets to unusable and unaffordable liabilities. Up to now, as far as we know, very few nations which had acquired nuclear weapons have subsequently and voluntarily surrendered such weapons. Three of these states were former members of the USSR, namely Belarus, Kazakhstan and Ukraine, and the weapons concerned were, of course, Russian and were returned to Russia or destroyed following the collapse of the USSR. The fourth was South Africa, which abandoned its limited nuclear arsenal in 1989 and acceded to the NPT two years later. In this last case, the reasons are more complex and perhaps largely *sui generis*.

Can this precedent be further extended? In particular, can it be extended to the major powers? If it cannot, there would be little point in embarking on this route in the first place. Would the major powers ever feel sufficient confidence and trust in one another to agree on a planned complete disposal of their arsenals? Whilst some will say that such confidence was found during the various rounds of the SALT and START talks, the case is not directly comparable, since there was then no question of either side ever losing a substantial deterrent capability, let alone being 'stripped naked'. The hope was that these treaties would increase confidence that disarmament could go much further. Moreover, as the recent behaviour of North Korea may demonstrate, any such move might be perceived to present an irresistible temptation to a rogue nuclear state, against which some nuclear 'insurance' might be desirable. It is, therefore, certainly possible that the progress towards total nuclear disarmament could even create a new, if possibly transient, instability which might present an even greater danger than the current situation.

But, some will say, this is no reason why those nations which do wish for nuclear disarmament should not disarm unilaterally, and moreover that this is the morally correct action to take and would set an example which might influence other nations. I do not dispute that, nor would I try to dissuade any nation from this course, although I am more dubious about its likely success in influencing the major powers. And, given that some lesser nuclear powers have reduced their conventional force structures in order to afford nuclear weapons, it is at least conceivable that such unilateral disarmament will increase the risk of conventional war at any rate for a period. While this may be less globally catastrophic than a major nuclear exchange, it is hardly an outcome over which to rejoice. There is, whether one likes it or not, a difficult moral argument to resolve as to whether the possible creation of greater instability and risk *en route* to a moral goal undermines the morality of the original purpose. This is a classic 'ends versus means' debate which cannot simply be ignored. Nor are morality and legality necessarily the same thing. The author tackles this question in his Chapter 5.

Approach 2 – nuclear control regimes

The problem has not, however, been ignored either in the United Nations or in individual countries. The alternative approach is that of incremental control and regulatory regimes, and this has been pursued for some considerable time now. Examples of this are the Partial Nuclear Test Ban Treaty (PTBT) of 1963, the Nuclear Non Proliferation Treaty (NPT) of 1968 (extended indefinitely in 1995), the Intermediate Nuclear Forces Treaty of 1987, the Comprehensive Nuclear Test Ban Treaty (CTBT) of 1996, the New START Treaty of 2010 and the Treaty on the Prohibition of Nuclear Weapons (TPNW) of 2017. In addition, there are, as we have already seen, other more limited bi-lateral agreements to try to enhance mutual deterrence and reduce the costs and the risk of nuclear use.

The first obvious problem is that either nations will not sign or ratify such agreements, or will subsequently ignore or withdraw from them, and this has certainly been one of the outcomes. There are several reasons for this, some of them worthier, or at least more plausible, than others. For example, China, France, and North Korea, *et alii*, have not signed the PTBT; the CTBT has not yet entered into force because five nations (USA, China, Israel, Iran and Egypt) have signed but not ratified it, and three nations (India, North Korea and Iran) have not even signed it, although some of these countries have thus far abided by its provisions. Nevertheless, the enforcement of international treaties and indeed international law generally is far from straightforward. In particular, where nations have not actually shared a common view either of morality or of the basis of the law, or where perceived national interest is at odds with the body of law, enforcement is a very difficult issue indeed.

The NPT is of somewhat greater interest in that it attempted to differentiate between peaceful and warlike use of nuclear technology. It is the case that, for the moment at least, nuclear power generation is indispensable, and that there are important medical applications of nuclear material. Clearly this issue is technically difficult to handle and provides opportunities for circumventing the provisions of the treaty, which are designed to prevent the spread of nuclear weapon technology beyond the five original overtly nuclear powers. 191 nations are states parties to the NPT; India, Israel, Pakistan and South Sudan have not signed it, whilst North Korea signed the treaty and subsequently withdrew from it in 2003.

Finally, the TPNW is the first attempt by the UN to commit nations to specifically outlaw nuclear weapons. However, some 69 nations have not adopted, let alone signed or ratified this treaty, including importantly all the current nuclear powers, and all US allies and NATO member countries. For it to enter into force, 50 nations must have signed and ratified it; so far 55 nations have signed and seven have done both, although the treaty was only adopted on 7 July 2017 and opened to signature on 20 September 2017.

Progress is therefore both encouraging and disappointing. For reasons that must by now be clear to the reader, there are considerable technical difficulties. There are political difficulties, too, not least because the current NPT can be seen as discriminatory, enabling just five nuclear states – which non-coincidentally are the permanent members of the UN Security Council – to enjoy the benefits of nuclear deterrence claimed by them until some utopian moment of their choosing, whilst trying to prevent other nations from doing so. It appears to many as a dispensation designed by the former and current masters of the world solely in their own interests. Moreover, it makes little allowance for shifts of power and influence around the globe, nor for the threats that specific nations perceive. Nevertheless, the fact remains that there has been no nuclear weapon detonated in anger for

73 years, and there is a clear and strong international majority view in favour of the control and ultimately the abolition of nuclear weapons. And in the 2017 TPNW one might argue that both approaches I have identified have begun to converge, despite the many difficulties and complications that lie in the way of achieving the final goal. This must surely be a reason for at least some limited optimism.

Will it all work?

Meanwhile some very big questions remain. Can we find a way through these great technical difficulties which is acceptable to all nations and provides adequate re-assurance to all? Can we get through this journey without creating great and dangerous instabilities *en route,* for example by contemplating, as the USA apparently is, deliberate pre-emptive nuclear use? In making this journey, can we avoid nuclear war through miscalculation or, just as likely in an era when split-second decisions are made by computers, through technical error or through what the stock markets call 'algorithmic action'? Conversely, can we reach a final position which does not simply make the world 'safer for conventional war'? Can we safely and with certainty separate the peaceful uses of nuclear technology, some of which can confer huge benefits on humanity, from the enormous dangers of military use which threaten humanity's survival? Perhaps above all, can we devise some method by which all this can be adequately policed and enforced? The current North Korean situation illustrates many of these points and highlights both the difficulties and the dangers, and the recent behaviour of stock markets shows the dangers of robotic decision-making without adequate human judgement and intervention. And of course, as I write this, the two great powers are both in the process of modernising their nuclear arsenals, making it very unlikely that they will be prepared to dispose of them, at least in the first half of this century.

All this needs to be approached with a level of humility, humanity, morality, understanding and ambition which is sadly rare in contemporary international politics; the art of statesmanship seems to have died, to be replaced by 'megaphone diplomacy'. This is typified by some shockingly loose and even crude use of social media, and by a failure to grasp the intellectual complexities of the subject, the various opposing arguments and, perhaps most of all, the immense and appalling consequences of failure. It almost seems that for some it is a 'reality TV' game in which their own personal success and ambition trump the interests of the human race, and indeed of our planet. In such a climate, serious and meaningful negotiation is very difficult. We are badly in need of statesmen of vision and courage.

For this reason and at this critical juncture in global affairs, a watershed indeed, I very much welcome this new edition of Rob Green's book, even though I do not agree with all his conclusions. I entirely share, however, his goal so that the gap between us is more about means than ends. Few people have devoted as much thought and effort, over so long a period of time, to the subject of reducing and ultimately removing the risks of nuclear war as he has; his views deserve to be carefully read and pondered, whatever one's own position may be. In the end, in this as in any crucial question which is part moral and ethical and part practical, we each have to make up our own mind. However, it is surely a serious error to think that, because one differs on means, one cannot share the same goal. It is worse still, whatever view of the matter one takes, to impugn the motives and moral standing of another thinker merely because one happens to disagree with his route map to achieving a shared objective. None of us is likely to be the owner of the 'whole and unvarnished truth'.

Rob Green tackles all these issues and more with a personal honesty, and with deep knowledge, clarity, and detail, and an impressive sense of purpose. He takes us movingly through his own journey of conscience and then, from the moral position he has reached, tackles all the issues I have briefly sketched out in this foreword. He analyses the historical development of nuclear weapons and more importantly nuclear 'theology', and considers whether the policies and actions of the various nations concerned are moral, honest, rational or effective. His answer to this question is very clear, and on the whole I share it. However, I am less sure that his detailed prescriptions are the right ones, in the sense of being capable of delivering safely and certainly the outcome all sensible and decent people must wish for. None the less, by addressing this deeply sensitive and controversial issue in so full and clear a manner, he has done us all a great service. Uncomfortable though the debate may be for some governments, there is no issue on which informed, open and widespread public debate can be more important. It has always been my own view, irrespective of other views I have from time to time held, that the nuclear protest movements performed, and perform, a critical function in ensuring that the subject is not 'buried'. This book is part of that vitally important tradition and brings authoritative intellectual support to the more emotional arguments.

Not everyone will agree fully with everything he proposes, nor with all his conclusions. I very much hope, however, that this revised and updated edition of his book will be read by those from both sides of the argument, as carefully and critically as it deserves. I hope that they will carefully distinguish fact from opinion and when they decide on their own views, they will be informed by what is fact and evaluate what is opinion – there is plenty of both. This is a most important contribution to the debate on a subject which is crucial to the survival of the human race, and it needs to be read with a degree of humility and with an open mind – qualities not always apparent amongst our decision makers and their advisers. So vital an issue deserves nothing less.

London
March 2018

Note

1   Sir Michael Quinlan, '*Quinlan's Law'*, 2008, unpublished but quoted in Hennessy, P., *Distilling the Frenzy: Writing the History of One's Own Time*, Biteback Publishing, London, 2012. For a more idiosyncratic and fuller treatment of the unexpected, readers may wish to read Taleb, N.N., *The Black Swan*, Penguin Books, London, 2007.

CHAPTER ONE

WHY I REJECTED NUCLEAR DETERRENCE

In 1969, I was a 25-year-old Royal Navy Lieutenant serving in the British aircraft-carrier *HMS Eagle* as back-seat aircrew in its Buccaneer nuclear strike jet squadron. 'Observer' is the Fleet Air Arm's traditional term for bombardier-navigator, whose job is to navigate the aircraft and help the pilot operate its weapons system. During the next three years, I accepted without question an elite role with my pilot as a 'nuclear crew', assigned a target from NATO's Single Integrated Operational Plan. Our task was to be ready to deliver a WE177 tactical free-fall nuclear bomb, of some ten kilotons explosive power, to detonate above a military airfield on the outskirts of Leningrad – which is now St Petersburg's airport.

Thirty years later, I landed there to speak at a conference reviewing nuclear policy and security on the eve of the 21st century. In a television interview, I apologised to the citizens of St Petersburg for having been part of a nuclear mission that would have caused appallingly indiscriminate casualties and long-term poisonous effects from radioactive fallout, and heavily damaged their beautiful ancient capital. By then I realised nuclear weapons would not save me – and they would not save the Russians either.

Following a decision by the British government that it could no longer afford strike carriers, in 1972 I switched to anti-submarine helicopters. A year later, I was appointed Senior Observer of a squadron of Sea King helicopters aboard the aircraft-carrier *HMS Ark Royal*. Our task was to use radar, variable-depth sonar and other electronic sensors, plus a variety of weapons, to detect and destroy enemy submarines threatening our ships. All was well until we were ordered to be ready to use a nuclear depth-bomb, an anti-submarine variant of the WE177 design. This was because our lightweight anti-submarine homing torpedoes could not go fast or deep enough to catch the latest Soviet nuclear-powered submarines. The explosive power of the depth-bomb was again ten kilotons, nearly that of the atomic bomb which devastated Hiroshima. If I had pressed the button to release it, it would have vaporized a large volume of ocean – and myself. Unlike a strike jet, my helicopter was too slow to escape before detonation. So this would have been a suicide mission. Furthermore, there would have been heavy radioactive fallout from the depth-bomb plus the nuclear submarine's reactor and any nuclear-tipped torpedoes it carried. That action could have escalated World War 3 to nuclear holocaust. All this, just to protect an aircraft-carrier.

Yet my concerns were brushed aside. Soothing responses included claims that 'going nuclear' would only be needed in deep water hundreds of miles from land, where nuclear submarines could use their speed advantage and no civilians would be involved; and 'the Soviets probably wouldn't even detect it.' Because I was ambitious, and was assured that there would almost certainly be no need to use it, I complied. No one else in my squadron raised objections. That peculiarly potent military tradition, carefully nurtured to carve out and hold down the British Empire, was immortalised by Tennyson in his Crimean War poem *The Charge of the Light Brigade* about an earlier suicide mission: 'Theirs not to reason why, theirs but to do and die.' That attitude was alive and well in the all-volunteer Royal Navy. However, my absolute trust in my leaders had been shaken. In the years which followed, I came to realise not only that nuclear weapons were militarily useless, but that the full consequences of their use had not been thought through.

In December 1979 in the House of Lords, a distinguished former military leader challenged the purpose of Britain's nuclear forces. Former UK Chief of Defence Staff Field Marshal Lord Carver declared:

> I have never heard or read of a scenario in which I would consider it right or reasonable for the Prime Minister or Government of this country to order the firing of our independent strategic force at a time when the Americans were not prepared to fire theirs – certainly not before Russian nuclear weapons had landed on this country. And, again, if they had already landed, would it be right and reasonable? All it would do would be to invite further retaliation.[1]

At the time I was a newly promoted Commander working in the Ministry of Defence in Whitehall, London, as Personal Staff Officer to an Admiral who had the responsibility of recommending the replacement for Britain's four Polaris nuclear-armed ballistic missile submarines. I witnessed the debate in the Naval Staff, and watched the nuclear submarine lobby campaign ruthlessly for a scaled-down version of the huge US Trident submarine-launched ballistic missile system. Yet it introduced a destabilising first-strike capability with its greater firepower and accuracy, and its massive cost threatened the future of the Royal Navy as a balanced, useful force.

Margaret Thatcher had just become Prime Minister. Addicted to all things nuclear, she forced the British nuclear energy industry to accept the US pressurised water reactor design that had recently failed at Three Mile Island. She welcomed the stationing of US nuclear-armed Cruise missiles on British soil in the face of huge public protest; and she decided to replace Polaris with Trident without consulting her Cabinet. Despite misgivings, the Chiefs of Staff were brought into line. One consequence was that the British surface fleet would shrink to become smaller than Japan's, while the nuclear submarine lobby's contribution to offsetting the cost of Trident was to allow a brand new class of conventionally powered submarines to be sold to the Canadian Navy.

Nevertheless, I still accepted the rationale for a nuclear submarine force like Polaris. This was a dangerous time in the Cold War: the Soviets had just invaded Afghanistan; the Polish trade union movement *Solidarnosc* was pioneering the East European challenge to Soviet hegemony; and new and more impressive Soviet warship designs were emerging almost every month. It was therefore also a very stimulating time to work in military intelligence. In my last appointment as Staff Officer (Intelligence) to Commander-in-Chief Fleet, I ran the team providing round-the-clock intelligence support to Polaris and the rest of the Fleet from the command bunker in Northwood just outside London.

In 1982, Britain suddenly found itself at war with an erstwhile friend, Argentina, over the Falkland Islands. The war was directed from Northwood; and at one point the outcome hung in the balance. If Argentine aircraft had sunk a troopship or aircraft-carrier before the landing force had got ashore, the British might have had to withdraw or risk defeat. What would Thatcher have done? Until the war, she had been the most unpopular Prime Minister in British history. Now she had become the Iron Lady, determined to show both the British and the world her leadership prowess. Nevertheless, Polaris had clearly not deterred Argentina's President Galtieri from invading. With victory in his grasp, it is doubtful he would have believed even Thatcher would have seriously threatened a nuclear strike on Argentina.

I was never aware of the location of the deployed Polaris submarines. However, after leaving the Navy I heard rumours of a very secret contingency plan to move a Polaris submarine south within range of Buenos Aires, which in the event was not required. More on Thatcher's probable intent emerged in a memoir by former French President François Mitterrand's psychoanalyst, Ali Magoudi. Apparently, Mitterrand told him about a phone call he received from Thatcher after a French-supplied Exocet missile fired by the Argentinians from a French-supplied Super Etendard strike jet disabled the British destroyer *HMS Sheffield*. The British Prime Minister threatened to carry out a nuclear strike against Argentina unless Mitterrand informed her of the secret codes that would enable the British to jam the missiles' acquisition system. Mitterrand had been so convinced of her seriousness that he had complied.[2]

Clearly, defeat would have been unthinkable for the proud British military against such a foe, and it would have consigned Thatcher to political oblivion. Furthermore, Thatcher was a true believer in nuclear deterrence. Had she so threatened, it is probable that Galtieri would have called her bluff very publicly and relished watching US President Ronald Reagan try to rein her in. The Polaris submarine's Commanding Officer, briefed by me on the Soviet threat before he went on so-called 'deterrent' patrol, would have been faced with a bizarre shift of target and new rules of engagement. In the last resort, would he have refused the firing order or faked a malfunction, and returned to face a court martial with a clear conscience?

Although this nightmare did not arise, for me the Falklands War raised major concerns relating to nuclear weapons. First, there was the huge danger of the dilemma for any leader of a nuclear-armed state faced with possible defeat, but especially by a non-nuclear state. For make no mistake: if the US had failed to restrain Thatcher, a nuclear strike – even with just a single 200-kiloton Polaris warhead – on the airbase for the Exocet-armed Super Etendard jets at Cordoba would not only have caused massively disproportionate collateral damage and long-term casualties from radioactive fallout, but would have redoubled Argentina's resolve to keep fighting. The horrific prospect would then have arisen of escalating to a nuclear strike on the capital, Buenos Aires. International outrage would have already made the UK a pariah state, its case for retaining the Falkland Islands lost in the political fallout from such a war crime. This led me to confront the realities of operating nuclear weapons on behalf of a leader in such a crisis. Had the Polaris Commanding Officer been given such an order and obeyed, the failure of nuclear deterrence would have compounded the ignominy of defeat with that of being the first to have broken the nuclear taboo since Nagasaki.

When the war was over I left the Navy at the end of 1982, taking the redundancy I had been granted in the government's 1981 defence review. I left for career reasons: having been promoted to Commander very early after a career spent almost exclusively in aviation, I was ill-equipped to succeed in the fierce competition to command a frigate, without which I could not reach the rank of Admiral. Underlying this, however, was my concern that I could not stay fully committed to the Navy if it had to operate Trident.

I was 38 years old. With a working wife and no children, I trained as a roof thatcher in Dorset where we were living. Enduring many bad puns from friends about the political regime at that time, I thatched for eight idyllic years. This proved vitally therapeutic following the bizarre, high-profile murder in 1984 of my aunt, Hilda Murrell. My mother's unmarried elder sister, Hilda had become my mentor and close friend after my mother's death when I was nineteen.[3]

The murky circumstances surrounding her murder, amid swirling opposition to nuclear power and weapons in the country, marked the beginning of a new journey for me. Hilda had convinced me that nuclear-powered electricity generation in its current form was unacceptably hazardous. She died a few weeks before she was due to testify at the first public British planning inquiry into a new nuclear power plant, at Sizewell in Suffolk. I presented her submission, criticising the government's plans for dealing with the radioactive waste, on her behalf. Then, following the Chernobyl nuclear power plant catastrophe in April 1986, I took up her campaign against nuclear-powered electricity generation. In the process, I learned that the British nuclear energy industry had begun as a cynical by-product of the race to provide plutonium for nuclear weapons. This pathway to acquiring nuclear weapons, and also warship propulsion, was followed by all the nuclear-armed states extracting fissile material from nuclear power plant spent fuel, despite no safe solution for highly radioactive waste storage or eventual disposal. This posed a new, potentially catastrophic risk to the environment and public health, with no consideration of power plant and spent fuel storage vulnerability to attack in conventional war or by extremists, let alone nuclear war. Nevertheless, I resisted taking the ultimate step of opposing nuclear weapons.

My case for supporting Polaris and nuclear deterrence crumbled with the Berlin Wall in 1989 followed by the dismantling of the Warsaw Pact. However, it took the 1990–91 Gulf War to break me out of the brainwashing that had sustained my belief in nuclear weapons. I realised that if I chose to speak out against them, I would be one of very few former British Navy Commanders with nuclear weapon experience to do so.

From the moment in November 1990 when the US doubled its original figure for ground forces assigned to eject Iraqi forces from Kuwait, I realised that this was to be a punitive expedition. My military intelligence training warned me that the US-led coalition's *blitzkrieg* strategy would give Iraq's President Saddam Hussein the pretext he needed to attack Israel in order to split the coalition and become the Arabs' champion. If sufficiently provoked, he could use Scud ballistic missiles with chemical or biological warheads. If such an attack caused heavy Israeli casualties, Israel's Prime Minister Shamir would come under massive domestic pressure to retaliate with a nuclear strike on Baghdad. Even if Saddam Hussein did not survive (he had the best anti-nuclear bunkers that Western technology could provide), the entire Arab world would erupt in fury against Israel and its allies, its security would be destroyed forever, and Russia would be sucked into the crisis.

In January 1991, I joined the growing anti-war movement in Britain and addressed a crowd of 20,000 people in Trafalgar Square. A week later, on the night of 17 January, the first Scud attack hit Tel Aviv two days after the Allied *blitzkrieg* began. For the first time, the second city of a *de facto* nuclear state had been attacked and its capital threatened. Worse still for nuclear deterrence dogma, the aggressor did not have nuclear weapons. The Israeli people, cowering in gas masks in basements, learned that night that their so-called 'deterrent' had failed in its primary purpose. Thirty-eight more Scud attacks followed.

The American journalist Seymour Hersh, in his bestseller *The Samson Option*, recounted how Israel reacted:

> The [US] satellite saw that Shamir had responded to the Scud barrage by ordering mobile missile launchers armed with nuclear weapons moved into the open and deployed facing Iraq, ready to launch on command. American intelligence picked up other signs indicating that Israel had gone on a full-scale nuclear alert that would remain in effect for weeks. No one in the Bush administration knew what Israel would do if a Scud armed with nerve gas struck a crowded apartment building, killing thousands. All Bush could offer Shamir, besides money and more batteries of Patriot missiles, was American assurance that the Iraqi Scud launcher sites would be made a priority target of the air war.

Such guarantees meant little; no Jews had been killed by poison gas since Treblinka and Auschwitz, and Israel, after all, had built its bomb so it would never have to depend on the goodwill of others when the lives of Jews were being threatened.

The escalation didn't happen, however; the conventionally armed Scud warheads caused – amazingly – minimal casualties, and military and financial commitments from the Bush administration rolled in. The government of Prime Minister Yitzhak Shamir received international plaudits for its restraint.

American officials were full of private assurances for months after the crisis that things had been under control; newsmen were told that Israel, recognising the enormous consequence of a nuclear strike, would not have launched its missiles at Baghdad.

The fact is, of course, that no one in America – not even its President – could have dissuaded Shamir and his advisers from ordering any military actions they deemed essential to the protection of their nation.[4]

Meanwhile, in Britain, the Irish Republican Army just missed wiping out the entire Gulf War Cabinet with a mortar-bomb attack from a van in central London. A more direct threat to the government could barely be imagined. What if instead they had threatened to use even a crude nuclear device? In such circumstances a counter-threat of nuclear retaliation would have no credibility whatsoever.

Belatedly forced to research the history of 'the Bomb', I learned that the British scientific-politico-military establishment bore considerable responsibility for initiating and spreading the nuclear arms race. Having alerted the US to the feasibility of making a nuclear weapon, the UK participated in the Manhattan Project. In 1947, on being frozen out of further collaboration by the 1946 McMahon Act, it began to develop its own nuclear arsenal. Thus the UK became a role model for Saddam Hussein: the first medium-sized power with delusions of grandeur to threaten nuclear terrorism. Also, the doctrine of nuclear deterrence had practical flaws; it was immoral and unlawful, and there were more credible and acceptable alternative strategies to deter aggression and achieve security.

Having given up thatching as the Gulf War loomed, later in 1991 I became Chair of the UK affiliate of the World Court Project. This worldwide network of citizen groups helped to persuade the UN General Assembly, despite desperate countermoves led by the three NATO nuclear weapon states, to ask the International Court of Justice for its Advisory Opinion on the legal status of nuclear weapons. In 1996, the Court confirmed that the threat, let alone use, of nuclear weapons would generally be illegal. For the first time, the legality of nuclear deterrence had been implicitly challenged.

One aspect of the Court's decision was especially important. It confirmed that, as part of international humanitarian law, the Nuremberg Principles applied to nuclear weapons. In particular, Principle IV states:

> The fact that a person acted pursuant to order of his government or of a superior does not relieve him from responsibility under international law, provided a moral choice was in fact possible for him.[5]

This has serious implications for all those involved in operating nuclear weapons – particularly military professionals who, unlike a President or Prime Minister, really would have to 'press the button'. What is at stake here is a crucial difference between military professionals and hired killers or terrorists: military professionals need to be seen to act within the law.

My research and experience led me to a fundamental contradiction underlying a willingness to use nuclear weapons, which cannot be wished away by any sophisticated rationalisations. In order to make nuclear weapons acceptable to political leaders, public opinion and those in the military who have to operate them, there has been a systematic effort to play down the appalling side effects and 'overkill' problem associated with even the smallest modern nuclear weapons. Added to such a ploy is the assurance that 'there would almost certainly be no need to use them.' Yet, simultaneously, support for nuclear deterrence demands belief in the terrorising power of nuclear weapons. In this respect, they are not weapons at all. They are utterly indiscriminate devices that combine the poisoning horrors of chemical and biological weapons of mass destruction, plus inter-generational genetic effects unique to radioactivity, with almost unimaginable explosive violence. This is why *a state practising nuclear deterrence is actually conducting a deliberate policy of nuclear terrorism.*

There is another fundamental objection to relying on nuclear deterrence. If deterrence based on conventional weapons fails, the damage would be confined to the belligerent states and the environmental damage would be reparable. What is at stake from the failure of nuclear deterrence is the devastation and poisoning of not just the belligerents but potentially most forms of life on Earth. Closely related to this is the crazy reality that nuclear deterrence is a scheme for making nuclear war less probable by making it more probable. Moreover, the danger of nuclear war under a regime of nuclear deterrence is greater than we think, especially when the US and Russia persist with a high-alert launch posture. One consequence is that, since Hiroshima, we have lived with what Jonathan Schell described as:

...the fissure that nuclear weapons have created between our political selves and our moral selves, [as a result of which] we are compelled to choose between a position that is politically sound but immoral and one that is morally sound but politically irrelevant.[6]

I will explain how I have resolved this dilemma by rejecting nuclear deterrence on the grounds that it is impractical, politically unsound and counterproductive to our real security needs, as well as immoral and illegal. Moreover, there are alternative, non-nuclear strategies to deter war and secure just and lasting peace.

Notes

1   Lord Carver, Hansard, House of Lords, v. 403 (18 December 1979), Cols. 1628-30.

2   Ali Magoudi, *Rendez-vous: La psychanalyse de François Mitterrand* (Maren Sell Editeurs, Paris, 2005). This account of Mitterrand's conversations with Magoudi is taken from John Follain, "The Sphinx and the curious case of the Iron Lady's H-bomb", *The Sunday Times*, 20 November 2005.

3   See http://www.hildamurrell.org for more information.

4   Seymour Hersh, *The Samson Option* (Random House, New York, 1991), p. 318.

5   These principles were first enunciated in the charter of the International Military Tribunal for the trial of Nazi leaders convened at Nuremberg, Germany under the terms of the London Agreement of 8 August 1945. The principles were unanimously adopted at the first session of the UN General Assembly in 1946 (Resolution 95), and their current text was agreed in 1950 by the International Law Commission, a UN body devoted to formulating and developing international law. See also Adam Roberts and Richard Guelff, eds, *Documents on the Laws of War* (Oxford University Press, 2000).

6   Jonathan Schell, *The Abolition* (Avon Books, New York, 1984), p. 98.

CHAPTER TWO

A BRIEF HISTORY

In the following brief history of nuclear deterrence, the focus is deliberately on the US, the UK and France. The reasons are primarily threefold: first, the greater difficulties of assessing and influencing Soviet/Russian and Chinese thinking; second, the guardians of nuclear deterrence are in the NATO nuclear states; and third, it is among those guardians that the mindset shift must begin.

From Monopoly to Massive Retaliation

Through the MAUD Committee Report of July 1941, the UK alerted the US both to the feasibility of building a nuclear weapon and to the urgency of doing so before Hitler obtained one.[1] President Roosevelt immediately authorised a US research programme to commence in October that year. Following the Japanese attack on Pearl Harbor two months later, the US swiftly outstripped the British atomic research programme. In August 1943, the US brought in both the UK and Canada as partners in the Manhattan Project, which assembled the first nuclear weapons in 1945. The first test, of a Plutonium 239 fission device, was carried out on 16 July at Alamogordo in New Mexico. On 6 August, a simpler Uranium 235 fission device obliterated the Japanese city of Hiroshima, developing an explosive power of 16 kilotons. Three days later, Nagasaki was destroyed by a 21-kiloton device of the type tested at Alamogordo.

Even before Hiroshima, scientists working on the first US nuclear weapons had addressed the idea of nuclear deterrence. In a report in September 1944, they had expressed doubt that nuclear deterrence would be effective.[2] From 1945 to the early 1950s, US strategic thinking saw free-fall nuclear weapons simply extending conventional bombing capabilities. In August 1949, the first Soviet test ended the US monopoly. This shock drove President Truman to order production of a thermonuclear weapon; and the first fusion explosion was achieved by the US at Enewetak Atoll in November 1952.[3]

Following the experience of the Korean War (1950-53), where nuclear weapons were found to be unusable in resolving a military stalemate, a new US doctrine of Massive Retaliation was announced by Secretary of State John Foster Dulles in January 1954 to try to restore the credibility of nuclear deterrence, and avoid future wars needing large numbers of US troops. This, the first US concept of nuclear deterrence, depended on the capacity to 'retaliate, instantly, by means and at places of our choosing.'[4]

The British Debate

The decision to develop an independent British nuclear capability emerged after the UK's exclusion from further collaboration with the US by the 1946 McMahon Act. Ironically, this Act was aimed at preventing nuclear proliferation. In October 1952, the UK became the world's third nuclear power when it detonated a fission nuclear device at Monte Bello in Australia. Meanwhile, in 1950, the UK had allowed British basing of US Air Force bombers equipped with nuclear weapons, without which the US could not threaten Moscow.

The British debate on nuclear deterrence pre-dated the US one, causing deep splits among military leaders and nuclear experts. As chronicled by Professor John Baylis, a historian of British nuclear weapons, the process began with the Labour Party Prime Minister Clement Attlee who had defeated Churchill in the 1945 election. At first Attlee had serious doubts: he was conscious that strategic bombing had been hailed as the great deterrent to war in the inter-war period, but had failed. He was concerned that things would be no different in the nuclear age. If deterrence did break down, he had no doubt nuclear weapons would be used. 'These deep anxieties about whether deterrence would work led the Prime Minister to argue that some form of international control of atomic weapons was urgently needed.'[5]

However, withdrawal of US collaboration in 1946 drove Attlee to pursue an independent UK nuclear arsenal, especially in light of worsening East-West relations and the growing Soviet threat. Another motivation was to preserve the UK's status as a 'Great Power'. Closely linked to that was Attlee's justification, at a time of uncertainty about the US commitment to West European security, that the British 'had to hold up our position vis-a-vis the Americans. We couldn't allow ourselves to be wholly in their hands.'[6]

Rear Admiral Sir Anthony Buzzard, Director of British Naval Intelligence in the early 1950s, argued publicly that the threat of mass destruction was dangerous and lacked credibility. It offered no incentive for restraint by the Soviet Union, and was destabilising because it put a premium on getting in the first blow. Instead, Buzzard advocated a form of graduated deterrence. In this, he drew a distinction between 'atomic' fission devices, which he proposed should be threatened only for tactical use against military targets, and 'hydrogen' thermonuclear devices, which should be reserved for strategic, all-out nuclear war. He contended that his alternative strategy was more credible and flexible in confronting a range of threats, and would allow the West to claim moral superiority over the Soviet Union by not threatening the immediate annihilation of another society.[7]

In 1954, having failed to change either the Royal Navy's or the government's policy from within, Buzzard retired and launched a remarkably effective public campaign of lectures and articles to influence both British and US nuclear strategy. At one point he enlisted the support of former Prime Minister Lord Attlee, who publicly condemned massive retaliation:

> The more absolute the sanction the greater the reluctance to use it... It would amount to bluff... I do not think it will by itself prevent wars. Indeed, there is a danger that people may chance making war in the belief that the weapon will not be used. The threat of its use is very dangerous because it may provoke anticipation.[8]

Buzzard's approach gained so much publicity and support that in 1955 the Chiefs of Staff directed their Joint Planners to assess its viability. The Joint Planning Staff responded with a report that concluded there was no distinction between tactical and strategic nuclear weapons. They also expressed anxiety that preparations to fight a limited nuclear war, on the lines suggested by Buzzard, would undermine the whole basis of deterrence.[9]

Another major disagreement within the UK defence establishment centred on the implications of the emerging nuclear stalemate between the US and the Soviet Union. One fear was that, in the age of nuclear parity, smaller regional wars were much more likely to occur, which would require more conventional forces.[10]

The Suez fiasco in 1956 and accelerating retreat from Empire as British colonies gained independence drove the UK to strive harder for an independent capability. Its first thermonuclear device, or 'hydrogen bomb', was tested near Christmas Island (now part of the

Republic of Kiribati) in May 1957, enabling the UK to announce its adoption of a doctrine of Massive Retaliation. Nevertheless, Prime Minister Harold Macmillan admitted privately: 'The H-Bomb is not important in the defence of Britain. We would never use it first.'[11]

Sir Solly Zuckerman, Chief Scientific Adviser to the Ministry of Defence at the time, recalled that his doubts set in when he read the 1957 Defence White Paper, which admitted that the country could not be protected against a nuclear strike. Zuckerman wrote:

> It was equally certain that we could not protect a handful of buried Blue Streaks [UK ballistic missiles under development, cancelled in 1960] in order that they might serve as retaliatory weapons in what Harold Macmillan once called an act of 'posthumous revenge'... either way, I argued, it made no difference to the future of the United Kingdom – were our missiles ever fired, we would be destroyed.[12]

By 1961, the government began to share those misgivings. The White Paper moved away from the past emphasis on Massive Retaliation and 'timidly formulated a "graduated deterrence" posture.'[13] In so doing, British nuclear policy effectively adopted Buzzard's view.

To sum up the British debate during this period, what emerged was a view of nuclear deterrence that was far more contested and subjective, and less rational, than is often suggested.

UK Dependence on the US

While it tried to resolve its nuclear doctrine, the UK quickly opted for nuclear dependence on the US, because the political and financial costs of independence were considered too great. The successful British H-Bomb test convinced the US to waive the strictures of the McMahon Act prohibiting UK collaboration and replace it with the 1958 *Anglo-American Agreement for Cooperation on the Uses of Atomic Energy for Mutual Defence Purposes*, which remains in force. Nonetheless, serious doctrinal difference with the US developed in 1961, when the Kennedy administration undertook a major reappraisal of strategy by the new Defense Secretary Robert McNamara. This resulted in a significant expansion of nuclear forces, and a new doctrine emphasising controlled nuclear responses and the need for larger conventional capabilities. McNamara condemned small nuclear forces as 'dangerous, expensive, prone to obsolescence and lacking in credibility as a deterrent.'[14]

The British were desperate to keep their place at the 'top table'. In December 1962, two months after the Cuban missile crisis, the US cancelled Skybolt, an air-launched ballistic missile on which the UK was relying for its delivery system. Macmillan had a crisis meeting with Kennedy at Nassau in the Bahamas, where the US agreed to provide the UK with the Polaris ballistic missile submarine system, which became operational in 1968.[15] Massive US assistance was needed to design and build the UK variants of both the Polaris and Trident submarines, each of which had 16 missile tubes instead of the 24 in the US submarines.

UK Polaris was portrayed as an 'independent nuclear deterrent', notwithstanding growing reliance on provision of US missiles, satellites and intelligence for targeting and avoiding detection. The UK remains unique among the five recognised nuclear states in not having developed its own space launch programme. National contingency plans were produced which identified 15 major cities to be attacked if, as a last resort, the UK was forced 'to go it alone' in a conflict with the Soviet Union. A number of top military and political figures, however, questioned whether such a concept of deterrence made any sense when the UK risked total annihilation if the Polaris force was ever used in this way. The scale of British dependence on the US also made the threat of independent action questionable. Yet such dependence made the UK a prime target for nuclear attack by the Soviet Union.

This charade of 'minimum deterrence' from a 'second centre of decision-making' was perpetuated by Margaret Thatcher's decision, in 1980, to replace Polaris with a UK variant of the US Trident system. The UK agreed to purchase Trident I C-4 missiles. The Reagan administration then quickly opted to replace them with the much more accurate and longer-range Trident II D-5, which made it a counter-force weapon, capable of destroying opposing nuclear weapon systems. In 1982, Thatcher had no choice but to accept the D-5 version, which the UK effectively leases from the US Navy's missile pool at the King's Bay submarine base in Georgia.

Since 1962 the UK has relied on US nuclear warhead testing facilities at Nevada, and the Royal Navy has used the US Eastern Test missile range off Florida after its Polaris force became operational between 1966–69. Following the 1993 US nuclear test moratorium, the UK was also obliged to stop testing. Instead, the UK Atomic Weapons Establishment at Aldermaston has received extensive US assistance in 'sub-critical' testing of warhead components at the Nevada test site. The US permits regular UK exchanges through joint working groups on all aspects of nuclear weapon development with its three leading nuclear weapon-related research laboratories, Lawrence Livermore, Sandia and Los Alamos.

The fourth and last *Vanguard* class submarine of the UK Trident force became fully operational by the end of 2000. The UK warhead is believed to be closely modelled on one of the US Trident warheads, W76, which has an explosive power of about 100 kilotons. Documents released under the US Freedom of Information Act indicate that in the early 1980s, when the UK was designing its Trident warhead, the Joint Atomic Information Exchange Group enabled the US to pass to the UK 'atomic information on the Mk-4 Re-entry Body and W76 warhead for the Trident Missile Systems.'[16] In 1987, the UK National Audit Office stated that most of the expenditure on the UK Trident warhead's development and production 'is incurred in the US.'[17]

Further details came to light in a 2005 report published by a consortium of UK NGOs called the WMD Awareness Programme.[18] For example, in 1988 the National Audit Office reported it was essential that Trident targeting software be produced in the UK. Then, as the first of the *Vanguard* class entered service in 1994, it was revealed that 'contractor support', almost certainly from the US, had been required to complete this work.

Targeting data in UK Trident submarines is processed in the fire control system by software produced in the US. This data is created in the Nuclear Operations and Targeting Centre in London, which again relies on US software. In 2002 the fire control systems in UK and US Trident submarines were modified. Just before this the computers in the London targeting centre were upgraded. It would be possible for US programmers to modify the software supplied to the UK, either openly or covertly, to restrict how UK Trident could be used.

There are special arrangements for supplying US nuclear targeting information to the UK. The UK Liaison Cell at US Strategic Command headquarters in Omaha plays a central role in this process. It follows that US support may also be required to produce plans for an independent attack. In addition, Trident missiles can only achieve the required level of accuracy if a special forecast of the weather over the target is available. This is supplied to UK and US submarines in compressed messages transmitted every 12 hours by the US Navy. Trident also relies on gravity information from US sources. Without this weather and gravity data the missiles would be less accurate.

The US Navy is upgrading communications to its submarines through provision of a new Extremely High Frequency (EHF) satellite system, in order to reduce the vulnerability of UHF/SHF satellite communications to disruption from very high altitude nuclear detonations. The UK Ministry of Defence considered adding an EHF facility to its satellite communication system Skynet 5, planned to replace Skynet 4. Instead the UK has joined the US Advanced EHF military satellite communications programme. So now the UK is dependent on the use of US satellites for EHF communications. Clearly, therefore, the UK Trident system is only as independent as Washington wants it to be.

Following a Strategic Defence Review by the newly elected Blair administration in 1998, it was decided to limit the number of deployed warheads to three per missile, and relax the notice to fire from 'minutes' to 'days'. At the same time, the UK government withdrew the WE177 tactical nuclear bombs I had been trained to operate. With Trident the sole remaining UK delivery system, there was a need for a tactical or 'sub-strategic' capability to maintain a degree of flexible response. This was apparently achieved by an announcement that the UK Trident warhead had the option of a lower yield, and that some missiles in the single deployed submarine would have only one warhead.

British dependence will inevitably increase with the Blair government's decision on 4 December 2006, implemented nearly ten years later by Parliament on 18 July 2016, to replace the current four *Vanguard* class Trident-equipped submarines with a successor programme to be called the *Dreadnought* class, as once again the UK will have to accept whatever system the US develops.[19] In exchange for all this US generosity, under the Mutual Defence Agreement it would appear that the only UK contributions are provision of some plutonium for the US in exchange for US highly enriched uranium for UK submarine propulsion reactors; investment of £100 million in the US National Ignition Facility as part of ensuring the safety and reliability of UK nuclear weapons; and some relatively minor research by the UK Atomic Weapons Establishment.

The UK Pay-back

However, when the track record of US defence involvement in the UK and its dependent territories plus UK support for US operations is examined, a clear trend emerges to explain how the UK has paid its share. The following case studies illustrate the costs of UK nuclear dependence on the US.

Diego Garcia. A British colony lying midway between Africa and Asia in the Indian Ocean, Diego Garcia is one of 64 coral islands forming the Chagos Archipelago. It once had an indigenous population of 2,000 until the US decided it needed a base there. During the 1960s, in exchange for acquiring the Polaris system at a reduced cost, Harold Wilson's Labour government secretly conspired with two US administrations to evict 1,200 of the islanders from Diego Garcia.[20]

To justify their removal, the UK Foreign & Commonwealth Office (FCO) invented the fiction that the islanders were merely transient contract workers who could be 'returned' to Mauritius, 1,000 miles away. In fact, many islanders traced their ancestry back five generations on the island. Files uncovered in 2006 in Washington DC and London confirmed that Wilson and at least three cabinet ministers approved this cover-up.[21] The islanders were dumped on the dockside in Mauritius, where they faced poverty and discrimination. More than a decade later, each person received less than £3,000 compensation from the British government.

The behaviour of subsequent British governments has been equally reprehensible. In 2000, the islanders won a historic victory in the High Court, which ruled that their expulsion more than thirty years earlier had been illegal. Within hours of the judgment, the FCO announced it would not be possible for the islanders to return to Diego Garcia because of 'our treaty commitments to the USA.'[22] In a follow-up High Court case in 2003, the islanders were denied compensation. Then in June 2004, the Government invoked the Royal Prerogative in order to crush the 2000 judgment. A decree was issued banning the islanders forever from returning to their home, or to any of the other islands. The islanders refused to accept this and were back in the High Court in 2005. On 11 May 2006, the Court ruled in their favour, describing the UK Government's behaviour as illegal, repugnant and irrational. The FCO appealed to the House of Lords, which in 2008 rejected the islanders' case by a 3–2 majority. The islanders went to the European Court of Human Rights in Strasbourg, where the UK government refused a 'friendly settlement.'[23]

Article 7 of the statute of the International Criminal Court describes the 'deportation or forcible transfer of population ... by expulsion or other coercive acts' as a crime against humanity.[24] Meanwhile, US storage of tactical nuclear weapons in Diego Garcia on UK territory is the major remaining obstruction to achieving a nuclear weapon-free Southern Hemisphere.

Menwith Hill. In 1966, the UK government allowed the US National Security Agency (NSA) to take control of 250 acres of farmland at Menwith Hill on the Yorkshire Moors. There, under cover of a confidential agreement with the Ministry of Defence, NSA built the largest electronic spy base in the world. Like 34 other US bases in Britain, it is disingenuously presented as a Royal Air Force station. In what is a major node of the US ECHELON global communications interception system, more than 1,200 US personnel operate antennas within over thirty large radomes targeting all international satellite telephone, fax and email traffic to and from Europe.[25] The base is also capable of intercepting microwave communications via US electronic spy satellites. Probably all unencrypted British communications are covered by what is almost certainly an illegal system, constituting an outrageous invasion of privacy and commercial confidentiality.[26]

In March 2003, a leaked email revealed that NSA had been involved in spying on the United Nations Security Council Missions. It asked for support for the operation from its British partner, the Government Communication Headquarters in Cheltenham, with the apparent expectation that this would be given as a matter of course.[27] This was during the US–UK attempt to obtain Security Council approval for their invasion of Iraq, which was not forthcoming. The Government did not deny a subsequent allegation by former Cabinet Minister Clare Short that the UK had spied on the UN Secretary-General.[28]

The 1986 US Strike on Libya. In April 1986, President Ronald Reagan ordered air strikes against the 'rogue' state of Libya, whose maverick leader Colonel Muammar Gaddafi had allegedly been the principal financier of international terrorism against US and Israeli citizens. Carrier-borne US Navy strike aircraft were launched from only a few hundred miles off the Libyan coast; but the USAF decided to use 24 F-111 tactical bombers. However, no southern European allies would let them operate from bases in their countries. British Prime Minister Margaret Thatcher enthusiastically authorised US bases in the UK to be used, but then the French and Spanish governments refused to allow the F-111s to overfly their territories. This meant they had to remain over the sea, and enter the Mediterranean via the Straits of Gibraltar using multiple in-flight refuelling involving 28 tanker aircraft.

The operation on 15–16 April was an embarrassing failure. Although the targets in Tripoli and Benghazi were allegedly military, bombs were dropped on civilian areas including the French embassy in Tripoli, killing and injuring scores of people, and one aircraft was lost with its crew. Gaddafi's home was hit, killing his adopted infant daughter, though Gaddafi himself was not there. In a clear attempt to assassinate him, pilots had been shown reconnaissance photographs indicating where he and his family were to be found.[29]

This episode was a propaganda gift for Gaddafi. Worldwide TV coverage produced an outburst of anti-American feeling, with the British implicated as willing accomplices in facilitating terror attacks such as those Gaddafi had allegedly sponsored.

The 2003 US–UK Invasion and Occupation of Iraq. The main elements are well-known of how the US, with the sole support of the UK (plus minor special forces involvement by Australia), invaded and occupied Iraq in 2003. The shifting justifications have also been fully aired, as it became clear that Iraq posed no immediate threat from weapons of mass destruction, to the fallback position: simply, that Saddam Hussein's cruel regime had to be replaced. However, it is now accepted that the Bush administration decided to invade and occupy Iraq soon after the terrorist attacks on New York and Washington on 11 September 2001.[30]

Sir Christopher Meyer, British Ambassador to Washington at the time, revealed what transpired between Tony Blair and Bush during Blair's visit soon after '9/11'.[31] Apparently, Blair secretly agreed then to support Bush in removing Saddam Hussein from power as soon as the Taliban had been overthrown in Afghanistan. While Blair probably needed no convincing, there is little doubt that Bush gave him no choice but to comply.

In a secret, leaked Downing Street memorandum published in the UK *Times* on 1 May 2005, this was confirmed by the following statement: 'The US saw the UK ... as essential, with basing in Diego Garcia and Cyprus critical...'[32] Thus Blair knew he had to make the best case he could for supporting the US plan, while deceiving both Parliament and the British people about his true intentions. Some of his official advisers warned that a pre-emptive invasion would be illegal, and that the UN Security Council would therefore not support it. An attempt to strong-arm Security Council members would backfire, leaving the US with just the UK and Australia as coalition partners. The European Union would be split; Israel would be emboldened to take an even harder line against the Palestinians; and the threat of international terrorist attacks on the UK would grow. All of these consequences eventuated.

UK Acceptance of US Ballistic Missile Defence Plans. On 25 July 2007, the British Government led by its new Prime Minister Gordon Brown announced that it had agreed to a US request for RAF Menwith Hill to be used as part of its ballistic missile defence (BMD) system.[33] This allows satellite warnings of potentially hostile ballistic missile launches to be fed into the US system. The UK Government had already given approval for the air defence radar at Fylingdales to be upgraded as part of the US sensor system for its BMD plans.[34]

The Pentagon wanted to deploy ten missiles in Europe, and considered the UK. However, Blair's declining popularity and the growing opposition to his support for the war in Iraq had been considerations in not asking the UK to host them as well.[35] Besides, a Central European location made more sense against missiles launched from the Middle East – or Russia.

The Bush Administration persuaded Poland to accept the missiles, and the Czech Republic to have an associated tracking radar system, despite vigorous public opposition in both countries. Russia responded angrily, arguing that it would upset the strategic balance between Moscow and Washington. President Putin countered by announcing that Russia had suspended its obligations under the Conventional Forces in Europe Treaty, and threatened to withdraw from the 1987 Intermediate-range Nuclear Forces Treaty.[36] Almost two years before this, Putin had announced that Russia would soon deploy a new ballistic missile, possibly with hypersonic manoeuvrable warheads, specifically designed to evade missile defences.[37] Now he warned of the US sparking a new arms race, and accused the US of aiming the BMD system at Russia, with obvious counterproductive implications for UK foreign policy. Inevitably, China also sees BMD as a shield behind which the US could conduct a first strike against its small nuclear forces, and can be expected to redouble its efforts to expand its arsenal, with knock-on effects in India and Pakistan. Meanwhile, a rampant US military-industrial complex forges ahead with plans to place both sensors and weapons in outer space as part of the Pentagon's strategy of 'full spectrum dominance'. A revived arms race looms, provoked by an aggressive US using double standards and contemptuous of international law, with the UK as uncritical accomplice.

By contrast, French President Jacques Chirac was able to take a position much more supportive of majority world opinion. France's independent nuclear stance – about which more later – was much less vulnerable to US pressure. This highlighted the speciousness of the British government's claim that its 'independent nuclear deterrent' is an essential guarantor of an independent foreign policy.

The US: From Massive Retaliation to Controlled Response

From the end of the Korean War until the early 1960s, the US embraced the doctrine of Massive Retaliation, with a 'trip-wire' linked to Soviet aggression against NATO territory in Europe. This was the first application of ***Extended Nuclear Deterrence***, and it meant that the US was committed to a massive first strike on behalf of NATO.

Extended deterrence is achieved by a nuclear weapon state extending its so-called 'nuclear umbrella' to cover the territories of its non-nuclear allies. The concept first arose in NATO during the Korean War. In 1952, the NATO Council set the unrealistic target of 96 army divisions to secure the conventional defence of Europe. It was never met: by 1954, only 15 divisions were in existence. The unwillingness, or inability, of West Europeans to address this conventional target gave birth to, and subsequently justified the continuing need for, extended nuclear deterrence. One important motive for establishing the Nuclear Non-Proliferation Treaty in 1968 was to convince the former Axis powers Germany, Japan and Italy that they had no need to develop nuclear weapons, because they would be covered by US extended deterrence.[38]

Extended deterrence has dogged US nuclear deterrence policy with respect to all its allies, including NATO, Japan, South Korea and Australia (and New Zealand until 1984). There were recurring doubts as to whether the US would risk nuclear war in order to protect an ally. Conversely, for Germany in particular there was a realisation that, despite its decision not to acquire nuclear weapons, it was likely to become a nuclear battlefield. Indeed, extended deterrence could even have the reverse effect of undermining security by *attracting* a nuclear strike because of membership of a nuclear alliance. Thereby, the nuclear 'umbrella' could become instead a 'lightning rod' for insecurity. Evidence of this, for example, is that US nuclear bases in Germany were targeted by Soviet nuclear planners.

In 1960 Atlas, the first US intercontinental ballistic missile (ICBM) became operational (a year after the first Soviet one), and the US Navy tested its first submarine-launched ballistic missile, Polaris. These effectively made nuclear strike aircraft obsolete. Besides, by 1965 the British V-bomber force was no longer able to penetrate improved Soviet air defences. Also in 1960, the US promulgated the first Single Integrated Operational Plan (SIOP) to co-ordinate the nuclear targeting of all three armed forces. This reflected improvements in satellite reconnaissance and accuracy of missile guidance technology.

In light of these rapidly growing options, especially the invulnerable second-strike capability of Polaris, and the shortcomings of Massive Retaliation, US Defense Secretary Robert McNamara introduced **Controlled Response**.[39] This echoed the argument for a form of 'graduated deterrence' proposed nearly ten years earlier by Admiral Buzzard in the UK. McNamara argued for movement away from the indiscriminate threats of Massive Retaliation to a strategy of a wide range of military capabilities, culminating in initial nuclear strikes against Soviet nuclear forces, whilst trying to rehabilitate extended deterrence. In so doing, he addressed damage limitation and civilian vulnerability for the first time by avoiding targeting Soviet cities, to allow war to stop short of an all-out nuclear exchange.

Another objective was to lower the likelihood of the US going to nuclear war. Both Kennedy and McNamara rightly saw Massive Retaliation as too destructive and inflexible, and incapable of deterring aggression short of all-out war. On the other hand, a superficially more rational strategy still held Soviet cities hostage through threatened use of nuclear weapons against civilian populations by second-strike forces, which would violate international humanitarian law. This stimulated fears in Europe that it would be detached for use as a nuclear battleground in exchange for the US restricting its nuclear targets to Soviet forces.[40] The concept of *'nuclear sharing'* was introduced partly to allay such fears.

From the early 1950s the US deployed strategic nuclear weapons among its air forces stationed in the UK. Then, in the late 1950s, additional US tactical nuclear weapons were provided to air forces of seven NATO allies in Europe, six of which were non-nuclear weapon states: Belgium, Germany, Greece, Italy, the Netherlands and Turkey. The seventh was the UK. (Denmark, Norway, Portugal, Iceland and Luxembourg decided not to participate.) While all such weapons were under US custody, in times of war they could be used by both US and specially assigned and trained allied air force units under secret bilateral agreements. In addition, European host states were invited to join NATO's Nuclear Planning Group, and its subsidiary body the High Level Group. These arrangements were designed to symbolise a US guarantee to sustain extended deterrence over European NATO, and the host members' commitment to sharing the benefits and risks.

From Controlled Response to MAD

Controlled Response contained further serious contradictions. McNamara introduced it at a time of US superiority as Polaris became operational. However, possession by only the US of such an assured capability forced the Soviets to target US cities as the only remaining politically coercive choice. Worse, the combination of a US first-strike counterforce strategy and invulnerable second-strike force placed the Soviets under huge pressure to strike first.

Within two years Controlled Response was superseded by a policy of **Assured Destruction**. A pre-eminent factor in this *volte-face* for McNamara was the Cuban missile crisis in October 1962. US declaratory policy reverted to Massive Retaliation, and US actions set up a trip-wire, jettisoning any pretence of damage limitation associated with avoiding the targeting of Soviet cities. In addition, by the mid-1960s the Soviets had achieved an enhanced second-strike capability in the form of greater numbers of widely dispersed intercontinental ballistic missiles and warheads.[41]

Meanwhile, improvements in Soviet intermediate-range ballistic missiles, which could only threaten Europe, prompted a rapid increase in their deployment. This made European NATO nuclear strike aircraft vulnerable, which forced NATO back to a 'launch under attack' status, making restraint impossible. This in turn undermined US extended deterrence because now, even if the Soviet Union was deterred from striking US cities, it would certainly strike European ones, while retaining in reserve an anti-US central force.[42] As these complexities and associated contradictions of US nuclear doctrine in relation to the USSR grew, in 1964 China became the fifth nuclear weapon state when it exploded its first device.

Three years later, the US forced NATO to enhance its conventional military options as part of a new NATO nuclear doctrine, **Flexible Response**. Assured Destruction had become feasible through the invulnerable Polaris submarine force and the sheer numbers of land-based ICBMs in hardened silos, backed up by long-range bombers. However, its credibility now relied on NATO's Flexible Response, which envisaged controlled escalation from conventional war to nuclear war in Europe backed by US strategic superiority.[43]

While marginally improving the conventional component, NATO remained committed to early reliance on US tactical nuclear weapons under nuclear sharing, backed up by the strategic threat. Flexible Response was meant to make war less likely by increasing the credibility of deterrence. In practice, it made war just that bit more likely by providing a possible opening, should war become unavoidable, for a Soviet *blitzkrieg* attack using conventional weapons only. Between 1969–75 the Soviets restructured their forces accordingly, to NATO's surprise and alarm.[44] Nonetheless, Flexible Response remained a key element of NATO's nuclear strategy until the end of the Cold War.

By now, the new US-Soviet relationship was regarded as one of **Mutual Assured Destruction**, with its fitting acronym MAD. It had always been acknowledged that Massive Retaliation would be credible only until the Soviet Union could match the US nuclear capability. When McNamara announced the shift to a policy of Assured Destruction, the Soviet arsenal stood at over 6000 warheads. Perversely, McNamara welcomed the effort by the Soviet Union to match the US, as he hoped that secure retaliatory capabilities on both sides would foster stability.[45]

However, MAD left both sides insecure because defence was impossible. Many strategists therefore rejected it on the grounds that it was not credible. To deter the Soviet Union, the US needed to be able to prevail at any level of conflict. This required a much larger arsenal and highly accurate missiles to destroy Soviet missiles in their silos as well as the underground bunkers where the political and military elite would take refuge in any conflict.[46]

Counter-value versus Counter-force

Some argued for a strategy based on aiming the weapons exclusively at the opponent's military forces and military assets, its *counter-force* targets. Others preferred that at least some of the weapons should be aimed at the opponent's population and social and economic infrastructure, its *counter-value* targets.

One difficulty with a counter-force strategy is that, to be effective, it is inseparable from a first-strike strategy – that is, initiating nuclear war. Furthermore, it places the enemy in a 'use it or lose it' dilemma at the outset of the crisis.

Proponents of counter-value targeting argue that Assured Destruction remains the only responsible policy. This is because, given the lack of civilian defences, the consequences of a nuclear war would be so unacceptable that neither side would initiate it. Also any use of nuclear weapons would almost certainly escalate quickly and uncontrollably. Indeed, much of the effectiveness of nuclear deterrence is claimed to rely on the fact that both sides know events are not entirely under anyone's control, and that nuclear war could start inadvertently.

The counter-force camp argues that the best deterrent posture is the operational capacity to wage nuclear war. Stability is allegedly assured through possession of a number of options, and the ability to dominate each level of war. This concept, known as Escalation Dominance, creates a situation where the potential opponent knows it cannot win a war, even if it is willing to accept the risks associated with various escalatory steps.

The main drawback to this philosophy is that the struggle for Escalation Dominance exacerbated the arms race. The ridiculous result was over 70,000 nuclear warheads at its peak in 1986, despite the signing of two arms-control agreements. The US alone spent over $5 trillion on its nuclear arsenal.[47]

First Use

While it had a nuclear monopoly, the US committed itself to the first use of nuclear weapons in order to defend Western Europe. When that monopoly was broken, the US still persevered with that policy. The Eisenhower administration formally adopted it in 1953, as did NATO in 1954, when it officially embraced the first use of tactical nuclear weapons to counter a conventional Soviet attack.[48] Flexible Response doctrine sustained this because, to deter conventional war and deny the opponent any advantage from it, NATO's nuclear posture had to include the threat to escalate a conventional war to the nuclear level by using nuclear weapons first.

In a crisis, mutual first-strike threats are likely to lead to actual first use, because of the pressure on both sides to destroy the opponent's first-strike system and to avert the destruction of one's own. Worse, US vulnerability to a Soviet nuclear counter-attack undermined the credibility of the US threat of first use, when the US could be devastated if the threat were carried out.

With the end of the Cold War and dissolution of the Warsaw Pact, NATO became vulnerable to criticism for persisting with its first-use option. NATO's conventional forces could deter conventional aggression by Russia.[49] In 1998, even *The New York Times* argued that 'NATO's first-use option ought to be reconsidered in the absence of the overwhelming conventional military threat posed by the old Soviet bloc.'[50]

Post-Cold War US Nuclear War Plan Changes

After the Cold War suddenly ended in 1989, unlike NATO the Warsaw Pact disbanded, followed by the break-up of the Soviet Union and the return of former Soviet nuclear weapons from the Ukraine, Belarus and Kazakhstan to Russia. All this, plus the experience of the 1990-91 Gulf War and the shock of discovering Iraq's nuclear weapon programme, forced major changes in the US nuclear war plan.

General Lee Butler, who played a pivotal role as Commander-in-Chief of US Strategic Air Command from 1991–92 and then of the amalgamated Strategic Command from 1992–94, recalled his reaction on first examining the US nuclear war plan in 1991:

> I finally came to understand the true meaning of MAD, Mutual Assured Destruction. With the possible exception of the Soviet nuclear war plan, *this was the single most absurd and irresponsible document I had ever reviewed in my life.* I was sufficiently outraged that as my examination proceeded, I alerted my superiors in Washington about my concerns... I came to fully appreciate the truth that now makes me seem so odd. And that is: *we escaped the Cold War without a nuclear holocaust by some combination of skill, luck and divine intervention,* and I suspect the latter in greatest proportion...[51] [emphasis added]

Finding 12,500 targets in the Soviet Union and China still destined to be hit almost simultaneously with 10,000 nuclear weapons, Butler cut the number of targets in the US nuclear war plan by no less than 75 percent.[52]

In September 1991, following a failed coup against the Soviet leader

Mikhail Gorbachev, Butler persuaded President George Bush Sr unilaterally to stand down Strategic Command bombers and some intercontinental ballistic missiles from high alert. Gorbachev reciprocated a week later. Both leaders also agreed to remove all tactical nuclear weapons from surface ships and attack submarines, and to drastically reduce the weapons deployed in Europe.

However, new emphasis on using nuclear weapons to counter the proliferation of weapons of mass destruction (WMD) among 'rogue' states in the Third World became a major driver in nuclear war planning. In 1993, a revised SIOP was published, which incorporated Third World WMD targets.[53]

Expanding nuclear deterrence to cover smaller and more diverse regional WMD contingencies, including, for the first time, targets in the Southern Hemisphere, meant nuclear planners would be faced with rapidly changing guidance and requirements. The solution was the creation of a completely new nuclear war planning apparatus based on *adaptive planning,* a concept which was also adopted by NATO.[54] Butler explained that, rather than identifying specific scenarios and enemies, options were matched to the range of threats: 'To ensure their completeness, these options consider the employment of both nuclear and conventional weapons.'[55]

What was dubbed the Living SIOP was implemented on 1 April 1994, to be used in conjunction with SIOP-95, the latest update of the traditional plan. The new Strategic War Planning System was scheduled to become initially operational in late 1998 and, when completed in 2003, would expand the US capability to incorporate the routine processing of WMD targets outside Russia in countries such as Iran, Iraq, Libya and North Korea.[56] This was despite the fact that all these countries were signatories of the Nuclear Non-Proliferation Treaty (NPT), and Libya had signed the Pelindaba African Nuclear Weapon Free Zone Treaty.[57]

US Nuclear Posture Review 1993–97

At the same time as this expansion of capabilities, a major review of US nuclear policy and force structure was initiated. However, when this first Nuclear Posture Review was completed in September 1994, little had changed. Reaffirming the importance of nuclear deterrence to US security, nuclear weapons featured prominently to 'deter WMD acquisition or use.' These conclusions were largely deleted from the public record to reflect the Clinton administration's line that the review had reduced the role of nuclear weapons.[58]

Sensitivity about using nuclear weapons to deter non-nuclear threats encouraged ambiguity in US nuclear deterrence policy thereafter. Also, expanding the target list globally would be difficult if nuclear weapon reductions were pursued below the 3,500 level agreed in the second Strategic Arms Reduction Treaty (START II) signed by Bush and the Russian president Boris Yeltsin in 1993.[59]

Consequently, in November 1997 Clinton signed a new secret Presidential Decision Directive, PDD 60, replacing one signed by Reagan in 1981. Russian conventional forces and industry were no longer targeted. Instead, the focus had shifted to destroying nuclear forces as well as the military and civilian leadership. Winning a nuclear war against Russia was no longer an objective. However, the PDD broadened targeting in China to include conventional forces and industry, deleted from the plan for Russia. It also identified specific regional contingencies where US nuclear forces could respond to WMD attacks.[60]

As US planning against Third World targets developed, US decision-makers found the old discredited policy of Controlled Response acquiring a new but still irresponsibly dangerous meaning. If regional nuclear deterrence was to add the credibility not able to be provided by the existing nuclear posture, then the new posture and strategy had to indicate more willingness than the old to use nuclear weapons.[61] By trying to revert to Cold War deterrence, but against less predictable, possibly non-nuclear armed opponents, US planners were lowering the threshold for use of US nuclear weapons, and increasing the risk of using them first.

NATO's Post-Cold War Nuclear Posture

Nervously following in the wake of these massive shifts in US nuclear policy and plans, NATO barely mentioned nuclear weapons in its new Strategy Concept published in April 1999. It could be inferred that its nuclear deterrence posture remained Assured Destruction but only as an extremely remote last resort, with no mention of Flexible Response. Nevertheless, it continued to deploy some less destructive sub-strategic or tactical nuclear weapons to 'provide an essential political and military link between Europe and the North American members of the Alliance.' In addition to US free-fall nuclear bombs deployed under the nuclear sharing agreements, for the first time 'a small number of United Kingdom Trident warheads' were specified as part of NATO's sub-strategic nuclear posture in Europe.[62] The UK government explained:

A sub-strategic capability is an essential element in ensuring that no nuclear-armed aggressor could gamble on us being self-deterred by fear of an inevitable strategic exchange. In such extreme circumstances this capability would allow the limited use of nuclear weapons to send an aggressor a political message of the Alliance's resolve to defend itself. The UK has a degree of flexibility in the choice of yield for the warheads on its Trident missiles.[63]

In the run-up to NATO's fiftieth anniversary summit in Washington in April 1999, the first evidence of dissension over its nuclear policy emerged. The previous December, a UN General Assembly resolution, 'Towards a Nuclear Weapon-Free World: The Need for a New Agenda', had resulted in every non-nuclear NATO member state except Turkey, and other close US allies Japan and Australia, abstaining despite heavy pressure from the US, the UK and France to oppose it. Such insubordination on nuclear policy was unprecedented.[64]

The sponsors of this resolution were a new coalition of eight middle-power governments from across the Cold War blocs, who had lost patience with the lack of progress towards the elimination of nuclear weapons. In June 1998, the Foreign Ministers of Brazil, Egypt, Mexico, Ireland, New Zealand, Slovenia, South Africa and Sweden issued a joint declaration calling for a new sense of urgency on nuclear disarmament. Dubbed the New Agenda Coalition, they criticised both the nuclear weapon states and the three nuclear-capable states of India, Israel and Pakistan and urged them all to agree to start work immediately on a programme of practical steps and negotiations required to eliminate their nuclear arsenals.[65] With Slovenia intimidated by NATO to drop out, the remaining seven governments followed through with the UN resolution, which was adopted by an overwhelming majority.

The primary objection to the resolution cited by the US, UK and France was that it was incompatible with nuclear deterrence. However, Canada was already reviewing its nuclear policy in light of the 1996 Advisory Opinion from the International Court of Justice on the legal status of the threat or use of nuclear weapons. Germany had recently changed its government to a coalition of Social Democrats and Greens, both of whom, in opposition, had called for changes in NATO's nuclear policy. Although they were US allies, both Canada and Germany, influenced by strong citizen group lobbying, decided on a joint abstention strategy, which succeeded.

Germany's Foreign Minister Joschka Fischer publicly challenged NATO's first use policy. A week after the vote, Canada's Parliamentary Standing Committee on Foreign Affairs and International Trade published their review of nuclear policy, which called for Canada to 'argue forcefully within NATO that the present re-examination and update as necessary of the Alliance Strategic Concept should include its nuclear component.'[66] The government of Canada responded by requesting NATO to review its nuclear policy as part of an ongoing major review of its strategy.

NATO's new strategy was published at the Washington Summit in April 1999. Paragraph 32 of the NATO Communique stated: 'In the light of overall strategic developments and the reduced salience of nuclear weapons, the Alliance will consider options for confidence and security-building measures, verification, non-proliferation and arms control and disarmament.'[67] Canada's Foreign Minister Lloyd Axworthy revealed that this vague language concealed reluctant acceptance by the US, the UK and France to conduct a nuclear policy review. NATO officials later denied this.

The New Agenda Coalition submitted a revised version of their resolution to the 1999 UN General Assembly. Again the NATO nuclear powers applied strong pressure to sustain NATO's apparently restored cohesion; but in the final vote, fourteen non-nuclear members out of the newly increased total of nineteen, plus Japan and Australia, abstained.[68] Two weeks later, NATO announced that its nuclear policy would be reviewed in what became known as the 'paragraph 32 process', with the outcome expected in December 2000.[69]

At the five-yearly NPT Review Conference in April–May 2000, the consensus final document listed thirteen practical steps towards a nuclear weapon-free world. These included the following:

* An unequivocal undertaking by the nuclear weapon states to accomplish the total elimination of their nuclear arsenals leading to nuclear disarmament to which all States parties are committed under Article VI.

* The further reduction of non-strategic nuclear weapons, based on unilateral initiatives and as an integral part of the nuclear arms reduction and disarmament process.

* Concrete agreed measures to further reduce the operational status of nuclear weapons systems.

* A diminishing role for nuclear weapons in security policies to minimise the risk that these weapons ever be used and to acilitate the process of their total elimination.[70]

These steps were all incompatible with NATO nuclear policy, because such an undertaking could not be reconciled with the following statements in NATO's 1999 Strategy Concept:

> The presence of United States... nuclear forces in Europe remains vital to the security of Europe... the Alliance will maintain for the foreseeable future an appropriate mix of nuclear and conventional forces based in Europe... Nuclear weapons make a unique contribution in rendering the risks of aggression against the Alliance incalculable and unacceptable. Thus, they remain essential to preserve peace... The supreme guarantee of the security of the Allies is provided by the strategic nuclear forces of the Alliance...[71]

The NPT Review final document also included, in the section on Article VII, the following paragraphs submitted by five NATO states (Belgium, Germany, Italy, the Netherlands and Norway):

> 2. The Conference reaffirms that the total elimination of nuclear weapons is the only absolute guarantee against the use or threat of use of nuclear weapons. The Conference agrees that legally binding security assurances by the five nuclear-weapon States to the non-nuclear-weapon States parties to the Treaty on the Non-Proliferation of Nuclear Weapons (NPT) strengthen the nuclear non-proliferation regime. The Conference calls on the Preparatory Committee to make recommendations to the 2005 Review Conference on this issue.
>
> 3. The Conference notes the reaffirmation by the nuclear-weapon States of their commitment to the United Nations Security Council resolution 984 (1995) on security assurances for non-nuclear-weapon States Parties to the Treaty on the Non-Proliferation of Nuclear Weapons.[72]

Such commendable leadership by these five NATO members was seriously undermined by NATO's insistence, as an integral part of Flexible Response, on retaining the option to use nuclear weapons first.

In December 2000, NATO released extracts from its report on the 'paragraph 32 process'. This simply reaffirmed that nuclear weapons 'make a unique contribution in rendering the risks of aggression against the Alliance incalculable and unacceptable. Thus, they remain essential to preserve peace.' It restated the need for nuclear sharing: '[T]he burden and risks of providing the nuclear element of NATO's deterrent capability should not be borne by the nuclear powers alone.'[73]

For the first time, however, NATO clearly felt the need to address accusations that its nuclear policy, and especially its sub-strategic capability, stimulated proliferation. Its rebuttals were weak and unconvincing, simply asserting that 'no evidence was found that proliferant nations acquire nuclear capabilities based on the fact that NATO maintains nuclear weapons in Europe... By contrast, the nuclear programmes [of proliferant states] have diminished, not strengthened security and stability within their regions and beyond.' It seemed unaware of the contradiction when later it stated that 'the Alliance's nuclear weapons will be maintained at the minimum level to preserve peace and stability. This enhances the security of the Euro-Atlantic region and beyond.' What message did this send to India, Pakistan and aspiring nuclear states? It went on to claim that 'NATO members support the entire Final Document of the May 2000 NPT Review Conference', and even cited the steps quoted earlier, which conflict with NATO nuclear policy.[74]

However, at a Senate Foreign Relations Committee hearing on the 2002 US Nuclear Posture Review, Admiral Bill Owens, former Vice Chair of the US Joint Chiefs of Staff, showed that some influential members of the US military saw no need for NATO nuclear weapons. He said:

> Now that we begin to see the Russians more like England and France than like the old Soviet enemy, then we should have very much on the table this issue of tactical nuclear weapons... and really get to the core of getting rid of them if we can. A part of this is our own problem... [because] many policymakers in this country believe the NATO nuclear force is critical to holding NATO together and to having a genuine capability against what I'm not sure, unless it's the Russians... It just seems to me that *we should find a way to come to grips with the fact that NATO does not need a nuclear force...* and that we should be step one in leading us to a decision to go to zero on tactical nuclear weapons and dramatically affect the business of proliferation.[75] [emphasis added]

US Doubts about Nuclear Deterrence

Underlying the shifts in US nuclear posture in the 1990s was a growing concern that the Cold War doctrines of MAD and Flexible Response were no longer reliable against 'rogue' regimes or extremists. With George W. Bush's inauguration as US President in January 2001, another major shift was heralded in US nuclear deterrence doctrine.

In April that year, British newspapers picked up on a *Washington Post* article headlined: 'US Studies Developing New Nuclear Bomb.' Walter Pincus wrote that the Pentagon was due to report to the Senate in July in response to a Republican request in the Defense Authorization Bill to find a way of destroying 'hardened and deeply buried targets.' The desire for such a capability was driven by the realisation that, for example, President Saddam Hussein would not be deterred by any of the nuclear warheads in the US arsenal, 'because he knows a US president would not drop a 100-kiloton bomb on Baghdad' in order to counter Iraq's WMD.[76]

Following the Gulf War in 1991, several leading US nuclear weapon experts reassessed the effectiveness of nuclear deterrence, especially against threats by 'rogue' states with WMD-armed ballistic missiles. Israel had become the first state with nuclear weapons to be directly struck by ballistic missiles, experiencing thirty-nine Scud attacks, some of them against its second largest city, Tel Aviv. For several weeks Israelis in gas masks had sheltered in basements, because it was known that a chemical warhead had been developed for Iraq's Scuds. Saddam Hussein had not been deterred by Israel's nuclear arsenal. Subsequently, the US, UK and France were further shocked to discover instead that Hussein had been provoked by Israel's clandestine acquisition of nuclear weapons – condoned and abetted by the three NATO nuclear states – to follow suit, despite the fact that Iraq was a signatory to the NPT.

In a 1991 article entitled 'Countering the Threat of the Well-Armed Tyrant', two Los Alamos National Laboratory nuclear weapon analysts argued that the US had no proportionate response to a 'rogue' dictator who uses chemical or biological weapons against US troops.[77] Nine years later, the consequent risk of self-deterrence was a supporting theme in an influential paper, *Nuclear Weapons in the 21st Century*, by Stephen Younger, Associate Laboratory Director for Nuclear Weapons at Los Alamos.[78] He challenged decades of military thinking by suggesting that precision-guided conventional munitions could replace nuclear warheads on most US strategic missiles. Because of improvements in accuracy, 'advanced conventional weapons delivered by ballistic or cruise missiles could defeat many [military sites] that are presently targeted by nuclear weapons', such as mobile missiles and manufacturing sites for chemical and biological weapons. However, no doubt concerned that he might be arguing away his job, he recommended that the US should consider developing a new generation of 'small' nuclear weapons to handle the few military tasks for which he claimed nuclear weapons to be indispensable.

In a speech at the US National Defense University on 1 May 2001, President George W. Bush showed he was sympathetic to these ideas when he called for deep cuts in the US nuclear stockpile, along with development of a still unproven ballistic missile defence system.[79] In some ways, this was a revived response to what Ronald Reagan had seen as the unacceptable and immoral prospect of relying forever on

MAD for US security. What had changed since the 'Star Wars' era was that Bush accepted the experts' potentially heretical thesis. He became the first US President publicly to doubt that nuclear deterrence alone would work against what was now seen as the greatest threat to Americans – extremists armed with WMD warheads intent on blackmailing the US:

> Cold War deterrence is no longer enough… We need new concepts of deterrence that rely on both offensive and defensive forces. Deterrence can no longer be based solely on the threat of nuclear retaliation.

Moreover, both his Vice-President Dick Cheney and Secretary of State General Colin Powell were known to have rejected use of nuclear weapons against Iraqi forces in the 1991 Gulf War.[80] Such perceived lack of faith in the utility of one's own weapons meant that any future US nuclear threat in a similar scenario would lack credibility.

The 2002 US Nuclear Posture Review

Responding to these challenges, after a year in office the Bush administration presented a new Nuclear Posture Review (NPR) to Congress in January 2002.[81] This established the broad outline of Pentagon planning for US nuclear strategy, force levels and infrastructure for the next ten years and beyond. Although the NPR report was secret, it was leaked to defence analyst William Arkin, who published his assessment in the *Los Angeles Times* on 10 March 2002.[82]

In the Foreword, Defense Secretary Rumsfeld confirmed that the NPR implemented a major change in the US approach to nuclear deterrence. A new 'Triad' had been established, composed of offensive strike systems (both nuclear and non-nuclear), defences (both active and passive), and a revitalized defence infrastructure to provide new capabilities to meet emerging threats. The old Triad had comprised a purely nuclear-armed combination of three delivery systems: land-based ICBMs, air-launched cruise missiles and free-fall bombs, and a relatively invulnerable second-strike capability with submarine-launched ICBMs. Rumsfeld argued that the new arrangement could both reduce dependence on nuclear weapons and improve the ability to deter attack in the face of proliferating WMD capabilities. By 'defences', he meant reviving Reagan's flawed dream of a ballistic missile defence (BMD) system in both its national and 'theatre' (regional) forms. To permit this, on 13 June 2002 the Bush administration withdrew the US unilaterally from the Anti-Ballistic Missile (ABM) Treaty, which had underpinned MAD by severely limiting BMD systems to one each around a single key target.[83]

Rumsfeld acknowledged that, in the decade since the collapse of the Soviet Union, US nuclear war plans had undergone only modest revision despite the new relationship with Russia, and few changes had been made to strategic nuclear forces. This would now change: 'As a result of this review, the U.S. will no longer plan, size or sustain its forces as though Russia presented merely a smaller version of the threat posed by the former Soviet Union.' Instead, planning for US strategic forces would be shifted from the threat-based approach of the Cold War to one based on capabilities. Furthermore, Rumsfeld stated:

> [W]e have concluded that a strategic posture that relies solely on offensive nuclear forces is inappropriate for deterring the potential adversaries we will face in the 21st century. Terrorists or rogue states armed with weapons of mass destruction will likely test America's security commitments to its allies and friends... A broader array of capability is needed to dissuade states from undertaking political, military, or technical courses of action that would threaten U.S. and allied security. U.S. forces must pose a credible deterrent to potential adversaries who have access to modern military technology, including NBC weapons and the means to deliver them over long distances...[84]

The review went on to cite seven countries that, by implication, were now targeted with US nuclear weapons:

> *North Korea, Iraq, Iran, Syria,* and *Libya* are among the countries that could be involved in immediate, potential, or unexpected contingencies. All have longstanding hostility toward the United States and its security partners; North Korea and Iraq in particular have been chronic military concerns. All sponsor or harbor terrorists, and all have active WMD and missile programs.
>
> Due to the combination of *China*'s still developing strategic objectives and its ongoing modernization of its nuclear and non-nuclear forces, China is a country that could be involved in an immediate or potential contingency...
>
> *Russia* maintains the most formidable nuclear forces, aside from the United States, and substantial, if less impressive, conventional capabilities. There now are, however, no ideological sources of conflict with Moscow, as there were during the Cold War. The United States seeks a more cooperative relationship with Russia and a move away from the balance-of-terror policy framework, which *by definition is an expression of mutual distrust and hostility*. As a result, a [nuclear strike] contingency involving Russia, while plausible, is not expected... Adjusting U.S. immediate nuclear force requirements in recognition of the changed relationship with Russia is a critical step away from the Cold War policy of mutual vulnerability and toward more cooperative relations... Russia's nuclear forces and programs, nevertheless, remain a concern. Russia faces many strategic problems

around its periphery and its future course cannot be charted with certainty. U.S. planning must take this into account. In the event that U.S. relations with Russia significantly worsen in the future, the U.S. *may need to revise its nuclear force levels and posture*.[85] [emphasis added]

Implications for US Nuclear Deterrence Doctrine

By combining BMD with augmented conventional strike systems, the Bush administration hoped to strengthen conventional deterrence and raise the threshold for use of strategic nuclear weapons. At first sight, this appeared to be a positive development, what with Bush and Russian President Vladimir Putin signing the Strategic Offensive Reductions Treaty (SORT) in Moscow, and the inauguration of a new NATO-Russia Council in May 2002.

Unfortunately, Bush's piecemeal approach with Russia excluded China, the only other nuclear-armed state with superpower potential. There were no plans for a NATO-China Council, or for sharing BMD technology with China. On the contrary, China correctly perceives current US collaboration with both Japan and Taiwan to develop theatre BMD systems as undermining MAD by threatening its land-based nuclear-armed ICBMs. As it modernises its arsenal of less than 300 nuclear warheads, China can be expected to use US theatre BMD plans to justify expanding its nuclear capability. This will inevitably spur India to expand its own, to which Pakistan will feel pressured to respond. Thus one long-term consequence of deploying BMD will be to stifle further progress in nuclear disarmament, because the US will argue it cannot make any more reductions in light of these developments. Russia will feel forced to follow suit.

Furthermore, the proposed US-Russian cuts in nuclear warheads in SORT were not what they seemed or should be. The reductions to between 1,700–2,200 on each side by 2012 were no advance on the third Strategic Arms Reduction Treaty (START III), guidelines for which were agreed in 1997 by Presidents Clinton and Yeltsin, to cut numbers to 2,000–2,500 by 2007. Progress on negotiating START III had been stymied by NATO's attack on Kosovo in 1999 followed by enlargement eastwards, and then by US plans for reviving BMD.

An early indicator of Russia's understandable response to the US Nuclear Posture Review came in August 2002. It announced a radical plan to overhaul 144 of its most powerful nuclear-armed Satan ICBMs destined for dismantling under START II. Instead of being dismantled by 2007, they would be kept fully operational until 2014, two years after SORT's agreed date of expiry. This announcement came despite ratification of START II by both the US and Russia.

When Bush and Putin signed SORT, no mention was made about standing down the 2,000 nuclear warheads which each side still held at minutes' notice to launch – evidence of the enduring legacy of the dogma of nuclear deterrence. This was an especially glaring omission, for two reasons. Bush had pledged to 'replace Mutual Assured Destruction with Mutual Cooperation' between Russia and the US. There was also a growing risk of false alarms from Russia's degraded early warning system following the break-up of the Soviet Union.

Another outcome of the revised US nuclear posture was making the use of nuclear weapons more likely. It recommended using low-yield nuclear weapons against hardened or deeply buried non-nuclear WMD targets or bunkers where conventional weapons could be ineffective. This might have been driven by the perceived need to restore US credibility in light of the Cheney/Powell decision to rule out use of nuclear weapons in the 1991 Gulf War. Such a recommendation was also an incitement to nuclear proliferation, as it would gut US assurances not to use nuclear weapons against non-nuclear NPT signatory states, including the 'axis of evil' trio of Iran, Iraq and North Korea, plus Libya and Syria. The UK government dutifully echoed its 'master's voice' by warning that it, too, was prepared to use nuclear weapons if its forces, not just national territory, were subjected to WMD attack.[86] In October 2003 the French government signalled its intention to follow suit.[87]

The Bush Doctrine of Pre-emption

Partly as a response to the '9/11' terror attacks on the centres of US economic and military power, just over a year later, on 20 September 2002, President Bush submitted to Congress a new National Security Strategy. At the heart of this was a controversial doctrine of 'pre-emptive' military action to counter proven, emerging or potential threats to US national security that might involve WMD. The justification for such a belligerent stance, euphemistically described by US administration officials as 'anticipatory self-defence', was driven by a fundamental recognition that nuclear deterrence is irrelevant against such a threat. The fifth section of the strategy spelt this out:

> Traditional concepts of deterrence will not work against a terrorist enemy whose avowed tactics are wanton destruction and the targeting of innocents; whose so-called soldiers seek martyrdom in death and whose most potent protection is statelessness.[88]

This Bush doctrine of pre-emption may have sounded the death-knell of nuclear deterrence.

In an effort to shore up its nuclear posture in relation to Iraq, on 11 December 2002 the Bush administration released a six-page document, *National Strategy to Combat Weapons of Mass Destruction*.[89] An unclassified summary of a new National Security Presidential Directive 17, it set out the practical ramifications of both the new US nuclear posture and national security strategy. PD17 authorised pre-emptive strikes on states and terrorist groups that are close to acquiring WMD or their long-range delivery systems. The 11 December statement also deliberately implied the possible use of nuclear weapons:

> The United States will continue to make clear that it reserves the right to respond with overwhelming force – including through resort to all of our options – to the use of WMD against the United States, our forces abroad, and friends and allies.[90]

This signalled to the world that, if anything, the US was increasing its reliance on nuclear weapons, while at the same time urging other countries to give up or forgo them. Thereby the US position so undercut the NPT that it essentially constituted an incitement to nuclear proliferation.

In January 2003, William Arkin revealed Pentagon plans for the possible use of nuclear weapons in Iraq.[91] The clearly understood implication was that an attack with crude chemical weapons, which might kill perhaps one hundred US troops in the Middle East, could result in some form of nuclear retaliation. This would kill or maim hundreds of thousands of non-combatants and make a vast area, possibly extending to other countries, uninhabitable for years. The other scenario involved attacking Saddam Hussein's deepest and hardest command bunkers. Many of these were in highly populated urban areas. The double standards involved were staggering: now part of the US strategy to combat WMD was to use such weapons of its own, risking provoking undeterrable opponents to use theirs too. Moreover, the pre-emption doctrine in this form flagrantly violated the principle of proportionality under the Geneva Conventions, which renders illegal the use of nuclear weapons in response to an attack with non-nuclear weapons.

Superimposed on all this was the fallacious lumping together of nuclear with chemical and biological weapons, as pointed out by Dr John Weinstein, Chief of the Futures and Initiatives Division of the US Nuclear Command and Control System Support Staff in Washington DC. In a 2001 essay called 'Ten Reasons Why Nuclear Deterrence Could Fail: The Case for Reassessing US Nuclear Policies and Plans', he argued for removal of 'the WMD shorthand from our deterrence vocabulary', because placing nuclear weapons in the same category prevents the development of clear deterrence concepts.[92]

Pentagon Confirms Plan for Pre-emptive Use of Nuclear Weapons

On the fourth anniversary of the 9/11 terror attacks, Walter Pincus reported in *The Washington Post* that the Pentagon had drafted a revised doctrine for the use of nuclear weapons as part of the National Strategy to Combat Weapons of Mass Destruction.[93] He drew upon an article by Hans Kristensen analysing a new draft of *Doctrine for Joint Nuclear Operations*, which he had found on the Pentagon website, but which was removed after the Pincus report appeared.[94]

The doctrine called for maintaining an aggressive nuclear posture with modernised weapons on high alert for a pre-emptive strike against adversaries armed with WMD. Conventional forces and BMD now merely complemented, instead of replacing, nuclear weapons. The addition of a chapter on regional nuclear operations reflected the struggle by US nuclear planners to find ways of deterring 'rogue' states armed with WMD. The result was nuclear pre-emption, not deterrence through threatened retaliation. Such a posture was an incitement to potential state and non-state adversaries, leading to more insecurity for all. What was driving the new doctrine was an acceptance that nuclear deterrence will fail sooner or later.

According to Kristensen, the doctrine identified four scenarios for pre-emptive use:

* An adversary intending to use WMD against US, multinational or allied forces or civilian populations.

* Imminent attack from an adversary's biological weapons, which only effects from nuclear weapons can safely destroy.

* Attacks on adversary installations including WMD destruction; deep, hardened bunkers containing chemical or biological weapons; or the command and control infrastructure required for the adversary to execute a WMD attack against the US or its allies.

* Demonstration of US intent and capability to use nuclear weapons to deter adversary WMD use.[95]

Interestingly, the new doctrine acknowledged that 'the belligerent that initiates nuclear warfare may find itself the target of world condemnation.' It then defiantly asserted that 'no customary or conventional international law prohibits nations from employing

Figure 1.	CHRONOLOGY OF NUCLEAR DETERRENCE DOCTRINE
1945-49	US nuclear monopoly: nuclear weapons simply extend conventional bombing capability.
1949	First Soviety test of fission device.
1951	First US test of thermonuclear davice.
1952	First UK test of a fission device. US announces doctrine of Massive Retaliation, and Extended Deterrence of non-nuclear NATO members.
1957	First UK test of thermonuclear device: adopts Massive Retaliation.
1960	First French test of fission device.
1962	US adopts Controlled Response.
1965	US shifts to docrtine of Assured Destruction.
1967	NATO adopts Flexible Response.
1968	First French test of thermonuclear device.
1974	First Indian test of fission device.
1979	Probable first Israeli/South African test of nuclear device.
1991	Israel's nuclear arsenal fails to deter Iraqi Scud attacks.
1995	Misidentified Norwegian research rocket brings Yeltsin within minutes of activating nuclear release codes.
1998	India and Pakistan test nuclear devices.
1999	India and Pakistan clash in Kargil: first by nuclear-armed states.
2002	Major confrontation between India and Pakistan, with nuclear threats. US and UK accept nuclear deterrence is unreliable against extremists; announce policy of first use against chemical or biological attack against their interests.
2003	Leaked Pentagon documents show plans for possible use of nuclear weapons in the US-UK invasion of Iraq. France aligns its nuclear deterrence policy with the US and UK.
2005	Leaked draft Pentagon doctrine for joint US nuclear operations implement Bush administration's 2002 National Strategy to Combat Weapons of Mass Destruction confirms pre-emptive choice because nuclear deterrence will fail sooner or later.

Figure 2. GLOBAL NUCLEAR ARSENALS, 1945-2018

Year	US	Russia	UK	France	China	Total
1945	6					6
1946	11					11
1947	32					32
1948	110					110
1949	235	1				236
1950	369	5				374
1951	640	25				665
1952	1,005	50				1,055
1953	1,436	120	1			1,557
1954	2,063	150	5			2,218
1955	3,057	200	10			3,267
1956	4,618	426	15			5,059
1957	6,444	660	20			7,124
1958	9,822	869	22			10,713
1959	15,468	1,060	25			16,553
1960	20,434	1,605	30			22,069
1961	24,126	2,471	50			26,647
1962	27,387	3,322	205			30,914
1963	29,459	4,238	280			33,977
1964	31,056	5,221	310	4	1	36,592
1965	31,982	6,129	310	32	5	38,458
1966	**32,040**	7,089	270	36	20	39,455
1967	31,233	8,339	270	36	25	39,903
1968	29,224	9,399	280	36	35	38,974
1969	27,342	10,538	308	36	50	38,274
1970	26,662	11,643	280	36	75	38,696
1971	26,956	13,092	220	45	100	40,413
1972	27,912	14,478	220	70	130	42,810
1973	28,999	15,915	275	116	150	45,455
1974	28,965	17,385	325	145	170	46,990
1975	27,826	19,055	**350**	188	185	47,604
1976	25,579	21,205	350	212	190	47,536
1977	25,722	23,044	350	228	200	49,544
1978	24,826	25,393	350	235	220	51,024
1979	24,605	27,935	350	235	235	53,360
1980	24,304	30,062	350	250	280	55,246
1981	23,464	32,049	350	274	330	56,467
1982	23,708	33,952	335	274	360	58,629
1983	24,099	35,804	320	279	380	60,882
1984	24,357	37,431	270	280	415	62,753
1985	24,237	39,197	300	360	425	64,519

Figure 2. Continued...

Year	US	Russia	UK	France	China	Total
1986	24,401	**45,000**	300	355	425	**70,481**
1987	24,344	43,000	300	420	415	68,479
1988	23,586	41,000	300	410	430	65,726
1989	22,380	39,000	300	410	**435**	62,525
1990	21,004	37,000	300	505	430	59,239
1991	17,287	35,000	300	**540**	435	53,562
1992	14,747	33,000	300	540	435	49,022
1993	13,076	31,000	300	525	435	45,336
1994	12,555	29,000	250	510	400	42,715
1995	12,144	27,000	300	500	400	40,344
1996	11,009	25,000	300	450	400	37,159
1997	10,950	24,000	260	450	400	36,060
1998	10,871	23,000	260	450	400	34,981
1999	10,824	22,000	185	450	400	33,859
2000	10,577	21,000	185	470	400	32,632
2001	10,527	20,000	200	350	400	31,477
2002	10,475	19,000	200	350	400	30,425
2003	10,421	18,000	200	350	400	29,371
2004	10,358	18,000	200	350	400	29,308
2005	10,295	17,000	200	350	400	28,245
2006	10,104	16,000	200	350	200	26,854
2009	9,400	13,000	160	300	240	23,100
2018	6,600	6,800	215	300	270	14,550

Figures prepared by Robert S. Norris of the Natural Resources Defense Council and Hans M. Kristensen of the Federation of American Scientists. See http://www.thebulletin.org for more details.

The US total comprises about 1,800 deployed warheads (1,650 strategic, 150 tactical), 2,200 in operational reserve (of which about 150 are tactical), and 2,600 awaiting disassembly. Russia's total comprises about 1,700 in its operational stockpile (all strategic) plus 2,600 in reserve or awaiting disassembly, of which about 1,800 are tactical. Norris and Kristensen explain that the halving of China's arsenal in 2006 from the 2005 figure came from new information. In 2018, the Arms Control Association offers the following estimates of the arsenals of the other four nuclear weapon states: Israel – 80; India – 130; Pakistan – 140; North Korea – 20.

nuclear weapons in armed conflict.' Yet Kristensen reported that, during the editing process, Strategic Command (STRATCOM) decided that counter-value targeting violated the Law of Armed Conflict. It therefore suggested changing 'counter-value' to 'critical infrastructure', offering the following argument:

> Many operational law attorneys do not believe 'counter-value' targeting is a lawful justification for employment of force, much less nuclear force. Counter-value philosophy makes no distinction between purely civilian activities and military related activities and could be used to justify deliberate attacks on civilians and non-military portions of a nation's economy. It therefore cannot meet the 'military necessity' prong of the Law of Armed Conflict. Counter-value targeting also undermines one of the values that underlies the Law of Armed Conflict – the reduction of civilian suffering and to foster the ability to maintain the peace after the conflict ends. For example, under the counter-value target philosophy, the attack on the World Trade Center Towers on 9/11 could be justified.[96]

In the end, the commands could not agree, so both terms were withdrawn. Kristensen pointed out how the doctrine contradicted the 1996 Advisory Opinion on the threat or use of nuclear weapons by the International Court of Justice.

Another important change was that the new doctrine did away with a separate regional role for non-strategic nuclear forces. Instead, it gave all nuclear weapons support roles in regional operations. The conclusion was that strategic nuclear weapons now had a regional role. Also, the planned fitting of conventional warheads to ICBMs, included in the doctrine for the first time, had serious implications for crisis stability. For example, a nuclear state under attack from a conventionally armed ICBM early in a conflict might conclude that it was under nuclear attack and launch a nuclear reprisal.

The doctrinal shift had progressed to the point where STRATCOM had implemented a new strike plan, Contingency Plan (CONPLAN) 8022: this made the Bush pre-emption policy operational, and the new nuclear doctrine codified it.[97]

France's *Force de Frappe*

France did not decide to go nuclear until December 1956. This was a month after the collapse of the Anglo-French Suez fiasco, which exposed the inability of either country to undertake any major military action if the US disapproved. The British opted for dependence, exploiting their special Anglo-Saxon relationship with the Americans. The French, still recovering from World War II, also had that option.

The French military had been discredited by a humiliating defeat, and the nation traumatised by Nazi occupation. A large part of the armed forces, especially the navy, had been seriously tarnished by its association with the Vichy regime, which had collaborated with the Nazi occupiers. It had taken time to rebuild the armed forces from General Charles de Gaulle's Free French forces, the Communist-dominated resistance and the former Vichy forces.[98] Then came the loss of French Indo-China, followed by the savage Algerian war of independence.

Despite this, de Gaulle, who became President in 1958, raised with the US the possibility of France sharing the UK's special treatment; but he was rebuffed. Nonetheless, although France did not decide to become a nuclear power until ten years after the UK, its nuclear research had kept pace with international developments; and it successfully tested its first nuclear device on 13 February 1960 in Algeria.

The Kennedy-Macmillan conference in December 1962, promising the Polaris system to the British, was decisive. It confirmed French suspicions of US-UK collusion on nuclear weapons, and ended any prospect of overt French co-operation with either country. On 14 January 1963, de Gaulle proclaimed full nuclear independence. The French nuclear programme became a key instrument in the attainment of de Gaulle's twin policy aims of reasserting France's independence from superpower hegemony and demonstrating its distinctive national identity. Another factor was that France could no longer allow its historic British rival to be the only European nuclear power.[99]

US opposition to what became known as the *force de frappe* angered de Gaulle. This opposition was epitomised by McNamara's 1962 University of Michigan speech in which he had introduced Kennedy's new nuclear policy of Controlled Response, and condemned small nuclear forces as 'dangerous' and 'lacking in credibility as a deterrent'. In 1966 de Gaulle removed France from NATO's military organisation, and evicted NATO's Europe HQ from Paris and other allied military facilities from French territory.

De Gaulle did not develop any nuclear philosophy other than that of giving France all options and relying primarily on the threat of nuclear use to deter any attack on its 'vital interests'. Unable or unwilling to challenge the orthodoxy bequeathed by him, his successors sought to emulate him and draw strength from his role and symbolism. Thus François Mitterrand, President from 1981–95, earned for himself the nickname '*Dieu*' (God) after he outrageously declared, '*La dissuasion, c'est moi*' ('I am deterrence').[100]

A distinctive characteristic of French doctrine is nuclear deterrence *tous azimuts* ('in all directions'). Its creator, General Ailleret, cited France's historic enemies, above all Britain, Germany and, almost as an afterthought, the Soviet Union (but only until Stalin's death in 1953). This helps explain why the French Pluton short-range ground-to-ground nuclear-tipped ballistic missile was specifically targeted on West German soil.[101]

Nevertheless, de Gaulle's decision to make France the world's fourth nuclear power was initially resisted, mainly by a strong Communist Party. For example, after the first French thermonuclear test on 24 August 1968 in the South Pacific, a national opinion poll recorded that 52 percent were opposed to a nuclear force. A broad consensus on defence was only established in the late 1970s. Thereafter, agreement on the desirability of avoiding disunity over defence issues spread throughout French society, with a striking absence of a strong protest movement against nuclear weapons. This was partly because, until recently, French governments described their nuclear arsenal as a deterrent which would definitely work and would therefore never be used.[102] The lack of public interest was closely linked to their ignorance, aided by the extreme secrecy with which the costly nuclear weapons programme has been pursued – as in the UK.

Another central article of faith driving France's nuclear ambitions was that many amongst the French see themselves as 'the oldest European nation', which predestines them to greatness and gives legitimacy to their quest for nuclear power. So convinced of this were they that, for many years, nuclear proliferation was encouraged. France not only supplied Israel and Iraq with their first nuclear reactor, but also assisted Argentina, Brazil, India and Pakistan with nuclear weapon-related technology. However, concern about nuclear proliferation increased during the 1980s and, following the 1991 Gulf War, France finally signed the Non-Proliferation Treaty in 1992.

The *Force de Frappe*, in the form of Mirage IV strike aircraft, became operational in 1964. France had to rely on this vulnerable and limited capability until 1971, when the first of its six ballistic missile submarines and land-based ballistic missiles came into service. The latter force did not constitute a credible deterrent, because of its small size. However, the submarines, especially once they had been replaced and re-equipped with the 5,000 km range M4 missile by 1993, are a formidable force. In 1996, the French decided to scrap their land-based ballistic missile force, and upgrade their bomber force to be capable of a sub-strategic role. In addition, the first of four new *Triomphant* class submarines, equipped with an upgraded version of the M4 missile, the M45, was launched in 1996, and the fourth submarine became operational in 2008. A new missile, the M51, with a range of 8,000-10,000 km and carrying up to six warheads, was successfully launched from *Le Triomphant* on 1 July 2016 as a replacement for the M45.[103]

Despite its claimed independence, France received US military and technological aid. Not only did the development of nuclear submarines require US assistance, but France also obtained 12 KC-135 tanker aircraft from the US for in-flight refuelling of the Mirage IV bombers. Only with this capability could they reach their targets in the Soviet Union.[104]

The Anglo-French *Entente Nucléaire*

Since 1992, a joint Anglo-French commission on nuclear co-operation has met regularly. This outwardly surprising development was driven by the need for both countries to support each other's increasingly questionable permanent membership of the UN Security Council, especially with Germany reunified, and to try to present a common position on the sensitive nuclear issue within the European Union.

A top priority has been to try to harmonise the two countries' deterrence doctrines. In particular, during 1993 there was a deep comparison of deterrence doctrines which, according to one French participant, showed there were no insurmountable differences between the two nations' approaches.[105] The new *Entente Nucléaire* became public during a meeting in the UK in 1995 between Prime Minister John Major and President Jacques Chirac, when Major refused to condemn France's resumption of nuclear testing in the South Pacific. The following joint announcement was made:

> We do not see situations arising in which the vital interests of either France or the United Kingdom could be threatened without the vital interests of the other also being threatened. We have decided to pursue and deepen nuclear co-operation between our two countries. Our aim is mutually to strengthen deterrence, while retaining the independence of our nuclear forces. The deepening of co-operation between the two European members of the North Atlantic Alliance that are nuclear powers will therefore strengthen the European contribution to overall deterrence. We have instructed our Joint Nuclear Commission to take this forward.[106]

The British *Financial Times* reported that agreement was reached on a broad definition of sub-strategic deterrence:

> ... in other words, the use of a low-yield 'warning shot' against an advancing aggressor, along with a threat warning of a massive nuclear

strike unless the attack halts. This warning shot would apparently be fired as soon as a country's 'vital interests' were threatened... French thinking has always placed more emphasis on the role of nuclear weapons as a strategic weapon of last resort, designed for deterrence rather than use. However, the end of the Cold War has prompted NATO to abandon the flexible response doctrine, and it has yet to define a new philosophy... The uncertainty about NATO's military doctrine has cleared the way for some rapprochement between British and French ideas – but UK defence experts doubt whether there can be a real meeting of minds unless France rejoins NATO's nuclear planning group. France has stayed aloof from all NATO's deliberations about the use of nuclear arms.[107]

Reflecting a clear decision to align French nuclear doctrine with that of the US and the UK, on 19 January 2006 Chirac made a speech at a nuclear submarine base in Brittany in which he said:

> The leaders of states who would use terrorist means against us, as well as those who could consider using weapons of mass destruction, must understand that they would lay themselves open to a firm and adapted response on our part. This response could be a conventional one. It could also be of a different kind.[108]

This was the first time a French President had publicly warned of possible nuclear retaliation against a state-backed terrorist strike. Chirac went further, warning that France's nuclear arsenal was now deployed not merely to ensure French independence but to protect 'strategic supplies' such as oil and the 'defence of allied countries'.[109] In an attempt to make this shift more credible, some of the French submarine-launched ballistic missiles were fitted with a reduced number of warheads, with the implication that these could also be of lower yield. This echoed the British policy.

Hitherto, the French nuclear debate had been ruled by surprisingly vague, metaphysical considerations. In France, nuclear weapons are believed to be the magic that keeps war at bay. The simplicity of the message at home – nuclear weapons equal peace, but also independence, international rank, and living up to France's glorious past – was bought at the price of the ambiguity of France's operational strategy and its operational relationship with NATO allies. At the beginning of the 21st century, with new threats to France's security, perhaps the French psyche had been healed by the nuclear drug administered by de Gaulle. French citizens were once again convinced of their country's greatness. So, as Heuser argued, 'Do they still need the medicine (or placebo) of nuclear prestige?'[110]

To this of course should be added, what example does the latest

French nuclear posture give to potential nuclear proliferators? And what evidence of French greatness and civilized values was portrayed by the sinking in 1985 by French secret agents of the Greenpeace ship *Rainbow Warrior* in Auckland, New Zealand, for opposing French nuclear testing in the South Pacific? In the words of David Lange, New Zealand's Prime Minister at the time, 'The leaders of the West expressed not a moment's outrage about terrorism directed by a government against opponents of nuclear deterrence.'[111]

On the night of 3–4 February 2009, the *Entente Nucléaire* suffered a deeply worrying setback that bordered on farce. The British Trident-equipped submarine *HMS Vanguard* collided with its French opposite number *Le Triomphant* while both were submerged on so-called 'deterrent' patrol in the Eastern Atlantic.[112] Because both were moving slowly, they sustained only minor damage. However, the fact that neither had detected the other showed how close this came to catastrophe. The embarrassing incident also demonstrated that coordination of patrols and water management had broken down.

Has Reality Begun to Prevail over Vested Interest?

Endorsement of some of my findings about nuclear deterrence came in 2007 from no less a former arch exponent of the dogma than Henry Kissinger. In an article headed 'A World Free Of Nuclear Weapons', published in the *Wall Street Journal*, he and co-authors George Shultz, William Perry and Sam Nunn wrote:

> The end of the Cold War made the doctrine of mutual Soviet-American deterrence obsolete. Deterrence continues to be a relevant consideration for many states with regard to threats from other states. But *reliance on nuclear weapons for this purpose is becoming increasingly hazardous and decreasingly effective*... the world is now on the precipice of a new and dangerous nuclear era... *non-state terrorist groups with nuclear weapons are conceptually outside the bounds of a deterrent strategy*...[113] [emphasis added]

What stimulated interest and excitement around the world was that their initiative placed an emphasis on the need to abandon nuclear deterrence doctrine and seriously plan for a nuclear weapon-free world. Also, these influential figures, all former proponents of nuclear deterrence as essential for security, appeared to have experienced a major mindset shift. A year later, the same four authors co-wrote a follow-up article, in which they challenged the nuclear weapon states to discard 'any existing operational plans for massive attacks that still remain from the Cold War days. Interpreting deterrence as requiring mutual assured destruction (MAD) is an obsolete policy in today's world.'[114]

In August 2008, the London-based International Institute for Strategic Studies published Adelphi Paper 396, *Abolishing Nuclear Weapons*.[115] Co-authored by George Perkovich and James Acton, it was a response to the call for fresh urgency in moving towards a nuclear weapon-free world expressed in the two *Wall Street Journal* articles by Shultz, Perry, Kissinger and Nunn. Perkovich and Acton sought to facilitate a debate on how complete nuclear disarmament could be achieved safely and securely. However, their approach was bedevilled by an implicit assumption that nuclear deterrence dogma will never be discredited, including the claimed role for extended deterrence. To their credit, a year later they published *Abolishing Nuclear Weapons: A Debate*, a selection of essays spanning a wide range of views on the issue.[116]

The Impact of Presidents Obama and Trump

When Barack Obama was elected US President in November 2008, he rode a tide of revulsion against the often belligerent, simplistic and insensitive foreign policy of the Bush administration. In the election campaign, Obama raised expectations among advocates of making progress towards a nuclear weapon-free world that he would show more constructive leadership.

In Prague on 5 April 2009, President Obama gave a speech in which he outlined the broad parameters of what he hoped to achieve in foreign policy.[117] On nuclear disarmament, he first correctly raised the alarm:

> The Cold War has disappeared but thousands of those weapons have not. In a strange turn of history, the threat of global nuclear war has gone down, but the risk of a nuclear attack has gone up. More nations have acquired these weapons. Testing has continued. Black markets trade in nuclear secrets and materials. The technology to build a bomb has spread. Terrorists are determined to buy, build or steal one.

He argued powerfully against accepting the inevitability of the spread of nuclear weapons, adding:

> Just as we stood for freedom in the 20th century, we must stand together for the right of people everywhere to live free from fear in the 21st. And as a nuclear power – as the only nuclear power to have used a nuclear weapon – the United States has a moral responsibility to act. We cannot succeed in this endeavor alone, but we can lead it. So today, I state clearly and with conviction America's commitment to seek the peace and security of a world without nuclear weapons.

Having thus acknowledged that a nuclear weapon-free world would be more secure, the US President pledged to 'ignore the voices who tell us that the world cannot change'. He continued: 'To put an end to Cold War thinking, we will reduce the role of nuclear weapons in our national security strategy and urge others to do the same.' However, he then declared:

> Make no mistake: as long as these weapons exist, we will maintain a safe, secure and effective arsenal to deter any adversary, and guarantee that defense to our allies...

This was reversion to old-style nuclear deterrence thinking.

In January 2010 a third article by Shultz, Perry, Kissinger and Nunn appeared in the *Wall Street Journal*.[118] This was a major disappointment, its title 'Protecting Our Nuclear Deterrent' no longer trying to hide their intent. It amounted to little more than lobbying for revived funding for the nuclear weapon laboratories, their vested interest.

NATO's guardians of nuclear deterrence further closed ranks in November 2010 with publication of NATO's current Strategic Concept.[119] This ignored all its contradictions with the 2010 NPT Review final document, the Action Plan of which incorporated most of the undertakings agreed at the 2000 NPT Review.[120] Since then, if anything NATO's position has hardened following Russia's annexation of Crimea in 2014.[121]

However, NATO nuclear war planners and military advisers to US President Donald Trump should be increasingly nervous about his irresponsibly belligerent, simplistic response to North Korean leader Kim Jong-un's determination not to echo the fate of Iraq and Saddam Hussein. The latest US Nuclear Posture Review, released on 6 February 2018, revives the Bush administration's enthusiasm for 'usable' low-yield warheads in response to strategic cyber attack, including a new warhead for Trident ballistic missiles, new nuclear-armed cruise missiles, and the possibility of pre-emptive use of more accurate B61-12 freefall nuclear bombs with lower variable yield and a fusing system capable of withstanding the shock of penetrating hardened and deeply buried targets.[122]

Allegedly responding to deployment of NATO reinforcements to the Baltic member states, also on 6 February Russia announced it had sent Iskander intermediate range ballistic missiles capable of delivering nuclear or conventional warheads to Kaliningrad – the timing was probably no coincidence.[123] These depressing developments, widely leaked beforehand, prompted the *Bulletin of the Atomic Scientists* on 25 January 2018 to move its Doomsday Clock thirty seconds closer to midnight. It now stands at 2358, the closest to nuclear catastrophe since 1953.

Summary

The twists and turns of nuclear deterrence dogma demonstrate how it was adjusted to accommodate the latest expansion of the nuclear arms race it had provoked. The leaders of the politico-military establishments of the nuclear powers, especially in the US and the UK, struggled to provide an intellectual coherence to a nuclear policy in an international atmosphere of paranoia and ideological confrontation. For British and French leaders, the added traumas of Suez and their crumbling empires drove them to clutch at nuclear deterrence to sustain their great power status and influence. In the case of France, this need was dire after the carnage of the First World War, followed by defeat and Nazi occupation less than a generation later.

The French chose to develop, at massive cost, their own nuclear weapons and delivery systems. The British decided they could not afford to pursue an indigenous nuclear weapon programme, so opted for dependence on the US in a Faustian bargain sealed between Macmillan and Kennedy in exchange for Polaris in 1962. The price proved exorbitant in terms of appeasing US demands, with extensive damage to the UK's independence, reputation and true security interests. In the US, in full denial over its nuclear atrocities at Hiroshima and Nagasaki, the Manhattan Project had created an unaccountable nuclear scientific and military monster. The Air Force, Navy and Army developed often competing projects in response to their inflated assessments of the threat. The engine propelling this forward was the confidence trick of nuclear deterrence.

When the Berlin Wall came down so unexpectedly, and President Gorbachev was briefly able to break the grip of Cold War security thinking, a window of opportunity opened to end the nuclear nightmare. However, as Communism gave way to the new threat of 'Islamic fundamentalism', a key source of festering conflict in the Middle East can be traced back to Israel's secret acquisition of a nuclear arsenal, assisted by France and condoned by successive US administrations. This had given Saddam Hussein the pretext to seek nuclear weapons, aided by Western technology and greed.

The Gulf War and Gorbachev's fall from power in 1991 signalled a US drive, uncritically supported by the UK, for a self-defeating new role for nuclear weapons: countering the spread of weapons of mass destruction. Exploiting the 9/11 terror attacks in the US, the Bush administration overtly incorporated this role into US nuclear policy, then reinforced and expanded it in Bush's Pre-emption Doctrine, which remains in force. Central to this doctrine, and echoed by the UK, France and Russia, has been an acceptance that nuclear deterrence will not work against 'rogue' regimes and other extremists armed with nuclear, chemical or biological weapons, which are now the primary threat to global security.

2007 saw the first signs that former advocates of nuclear deterrence, like Shultz, Kissinger, Perry and Nunn, were having second thoughts. Two years later Barack Obama became the first US President to call formally for a nuclear weapon-free world; but he remained trapped in old thinking about nuclear deterrence, which is still cited as the bedrock justification for maintaining nuclear arsenals.

Paradoxically, Donald Trump's wildly incoherent taunting of Kim Jong-un has brought the frailties of nuclear deterrence back into the mainstream media spotlight. One encouraging consequence in the UK is that a new generation with no experience of the anxieties of the Cold War enabled the leader of the Labour Opposition, Jeremy Corbyn, to gain votes in the 2017 election despite openly rejecting nuclear deterrence.

Notes

1. MAUD, not an acronym, was named after Maud Ray, a British governess to the children of Niels Bohr, a Danish physicist closely involved in the early development of the atomic bomb. See Margaret Gowing, *Britain and Atomic Energy, 1939-45* (Macmillan, London, 1964), p. 45.
2. Lawrence Freedman, *The Evolution of Nuclear Strategy* (Macmillan, London, 1981), p. 41.
3. The first true fusion device, *Ivy Mike*, achieved an explosive power of over ten megatons. Modern thermonuclear weapons are much less destructive, of the order of 300-500 kilotons; but this is still some twenty times the explosive power of the Nagasaki device.
4. John Foster Dulles, Speech 'The Evolution of Foreign Policy', Department of State Bulletin, Vol. XXX, 25 January 1954, pp. 107–110.
5. John Baylis, *Ambiguity and Deterrence* (Oxford University Press, 1995), pp. 37–38.
6. F. Williams, *Twilight of Empire: Memoirs of Prime Minister Clement Attlee* (A.S. Barnes & Co, New York, 1962), pp. 118–119.
7. Baylis (1995), pp. 197–202.
8. A.J.R. Groom, *British Thinking About Nuclear Weapons* (Frances Pinter, London, 1974), p. 139.
9. Baylis (1995), p. 202.
10. Ibid, pp. 269–271.
11. Prime Minister Harold Macmillan in private interview with Henry Brandon in July 1957: H Brandon, *Special Relationships: A Foreign Correspondent's Memoirs from Roosevelt to Reagan* (Macmillan, London, 1988), p. 138.
12. Solly Zuckerman, *Monkeys, Men and Missiles: An Autobiography 1946-88* (W.W.Norton & Company, New York/London, 1988), p. 234.
13. Groom (1974), p. 481.
14. Baylis (1995), pp. 300–301.
15. Nassau Agreement, http://en.wikipedia.org.uk/wiki/Nassau_Agreement.
16. Annual Historical Summary (U), Joint Atomic Information Exchange Group, HQ, Defense Nuclear Agency, 1 October 1982–30 September 1983.
17. "Report by the Comptroller and Auditor General [National Audit Office], 'Control and Management of the Trident Programme', July 1987, HC27, para. 3.27.
18. John Ainslie, *The Future of the British Bomb* (the WMD Awareness Programme, October 2005), www.comeclean.org.uk. See also Dan Plesch, *The Future of Britain's WMD* (The Foreign Policy Centre, London, 2006), www.danplesch.net.
19. UK's Nuclear Deterrent, Commons Debate, 18 July 2016, hansard.parliament.uk/commons/2016-07-18/debates/7B7A196B-B37C-4787-99DC-098882B3EFA2/UKSNuclearDeterrent; Ministry of Defence, 'New Successor Submarines Named', 21 October 2016, www.gov.uk/government/news/new-successor-submarines-named..
20. Under an *Exchange of Notes between the UK and US concerning the Availability for Defence Purposes of the British Indian Ocean Territory* of 30 December 1966 (Cmnd 3231), the whole territory is to remain available to meet the possible defence needs of the two countries for an initial period of fifty years from 1966, and thereafter for a further period of twenty years unless either party has given prior notice to terminate it. A further Exchange of Notes concluded in 1976 (Cm 6413) regulates the establishment and functioning of the US in Diego Garcia and related matters. See also *The Sunday Times*, 25 January 1976, cited in Duncan Campbell, *The Unsinkable Aircraft Carrier: American Military Power in Britain* (Michael Joseph Publications, London, 1984), p. 110.
21. John Pilger, 'Out of Eden', *The Guardian*, 31 May 2006.
22. Memorandum submitted by the Foreign & Commonwealth Office on British Indian Ocean Territories (BIOT) (31 July 2000) appended to the House of Commons Foreign Affairs Committee First Special Report, 19 December 2000,

	www.parliament.the-stationery-office.co.uk/pa/cm200001/cmselect/cmfaff/78/7803.htm.
23	Sean Carey, 'The UK's role in Diego Garcia: green fingers or red faces?', *The New Statesman*, 7 September 2009, www.newstatesman.com/international-politics/2009/09/diego-garcia-chagos-british.
24	Pilger (2006).
25	See European Parliamentary Temporary Committee on the Echelon Interception System, 'Report on the existence of a global system for the interception of private and commercial communications' (ECHELON interception system) (2001/2098(INI)), 11 July 2001. For more details on the ECHELON system, see Nicky Hager, *Secret Power: New Zealand's Role in the International Spy Network* (Craig Potton Publishing, Nelson, New Zealand, 1996).
26	See website of the Campaign for the Accountability of American Bases www.caab.org.uk: click on 'The American Bases', then 'QPSW briefing: US bases on British territory' for a June 2004 analysis by David Gee.
27	Email from NSA to GCHQ requesting help with UN spying mission, in 'US plan to bug Security Council: the text', *The Observer*, 2 March 2003. Confirmation of such activities was recently provided by the ex-NSA whistleblower Edward Snowden.
28	Transcript of Clare Short interview, *BBC News online*, 26 February 2004.
29	Stephen Shalom, 'The United States and Libya, Part 2: The Qaddafi Era', *Z Magazine*, June 1990, www.zmag.org/zmag/articles/ShalomLyb2.html.
30	'Bush obsessed with Iraq', *Los Angeles Times*, 23 March 2004. See also Richard A. Clarke, *Against All Enemies* (Free Press, New York, 2004).
31	David Rose, 'Bush, Blair's secret pact for Iraq war', *The Observer*, 4 April 2004.
32	For the memo text see http://www.timesonline.co.uk/article/0,,19809-1593637,00.html.
33	'UK agrees missile defence request', BBC News, 25 July 2007, http://news.bbc.co.uk/1/hi/uk_politics/6916262.stm.
34	Tom Baldwin, 'US turns back to Britain as its base for Son of Star Wars', *The Times*, 5 August 2006, http://www.timesonline.co.uk/article/0,,11069-2315036,00.html.
35	Ian Bruce, 'Son of Star Wars' missiles will not be sent to UK', *The Herald*, 23 May 2006, http://www.theherald.co.uk/news/62478.html.
36	'No defence against missiles', *The Guardian*, 16 July 2007, http://www.guardian.co.uk/usa/story/0,,2127230,00.html. See also Demetri Sevastopulo et al, 'Russia threatens to quit arms treaty', *Financial Times*, 15 February 2007, http://www.ft.com:80/cms/s/289ed728-bd26-11db-b5bd-0000779e2340.html.
37.	Steven Lee Myers, 'Putin Says New Missile Systems Will Give Russia a Nuclear Edge', *The New York Times*, 18 November 2004.
38	Erwin Hackel, 'Towards non-nuclear security: costs, benefits, requisites', Regina Cowen Karp ed., *Security Without Nuclear Weapons? Different Perspectives in Non-Nuclear Strategy* (Oxford University Press, 1992), p. 58.
39	Robert S. McNamara, 'Defense Arrangements and the North Atlantic Community', Address given at the University of Michigan, Ann Arbor, 16 June 1962, Department of State Bulletin 47 (9 July 1962), pp. 67–68.
40	Philip Bobbitt, *Democracy and Deterrence – The History and Future of Nuclear Strategy* (Macmillan, London, 1988), pp. 47–51.
41	Ibid, pp. 60–61.
42	Ibid, p. 62.
43	Ibid, p. 66.
44	Michael MccGwire, *Nuclear Deterrence*, Canberra Commission on the Elimination of Nuclear Weapons, Background Papers, August 1996, p. 234.
45	R. Ned Lebow and Janice Stein, *We All Lost the Cold War* (Princeton University Press, 1994), p. 349.
46	Ibid, pp. 349–350.

47	Stephen I. Schwartz ed., *Atomic Audit: The Costs and Consequences of U.S. Nuclear Weapons since 1940* (Brookings Institution Press, Washington, D.C., 1998).
48	Regina Cowen Karp ed., *Security with Nuclear Weapons?* (Oxford University Press, 1991), p. 72.
49	Robert O'Neill, 'Britain and the Future of Nuclear Weapons' (*International Affairs*, vol .71, no. 4, October 1995), pp. 747–761.
50	'Confusion about NATO', editorial, *The New York Times,* 8 December 1998.
51	General Lee Butler USAF (Ret), address to the Canadian Network Against Nuclear Weapons, Ottawa, 11 March 1999.
52	Ibid.
53	*Nuclear Futures: Proliferation of Weapons of Mass Destruction and US Nuclear Strategy,* British American Security Information Council [BASIC] Research Report 98.2 (March 1998), pp. 5–6.
54	Ibid, pp. 8–9.
55	Barbara Starr, 'Targeting Rethink May Lead To Non-Nuclear STRATCOM Role', *Jane's Defence Weekly,* 22 May 1993, p. 19.
56	BASIC (1998), pp. 9–10.
57	Of course, subsequent revelations about covert nuclear weapon programmes in all these countries cast fresh doubt on the effectiveness of the NPT, and tend to vindicate the decision by Israel, India and Pakistan not to sign such a discriminatory treaty which, in any case, is not being honoured by the permanent members of the UN Security Council.
58	Ibid, pp. 11–12.
59	Ibid, pp. 15–16.
60	Ibid, p. 16.
61	Ibid, pp. 19–20.
62	*The Alliance's Strategy Concept* [NAC-S (99) 65], April 1999.
63	'Sub-Strategic Use of Trident'; letter from C H J Davies, UK Ministry of Defence, to Dr E Waterston, 27 October 1998.
64	UN General Assembly Resolution 53/77Y, adopted on 4 December 1998 by 114 votes to eighteen, with thirty-eight abstentions.
65	Joint Declaration 'Towards A Nuclear-Weapon-Free World: The Need For A New Agenda', 9 June 1998, *The Ploughshares Monitor,* June 1998, vol. 19, no. 2, www.ploughshares.ca/libraries/monitor/mon/98f.html.
66	The report was requested by Canada's Foreign Minister Lloyd Axworthy to the Select Committee to review Canada's nuclear weapons policy in light of the World Court Advisory Opinion – the only government to do so. Axworthy's initiative was also stimulated by a report from Project Ploughshares following a series of Roundtables conducted by former Disarmament Ambassador Douglas Roche in eighteen cities across Canada in September 1996 to consider the issue, which found a strong civil society consensus for Canada to place its support for international law and abolition of nuclear weapons above its allegiance to NATO.
67	*An Alliance for the 21st Century,* NATO Washington Summit Communique, 24 April 1999, para. 32.
68	UN General Assembly Resolution 54/54G, adopted 2 December 1999 by 111 votes to thirteen, with thirty-nine abstentions.
69	Communique of the Meeting of NATO Foreign Ministers, 15–16 December 1999.
70	*2000 Review Conference of the Parties to the Treaty on the Non-Proliferation of Nuclear Weapons,* Final Document NPT/CONF.2000/28, vol. I, part I, 'Article VI and preambular paragraphs 8 to 12', para. 15.
71	*The Alliance's Strategy Concept* [NAC-S(99) 65], April 1999.
72	*2000 Review Conference,* 'Article VII and the security of non-nuclear-weapon States'.
73	NATO Press Release M-NAC-2 (2000)121, *Report on Options for Confidence and Security Building Measures (CSBMS), Verification, Non-Proliferation, Arms Control and Disarmament,* December 2000, paras. 72 and 98.

74	Ibid, paras. 100, 102 and 106.
75	Extract from transcript of Hearing on Nuclear Posture Review of Panel One of the Senate Foreign Relations Committee, chaired by Sen. Joseph Biden, 16 May 2002.
76	Walter Pincus, 'US Studies Developing New Nuclear Bomb', *The Washington Post*, 15 April 2001.
77	See Robert W. Nelson, 'Low-Yield Earth-Penetrating Nuclear Weapons', *The Journal of the Federation of American Scientists* 54, 1, (January/February 2001), http://www.fas.org/faspir/2001/v54nl/weapons.htm.
78	Walter Pincus, 'Nuclear Expert Challenges US Thinking on Warheads', *The Washington Post*, 24 October 2000.
79	Remarks by the President to Students and Faculty at National Defense University, 1 May 2001, http://www.whitehouse.gov/news/releases/2001/05/20010501-10.html.
80	Colin Powell, *A Soldier's Way* (Hutchinson, London, 1995), p. 324.
81	Public briefing on 9 January 2002 by J.D.Crouch, Assistant Secretary of Defense for International Security Policy, available at http://www.defenselink.mil.
82	Excerpts from the report are available at http://www.globalsecurity.org.
83	Ibid.
84	Ibid.
85	Ibid.
86	On 20 March 2002, UK Secretary of State for Defence Geoff Hoon appeared before the House of Commons Select Committee on Defence (see transcript paras. 234–237 at http://www.publications.parliament.uk/pa/cm200102/cmselect/cmdfence/644/2032001.htm). When asked whether he thought a state like Iraq 'would be deterred by our deterrent from using weapons of mass destruction against our forces in the field?' he replied: 'I think… that there are clearly some states who would be deterred by the fact that the United Kingdom possesses nuclear weapons and has the willingness and ability to use them in appropriate circumstances. States of concern, I would be much less confident about… *They can be absolutely confident that in the right conditions we would be willing to use our nuclear weapons.* What I cannot be absolutely confident about is *whether that would be sufficient to deter them* from using a weapon of mass destruction in the first place.' [emphasis added]
87	Philip Delves Broughton, 'France to aim nuclear arms at rogue states', *Daily Telegraph*, London, 28 October 2003.
88	Excerpts from the US National Security Strategy are available at . See Section V, 'Prevent Our Enemies from Threatening Us, Our Allies, and Our Friends with Weapons of Mass Destruction'.
89	See http://www.whitehouse.gov/news/releases/2002/12/WMDStrategy.pdf.
90	Ibid.
91	Paul Richter, 'U.S. Weighs Tactical Nuclear Strike on Iraq', *Los Angeles Times*, 26 January 2003.
92	John M. Weinstein, 'Ten Reasons Why Nuclear Deterrence Could Fail: The Case for Reassessing US Nuclear Policies and Plans', *Deterrence in the 21st Century*, Max G. Manwaring ed. (Frank Cass & Co Ltd, London, 2001), p. 37.
93	Walter Pincus, 'Pentagon Revises Nuclear Strike Plan', *The Washington Post*, 11 September 2005.
94	Hans M. Kristensen, 'The Role of U.S. Nuclear Weapons: New Doctrine Falls Short of Bush Pledge', *Arms Control Today*, September 2005, http://www.armscontrol.org/act/2005_09/Kristensen.asp?print.
95	Ibid.
96	Chairman of the Joint Chiefs of Staff, 'JP 3-12, Joint Staff Input to JP 3-12, Doctrine for Joint Nuclear Operations (Second Draft)', 28 April 2003, pp 34–35.
97	Perhaps reflecting the Bush Administration's perceived need to counter widespread criticism of the 2001 Nuclear Posture Review and consequent changes in US nuclear doctrine, Keith Payne, president of the National

	Institute for Public Policy and a former Deputy Assistant Secretary of Defense 2002–3, published an apologia, 'The Nuclear Posture Review: Setting the Record Straight', *The Washington Quarterly*, Summer 2005, 28:3, pp. 135–151. In it he argued that critics, locked in Cold War thinking, had misunderstood it. My response is that they understood it only too well. Payne seemed driven by an unshakeable faith in the continuing US ability to adapt and control its nuclear strategy, when the threats had shifted and become so diffuse, and the cost of deterrence failure was too high. Also, he was in denial about inciting proliferation, with no mention of Israel.
98	Robert H. Paterson, *Britain's Strategic Nuclear Deterrent* (Frank Cass & Co Ltd, London, 1997), p. 135.
99	Ibid, p. 138.
100	Beatrice Heuser, *Nuclear Mentalities? Strategies and Beliefs in Britain, France and the FRG* (Macmillan Press, London, 1998), pp. 75–80.
101	Ibid, p. 127.
102	Ibid, p. 92.
103	See http://www.navyrecognition.com/index.php/news/defence-news/2016/july-2016-navy-naval-forces-defense-industry-technology-maritime-security-global-news/4155-successful-m51-ballistic-missile-slbm-test-in-operational-conditions-from-french-navy-ssbn.html.
104	Karp (1991), p. 175.
105	'Franco-British Nuclear Weapons Cooperation', Briefing Notes, Centre for European Security and Disarmament, Brussels, 6 November 1995.
106	British and French Joint Statement on Nuclear Co-operation, issued at Anglo-French Summit, Chequers, UK, 29-30 October 1995.
107	Bruce Clark, 'Nations draw closer on use of nuclear weapons', *Financial Times*, London, 31 October 1995.
108	Ariane Bernard, 'Chirac hints at nuclear retaliation', *The New York Times*, 19 January 2006.
109	John Lichfield, 'Chirac threatens nuclear attack on states sponsoring terrorism', *The Independent*, London, 20 January 2006. Apparently, Chirac was also under pressure to head off his main political rival for the Presidency, Interior Minister Nicolas Sarkozy, who was the most prominent among several critics of spending 10 percent of France's defence budget on the nuclear arsenal with French public spending facing drastic cuts.
110	Heuser (1998), p. 144.
111	David Lange, *Nuclear Free – The New Zealand Way* (Penguin Books, Auckland, 1990), p. 122.
112	Rachel Williams, Richard Norton-Taylor, 'Nuclear submarines collide in Atlantic', *uardian*, 16 February 2009, http://www.guardian.co.uk/uk/2009/feb/16/nuclear-submarines-collide.
113	George P. Shultz, William J. Perry, Henry A. Kissinger and Sam Nunn, 'A World Free Of Nuclear Weapons', *The Wall Street Journal*, 4 January 2007, http://www.fcnl.org/issues/item.php?item_id=2252&issue_id=54.
114	Shultz, Perry, Kissinger and Nunn, 'Toward a Nuclear-Free World', *The Wall Street Journal*, 15 January 2008, http://online.wsj.com/article/SB120036422673589947.html .
115	George Perkovich and James M. Acton, *Abolishing Nuclear Weapons*, Adelphi Paper 396, The International Institute for Strategic Studies (Routledge, August 2008).
116	George Perkovich and James M. Acton, *Abolishing Nuclear Weapons: A Debate* (Carnegie Endowment for International Peace, Washington D.C., 2009).
117	Remarks of President Barack Obama, Hradcany Square, Prague, Czech Republic, 5 April 2009, http://i.usatoday.net/news/TheOval/Obama-in-Prague-4-5-2009.pdf.
118	Shultz, Perry, Kissinger and Nunn, 'Protecting Our Nuclear Deterrent', *Wall Street Journal*, 19 January 2010, http://online.wsj.com/article/SB1000142405274

8704152804574628344282735008.html?mod=googlenews_wsj#printMode.
119 See *Active Engagement, Modern Defence: Strategic Concept for the Defence and Security of the Members of the North Atlantic Treaty Organisation adopted by Heads of State and Government in Lisbon*, 19 November 2010, http://www.nato.int/cps/en/natolive/official_texts_68580.htm.
120 Action Plan from the Final Document adopted by the 2010 Review Conference of the Parties to the Treaty on the Non-Proliferation of Nuclear Weapons, http://www.reachingcriticalwill.org/images/documents/Disarmament-fora/npt/revcon2010/2010NPTActionPlan.pdf.
121 See https://en.wikipedia.org/wiki/Annexation_of_Crimea_by_the_Russian_Federation.
122 Nuclear Posture Review February 2018, Office of the Secretary of Defense, https://www.defense.gov/News/SpecialReports/2018NuclearPostureReview.aspx. For more on the B61-12 bomb, see https://en.wikipedia.org/wiki/B61_nuclear_bomb. For an authoritative commentary, see John Burroughs, 'Trump's Nuclear Posture Review is a Dangerous Step Backward', Lawyers' Committee on Nuclear Policy, 3 February 2018, http://www.lcnp.org/Trump's%20NPR.pdf.
123 See https://www.reuters.com/article/us-russia-nato-missiles/russia-deploys-iskander-nuclear-capable-missiles-to-kaliningrad-ria-idUSKBN1FP21Y.

CHAPTER THREE

NUCLEAR DETERRENCE IN THE REAL WORLD

When considering the practicalities of nuclear deterrence, it is important to bear in mind the cautionary teachings of Colin Gray, Director of the Centre for Strategic Studies at the University of Reading in the UK. As he argues, deterrence is inherently unreliable because it involves trying to influence states of mind; and this fundamental uncertainty is redoubled in the current international situation where the top priority is to deter the leaders of desperate regimes or extremists. This suggests it would be wise to consider the consequences of failure, and not to rely on nuclear deterrence working.[1]

The Cuban Missile Crisis

In October 1962, after Soviet President Khrushchev decided to send missiles to Cuba, US President Kennedy warned that he would not tolerate the introduction of Soviet missiles in the region. Kennedy issued his threat in the belief that Khrushchev had no intention of establishing missile bases in Cuba. Despite Kennedy's warnings, Khrushchev nevertheless proceeded with the secret deployment. He was convinced they were necessary to protect Cuba from invasion, redress the strategic balance and establish psychological equality with the US. The crisis was resolved when Khrushchev agreed to withdraw the missiles, with the understanding that the US would dismantle its own missiles in Turkey, regarded by Khrushchev as a threat to the Soviet Union.

Despite this apparent US success, Khrushchev's willingness to deploy missiles in the first place was a dramatic failure of nuclear deterrence, occurring in the face of US superiority in strategic nuclear forces. Although no attack on the US resulted, if deterrence supposedly prevents provocations that could lead to nuclear war (as the installation of missiles in Cuba almost did), then it failed.[2] Moreover, nuclear deterrence had provoked the most acute crisis of the Cold War.[3]

Thirty years later, Robert McNamara told a London audience that the surviving decision-makers on both sides had met annually since 1987. He had learned from these reunions that the Soviets' clear intent had been to deceive; but no one had intended to go to the brink. Khrushchev had been reckless, but all had been captive to huge miscalculations:

1) The Soviet Union had believed that the US would invade Cuba.
2) The US had believed that the Soviet Union would never move nuclear weapons outside the homeland.
3) The Soviet Union had thought its missiles would not be detected.
4) The US had thought the Soviet Union would not retaliate – but the Soviet Union was preparing to attack US missiles in Turkey.

Saturday 27 October 1962 had been the crisis moment: both sides had felt there was no way back. Castro had sent a signal to Khrushchev that he intended to use Soviet nuclear weapons in self-defence. McNamara had been horrified to discover on 29 October, the day after the crisis was resolved, that not only were there thirty-six strategic nuclear-tipped Soviet missiles in Cuba but also nine tactical nuclear warheads, with authority delegated to use them against a US invasion force, which was not nuclear-armed.[4]

After the shock of that crisis, there is little doubt that fear of nuclear war made the leaders of the superpowers inwardly more cautious. However, any benefit from this was eroded by the inherent contradictions and dynamics of nuclear deterrence, in an inevitable process that is still continuing long after the end of the Cold War. What is more, the crisis had been provoked by the dictates of nuclear deterrence dogma. The Soviet missile deployment in Cuba had been a response to US deployment of Jupiter missiles in Turkey, as well as plans, announced in 1961, to deploy 1,000 Minuteman ICBMs in hardened silos in the US Midwest.

The 1996 Canberra Commission on the Elimination of Nuclear Weapons, of which McNamara and General Lee Butler were members, showed evidence of this pernicious process. Having demolished almost every argument in favour of nuclear deterrence, their report limply stated that 'the only apparent military utility that remains for nuclear weapons is in deterring their use by others.'[5] With a former French Prime Minister among them, perhaps this was the best that could have been expected in order to achieve consensus. The evidence for challenging this assertion follows.

A Question of Credibility

For deterrence to work, the aggressor must be convinced that the deterrent force can and will be used, and will be effective. Furthermore, the deterrer must have reasonable confidence that the force can be used without dire consequences to himself. It is impossible for a rational leader to make a credible nuclear threat when directed against a nuclear adversary capable of a retaliatory second strike. Ultimately, as Sir Lawrence Freedman, Professor of War Studies at Kings College, London, and a leading UK expert on nuclear deterrence, wrote in 1981:

> The question of what happens if deterrence fails is vital for the cohesion and credibility of nuclear strategy. A proper answer requires more than the design of means to wage nuclear war in a wide variety of ways, but something sufficiently plausible to appear as a tolerably rational course of action which has a realistic chance of leading to a satisfactory outcome. It now seems unlikely that such an answer can be found.[6]

This contradiction is one from which nuclear deterrence dogma cannot escape. Jonathan Schell cut to the heart of the problem when he stated:

> In the last analysis, there can be no credible threat without credible use – no shadow without an object, no credit without cash payment. But since use is the thing above all else that we don't want, because it means the end of all of us, we are naturally at a loss to find any rationale for it. To grasp the reality of the contradiction, we have only to picture the circumstances of leaders whose country has just been annihilated in a first strike.[7]

Nuclear deterrence between opponents equipped with a survivable retaliatory capability is unique in history, because never before have threats of unacceptable destruction been mutual. It is generally agreed that the ultimate threat would only be made in the face of extreme provocation. Therefore the need arose for a doctrine to respond to more limited provocation, such as Admiral Buzzard's graduated deterrence or NATO's Flexible Response. This brings us back to the problem of initiating a nuclear exchange, however limited. Any rational leader would tend to be self-deterred from 'breaking the nuclear taboo', and provoking uncontrolled escalation to all-out nuclear war. To these should be added the likelihood that nuclear possessor states would use the territory of their forward-based allies as a nuclear battlefield, making a mockery of the alleged security benefits of extended deterrence.

In an effort to shore up credibility, the US theorist Herman Kahn – who himself doubted the stability of mutual deterrence – argued in 1960 for a credible first-strike capability, backed up by adequate civil defence preparations demonstrating the will to 'ride out' any retaliation.[8] However, the Cuban missile crisis two years later showed that a counter-force strategy was irrelevant, because Kennedy threatened the Soviets with full retaliation and deployed US bombers to civilian airfields, thereby denying the USSR a counter-force option.[9] Instead, the US moved to Assured Destruction while exploring efforts to control the arms race and avoid war.

Nevertheless, counter-force advocates continued to argue that the most credible form of deterrence would be to demonstrate the capability and will to fight and even win a nuclear war. In this respect they were close to the Soviet position, which was reinforced by concerns that deterrence would not hold. This helped to explain the Soviet emphasis on deterrence by denial – by forestalling, disrupting, and withstanding an enemy nuclear strike – rather than by punishment. Soviet strategists were also healthily sceptical of Assured Destruction, arguing that it had no answer to the problem of what to do if deterrence failed, and to the fact that the initiator of nuclear war would be committing suicide.[10] They found eloquent support in the early 1970s from US defence scientists such as Fred Ikle and Herbert York.[11]

Fred Ikle believed that a threat which, if carried out, would lead to mutual destruction was not inherently credible. Such a threat also neglected the persistent danger of the 'fatal accident or unauthorized act', and meant a never-ending posture of hostility:

> The jargon of American strategic analysis works like a narcotic. It dulls our sense of moral outrage about the tragic confrontation of nuclear arsenals, primed and constantly perfected to unleash widespread genocide. It fosters the current smug complacency

regarding the soundness and stability of mutual deterrence. It blinds us to the fact that our method for preventing nuclear war rests on a form of warfare universally condemned since the Dark Ages – the mass killing of hostages.[12]

Here he correctly alluded to the analogy with terrorism.

Herbert York felt that to accept a substantial chance that the world would 'go up in nuclear smoke' was 'too frightful and dangerous a way to live indefinitely; we must find some better form of international relationship than the current dependency on a strategy of mutual assured destruction.'[13]

Ultimately, the insoluble core problem for those advocating nuclear deterrence is that credibility resides in the mind of the beholder or recipient rather than in those attempting to deter. This relies on convincing the recipient that executing a retaliatory threat would be rational, when a second strike would amount to what British Prime Minister Harold Macmillan described as no more than 'posthumous revenge'. In the case of threatening first use, which means escalating from conventional to nuclear warfare, credibility is undermined by the risk of self-deterrence prompted by concern about disproportionality. The danger then arises of the need to compensate by demonstrating sufficient resolve, which invites the non-nuclear armed enemy to call the deterrer's bluff. Moreover, current US nuclear policy seems designed to do just this, despite the huge consequences if nuclear deterrence is seen to have failed.

Nuclear Deterrence and the Absence of War between the Major Powers

Since the credibility of nuclear deterrence is seriously at issue, what does one make of the pro-nuclear lobby's assertion that nuclear weapons have prevented war between the major powers?

The first problem with this is that it is impossible to prove a negative – which is why such a claim is so popular a justification for retaining nuclear weapons. However, it is worth considering whether there would have been a war between the US and Soviet Union if only conventional weapons had been available. In so doing, it is important to consider what incentive the Soviet Union had for going to war again: after all, it had just regained territories lost in 1918–21 and had restored the old imperial borders.

The Soviets, particularly in the immediate post-war period, were having enough trouble consolidating their hold at home and on Eastern Europe. They had no immediate need for more hostile territory to oversee, and there was a major famine in the Ukraine in 1946–47. As the Soviet people tried to recover from World War II in which they had suffered over 20 million dead, they were hardly in the mood for more. The Soviet leader Josef Stalin's declaration of war on Japan three months after the defeat of Germany was met with great dismay within the Soviet Union. To launch an adventurist war in the West might have risked discontent to the point of insurrection in Eastern Europe, and revolution at home. Stalin would not have forgotten that many Soviet citizens, particularly in the Ukraine, had initially welcomed the Germans as liberators.

Even if the Soviet Union had had the ability to overrun Western Europe (which it did not), it could not have stopped the US from repeating what it had done after Pearl Harbor in 1941. The US ability to threaten a long war of attrition from the south, west and east would have deterred them, without nuclear weapons. The reality was that the Soviet Union could barely feed its people, and had adopted the expedient of removing the second track of German railways to help restore the rail system in Russia.[14]

No doubt Stalin was shocked by Hiroshima and Nagasaki; but it is not clear that these events intimidated him or limited his behaviour, particularly in the crucial area of Eastern Europe. As to whether the Soviet leader was restrained from greater provocations, George Kennan, US Ambassador to the Soviet Union in 1952, offered this authoritative verdict in 1984:

> I consider this sheer nonsense. There are many reasons why the Soviet leaders would not see such an adventure as being in their interests, not the least of them being the extreme military-political isolation in which their country finds itself at this period in history. Remember that the Soviet Union does not have a single ally among the great powers. Its only allies are secondary client states, generally resentful of their dependence on Moscow, weak and unreliable for any serious military encounter. It is entirely clear to me that Soviet leaders do not want a war with us and are not planning to initiate one. In particular, I have never believed that they saw it as in their interests to overrun Western Europe militarily, or that they would have launched an attack on that region in these postwar decades even if the so-called nuclear deterrent had not existed.[15]

Former USAF General Lee Butler, a Russian linguist, also studied this claim:

> Access to Soviet archives continues to shed critical new light on the intentions and motivations of Soviet leaders during the tensest moments of the Cold War. For instance, Vojtech Mastny, as senior research scholar with the Cold War International History Project of

the Woodrow Wilson Center, analyzed the deterrence argument and concluded that the much-vaunted nuclear capability of NATO turns out to have been far less important to the eventual outcome than its conventional forces. But above all, it was NATO's soft power that bested its adversary. Nuclear weapons did not and will not, of themselves, prevent major wars, and their presence unnecessarily prolonged and intensified the Cold War. In today's environment, the threat of use has been exposed as neither credible nor of any military utility. In Korea, in the Formosa Strait, in Indochina, and in the Persian Gulf, presidents – Democratic and Republican – have categorically rejected the use of nuclear weapons, even in the face of grave provocation.[16]

Sir Michael Quinlan, a leading British champion of nuclear deterrence, disagreed. In his 2009 book *Thinking About Nuclear Weapons: Principles, Problems, Prospects*, a central tenet of his case was that nuclear deterrence makes major war between nuclear-armed adversaries irrational, and therefore that nuclear weapons are needed to keep the peace.[17] However, he ignored the contradiction between his claim that fear of nuclear war induces caution, and his complacency that nuclear deterrence works. An added constraint not mentioned by him is that conventional war between major industrialised nations now risks devastating consequences from attacks on nuclear power plants.

Michael MccGwire, a widely respected British expert on Soviet military thinking and consultant to the Canberra Commission on nuclear deterrence issues, reinforced the historical assessments mentioned above with a more satisfactory explanation for Quinlan's claim.[18] He argued that by the end of the nineteenth century, the drive for overseas possessions by the long-established 'great powers' had peaked, and their rivalry in Europe had passed. However, three new colonising nations – Italy, Germany and Japan – were not satisfied. Their ambitions led to the unprecedented destruction of the wars that ended in 1945. An understanding that war between industrially advanced nations was dysfunctional was proved correct by World War I, and was finally assimilated after World War II. For such nations, henceforth power would derive from export industries and currency markets. This was exemplified by Germany and Japan, which secured through their post-war economic performance much of what they had sought through war in the 1930s and 1940s. Now China is applying this lesson.

MccGwire then argued that the nature of the ideological conflict after 1945 was a major restraint on war. While the West defined it as an absolute struggle between good and evil, the Soviets kept the Marxist faith that history was on their side, and that the emerging system of world socialism would prevail against an outmoded capitalist imperialism. Moreover, the revolution could not be spread by military domination. Unless the security of the homeland was at risk, the Soviets were always ready to cut their losses in the competition for world influence. There is now a consensus that Soviet occupation of Eastern Europe was driven by the need to crush Nazi Germany and then create a buffer zone against any repeated attempt to invade Russia from the west. After the end of the Cold War, no evidence emerged of any plans for further expansion.

Four examples, cited by MccGwire in support of his rebuttal of Quinlan, point to US restraint regarding provoking the Soviets into conventional war. In 1948, the US established an air bridge rather than risking an armoured thrust to lift the Berlin blockade. In 1951–52 it kept secret the involvement of Soviet-manned aircraft in the Korean War; and it did not intervene when East German riots broke out in 1953, nor during the Hungarian uprising in 1956. In the first three, the Soviets had yet to deploy an effective strategic nuclear capability. Of course, these could be further instances where the US was self-deterred; but it certainly had no fear of nuclear escalation. Even in the 1956 case, MccGwire concluded that the danger of becoming embroiled in a conventional war with the Soviet Union was a major, and probably decisive, factor. Moreover, one case where nuclear weapons did not keep the peace between major powers was when China was not deterred by the US nuclear monopoly from entering the Korean War.

By 1959, despite periodic belligerent statements from US hawks keen to exploit the US nuclear advantage, the Soviets had discounted the threat of a premeditated Western attack. Instead, they feared inadvertent or accidental war, which could be avoided but *not deterred*. Soviet policy was therefore directed at crisis avoidance. It took Mikhail Gorbachev to recognise the dangerous absurdity of the US-Soviet arms race. Also, he saw through Reagan's wild rhetoric about an 'evil empire' justifying US development of an ambitious anti-ballistic missile system called the Strategic Defense Initiative (SDI), known as 'Star Wars'. In 1987–88, Gorbachev walked away from the arms race and withdrew Soviet forces from Eastern Europe, thus opening the way for the end of the Cold War.

The 1986 Reykjavik Summit

Indeed, further evidence that nuclear deterrence was not just irrelevant, but counterproductive to keeping the peace at the height of the Cold War, emerged in a remarkable speech by Gorbachev on

Soviet Television on 14 October 1986, in which he explained what had happened at the famous meeting, at his own invitation, with Reagan on 10–11 October in Reykjavik, Iceland.[19] Ten years later, Gorbachev provided further reflections on this in his memoirs.[20] He had proposed a set of major measures which, if accepted, would have ushered in a nuclear weapon-free era between the two superpowers. The talk was no longer about limiting nuclear weapons, but eliminating them.

Gorbachev explained in his memoirs how he had hinted at this initiative at his first meeting with Reagan in Geneva in November 1985, before publishing it at the 27th Party Congress on 15 January 1986. He recalled that it was 'met [by Western leaders] with mistrust and jeering, as just another propaganda trick', but he had refused to be deflected.[21] As he told Jonathan Schell, when he had first arrived in the Kremlin in 1980 as a full member of the Politburo, he had seen 'the monster that we and the United States had created as a result of the arms race, with all its mistakes and accidents with nuclear weapons and nuclear power' – and this was six years before Chernobyl: 'I finally understood what the consequences, including global winter, would be.' This was why, in London in 1984, he had first spoken about his 'new thinking' that a nuclear war could not be won. This conclusion was reflected in his January 1986 proposal to abolish nuclear weapons.[22]

In driving this forward, he had been encouraged by Reagan's condemnation in Geneva of nuclear deterrence for triggering the arms race and leading humanity to the brink of destruction. However, Reagan then tried to reassure Gorbachev that his answer, SDI, posed no threat to the Soviet Union. Gorbachev responded that, from the Soviet perspective, SDI was an attempt to create a shield that would allow a first strike without fear of retaliation, and would stimulate a new arms race in space. He added, 'I think you should know that we have already developed a response. It will be effective and far less expensive than your project, and be ready for use in less time.' Declining to be more specific, he was referring to what became the 15 January 1986 proposal; and at Reykjavik he put it formally to Reagan.

Gorbachev told Schell: 'The real watershed was the summit at Reykjavik. It turned things completely upside down. It upset all those decades of calculations and unserious negotiations.' He expressed Soviet readiness to reduce strategic nuclear forces by 50 per cent in five years, and to go to zero in ten years. In so doing, he withdrew a previous Soviet demand that these should include US medium-range ICBMs and forward-based systems capable of reaching Soviet territory. In addition, the Soviet leader proposed the elimination of all US and Soviet medium-range missiles in Europe. Here, too, he included the substantial concession that British and French nuclear systems need not be taken into account: 'We proceeded from the necessity to pave the way to *détente* in Europe, to free the European nations of the fear of a nuclear catastrophe, and then to move further.' Finally, he argued for a prohibition on all nuclear testing.[23]

The only Soviet condition was that the US agree to a mutual ten-year undertaking not to pull out of the ABM Treaty, during which time strategic nuclear forces would be abolished. Given Reagan's commitment to SDI, Gorbachev did not demand that work should cease, but that it should not go beyond laboratory research. He warned:

> If the United States creates a three-tiered ABM system in outer space, we shall respond to it. However, we are concerned about another problem: the SDI would mean the transfer of weapons to a new medium, which would destabilize the strategic situation, make it even worse than it is today. If this is the United States' purpose, this should be stated plainly. But if you really want reliable security for your people and for the world in general, then the American stand is totally ungrounded.[24]

In his memoirs, Gorbachev recalled that his far-reaching proposals seemed to catch Reagan off-guard:

> The US President appeared confused, although we had suggested something the United States has always wanted to do, i.e. a radical cut in our intercontinental ballistic missiles. But since this proposal was part of a package, the American President apparently feared some sort of trick… Both the negotiating teams and the media realized that this was a unique opportunity to break out of the vicious circle of the nuclear arms race. But the moment we had seemingly reached an agreement, some invisible force suddenly stayed the hand of the President of the United States.[25]

It became clear to Gorbachev that the US delegation was not going to give any ground, especially on SDI. He recorded the following final exchange:

> Reagan reproached me: 'You planned from the start to come here and put me in this situation!' 'No, Mr President,' I replied. 'I'm ready to go right back into the house and sign a comprehensive document on all the issues agreed if you drop your plans to militarize space.' 'I am really sorry,' was Reagan's reply.[26]

As a result, this potentially historic breakthrough for nuclear disarmament and peace collapsed. In his televised address, Gorbachev summed up his explanation:

[T]he leadership of that great country [the US] relies too heavily on the military-industrial complex, on the monopolistic groups which have turned the nuclear and other arms races into a business, into a way of making money, into the object of their existence and the meaning of their activities... The United States seeks to exhaust the Soviet Union economically with a build-up of sophisticated and costly space arms.[27]

Noting that 'the opponents of peace across the ocean are strong and influential', he added that, after Reykjavik, 'the infamous SDI became even more conspicuous as an epitome of obstructing peace, as a strong expression of militaristic designs and an unwillingness to get rid of the nuclear threat looming over mankind. It is impossible to perceive this programme in any other way.' Nevertheless, he was even more convinced that 'the path we have chosen is correct and that a new mode of political thinking in the nuclear age is necessary and constructive.'[28]

Hypocritically, the Reagan administration's drive for ballistic missile defence was claimed to be based on the immorality of MAD. This provided another argument, however disingenuous, to undermine the centrality of nuclear deterrence in preventing war between the major powers. Subsequently it became clear that a major stumbling block to an agreement between the US and the Soviets was US allies' fear that extended nuclear deterrence would be withdrawn. The monstrous hoax of nuclear deterrence had helped prevent peace.

The Experience of India and Pakistan

Meanwhile, the experience of India and Pakistan provided little support for Quinlan's claim that nuclear deterrence induced caution about going to war. Instead, their nuclear weapons have become an illusory shield behind which to carry out limited conventional wars that could go nuclear in a moment of stress, miscalculation or defeat. The proximity of India and Pakistan makes the risk of accidental nuclear war and radiation fallout even more dangerous.

When India tested its first 'peaceful' nuclear device in 1974, the US Ambassador in New Delhi, Daniel Patrick Moynihan, wrote to Prime Minister Indira Gandhi: 'India has made a huge mistake. Now in a decade's time some Pakistani General will call you up and say, I have four nuclear weapons and I want Kashmir. If not, we will drop them on you and we will all meet in heaven. And then what will you do?'[29] The ten-month confrontation between India and Pakistan in 2002 over Kashmir came close to that in propaganda terms, with over ten times that number of nuclear weapons assessed to be available on both sides (see Chapter 4). Since then their arms race has added another hundred warheads to each side's nuclear arsenals.

Rivalry between the US and the Soviet Union, plus US possession of nuclear weapons, drove the Soviets to acquire them; but nuclear deterrence doctrine then perpetuated a state of hostility and mistrust. Now we witness the same dynamic with India and Pakistan. Emma Rothschild, in a 1983 article titled 'The Delusions of Deterrence', put her finger on this fundamental weakness when she wrote that nuclear deterrence 'has not prevented – in fact, it has required – the deterioration of political relationships, and the expansions of fear and hatred, which are most likely, I believe, to bring us to war.'[30] MccGwire went further:

> Deterrence dogma stunted the development of US foreign policy. Because deterrence and its corollary, containment, were the dominant concepts in foreign and defence policy, perceptions of threat remained frozen in the mould of the 1947–53 period. The dogma provided the intellectual casing that made this worldview impervious to contradictory evidence and analysis.
>
> In sum, deterrence dogma fostered an assertive apolitical style that favoured preventive and punitive instruments, was distrustful of negotiations, and saw compromise as weakness. The possibility that US interests might be served by cooperating with the Soviet Union in dealing with problems around the world was excluded from consideration, and long-term objectives designed to shape future Soviet policies were simply not addressed.[31]

Moreover, a nuclear deterrence relationship can have unpredictable consequences. This is best illustrated by the daunting problems facing India and Pakistan. Even if they were each to succeed in building an invulnerable second-strike capability, they will be trapped in a nightmare graphically portrayed by Stephen Cimbala:

> [M]utual survivability of forces might help to defuse the crisis by facing each prospective attacker with the apparent hopelessness of knocking out the other side's retaliatory arsenal; but *it might have the opposite effect*. If national leaders are not calculating, rational actors, but are prone to launch into war for reasons of pride or fear, then calculations of the prewar balance might not deter them, but *attract them* to war. There is a fine line between deterrence and provocation. Forces felt to be secure deterrents in normal peacetime conditions may, during a crisis with potentially ultimate values at stake, turn into provocations in the minds of the opponents.[32] [emphasis added]

There is considerable evidence that belief in nuclear deterrence dogma emboldened Pakistan to initiate the Kargil confrontation in

1999. It was also a major factor in the huge mobilisation of military forces on both sides in 2002. In both cases, war was only averted by US intervention.

Self-Deterrence

A nuclear strike would mean taking over territory made useless through devastation and radioactive poison, with unmanageable survivors amid a public health catastrophe. Churchill warned after the Allied air-raid on Dresden in February 1945 that the Allies risked 'taking over an utterly ruined land' – and that was conventional bomb damage. Nine years later, Dwight Eisenhower brought this reality into the atomic age when he spoke to a group of senior officers about the consequences of a nuclear strike on the Soviet Union:

> [G]ain such a victory, and what do you do with it? Here would be a great area... torn up and destroyed, without government, without its communications, just an area of starvation and disaster. I ask you what would the civilized world do about it?[33]

He omitted to mention the long-term health effects of radioactive fallout. Moreover, even a low-yield nuclear strike – now official US, UK and French policy in defence of their 'vital interests' anywhere against chemical or biological weapon attack – would so outrage world opinion that it would be self-defeating.

In the case of a nuclear state facing defeat by a non-nuclear state, there is evidence that nuclear weapons are again self-deterring. The US in Korea and Vietnam, and the USSR in Afghanistan, preferred withdrawal to the ultimate ignominy of resorting to nuclear weapons to secure 'victory' or revenge. Similarly, if NATO were faced with a crisis in which the use of US nuclear weapons in Europe became imminent, the leaders of its member states might well refuse their assent. David Yost argued that 'the overriding imperative would probably be to find conventional ways to deal with the challenge which provoked the crisis, and to avoid a decision on using nuclear weapons. In the aftermath of the crisis, US nuclear weapons in Europe might be seen as a source of trouble and risk, rather than as one of the means of ensuring NATO's security.'[34]

Recognition that a nuclear exchange could spell devastation for his own country was a powerful argument in favour of self deterrence for former French President Giscard d'Estaing. While France – its people and culture – had made a full recovery after the experience of defeat and occupation by Nazi Germany, the prospects of its survival following a nuclear war would be in doubt. Sharing his reflections on the subject in his memoirs in 1991, d'Estaing wrote:

> And then, as far as mutually assured destruction is concerned, whatever may happen – and I write this in brackets to stress that this decision was always buried deep inside me – whatever may happen I will never take the initiative of doing something that would lead to France's annihilation. If her destruction was begun by the enemy, I would immediately make the decision necessary to avenge her. But otherwise, I would wish to give some chance to France's landscape, houses, trees, ponds, rivers and to her inhabitants' hidden loyalty to their convictions... I would wish to give them a final chance to revive French culture some day.[35]

'Sub-Strategic' Nuclear Deterrence

To circumvent the problem of self-deterrence, the proponents of nuclear weapons and deterrence theory have sought to develop arguments in favour of a separate class of 'usable' or *sub-strategic* nuclear weapons. However, in his last speech before he was assassinated in 1979, Admiral of the Fleet Earl Mountbatten echoed what several leading members of the UK establishment had conceded back in the 1950s: 'I have never been able to accept the reasons for the belief that any class of nuclear weapons can be categorised in terms of their tactical or strategic purposes.'[36] The argument that more usable nuclear weapons make nuclear war more likely must be addressed by proponents of nuclear deterrence. In order to uphold the logic of nuclear deterrence, they have to state a clear preference for usable nuclear weapons, or admit that nuclear deterrence relies on bluff. At present, they are trying to have their cake and eat it.

The Bush administration, echoed by the UK and French governments, warned that it reserved the option to use nuclear weapons in response to an attack with WMD against their military forces anywhere in the world; and this policy has now been extended to include strategic cyber attack. Meanwhile, mirroring NATO's posture in the Cold War, Russia has revived its dependence on its arsenal of tactical nuclear weapons to compensate for its conventional military inferiority. The UK Trident ballistic missile submarine force may still have a sub-strategic role, in which some missiles are apparently fitted with maybe only a single, lower-yield warhead. In 1999, NATO announced that 'a small number of United Kingdom Trident warheads' were now part of NATO's sub-strategic posture in Europe.[37] The UK government explained:

> A sub-strategic capability is an essential element in ensuring that no nuclear-armed aggressor could gamble on us being self-deterred from

crossing the nuclear threshold in extreme circumstances of self-defence by fear of an inevitable strategic exchange. In such circumstances this capability would allow the limited use of nuclear weapons to send an aggressor a political message of the Alliance's resolve to defend itself. The UK has a degree of flexibility in the choice of yield for the warheads on its Trident missiles.[38]

Nothing more is publicly known about this warhead – yet it is the most likely British one to be used (more is known on almost every other deployed nuclear weapon, including Russian and Chinese ones).

There is another problem here for both the UK and US governments. Notwithstanding the former's efforts to appear to be independent, there is a major risk that use of a UK Trident missile would be indistinguishable from a US Trident launch. What is more, how does the UK government distinguish sub-strategic nuclear deterrence from strategic in the perceptions of a potential aggressor? The range of the system is the same in both cases. There is no identification of the platform, and presumably no indication to surveillance systems on launch that an attack is sub-strategic, other than counting the number of detonations. Also, the launch would reveal the location of the submarine, exposing it to potential counter-attack.

Thus, if a UK Trident sub-strategic strike is directed at a nuclear-armed state, its government would probably not wait to discover what the explosive power is, but would regard it as a strategic first strike and retaliate strategically. The deduction from this is that a sub-strategic role should be confined to threatening only non-nuclear states (the March 2002 statement by UK Defence Secretary Geoff Hoon appeared to endorse this approach).[39] However, this would be unlawful.

The difficulties proliferate. The UK government's announced policy will raise fears among non-nuclear states that its negative security assurances given under the Non-Proliferation Treaty are worthless. Further confusion was sown by UK Secretary of State for Defence Des Browne in a speech on 26 January 2007, when he argued that Britain has

> ...never sought to use [its] nuclear weapons as a means of provoking or coercing others. [It] will never do so. Nor are [its] weapons intended or designed for military use during conflict. Indeed, [it] has *deliberately chosen to stop using the term 'sub-strategic Trident'*, applied previously to a possible limited use of [its] nuclear weapons. I would like to take this opportunity to reaffirm that the UK would only consider using nuclear weapons in the most extreme situations of self-defence.[40] [emphasis added]

Yet the policy may not have changed. In the UK Government's White Paper *The Future of the United Kingdom's Nuclear Deterrent*, published only a month earlier, in December 2006, the option of a lower-yield warhead remained:

> Retaining some degree of uncertainty over the nature and scale of [the UK's] response to any particular set of circumstances is an important part of our deterrent posture... [T]he ability to vary the number of missiles and warheads which might be employed, coupled with the *continued availability of a lower yield from our warhead*, can make [the UK's] nuclear forces a more credible deterrent against smaller nuclear threats.[41] [emphasis added]

An interesting example of what might happen in a real scenario was recounted by former French President Giscard d'Estaing. To 'clarify the use of the tactical nuclear weapon', he instructed his army chiefs in 1980 to organise a 'full-scale exercise, in which we would test the decisions that had to be taken.'[42] The war game began in the French Zone of West Germany. The generals, who at first hoped that they could 'play their trump card', concluded that, when forced to retreat by a more numerous enemy, the High Command would not ask the President to authorise the use of tactical nuclear weapons as a final warning demonstration: 'They considered that it was better to keep our battle forces intact and available rather than expose them to nuclear destruction.' D'Estaing commented:

> So, no request goes to the President! The demonstration is not complete. But progressively, as we pull back towards our own frontier, we leave the domain of 'final warning' and enter the domain of strategic deterrence. A limited strike by us would immediately trigger retaliation direct onto French soil. Then there would remain only the choice between the white flag of surrender and 'mutually assured destruction'. A better choice would be to keep our remaining cards in our hands, unplayed.[43]

He went on to admit that he would have chosen surrender, as mentioned earlier under 'self-deterrence'. As he indicated, the enormity of 'crossing the nuclear threshold' should not be underestimated. Here is what Colin Powell discovered in 1986 as a General in a war-game in West Germany:

> No matter how small these nuclear payloads were, we would be crossing a threshold. Using nukes at this point would mark one of the most significant political and military decisions since Hiroshima. The Russians would certainly retaliate, maybe escalate. At that moment, the world's heart was going to skip a beat. From that day on, I began rethinking the practicality of these small nuclear weapons.[44]

Extended Nuclear Deterrence

The unintended consequences of strategies based on deterrence theory are also central to a critique of the strategy of *extended nuclear deterrence*. The dangerous dilemma is that the state providing a so-called 'nuclear umbrella' for non-nuclear allied states risks being pushed through the nuclear threshold when its own security is not directly threatened. Furthermore, 'umbrella' is a misnomer: it is in reality a *lightning rod for insecurity* because of the near-certainty of rapid, uncontrollable escalation to full-scale nuclear war.

A particularly damning indictment of extended deterrence follows from Stephen Cimbala:

> Henry Kissinger once made an unfortunate speech in Brussels, in which he said that the United States should not make threats it does not mean (nuclear threats to deter conventional war in Europe) or, if it means them, cannot execute, because if it executes, it risks the destruction of civilization. The only saving grace of this statement was that it was made by Kissinger while out of office, but it still commits almost every sin imaginable from the standpoint of reassurance to Europeans and deterrence of the Soviet Union.[45]

In an appendix to his 1988 book *Democracy and Deterrence*, Philip Bobbitt drew attention to a significant factor in the political fallout from the failed Reykjavik summit in October 1986 between Reagan and Gorbachev, which is relevant here. As mentioned earlier, US allied governments were stunned to learn from the media that withdrawal of US extended nuclear deterrence had almost been agreed upon with no consultation. While most of their citizens welcomed Gorbachev's proposal to eliminate all Russian and US nuclear weapons within ten years, the very foundations of NATO and the bilateral security treaties with Japan, South Korea and Australia were shaken. Here was powerful evidence of the pernicious influence of extended nuclear deterrence as the 'nuclear glue' in sustaining military alliances and blocking progress to a nuclear weapon-free world.[46]

Escalation is Inevitable

Both sub-strategic and extended nuclear deterrence entail a huge risk. Mountbatten described it thus in 1979: 'I repeat in all sincerity: as a military man, I can see no use for any nuclear weapons which would not end in escalation, with consequences that no-one can conceive.'[47] Three years later, McGeorge Bundy, George Kennan, Robert

McNamara and Gerard Smith were alarmed enough to write jointly: 'No one has ever succeeded in advancing any persuasive reason to believe that any use of nuclear weapons, even on the smallest scale, could reliably be expected to remain limited.'[48] This is because of communication difficulties in the midst of nuclear war. Even if crucial command system components are not targeted, they are vulnerable to the environmental disturbances caused by the Electro-Magnetic Pulse effects of nuclear explosions.

Nuclear Deterrence against Chemical and Biological Weapon Attacks

In 1996, US Defense Secretary William Perry told a Senate Foreign Relations Committee hearing on chemical and biological weapons that the Pentagon favoured using a new earth-penetrating nuclear weapon against an alleged underground chemical weapon plant in Tarhunah, Libya.[49] Although the statement was later withdrawn, this indicated that the US was contemplating using nuclear weapons to deter any attacks with chemical or biological weapons against their 'vital interests' anywhere in the world. With publication in December 2002 of the Bush administration's National Strategy to Combat Weapons of Mass Destruction, this was confirmed as US policy.

The justification was that only a nuclear weapon has the explosive power to destroy such a target, especially if underground, and its enormous heat would incinerate germ warfare agents. The extreme dangers of such an approach, amounting to military incompetence, are as follows:

* The nuclear explosion would create and disperse massive amounts of radioactive fallout.
* Any chemicals or biological toxins not destroyed in the blast could be dispersed with catastrophic effects.
* Any state with chemical or biological weapons is unlikely to store them in one place. Thus any attempt to destroy them would require several nuclear weapons, multiplying the risk of civilian casualties and environmental damage.
* Instead of deterring the possession or use of chemical or biological weapons, the mere threat to use a nuclear weapon would give that state the political and military justification to use their own weapons of mass destruction.[50]

In a US confrontation with Iraq in February 1998, the possibility of using nuclear weapons against suspected underground Iraqi chemical and biological weapon production and storage sites caused a worldwide outcry. General Butler, who in the 1991 Gulf War had helped convince General Colin Powell to rule out plans to use nuclear weapons, angrily responded with the following volley of questions:

> What better illustration of misplaced faith in nuclear deterrence is there than the persistent belief that retaliation with nuclear weapons is a legitimate and appropriate response to post-Cold War threats posed by weapons of mass destruction? What could possibly justify our resort to the very means we properly abhor and condemn? Who can imagine our joining in shattering the precedent of non-use that has held for more than fifty years? How could America's irreplaceable role as leader of the campaign against nuclear proliferation ever be rejustified? What target would warrant such retaliation? Would we hold an entire society accountable for the decision of a single demented leader? How would the physical effects of the nuclear explosion be contained, not to mention the political and moral consequences? In a single act, we would martyr our enemies, alienate our friends, give comfort to the non-declared nuclear states and impetus to states who seek such weapons covertly.[51]

Clearly, the threatened use of nuclear weapons in reprisal for an attack with chemical or biological weapons would exacerbate the danger of nuclear proliferation by effectively telling non-nuclear states that nuclear weapons are necessary to deter a potential US nuclear attack, and by sending a green light to other nuclear states that it is permissible to use them.

The first indication that this was happening came in March 2002 with the statements by the UK Secretary of State for Defence, Geoff Hoon, to the effect that the UK government would be prepared to use nuclear weapons in response to a CB attack against British troops deployed overseas.[52] A year later, the French government followed suit.[53]

The new US nuclear posture envisaged a role for nuclear weapons against hardened and deeply buried targets (HDBTs):

> The United States currently has a very limited ground penetration capability with its only earth penetrating nuclear weapon, the B61 Mod 11 gravity bomb. This single-yield, non-precision weapon cannot survive penetration into many types of terrain in which hardened underground facilities are located... For defeat of very deep or larger underground facilities, penetrating weapons with large yields would be needed to collapse the facility... Investment and organization will yield a new level of capability for the stated objectives by 2007, with new technologies deployed by 2012.[54]

More than any other aspect of the new US nuclear posture, this signalled a massive shift in thinking about the utility of nuclear weapons. The Bush administration appeared to have been persuaded by the weapon laboratories that such a role for a nuclear warhead was feasible, though it was yet to be demonstrated. Almost no consideration seems to have been given to the drawbacks of using a nuclear weapon like a conventional munition.

On 26 January 2003, US defence analyst William Arkin revealed in the *Los Angeles Times* that the Pentagon was preparing for the possible use of nuclear weapons in a war against Iraq. Specifically, options were under consideration for use of tactical nuclear weapons against HDBTs to pre-empt a chemical or biological attack by the Iraqis. These plans suggested a new recklessness in Pentagon thinking, probably with the aim of exploiting the invasion of Iraq in order to validate new roles for nuclear weapons. Yet the US proved that it had no military need of them there. Its formidable arsenal of conventional munitions successfully neutralised all underground targets, including the best anti-nuclear bunkers that Western technology could provide. It was therefore a relief when the Bush administration announced in October 2005 that it had abandoned research into a nuclear 'bunker-buster' warhead, deciding instead to pursue a similar device using conventional weaponry.[55]

Nuclear Deterrence is a Two-Way Street

The proponents of deterrence expect it to work in accordance with the script they have written for it. The fallacy of such a premise might not hold in the real world, where particular histories define the motivations and behaviour of particular actors who, in the heat of an escalating conflict, may not perform as expected.

General Lee Butler drew attention to this difficulty when he pointed out that '[deterrence] in the Cold War setting was fatally flawed at the most fundamental level of human psychology in its projection of Western reason through the crazed lens of a paranoid foe.'[56] He went on to ask:

> How is it that we subscribed to a deterrence strategy that required near-perfect understanding of an enemy from whom we were deeply alienated and largely isolated? How could we pretend to understand the motivations and intentions of a Soviet leadership, absent any substantive personal association? Why did we imagine a nation that had survived successive invasions and mind-numbing losses would accede to a strategy premised on fear of nuclear war? Little wonder that intentions and motives were consistently misread. While we clung to the notion that nuclear war could be reliably deterred, Soviet leaders became convinced that such a war might be thrust upon them and, if so, it must not be lost. Driven by fear, they took Herculean measures to fight and survive no matter the odds or the cost.[57]

In determining the most likely threat, my military intelligence training taught me always to examine my own forces' proposed actions or declared intentions from the enemy's point of view, answering the question: 'How would I react if I was on the receiving end of my own actions?' To take a relevant example, picture the accumulated paranoia in the US if, instead, the Soviets had without warning dropped two nuclear weapons on Japan in 1945. The Americans, reeling from having lost over 20 million dead repulsing the Nazis, would take four years to develop one. In that time the Soviet Union had proceeded to invade Japan, declared that the US was its new foe, and then established a string of airbases in Canada, Mexico and the Caribbean within bomber range of Washington and the main centres of population... It is instructive to view the 1962 Cuban missile crisis with this 'mirror' scenario in mind.

Here is the verdict by Lebow and Stein, who examined the role of general deterrence in Soviet-American relations on the eve of the crisis:

> We found that deterrence was provocative instead of preventive. Soviet officials testified that the American strategic build-up, missile deployment in Turkey and assertions of strategic superiority exacerbated their insecurity. President Kennedy considered all these actions as prudent, defensive measures against Soviet threats, especially in Berlin. Instead of restraining Khrushchev, they convinced him of the need to do more to protect the Soviet Union and Cuba from American military and political challenges. Through their avowedly defensive actions, the leaders of both superpowers made their fears of an acute confrontation self-fulfilling... [The Americans] rejected a defensive interpretation of Khrushchev's action in part because they could not empathize; they did not understand the perception of threat their strategic and Caribbean policies engendered in Moscow.[58]

Even a pro-nuclear US report warned in 1998: 'What is required to deter and how effective deterrence will be depends upon the party you are trying to deter and the context. Threats and actions that may seem to the United States as a credible deterrent may not deter others because their value system is different.'[59]

Leading on from this, the same report spelt out a fundamental difficulty regarding the most likely target for nuclear deterrence, a paranoid regime or extremists:

> Deterrence based on a generically rational and sensible foe will not be adequate in the decades ahead. Differences in leaderships, decision-making processes, risk tolerances, threat perceptions, goals, values, and determination, and simply the potential for idiosyncratic behaviour, limit the reliability of any general formula for deterrence.

Detailed intelligence information will be essential to the effectiveness and reliability of deterrence policies. In the absence of such information, there can be little basis for confidence in making informed recommendations about how to deter any particular foe from a specific act.[60]

In 1993, the UK Secretary of Defence agreed:

[I]n the absence of an established deterrent relationship... [w]ould the threat be understood in the deterrent way in which it was intended; and might it have some unpredictable and perhaps counter-productive consequence? Categoric answers to these questions might be hard to come by, and in their absence the utility of the deterrent threat as a basis for policy and action would necessarily be in doubt... *it is difficult to see deterrence operating securely against proliferators.*[61] [emphasis added]

Was Iraq Deterred in the First Gulf War?

The case of Iraq demonstrates these difficulties. Because Iraq did not use its chemical or biological weapons during the 1991 Gulf War, officials argued that US nuclear threats had worked. They cited comments by Iraq's Deputy Prime Minister Tariq Aziz in August 1995 that fear of nuclear attack had been why Iraq had not used its chemical arsenal. There are reasons to doubt this claim.

Rolf Ekeus, then head of the UN Special Commission in Iraq and to whom Aziz had commented, told independent military analyst William Arkin six months later that he was quite sure it was not a decisive factor. Rather, it was a line Iraq had taken to try to end UN sanctions by claiming that it was a victim of the US. Ekeus had learned that, shortly before the allied air blitz began, Iraq deployed biological weapons to airfields in western Iraq. However, it had been caught off-guard by the speed and ferocity of the war. The widespread destruction, especially of command and control systems, probably prevented Iraq from mounting a successful attack. Furthermore, the adverse weather, with winds that would have carried a biological or chemical attack back over Iraqi ground forces who were poorly equipped with defensive measures, had almost certainly been a major factor.[62]

Moreover, as Scott Sagan pointed out, the note from President Bush, delivered by Secretary of State James Baker to Aziz (then Iraq's Foreign Minister), did not threaten a devastating response only in retaliation to Iraqi use of chemical or biological weapons. It also listed Iraqi support for terrorist activities or the destruction of the Kuwaiti oilfields as actions that would cause the US public to 'demand the strongest possible response'. Yet Saddam Hussein did order terrorist attacks against US targets, and Iraqi special forces set fire to the Kuwaiti oilfields.[63]

The doubts deepen with US officials' subsequent claims that the note had been a bluff. This is consistent with the fact that Generals Lee Butler and Colin Powell both publicly confirmed that, as the chief nuclear planners, they ruled out any use of nuclear weapons in the war. An extract from Powell's autobiography follows:

> 'Let's not even think about nukes,' I said. 'You know we're not going to let that genie loose.'
>
> 'Of course not,' Cheney [Secretary of Defense] said. 'But take a look to be thorough and just out of curiosity.'
>
> I told Tom Kelly to gather a handful of people [including General Lee Butler] in the most secure cell in the building to work out nuclear strike options. The results unnerved me. To do serious damage to just one armored division dispersed in the desert would require a considerable number of small tactical nuclear weapons. I showed his analysis to Cheney and then had it destroyed. If I had had any doubts before about the practicality of nukes on the field of battle, this report clinched them.[64]

One significant conclusion is that a US track record of failure to carry out any of several known threats to use nuclear force, dating back to the Soviet blockade of Berlin in 1948, was sustained. This means that any future threat by the US to use nuclear weapons in a similar scenario will lack credibility.

Terrorists are Undeterrable with Nuclear Weapons

The terror attacks against the World Trade Center and the Pentagon on 11 September 2001 drew attention to the far more catastrophic consequences of the detonation of even a small nuclear device in such locations. Nuclear blackmail is the ultimate expression of megalomania and terrorism, which is why a nuclear device would be so attractive to terrorists.

Deterrence of terrorist groups presents some unique problems that do not exist in deterring a state. They may operate on their own, and on a very small scale, or as agents of a state in which case they could pose a larger and more sophisticated threat. Terrorists, especially suicide bombers, generally operate within a value system not susceptible to deterrence. As Kissinger said, 'nothing can deter an opponent bent on self-destruction.'[65] Also, the targeted state may not know the source of a terrorist attack, and thus there may be nowhere at which to direct retaliatory threats.

At the lowest yield currently deployed by the US – 0.3 kilotons, or 300 tons of TNT – a nuclear weapon is hundreds of times more powerful than the largest conventional bomb. It is therefore too indiscriminate to use as a discreet instrument of retribution. With no clear target anyway, a threat to do so would not be credible. This reality was acknowledged by the Bush administration in its 2002 National Security Strategy.

Nuclear Deterrence Undermines Security

This leads on to a wider reality. Nuclear deterrence directly threatens the security of both those who depend on it and those whom it is meant to impress. Nuclear weapons are, in fact, a security problem, not a solution. This is because they undermine a possessor's security by provoking the most likely and dangerous threat: proliferation to undeterrable extremists.

The decision by Israel, India, Pakistan and North Korea to go nuclear, and concerns about Iran, vindicated Ken Booth and Nicholas Wheeler when they wrote in 1992 that 'nuclear weapons, by their very nature, are offensive devices of mass destruction which feed the security dilemma, and which are likely, slowly, to proliferate to a larger number of states.'[66] Kennan added:

> The nuclear weapon is recognized as a suicidal device, capable of bringing nothing less than disaster to whoever might venture to use it. It can serve neither offensive nor defensive purposes. So long as it remains in national arsenals, and to the extent that it does, it is a menace to all of us. *Nor is there any security to be gained from the effort to diminish the security of anybody else. The other fellow's security is in fact one's own.* The striving for military superiority thus serves no purpose; it is only a means of 'chasing one's own tail'.[67] [emphasis added]

Evidence of this reality materialised on 9 October 2006 when North Korea carried out its widely advertised first nuclear test. Peter Hayes characterised North Korean behaviour as follows:

> Currently, the United States has no common language for discussing nuclear weapons with the North Korean military in the context of the insecurities that bind the two sides together at the Demilitarized Zone.
> Continued rebuffing of Pyongyang's overtures may lead to more 'nuclear stalking' – that is, the development of creative and unanticipated ways of using nuclear threats, deployments, and actual use in times of crisis or war. There are no grounds to believe that the

DPRK will employ a US or Western conceptual framework of nuclear deterrence and crisis management in developing its own nuclear doctrine and use options. Indeed, US efforts to use 'clear and classical' deterrent threats to communicate to North Koreans that 'if they do acquire WMD, their weapons will be unusable because any attempt to use them will bring national obliteration' – as Condoleezza Rice put it in her Foreign Affairs essay in 2000 – serve to incite the DPRK to exploit this very threat as a way to engage the United States, with terrible risks of miscalculation and first-use on both sides.

In fact, the scenario of nuclear next-use in Korea that is most worrisome is not the result of war involving the United States with its allies, and the DPRK: rather, it involves the consequences of the DPRK falling into a state of war with itself. Should the DPRK collapse violently, then its nuclear weapons or fissile material might be commandeered either for provocative use in order to draw the ROK into such a war by one or other faction in the DPRK, or simply spirited out of the country by the residual narco-criminal networks operating out of the DPRK and become available to another proliferating state or a non-state actor with nuclear aspirations. For this reason alone, it is urgent that the international community cooperate to stabilize the political and economic situation of the North Korea.

Such is the awesome power of nuclear weapons that there is no alternative.[68]

The course of the North Korean crisis since then seems to have borne out this assessment.

Nuclear Deterrence Creates Instability

Another quest doomed to failure is that of 'stable' nuclear deterrence. Indeed, the expression is a contradiction in terms.

As Keith Payne pointed out, confident claims that any particular strategic nuclear balance is 'stable' should be viewed with great scepticism, because deterrence involves much more than comparing relative force capabilities. It includes decision-making factors typically ignored in Cold War 'stability analyses', such as a desperate leadership's unwillingness to take inconvenient facts into account. Nevertheless, confidence persists that mutual vulnerability will assuredly produce deterrence 'stability'.[69]

There are two forms of instability caused by nuclear deterrence. The first, through *arms racing*, was recognized by theorists as early as the 1950s, with the emergence of the 'original' nuclear weapon states following the lead set by the US. It was then demonstrated by the continuing strategic arms race long after both sides had the capacity to destroy each other several times over. It became clear that instability was a function of psychological and political factors, which were exacerbated by asymmetries in the nature and timing of weapons programmes.[70]

The second form, *crisis* instability, arises when nuclear deterrence itself transforms a conflict or clash of interests into a major crisis. The Cuban missile crisis is the supreme example. Nuclear deterrence strategy encourages both sides to adopt a high state of alert early in a serious crisis in order to discourage adversarial pre-emption, thereby increasing the risk of accidental nuclear war.[71]

On nuclear deterrence's influence on the arms race, General Lee Butler commented:

> Deterrence failed completely as a guide for setting rational limits on the size and composition of forces. The appetite of deterrence was voracious, its capacity to justify new weapons and large stocks unrestrained... I saw the arms race from the inside, watched as intercontinental ballistic missiles ushered in mutual assured destruction and multiple-warhead missiles introduced genuine fear of a nuclear first strike. I was responsible for nuclear war plans with more than 12,000 targets, many of which would have been struck with repeated nuclear blows.[72]

The most extreme current example of instability in both forms is between India, Pakistan and China. Pakistan is heavily disadvantaged with respect to India's conventional military strength. This asymmetry is unaffected by India's claim to be developing a 'minimum deterrent', because India's minimum will be assessed with respect to China, not Pakistan. American persistence in developing a Theatre Missile Defence system with Japan means that China will be driven to counter it by expanding its nuclear arsenal. Inevitably, India's 'minimum' will therefore always exceed Pakistan's.

Until Pakistan builds a survivable second-strike capability (if it can afford one), it will be faced with a 'use them or lose them' situation in the face of India's ability to launch a 'decapitating' strike. Meanwhile, if India succeeds in its announced plan to build a triad of air, land and, especially, invulnerable submarine-delivered nuclear weapons that can reach key Chinese targets, then China may well explore a closer nuclear relationship with Pakistan.

These developments mean a nuclear arms race amid severe political tension in South Asia, with increasing probability of accidents and misunderstandings as the Kashmir crisis festers. This creates deepening instability, in which the illusions of nuclear deterrence will play a central role.

Nuclear Deterrence Provokes Proliferation

The case of India and Pakistan also serves as the most dramatic recent evidence in support of the charge that nuclear deterrence provokes proliferation. As the former colonial power whose example continues to be deeply influential, the UK carries a heavy responsibility for this. In addition, NATO's insistence that nuclear weapons are essential for its security cannot be excluded as another motive for India's decision to go nuclear. Here is the view of a former Foreign Minister of Canada: 'We should be circumspect about the political value we place on NATO nuclear forces, lest we furnish arguments proliferators can use to try to justify their own nuclear programs.'[73] General Lee Butler observed:

> [W]ith respect to the central issue of proliferation, we risk summoning the very nightmare we have worked so fervently to forestall. First-use policies and high alert postures are in direct contradiction to our self-interest, the objectives of the Non-Proliferation Treaty, and the patent rejection of the use of nuclear weapons by American presidents in conflicts from Korea to Indochina to the Persian Gulf...
>
> India and Pakistan have thrust themselves into the nuclear arena, casting aside pretense, brandishing their fledgling arsenals and declaring themselves cloaked in the security of the self-same deterrence proclaimed so insistently by the charter members of the nuclear club... it is painfully evident that no amount of protest would suffice coming from an American president hoist on the petard of his own nuclear weapons policy.[74]

Nuclear Deterrence Threatens Democracy

Democracy depends on responsible use of political and military power, with leaders held accountable to the will of the majority of the people. If a democratic nation is forced to use state-sanctioned violence to defend itself, its leaders must stay within internationally recognised moral and legal limits. Yet nuclear deterrence is about threatening the most indiscriminate violence possible, unrestrained by morality or the law. It is therefore a policy of gross irresponsibility, and the antithesis of democratic values.

Furthermore, democracy within a nation operating a nuclear deterrence policy is inevitably undermined by the need for secrecy and tight control of technology, equipment and personnel. For example, the history of the UK's nuclear arsenal shows that every major decision was taken without even full Cabinet knowledge, let alone approval. Francis Boyle, an expert in international law, wrote about the US experience:

There has never been any form of meaningful democratic accountability applied to the U.S. nuclear weapons establishment. The American people as individuals or as a whole have never had any significant input into the process of developing nuclear weapons systems except to the extent that Congress has voted blank checks. The very existence of nuclear weapons systems and their requisite degrees of super-secrecy require that our system of nuclear government be kept stealthily anti-democratic... Finally, the same principle holds true for the Constitution. Constitutional protections became meaningless when nuclear weapons were integrated into the U.S. foreign affairs and defense establishment. Indeed, the U.S. Constitution has become a farce and façade in the name of national security as a direct result of nuclear weapons.[75]

Launch On Warning

Nearly thirty years after the Cold War ended, the US and Russia continue to threaten each other with nuclear annihilation. As General Lee Butler pointed out in 1999:

> Today we find ourselves in the almost unbelievable circumstance in which the United States nuclear weapons policy is still very much that of 1984, as introduced by Ronald Reagan. Our forces with their hair-trigger postures are effectively the same as they have been since the height of the Cold War.[76]

One dangerous consequence of Mutual Assured Destruction and retaining the option of first use is that both the US and Russia still sustain a posture of 'launch on warning' for their strategic nuclear forces. Even after signing the New START Treaty in 2010, the two nuclear superpowers each remain ready to fire over 1,500 nuclear weapons at each other within about half an hour.[77] Each side is poised to release a massive retaliatory salvo after detecting an enemy missile attack but before the incoming warheads arrive – which might take just fifteen minutes if fired from submarines deployed nearer to the other side's territory. Although it has thousands of warheads securely deployed at sea, the US adheres to this stance because of the vulnerability of its missile silos and command apparatus, including its political and military leadership in Washington, D.C.

The Russians feel much more vulnerable, because lack of resources means that currently only two of their submarines are at sea on patrol at any time. What is more, the Russian warning time is reduced by the relative proximity of NATO submarines; and the performance of its early warning system has been eroded with the break-up of the Soviet Union and technical problems. As a result, five of the eight radar stations that formed the Soviet system are now outside Russia.

Mutual de-targeting agreements in 1994 helped to ease the problem, but have little military significance. Missile commanders can reload target coordinates into guidance computers within seconds; and apparently an unprogrammed Russian missile would automatically switch back to its primary wartime target. Moreover, both US and Russian missiles cannot be ordered to self-destruct once they are launched, presumably because of the risk of radioactive fallout in the possessor state.

There is also the problem of confusion following such an accidental launch, with so little time to decide on a course of action. On 25 January 1995, the world came close to accidental nuclear weapon use when the Russian military detected an unidentified ballistic missile over Norway, possibly heading for Russia. For the first time, the Russian 'nuclear briefcase' carried by the President was activated as Yeltsin prepared to respond. Orders were given to Russian ballistic missile submarines to go to battle stations. Disaster was averted by only a few minutes when the missile was reassessed as harmless, as it continued north over the Arctic to observe the Northern Lights. Its identity and research mission had not reached the Russian early warning system.[78] In fact it was a US manufactured Norwegian research rocket, with a missile trail signature which Russian detectors would have identified as potentially hostile.

This is what happens when two superpowers have the resources to pursue the logic of nuclear deterrence dogma. Paradoxically, the need to deploy nuclear forces in such a way as to convince the opposing side that they could not defeat a second strike nor withstand its destructiveness turns the dogma on its head. This is because, as General Lee Butler explained to Jonathan Schell in 1998,

> [t]he things that you do in the quest to convey the reality of your retaliatory threat will be seen, through the prism of your enemy's perspective, as a hostile capability to launch a first strike. And that perception forces him, once again, to try to trump your ace... Thus your quest for security, by building a highly credible deterrent force, is unhinged by your opponent's need to respond in kind. In my view, that paradox is the fundamental problem at an operational level with deterrence.[79]

This dynamic is fed by another disturbing reality. In 1985, the nuclear analyst and former USAF launch control officer for Minuteman nuclear-armed ICBMs, Bruce Blair, published a book, *Strategic Command and Control*, in which he demonstrated that the US could not reliably deliver a retaliatory strike because of the extreme vulnerability of its command and control systems. This meant that not only the nation's declared policy of flexible response but also the entire policy of deterrence was vitiated. Moreover, in a follow-up book *The Logic of Accidental Nuclear War*, Blair took advantage of the end of the Cold War to research the situation in the USSR and later Russia, and found that Moscow's command and control system was at least as vulnerable as Washington's. Hence, as Blair's findings show, it would be justifiable to conclude that, far from 'working', nuclear deterrence in the form of MAD never properly existed! The military leaders on both sides in charge of operating nuclear forces knew this. Their response was to adopt 'launch on warning', despite the huge pressures it imposed on decision-makers.

To facilitate that decision-making process, the military introduced a deeper deception. In a 2004 article entitled 'Keeping Presidents in the Nuclear Dark', Blair described how the President's supporting command system is so biased in favour of launch that

> it would take enormously more presidential will to withhold an attack than to authorize it. The option to 'ride out' the onslaught and then take stock of the proper course of action exists only on paper. That is what presidents never learn during their tenures. Their real control is illusory. What's more, the truth has been kept from the presidents intentionally.[80]

The military designed the hardware and procedures to ensure that no President could opt to ride out a first strike, even though the essential part of US nuclear deterrence policy is second-strike retaliation. General Lee Butler corroborated this with Schell, adding that the consequence was that neither side would survive. The Russian response was to introduce *Perimetr* to ensure that, if a US first strike decapitated the Russian command and control system, their forces would be launched automatically by what is known as the 'dead hand'.[81] Butler commented, 'Where's the deterrence in that?'[82]

This is why it is irresponsible for both nuclear superpowers to sustain their addiction to the dogma of nuclear deterrence, when the top priority should be to eliminate the possibility of accidental nuclear war between two alleged partners in the struggle against terrorism.

Summary

Over sixty years after the first claims were made for the indispensability of nuclear deterrence, there are substantial grounds for doubt that it has worked as a guarantor of security policy. Indeed, the ultimate irony of nuclear deterrence may be the way in which it undercuts much of the political stability its proponents claim it creates. The arms race, threatening military deployments, confrontational rhetoric and often reckless posturing that characterise its application are self-defeating, provoking precisely the response it is designed to prevent. Underlying all this is a fundamental, insoluble lack of credibility.

Because the governments of the US-allied states have been intimidated into blind allegiance to nuclear deterrence, its underlying assumptions have been difficult to challenge, especially during the Cold War. The concept has been likened to an intellectual tranquilliser, its increasingly sophisticated logic imparting a sense of false certainty.

A more realistic verdict is that the great achievement of the last fifty years was to have avoided major war between the nuclear weapon states *despite* the corrosive effect of nuclear deterrence doctrine on all aspects of East-West relations. In the case of India and Pakistan, there is evidence that naive belief in nuclear deterrence actually caused the 1999 Kargil confrontation, and could yet provoke all-out war.

The George W. Bush administration pursued new war-fighting roles for nuclear weapons. In so doing, it was the first to acknowledge that nuclear deterrence probably will not work against the greatest current threat to Americans: attacks by extremists with weapons of mass destruction. Evidence is accumulating that nuclear weapons do not provide security; on the contrary, they are now the central security problem for the international community.

Tragically, the example set by the US, the UK and France as the guardians of nuclear deterrence dogma has been followed by Israel, Iraq, India, Pakistan, and North Korea. Until the government of one of the NATO nuclear states is persuaded that the arguments presented in this chapter outweigh the perceived status of possessing nuclear weapons, the prospect is for further proliferation, most likely to regimes or terrorist groups who will not be deterrable.

Notes

1   See Colin Gray, 'Deterrence and the Nature of Strategy', in *Deterrence in the 21st Century*, edited by Max G. Manwaring, Professor of Military Strategy, US Army War College (Frank Cass, London, 2001), pp. 17–26.

2   Stephen J. Cimbala, *Nuclear Strategizing – Deterrence and Reality* (Praeger Publishers, New York, 1988), p. 18.

3   R. Ned Lebow and Janice Stein, 'Nuclear lessons of the Cold War' (Ken Booth ed., *Statecraft and Security – The Cold War and Beyond*, Cambridge University Press, 1998), p. 74.

4   The occasion was a meeting attended by the author at the Royal Society on 11 December 1992, when the Pugwash Conferences on Science and World Affairs invited McNamara to speak on 'A Nuclear Weapon-Free World: Desirable? Feasible?' The points are from the author's notes.

5   Report of the Canberra Commission on the Elimination of Nuclear Weapons (Australian Ministry of Foreign Affairs & Trade, August 1996), p. 10. The 17-member Commission, established by the Australian government in October 1995, comprised nuclear weapon experts and nuclear disarmament advocates from the five recognised nuclear weapon states, plus Japan and Australia, and included General Lee Butler and Sir Joseph Rotblat.

6   Lawrence Freedman, *The Evolution of Nuclear Strategy* (The Macmillan Press Ltd, London and Basingstoke, 1981), p. 395. For an authoritative update on all aspects of nuclear deterrence, see also Lawrence Freedman, *Deterrence* (Polity Press, Cambridge UK, 2004).

7   Jonathan Schell, *The Fate of the Earth* (Pan Books Ltd, 1982), p. 203.

8   Herman Kahn, *On Thermonuclear War* (Princeton University Press, 1960), pp. 559–560.

9   George Quester, *Nuclear Diplomacy: The First Twenty-Five Years* (Dunellen, New York, 1970), p. 246.

10   Freedman (1981), p. 270.

11   Ibid, pp. 349–351.

12   Fred Ikle, 'Can nuclear deterrence last out the century?', *Foreign Affairs*, LI: 2 (January 1973).

13   Herbert York, 'Reducing the overkill', *Survival*, XVI: 2 (March/April 1974).

14   Michael MccGwire, *Nuclear Deterrence* (Canberra Commission Background Papers, 1996), p. 236.

15   George F. Kennan, 'American Policy Toward Russia on the Eve of the 1984 Presidential Election' (*At A Century's Ending: Reflections 1982-1995*, W.W. Norton & Company, New York, 1996), p. 105.

16   General Lee Butler USAF (Ret), 'Zero tolerance' (*The Bulletin of the Atomic Scientists*, January/February 2000), pp. 21 and 72. After commanding all US strategic nuclear forces in his final post as the first Commander-in-Chief Strategic Command 1992-94, General Butler was an unrivalled authority on the complexities of running a nuclear war machine. However, when he had examined it in detail, he became so horrified by the incoherent madness of nuclear deterrence thinking that, after retiring, he spoke out against it in a series of speeches to influential audiences. After serving with Robert McNamara on the Canberra Commission on the Elimination of Nuclear Weapons 1995-96 sponsored by the Australian government, he made a prodigious personal effort to bring some wisdom to the nuclear weapon debate, lobbying decision-makers in all the nuclear powers. Also, in November 1999 the author accompanied Butler and McNamara to the Japanese Foreign Ministry as part of a Track 2 initiative to urge Japan to review its dependence on US nuclear protection (see photo page III). Yet, despite recruiting over a hundred former international military leaders in support, he found he could not prevail against years of pro-nuclear hubris, indoctrination and outmoded thinking.

17   Michael Quinlan, *Thinking About Nuclear Weapons: Principles, Problems, Prospects* (Oxford University Press, 2009), pp. 9–10.

18	See Michael MccGwire, 'The Elimination of Nuclear Weapons', *Alternative Nuclear Futures: The Role of Nuclear Weapons in the Post-Cold War World*, edited by John Baylis and Robert O'Neill (Oxford University Press, 2000), pp. 148–157.
19	See an English translation of the text in 'The results and lessons of Reykjavik': speech by Mikhail Gorbachev, General Secretary of the CPSU Central Committee, on Soviet Television on 14 October 1986, *DDR: Our Point of View* (Panorama DDR, October 1986), pp.11–28.
20	Mikhail Gorbachev, *Memoirs* (Doubleday, London, 1996), pp. 416–420.
21	Ibid, p. 412.
22	Jonathan Schell, *The Gift of Time: The Case for Abolishing Nuclear Weapons* (Metropolitan Books, New York, 1998), pp. 161–162.
23	Gorbachev (1986), pp. 13–15.
24	Ibid, p. 16.
25	Gorbachev (1996), pp. 417–418.
26	Ibid p. 419.
27	Gorbachev (1986), p. 27.
28	Ibid, p. 24.
29	Ahmed Rashid, 'The Indian Nuclear Ambition' (*The Nation*, 24 March 2000).
30	Emma Rothschild, 'The Delusions of Deterrence' (*The New York Review*, 14 April 1983), p. 41.
31	Michael MccGwire, *Nuclear Deterrence* (Canberra Commission Background Papers, 1996), pp. 231–233.
32	Cimbala (1988), p. 21.
33	Philip Bobbitt, *Democracy and Deterrence – The History and Future of Nuclear Strategy* (Macmillan Press, London, 1988), p. 41.
34	David S. Yost, 'The US and Nuclear Deterrence in Europe', *Adelphi Paper 326* (The International Institute of Strategic Studies, London, 1999), p. 48.
35	Giscard d'Estaing, *Le Pouvoir et la Vie* (vol. II) (Cie 12, Paris, 1991), p. 210.
36	Admiral of the Fleet Earl Louis Mountbatten of Burma, 'On Nuclear Arms and War', speech to the Stockholm International Peace Research Institute, Strasbourg, 11 May 1979.
37	*The Alliance's Strategy Concept* [NAC-S (99) 65], April 1999.
38	Letter 'Sub-Strategic Use of Trident' from C H J Davies, UK Ministry of Defence, to Dr E Waterston, 27 October 1998.
39	See Chapter 2, note 85.
40	Made at King's College, London, 'The United Kingdom's Nuclear Deterrent in the 21st Century',http://www.mod.uk/Defence Internet/AboutDefence/People/ Speeches/SofS/TheUnited KingdomsNuclearDeterrentInThe21stCentury.htm.
41	Ministry of Defence and Foreign & Commonwealth Office, *The Future of the United Kingdom's Nuclear Deterrent.* Presented to Parliament by The Secretary of State for Defence and The Secretary of State for Foreign & Commonwealth Affairs, by Command of Her Majesty. Command 6994, December 2006 (Norwich: The Stationery Office).
42	Giscard d'Estaing (1991), p. 203.
43	Ibid, p. 210.
44	Colin Powell, *A Soldier's Way* (Hutchinson, London, 1995), p. 324.
45	Cimbala (1988), p. 90. Kissinger made the speech in 1979.
46	Philip Bobbitt, *Democracy and Deterrence – The History and Future of Nuclear Strategy* (Macmillan, London, 1988), pp. 329–338.
47	Mountbatten (1979), op cit.
48	McGeorge Bundy, George Kennan, Robert McNamara and Gerard Smith, 'Nuclear Weapons and the Atlantic Alliance' (*Foreign Affairs* 60, no. 4, Spring 1982), p. 757.
49	*Nuclear Futures: Proliferation of Weapons of Mass Destruction and US Nuclear Strategy* [British American Security Information Council (BASIC) Research Report 98.2, March 1998], p. 18.
50	See also animation by the Union of Concerned Scientists and Physicians for Social Responsibility with supporting material at http://www.ucusa.org/

	globalsecurity/nuclear_weapons/page.cfm?pageID=1781.
51	Butler (1998), p. 61.
52	See Chapter 2, note 86.
53	John Lichfield, 'France may allow "first strikes" on rogue states in policy shift', *The Independent*, London, 28 October 2003, http://news.independent.co.uk/europe/story.jsp?story=457980.
54	Excerpts from the original NPR report are available at: http://www.globalsecurity.org.
55	H. Joseph Hebert, 'Bush Administration Drops "Bunker-Buster" Plan', *The Washington Post*, 25 October 2005.
56	General Lee Butler, Erich Geiringer Memorial Oration, Wellington, New Zealand, 1 October 1997.
57	Butler (1998), op cit.
58	Lebow and Stein, *We All Lost the Cold War* (Princeton University Press, 1994), pp. 92 and 329.
59	National Defense University/Lawrence National Laboratory (1998), p. 2.8.
60	Ibid, pp. 2.8–2.9.
61	Sir Malcolm Rifkind, 'UK Defence Strategy: A Continuing Role for Nuclear Weapons?', speech in King's College, London, 16 November 1993.
62	Schwartz (1998), p. 12.
63	Scott D. Sagan, 'The Commitment Trap', *International Security*, vol. 24, no. 4, Spring 2000, pp. 85–115.
64	Colin Powell, *A Soldier's Way* (Hutchinson, London, 1995), pp. 485–486.
65	Henry A. Kissinger, *Nuclear Weapons and Foreign Policy* (W.W. Norton & Company, New York, 1969), p. 109.
66	Ken Booth & Nicholas J. Wheeler, 'Beyond nuclearism', Regina Cowen Karp ed., *Security Without Nuclear Weapons? Different Perspectives on Non-Nuclear Security* (Oxford University Press, 1992), p. 44.
67	Kennan (1996), p. 223.
68	Peter Hayes, *The Stalker State: North Korean Proliferation and the End of American Nuclear Hegemony*, Nautilus Institute Policy Forum Online, 4 October 2006, http://www.nautilus.org/fora/security/0682Hayes.html.
69	Keith B. Payne, *The Fallacies of Cold War Deterrence and a New Direction* (The University of Kentucky Press, Lexington, 2001), pp. 30–31 and pp. 80–82. Much of his book, which anticipated the thrust of the 2002 US Nuclear Posture Review, is devoted to a case study of a US-China crisis over Taiwan.
70	MccGwire (1996), p. 235.
71	Ibid, p. 236.
72	Butler (1998), op cit.
73	Lloyd Axworthy, Canada's Foreign Minister, address to the North Atlantic Council, Brussels, 8 December 1998.
74	General Lee Butler, 'Ending the Nuclear Madness', acceptance speech on receiving the Nuclear Age Peace Foundation's 1999 Distinguished Peace Leadership Award (*Waging Peace Series*, September 1999), pp. 4–5.
75	Francis A. Boyle, *The Criminality of Nuclear Deterrence* (Clarity Press, Inc., Atlanta, 2002), p. 76.
76	General Lee Butler, address to the Canadian Network Against Nuclear Weapons, 11 March 1999. For further revelations about the dangers of US nuclear policies, see Dan Ellsberg, *The Doomsday Machine: Confessions of a Nuclear War Planner* (Bloomsbury USA, 2017).
77	See https://www.armscontrol.org/factsheets/NewSTART.
78	Bruce G. Blair, Harold A. Feiveson and Frank N. von Hippel, 'Taking Nuclear Weapons off Hair-Trigger Alert' (*Scientific American*, November 1997), pp. 74–80.
79	Schell (1998), pp. 72–74.
80	Bruce Blair, 'Keeping Presidents in the Nuclear Dark', 16 February 2004, http://www.cdi.org/blair/launch-on-warning.cfm.
81	See Valery Yarynich, *C3: Nuclear Command, Control, Cooperation* (Center for

Defense Information, Washington D.C., 2003), pp. 157–158. During a high-level alert, the National Command Authority (NCA) issues preliminary authorisation to a super hardened radio command and control centre. The centre prepares to transmit a launch order by means of *Perimetr* command missiles that radio the launch codes to the silos. The launch order is transmitted only if three conditions are simultaneously met: the preliminary authorisation has been received, there has been a complete loss of communications with the NCA, and positive signals of nuclear detonations are received from the different types of sensors.

82   Schell (1998), p. 196.

Above: Buccaneer nuclear strike jet over aircraft-carrier HMS *Ark Royal*, 1972.
Royal Navy

Above: Royal Navy Staff Course prizewinners with the First Sea Lord, 1978 (author at the front right).
Royal Navy

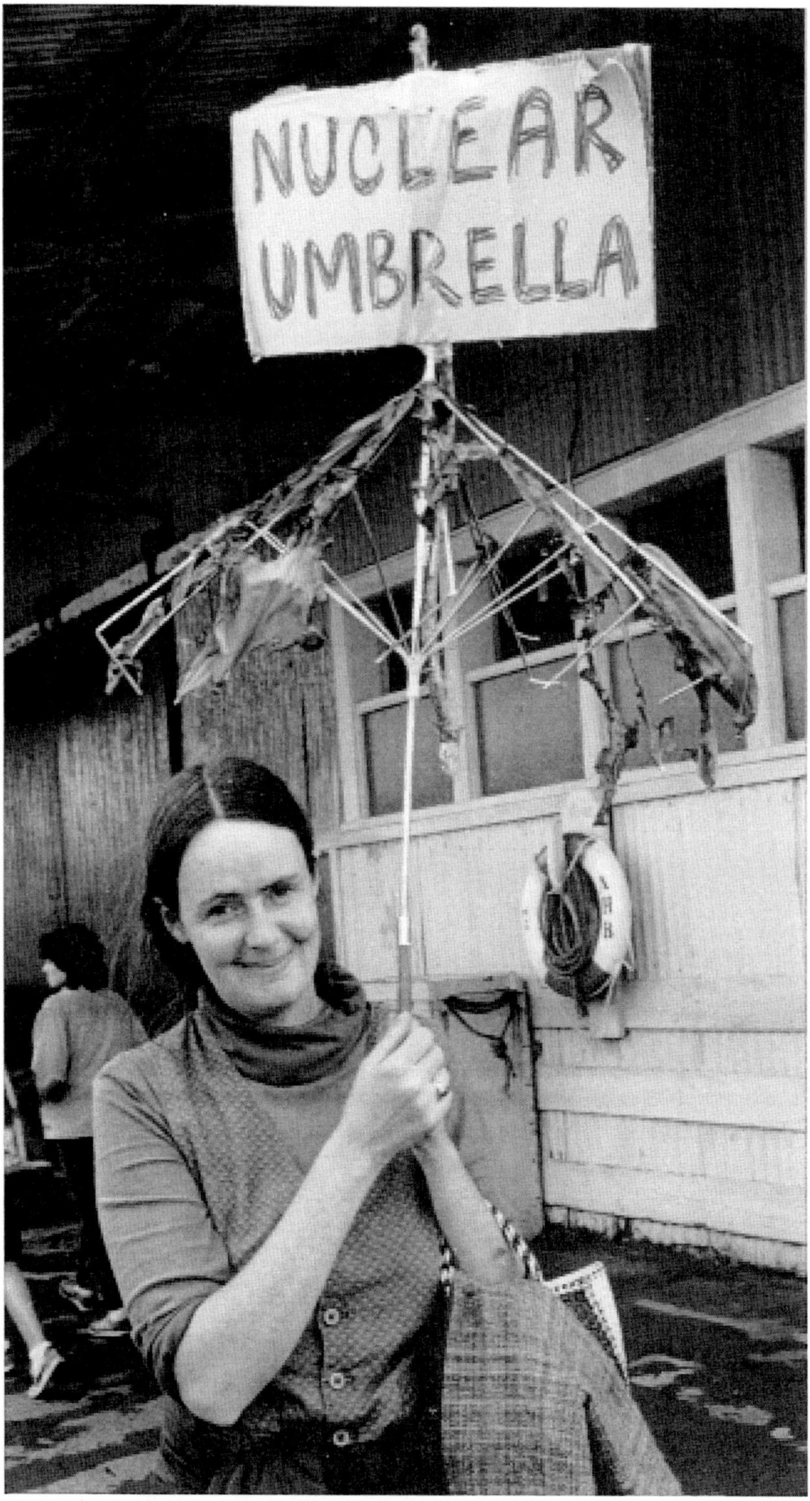
NUCLEAR
UMBRELLA

Above, left to right: General Lee Butler, Robert McNamara and the author before a meeting in the Japanese Foreign Ministry, November 1999.
Photo in author's possession

Facing Page: 'Nuclear Umbrella' anti-nuclear demonstration, Auckland, New Zealand.
Gil Hanly

Above: Rainbow Warrior, sunk by French government agents, 10 July 1985.
Gil Hanly

Above: Miniature nose cones represent the warheads in the US nuclear arsenal in the early 1980s.

Amber Waves of Grain: Barbara Donachy, Boston Science Museum.

Robert Del Tredici

Above: David Lange welcomed at Auckland Airport after the Oxford Union debate, March 1985.
Gil Hanly

Above: The author (far right) and others outside the International Court of Justice in November 1995 with the NZ Attorney General, Paul East, shaking hands with Dr Kate Dewes before presenting the NZ case for illegality of the threat or use of nuclear weapons.
Photo in author's possession

Above: The International Court of Justice in session on 8 July 1996.
Martin Duckerman, World Court Project

Above: The author (far right) joins other members of the New Zealand delegation at the United Nations during negotiations on the Nuclear Ban Treaty, 2017.
Photo in author's possession

CHAPTER FOUR

NUCLEAR DETERRENCE AND PROLIFERATION: ISRAEL, INDIA AND PAKISTAN

On United Nations Day, 24 October 2008, UN Secretary-General Ban Ki-moon gave an important speech, in which he unveiled a five-point plan to revive the nuclear disarmament agenda.[1] He included these words:

> Unfortunately, the doctrine of nuclear deterrence has proven to be contagious. This has made non-proliferation more difficult, which in turn raises new risks that nuclear weapons will be used.

Not surprisingly, the thesis that nuclear weapons deter aggression and secure peace has proved seductive for states which seek to follow where the US, Russia, the UK, France, and China have led.

The Non-Proliferation Treaty has not been a sufficient impediment because it is based on a double standard, acknowledging the possession of nuclear weapons by the original five while prohibiting their acquisition by any others on the grounds that proliferation would threaten international security. Yet if nuclear deterrence works, then why should it not do so for other states that feel equally threatened and insecure? Indeed, it is this desire for invincibility, the qualitative transformation in the balance of power that nuclear deterrence promises, which is the driving force behind the proliferation of nuclear weapon states.

Several states outside the official nuclear club embarked on the road to nuclear weapons. For varying reasons a few abandoned the quest: Brazil, Argentina and post-apartheid South Africa voluntarily dismantled their nuclear weapon programmes; Iraq's nuclear weapon programme in the Middle East was damaged by Israel's air strike in 1981, and then neutralised by a combination of UN sanctions and inspection initiatives, as confirmed after the 2003 US-UK invasion and occupation. Others like North Korea and Iran held out against all blandishments and threats and have not surrendered their right to build nuclear weapons for self-defence (North Korea) or to pursue nuclear research activities for 'peaceful' purposes (Iran). In the latter case, Israel's hypocritical allegations that Iran was secretly developing nuclear weapons, and irresponsible Israel-US interference with its computer-controlled uranium enrichment facilities, were defused by successful negotiation of a Joint Comprehensive Plan of Action (JCPOA) in 2015 with the P5 plus Germany and the European Union, whereby Iran agreed to restrict its uranium enrichment programme under IAEA supervision, in exchange for relief from nuclear-related economic sanctions.[2]

As the North Korean and Iranian dramas play out, it is instructive to trace why and how three other states which have got away with nuclear proliferation did so. First Israel, and then India followed by Pakistan, acquired nuclear arsenals in defiance of the non-proliferation regime established by the international community. How they did so makes salutary reading for two reasons. First, they expose the contradictions and thus the ineffectiveness of existing non-proliferation policies. More importantly they show that, in chasing the delusion of power and security through nuclear deterrence, these states – like the major powers they seek to emulate – have made the world much more dangerous. Indeed, perhaps the greatest risk of the first use of a nuclear weapon since Nagasaki is to be found in the Middle East or South Asia.

Israel and the 'Samson Option'

Israel's status as a nuclear power is based on a distinctive version of the concept of *existential nuclear deterrence,* a deliberately opaque and contradictory posture of refusal to acknowledge possession, let alone deployment, of a nuclear arsenal.[3] Understanding the evolution of this particular, perverse notion is essential because it poses a grave danger for Israel, the Middle East and the United States. Indeed, it was this key issue that first convinced me to speak out against nuclear weapons.

In the afterword to the third edition of his ground-breaking book on Israel's nuclear programme, published in 1993, Seymour Hersh noted that in researching and writing *The Samson Option* he came to understand that the pursuit and ultimate possession of nuclear weapons seems inherently to lead to various forms of denial and self-deceit:

For more than three decades, successive American administrations of both parties, the bureaucracy, and the diplomatic service have ignored the existence of the Israeli nuclear arsenal... The current official position of the United States and its nuclear allies is, astonishingly, that there is no positive evidence that Israel is, in fact, in possession of nuclear arms. *The Samson Option* did not change any official positions, but it did expose them to be ludicrous.[4]

On 7 June 1981, Israeli F-16 fighter-bombers – provided by the US for 'defensive purposes only' – destroyed an Iraqi nuclear research reactor at Osirak, twelve miles from Baghdad, for which the French had supplied nuclear materials and expertise in exchange for oil.[5] By then, Israel had been manufacturing nuclear weapons for 13 years at Dimona, in the Negev desert. Also aided by the French and British, it had constructed a nuclear reactor as well as a separate facility, hidden beneath it underground, for reprocessing the reactor's most important by-product: weapons-grade plutonium.

The state of Israel had been created by force in 1948. David Ben-Gurion, who served as its first Prime Minister and Defence Minister almost continuously from 1948–63, feared a second Holocaust, this time at the hands of the Arabs. When Gamal Abdel Nasser seized power in Egypt in 1954, many of those Israelis who had survived the Nazi concentration camps believed that Hitler and Nasser were interchangeable, and that there was no alternative but to prepare to strike against Nasser and his Pan-Arab friends.[6] For them, a nuclear arsenal was essential to Israel's survival – but they discovered that the US would not provide it. In 1954, Israel signed an agreement under the Eisenhower administration's 'Atoms for Peace' programme through which the US provided a small research reactor near Tel Aviv. However, the agreement gave the US inspection rights to monitor an Israeli guarantee that nuclear materials would not be diverted to weapons research.

In the 1950s, Israel and France had similar needs. French scientists, despite extensive experience in pre-World War II nuclear fission research, had been excluded from any major role in the Manhattan Project. Later President de Gaulle was rebuffed by the US when he tried to gain a share for France of the UK's special treatment. However, French nuclear research was at the forefront of developments. Israeli scientists therefore approached the French for training and collaboration, just when France needed technical assistance in building its first, secret plutonium plant at Marcoule in 1952.[7] Israeli computer skills were such that the French became dependent on them for their own nuclear weapon programme until the 1960s – and the first French nuclear device was tested in 1960. At the same time, many of France's leading nuclear scientists were Jewish, had served in the Resistance and maintained intense feelings about the Holocaust, and were therefore strong supporters of Israel.[8] In 1953, a formal agreement for cooperation in nuclear research was signed between the two countries.

Israel was fully involved in the Anglo-French Suez operation in 1956 after Nasser nationalised the Suez Canal. Ben-Gurion took advantage of this to seek French help in developing Israel's 'bomb' by asking them to provide a reactor. He sent Shimon Peres, then director-general of the Ministry of Defence, and Ernst Bergmann, Israel's leading nuclear weapon scientist, to meet a top French colleague, Francis Perrin, in Paris. Perrin, when interviewed later, was the first to express what became known as the 'Samson Option':

> We thought the Israeli bomb was aimed against the Americans. Not to launch it against America but to say, 'If you don't want to help us in a critical situation we will require you to help us. Otherwise we will use our nuclear bombs.'[9]

When Eisenhower forced the British and French into a cease-fire, Israel had to follow suit, despite being poised to take Cairo and topple Nasser.[10] Ben-Gurion learned that the pro-Israeli elements within and outside the American Jewish community were unable to exert enough pressure on the US administration. One US defence analyst, many years later, discussing Israel's drive for the nuclear option after Suez, said that the lesson for the US was as follows: 'It is terribly dangerous to stop Israel from doing what it thinks is essential to its national security.'[11]

France's failure to stand by Israel led to a trade-off. Ben-Gurion agreed to withdraw Israeli forces from Sinai and accept UN peacekeepers in exchange for France's help in building the reactor and underground reprocessing plant at Dimona. A French chemical firm led the building of the latter, in total secrecy. At the same time, for similar reasons France decided to pursue its own nuclear weapon programme: thus France's *force de frappe* became the role model for Israel.[12] Meanwhile, the UK secretly sold Israel twenty tons of heavy water, without which the reactor could not have been started up.[13] Then in 1966 the UK Atomic Energy Authority sold a small quantity of plutonium to Israel, which enabled it to accelerate its weapon programme significantly.[14]

As in France, there was internal opposition to the prospect of Israel, struggling economically and with a huge defence budget, becoming a nuclear power.[15] Construction of Dimona diverted many of the most skilled scientists and technicians from its industry.[16] To sidestep some of this criticism, Ben-Gurion instructed Peres to recruit a discreet international group of wealthy Jews who quietly raised funds for the 'special weapons' project.[17] However, these covered only a small fraction of the massive cost, estimated by the mid-1960s at over US$500 million a year – more than 10 per cent of the military budget.[18]

When de Gaulle became French President in 1958, he was so concerned about the commitment to Dimona that he ordered all French work on the reprocessing plant to cease. As a sop to Ben-Gurion, de Gaulle offered to sell him the latest French fighter aircraft and undertook to defend Israel if it was attacked. However, Ben-Gurion was not prepared to trade Israel's bomb for military aid. Instead, the Israelis agreed to reveal to the world the existence of Dimona as a 'research' reactor for peaceful development of the Negev desert, but assured France that they had no intention of building nuclear weapons and would not reprocess any plutonium.[19] Ben-Gurion announced this cover story in the Knesset on 21 December 1960: no parliamentarian dared ask why, if Dimona was for peaceful research, it was so secret.[20] Israel formally took over construction – but French contractors continued work on the site, completing the plant in 1965.

The Eisenhower administration, though aware from aerial reconnaissance of suspicious construction work at Dimona, accepted the cover story, and then moved to dampen media interest: Eisenhower was about to lose the Presidency to John F. Kennedy. At first, Kennedy demanded that an IAEA inspection team be given full access to Dimona, consistent with his commitment to halting the spread of nuclear weapons and as a way to reassure Egypt, which had reacted belligerently after the December 1960 revelations.[21] Ben-Gurion refused, protesting that Israel was not pursuing a nuclear weapon programme. A deal followed in 1961: in exchange for US military aid for the first time (risking a political crisis in the Middle East), Israel allowed a US inspection team to visit the incomplete Dimona site annually to a pre-arranged schedule, whereupon they were shown a fake control room. Each time, they duly reported nothing suspicious. Kennedy was not convinced and sustained an increasingly acrimonious correspondence with Ben-Gurion until the latter resigned in 1963. Kennedy was assassinated a few months later on 22 November 1963.[22] His successor Lyndon Johnson was far more sympathetic to Israel, but continued Kennedy's call for IAEA inspection of Dimona.

As Dimona approached completion, a real nuclear debate about the way ahead took place in 1962 behind closed doors within the Israeli government.[23] The chief advocates of weaponisation were Ben-Gurion's protégés Peres and General Moshe Dayan in the Ministry of Defence, who argued for 'stable' nuclear deterrence as an independent security guarantee under a 'doctrine of self-reliance', instead of a debilitating conventional arms race with the Arabs. Their opponents, led by former military heroes from the War of Independence Yigal Allon and Israel Galili, dismissed the pessimism underlying the belief that nuclear weapons were the only solution to Israel's long-term security. More importantly, they doubted the applicability of nuclear deterrence to the Middle East because of the asymmetries between the antagonists, and they warned that a nuclear monopoly would inevitably be temporary because it would incite a regional nuclear arms race. They were also concerned that investment in nuclear weapons might encourage the Arabs to wage another war. (Both predictions were borne out by subsequent events.) Ben-Gurion headed off their opposition by supporting their request for Israel's conventional forces to be strengthened with new armour and strike aircraft.

In 1964, Dimona became operational. Its supporters had convinced most of Israel's leadership that only nuclear weapons could provide an absolute deterrent to the Arab threat. Also, only nuclear weapons could persuade the Arabs – now receiving rapidly growing Soviet or US economic and military aid – that they must renounce their plans for military conquest of Israel and agree to a peaceful settlement of the Palestinian conflict. This was when what Ben-Gurion's successor Levi Eshkol dubbed the 'Samson Option' was introduced, to justify the fateful decision to start building nuclear weapons.[24] In the Bible's Old Testament, Samson had been captured by the Philistines and put on public display in Dagon's Temple in Gaza. He asked God to give him back his strength for the last time, and pushed apart the temple pillars, bringing down the roof and killing himself and his enemies.[25]

Under heavy pressure from Kennedy for Dimona to be opened to more intrusive semi-annual US inspections, Eshkol decided that denial was no longer feasible, and he therefore moved to a nuclear policy of ambiguity.[26] He considered three postures: to build nuclear weapons but keep them in store; to manufacture the components but not assemble them; or only to conduct further research. He avoided a showdown by agreeing in principle to US visits without undermining Israel's future nuclear option. The penalties were infringement of Israel's sovereignty and further movement towards nuclear opacity.

After Kennedy's assassination, Eshkol told Johnson that he would defer a decision on going nuclear in return for a US commitment to supply offensive arms to match those being supplied by the Soviets to

Egypt.[27] The blackmail worked: in 1966 the US sold Israel 48 advanced A-4E Skyhawk strike jets, with the justification that Israel had become a US surrogate in the Cold War confrontation in the Middle East while the US was preoccupied by the Vietnam War.[28] From then on the US was Israel's chief arms supplier.

It was in the Memorandum of Understanding relating to this agreement that the Israeli government first committed to writing its notorious lie that 'Israel will not be the first to introduce nuclear weapons into the Arab-Israeli area', later amended to the Middle East.[29]

Reports in 1966 that Israel had purchased medium-range ballistic missiles from France raised Arab fears that they were part of Israel's nuclear programme, and prompted a public debate in the Arab press led by Mohammed Heikal, editor of *Al-Ahram*, Cairo's largest newspaper.[30] While Heikal was a nuclear hawk, several influential Syrians argued that nuclear weapons ultimately were not militarily credible – but that the Arabs should not allow Israel to play the nuclear card. This coincided with a visit to Egypt by the Soviet first deputy defence minister, Marshal Andrei Grechko, who offered extended nuclear deterrence.

A year later, miscalculations on both sides led to a failure of conventional deterrence, when Israel pre-emptively routed Arab forces in the Six-Day War (5–10 June 1967). None of the accounts considered that the nuclear issue played a role in the outbreak of war. However, Cohen argued persuasively that, as Israel completed its nuclear weapon infrastructure in 1966, it was concerned that Dimona could cause hostilities with Egypt.[31] This led to pressure to pre-empt an Egyptian attack, especially after two Egyptian aircraft flew over Dimona on a high-level reconnaissance mission on 17 May. The resulting escalation by both sides was a classic example of how attempts to deter can be misunderstood as provocation. Significantly, the role of Dimona in the crisis has been suppressed in Israeli accounts.

Shortly before the Six-Day War, US intelligence learned that Israel had completed its basic weapon design and was capable of manufacturing warheads for deployment on both aircraft and missiles.[32] Indeed, Cohen claimed that Israel 'had a rudimentary, but operational, nuclear weapons capability' in the form of two deliverable nuclear devices.[33] These were readied for use, to be delivered by a French-Israeli version of the ballistic missile supplied by Dassault, known as the Jericho I.[34] However, Israel had given no indication that it was deploying its nuclear capability; and neither Egypt nor the US appeared to have taken the Israeli nuclear potential into their crisis calculations.

On 1 June, de Gaulle imposed an arms embargo on Israel, ending twelve years of close French support. Four days later, Israel launched a pre-emptive air attack in which most of the Egyptian air force was destroyed on the ground within the first three hours. Following a brilliant Israeli campaign, the US joined de Gaulle and embargoed all arms deliveries to Israel for 135 days. The Soviets immediately began re-arming their Arab clients, and this was completed within a year. In the process, they were granted virtual control of seven Egyptian air bases, and preferential access to four Mediterranean ports.[35] Meanwhile, the most important lesson was the inapplicability of nuclear weapons to almost all military situations for Israel.[36]

In an attempt to respond to these realities, after the 1967 war Israel moved towards a 'bomb in the basement' posture.[37] General Moshe Dayan, now a war hero and Defence Minister, argued that if the Soviets could be persuaded that the Israeli nuclear threat was credible, they would be deterred from jeopardising Israel's survival. At that moment, he learned that President Johnson had publicly disavowed any firm commitment to defend Israel in a crisis.[38]

Johnson tried to persuade Israel to accept the nascent nuclear Non-Proliferation Treaty (NPT) in exchange for fifty F-4 Phantom fighter-bombers, then the most advanced of its type in the US arsenal, plus twenty-eight more A-4 Skyhawks to replace war losses and French Mirage Vs under embargo. The Israelis refused to sign the NPT, but still got the aircraft – and the F-4 was capable of a one-way nuclear mission from Israel to Moscow.[39] Soon after Richard Nixon's inauguration as US President in January 1969, his Secretary of State Henry Kissinger perversely told his staff that not only Israel, but also Japan, would benefit from acquiring nuclear weapons. He considered that the NPT was a futile exercise in morality.[40] Kissinger and Nixon ended the charade of Dimona inspection visits by judging that Israel had gone nuclear, and there was nothing that the US could, or wanted to, do about it. One serious consequence was that thereafter US policy on the NPT was to a large extent vitiated by this double standard.[41]

At a summit meeting in Khartoum in August 1967, Arab leaders had agreed on three 'no's': no recognition, no negotiations and no peace agreement with Israel. In 1968, following the rapid Soviet replacement of equipment losses, Nasser had initiated what became known as the War of Attrition to recover the Sinai territory lost in the Six-Day War. Israel responded with air strikes deep into Egypt. As Egyptian losses mounted, Soviet air force units and anti-aircraft batteries were sent, and became involved in hostilities. In early 1970, while the US urged Israeli restraint, the Soviets moved anti-aircraft missiles closer to the Suez Canal, enabling the Egyptians to cross it and directly threaten invasion of the Sinai. In July 1970 Israel ambushed some Soviet aircraft, shooting down five for no loss. Days later a US-sponsored ceasefire brought the war to an end. This experience led to the Israeli decision to acquire the capability to target Moscow with nuclear weapons.[42]

In 1968, Dimona had begun full-scale production, producing about five warheads a year. By 1971, Jericho I missiles were deployed capable of hitting targets in Southern Russia as well as Arab capitals, while nuclear-armed F-4s were targeted on Moscow. Miniaturised low-yield tactical warheads had been developed for battlefield use in heavy artillery provided by the US. More than twenty nuclear warheads of various types were available for the Yom Kippur War in 1973.[43] Nevertheless, this nuclear capability did not deter Israel's enemies from attacking, not least because of the posture of opacity.[44]

Anwar Sadat had succeeded Nasser in 1970 on the latter's death. He had made peace overtures to Israel but had been rejected. He then evicted the Soviets in order to boost his non-aligned posture; but this was misunderstood by Nixon and Kissinger as a reward for their pro-Israel policy. This led Sadat to go to war with Israel as the only way to be taken seriously.[45]

The Israelis had become complacent, and were taken completely by surprise when Egyptian and Syrian forces attacked on 6 October 1973, the holiest day of the Jewish year. Israel suffered heavy losses, and Syrian forces moved to the edge of Galilee. Israel responded by starting to arm its nuclear arsenal (appropriately codenamed the 'Temple' weapons), tipping off the Egyptians who would inform the Soviets, and blackmailing the US by reporting this and demanding an emergency airlift of military aid. Israel calculated that the Soviets would ensure that the US knew about the nuclear escalation, and would order their Arab clients not to advance beyond the 1967 borders. The ploys worked – though it later became clear that Syria had not intended to advance further, and indeed had stopped its forces before Israel decided to go on nuclear alert. By mid-October, following a massive US airlift, the Israeli military had successfully counter-attacked on both fronts, and a cease-fire was negotiated.[46]

Before that, at one point Israeli forces had surrounded the Egyptian Third Army east of the Suez Canal and were within sixty miles of Cairo. The Soviets responded by raising the alert status of their airborne divisions, while the Arab oil-producing countries announced a dramatic price increase and boycotted oil sales to the US. Nixon, mired in the Watergate scandal, ordered Kissinger to ensure that Israel accepted a cease-fire; but he also placed US nuclear forces on high alert until the cease-fire was secured.[47]

After this experience, the US and Israel reverted to their policy of mutual denial, even when Sadat announced in 1974 that he had intelligence that Israel had developed tactical nuclear weapons.[48] Meanwhile, following the split with France, Israel had turned to South Africa, which had similar problems of alienation from its neighbours. Israel was able to trade its nuclear expertise for uranium ore. This culminated in a joint nuclear test, probably of a low-yield artillery shell, in the South Indian Ocean on 22 September 1979, which was detected by a US satellite. The Carter administration, only months away from a Presidential election and amid delicate peace negotiations between Israel and Egypt, deflected attention from it and suppressed reliable US intelligence reports.[49]

Israel's ruthless pursuit of a nuclear arsenal provided a clear pretext and incitement for Iraq to follow its example. This in turn meant that Iraq's bitter rival, Iran, where an Islamic fundamentalist regime led by Khomeini had overthrown the Shah in 1979, would see the need to do likewise. Three months after the June 1981 Israeli raid on Iraq's nuclear plant at Osirak, Israel's Prime Minister Menachem Begin and his new Defence Minister, Ariel Sharon, visited Washington to propose to President Reagan that Israel formally become a US military partner and its surrogate in the Middle East and Persian Gulf. Reagan agreed, but was later overruled by his horrified advisers. Sharon insisted on giving a briefing in which he called not only for joint use of airfields and Navy ports but also formal Israeli access to the US KH-11 high-resolution photographic satellite, desperately sought by Israel for its nuclear targeting of the Soviet Union. US Defense Secretary Caspar Weinberger headed Sharon off in negotiations, and he did not get what he wanted.[50] Sharon apparently returned to Israel in an anti-American frame of mind and began to argue that US passivity was indirectly responsible for Soviet advances in the Middle East and Africa. He called for Israel to broaden its national security interests, and meet the growing and expanding Soviet threat by increased reliance on its nuclear arsenal.[51]

At about this time, an Israeli defector who had worked inside Dimona provided the US with the first photographs of complete Israeli thermonuclear weapons in storage there – and reported that Israel had more than a hundred of them. From these photographs, plus extensive documentary evidence, his American handlers were alarmed to learn that the Israelis 'can do anything we or the Soviets can do'. Yet this intelligence was not even shared with the State Department's proliferation experts.[52]

In June 1982, Sharon led Israeli forces into Lebanon in an effort to destroy the Palestine Liberation Organisation. This disastrous campaign, resulting in the massacre of Palestinians in the Sabra and Shatila refugee camps, reflected the determination by Begin and Sharon to use Israel's military dominance to redraw the political map of the Middle East without the help of Washington.[53]

The Dimona bomb-making plant's existence, and confirmation that Israel was producing hundreds of nuclear warheads there, were not publicly established until 1986. On 5 October, the UK *Sunday Times* published an extraordinary inside account from interviews with a Moroccan-born technician called Mordechai Vanunu, who had worked in Dimona from 1977–85. Soon after the story broke, he was lured to Rome, abducted by Mossad and taken back to Israel, where a secret court sentenced him to eighteen years in a maximum-security prison, mostly in solitary confinement. Vanunu claimed that over 200 warheads had been made, including low-yield neutron bombs utilising enhanced radiation and minimal blast to maximise casualties while limiting property damage. Yet no major US media outlet picked up the story.

In 1988, Israel launched several Ofek intelligence satellites into orbit on Shavit three-stage rockets derived from the Jericho II missile.[54] This brought it closer to an ICBM capability and marked an end to reliance on the US for satellite targeting information. On 26 June 2002, the Israeli newspaper *Ha'aretz* cited Avi Har-Even, the director-general of the Israeli Space Agency, who reported that it had recently launched the Ofek 5 satellite, which provided Israel with an independent spy satellite capability to monitor military activities in targeted countries throughout the entire Middle East.

As cited earlier, Seymour Hersh alleged that in the 1991 Gulf War Israel had blackmailed the US, by indicating that it might use its nuclear arsenal in retaliation for Iraqi Scud missile attacks if they were fitted with chemical or biological warheads. On 2 February 2000, in the first debate to be held in Israel's Parliament on its nuclear policy, this posture of existential nuclear deterrence combined with opacity/ambiguity had been challenged when Knesset Member Issam Makhoul said:

> Nuclear ambiguity is nothing but self-delusion, and has long ago ceased to be effective. The entire world now knows that Israel has a huge stockpile of nuclear, biological and chemical weapons and that it serves as the cornerstone for the nuclear arms race in the Middle East. In Israel there is frequent mention of the 'Iranian and Iraqi danger', while ignoring the fact that it was Israel that introduced nuclear weapons to the Middle East in the first place, and created the legitimacy for other states in the region to obtain nuclear weapons.
>
> One obvious proof that the ambiguity and deterrence which formed the basis for Israel's nuclear policy have become redundant

is Israel's acquisition of the German submarines that have recently arrived in this country and which, according to the media, will be equipped with nuclear missiles. The purpose of these submarines is to cruise deep in the sea and constitute the 'second strike' force, in the event that Israel is attacked with nuclear weapons. That means that not only do the hundreds of nuclear bombs that Israel possesses not pose a defence – they actually caused the military establishment to fear a nuclear early strike, which escalates the spiral of the non-conventional arms race further and further, at the cost of billions of dollars.

Today the so-called ambiguity applies only to the citizens of Israel. They are unable to act as democratic critics of their government because the latter conceals from them the truth about an issue on which their lives depend. We have no information about the people who have their fingers on the nuclear button, what is their chain of command, or what is our defence if a nuclear Barukh Goldstein [*who committed a massacre of Muslims at a mosque on the West Bank*] should infiltrate the system and, equipped with a religious sanction from some rabbi, launch a nuclear Armageddon.

Mr. Chairman, the dangers to the citizens of Israel and to our neighbours exist not only in the event of a nuclear war. Even without a war, we face the constant danger of the eruption of the nuclear volcano that we have built on our own doorstep.[55]

In June 2000, Israeli defence sources had claimed that the first test launches of its own design of cruise missile capable of carrying nuclear warheads had been successfully conducted in the Indian Ocean from one of its three German-built Dolphin class diesel-powered submarines. Apparently the missile hit a target more than 900 miles away.[56] In October 2003, the *Los Angeles Times* reported that Israeli and US officials had confirmed that nuclear-armed cruise missiles were now deployed as the third, second-strike leg of Israel's nuclear triad – contrary to previous assurances given to the Germans. Apparently its seaborne nuclear doctrine aimed to place one submarine in the Persian Gulf and another in the Mediterranean, with the third on standby.[57] In 2016, Israel received its fifth submarine from Germany, the most advanced variant of the Dolphin 2 class.

Israel has long been suspected of attacking what it alleges was a secret Syrian nuclear reactor for producing plutonium, in much the same way as it destroyed Iraq's research reactor at Osirak in 1981. Syria reported at the time that, early on 6 September 2007, its 'air defences had repelled an incursion by Israeli warplanes', with no further details, and Israel declined to comment. On 21 March 2018, Israel's Prime Minister Benjamin Netanyahu confirmed that Israeli F-15 and F-16 strike jets, supplied by the US, destroyed the Al-Kubar facility near Deir al-Zor in eastern Syria, which had been built with help from North Korea. Netanyahu, who had been repeatedly urging the US to take tougher action regarding the alleged nuclear weapon programme of Syria's ally Iran, added that Israel remained determined to prevent its enemies from obtaining nuclear weapons.[58] This admission, and its timing, amounted to a veiled threat to both Iran and the US regarding the Joint Comprehensive Plan of Action to curb Iran's nuclear programme negotiated with the P5, Germany and the European Union in 2015.

In its 2018 assessment of global nuclear stockpiles, the Arms Control Association estimates that Israel has 80 nuclear warheads, and has produced enough fissile material for up to 200, equivalent to the UK nuclear arsenal.[59] Yet the official position of the US, UK and France, condoned by their allies, remains that there is no positive evidence that Israel possesses nuclear weapons. Incredibly, a January 2001 Pentagon report *Proliferation: Threat and Responses* omitted Israel from its review of the Middle East.

India and Pakistan

Like the Soviet Union, the UK, France, China and Israel – which all followed the US example – the stories of India and Pakistan's acquisition of nuclear weapons turn any notion of an effective non-proliferation policy on its head. They also offer lessons about the consequences of two rival nations who desperately need to coexist, but now find that need threatened by the dogma of nuclear deterrence, thereby diverting crucial resources from the basic needs of their impoverished citizens.

What happened in South Asia was not simply a consequence of the interplay between the US, the Soviet Union and China manoeuvring for regional influence under Cold War conditions. It is the story of how great and lesser powers cannot possibly stem nuclear proliferation while at the same time ruthlessly advancing their own nuclear capabilities. India's and Pakistan's experiences show this paradox in all its fullness.[60]

For reasons of sheer size, wealth and resources, India has always led the way, with Pakistani governments responding to developments across the border which, from their perspective, affected Pakistan's national interest. During the early period from independence in 1947 to the mid-1960s, India and Pakistan were in dispute over Kashmir; but Pakistan was no threat as it struggled to recover from the disarray of partition. India's Prime Minister Jawaharlal Nehru – Mahatma Gandhi's heir in sustaining his vision of non-violence – was publicly opposed to nuclear weapons on moral, political and strategic grounds, and demanded that their possession be declared a 'crime against humanity'. However, he was persuaded by the brilliant Cambridge-trained physicist Homi Bhabha that a vigorous nuclear electricity generation research programme could lift India out of poverty, and authorised special priority to state investment in the nuclear establishment.[61] Tragically, these hopes were not realised despite massive diversion of resources badly needed elsewhere in India.

Nehru was aware of the ambiguity that India's nuclear research opened up in terms of military potential, and the associated temptation to use it as a short cut to major power status.[62] After Bhabha became the first chairman of India's Atomic Energy Commission in 1948 and secretly planned to exploit this (specifically by extracting plutonium from spent fuel), Nehru did not stop him.[63] Bhabha also played a key role in ensuring that the safeguards regime written into the statute of the International Atomic Energy Agency did not preclude nations from diverting plutonium for weapon use. He was an eloquent critic of the double standard over safeguards established by the leading nuclear powers, which later extended to their attempts to prevent proliferation.

In 1959, when it became clear that China was developing nuclear weapons, Bhabha told a parliamentary committee that India could make nuclear weapons without external assistance if required. The following year, Nehru himself announced that India would build a plutonium separation plant to provide part of the combined plutonium-thorium fuel for its first fast breeder reactor. In 1961, the US secretly considered assisting Bhabha with nuclear weapons technology as a counterweight, but decided against it because of Nehru's opposition.[64] Even after India was defeated by China in a war over a territorial dispute in November 1962, Nehru resisted the first public demands for a nuclear weapon programme because it would destroy India's reputation as a leader in promoting nuclear disarmament, quite apart from the impact on its hard-won legacy as a democracy espousing non-violence.

Pakistan, dissatisfied with the level of US aid it was receiving, signed a border agreement with China in December 1962. Nehru died in May 1964; in October, China conducted its first nuclear test. From then on, India, deeply shaken by its 1962 defeat, began quietly pursuing a nuclear weapon capability while publicly opposing nuclear deterrence. However, in 1964, two years before he died, Bhabha argued persuasively that if the US and USSR did not wish India to acquire nuclear weapons, they had to either guarantee its security or take a lead in nuclear disarmament.[65]

Bhabha's more determined efforts to achieve a nuclear weapon capability after Nehru's death were among the factors that tempted Pakistan's President Ayub Khan to risk the second war with India over Kashmir in 1965, which resulted in a stalemate but at the cost of disproportionately heavy Pakistani military losses. During that war, Pakistan's Foreign Minister Zulfikar Ali Bhutto made his notorious remark that, if India produced nuclear weapons, Pakistanis would have to get them too, even if 'we should have to eat grass'.[66]

Speculation about Pakistan's nuclear ambitions had first appeared in about 1960, when the US 'Atoms for Peace' programme had resulted in training over a thousand Pakistani scientists and engineers in nuclear physics, chemistry and engineering and practical applications. Despite Bhutto's comments in 1965 about the need for Pakistan to match India's nuclear ambitions, the actual decision to develop a nuclear arsenal was not taken until after the defeat and dismemberment of Pakistan in the third major war with India in 1971–72, when Bangladesh was formed.

During this period France agreed to supply Pakistan with a plutonium reprocessing plant at Chashma. Bhutto successfully persuaded the US, to the fury of India, to resume military aid to obviate Pakistan's need for nuclear weapons to compensate for its conventional military inferiority to India. At the same time the US pressed France for restraint in supplying Pakistan's nuclear programme, to the extent that, in 1978, France revoked the contract for the Chashma plant. For help in other aspects of its nuclear weapon project, Pakistan turned to China as early as 1965.[67]

Meanwhile, in India the death of Bhabha and the rise to power of Nehru's daughter, Indira Gandhi, in 1966 had stimulated a public nuclear debate. Vikram Sarabhai, who had succeeded Bhabha after he died in a plane crash in January 1966, had initially questioned the benefits for India of building nuclear weapons.[68] He had received powerful support from the first director of India's Institute for Defence Studies and Analyses, Major General Som Dutt in a November 1966 Adelphi Paper for the Institute of Strategic Studies in London. Pointing out that US nuclear weapons had not prevented China from assisting the Viet Cong, Dutt doubted that Indian nuclear weapons could alter China's ambitions in Asia. He correctly predicted that a quest for nuclear weapons by India would force Pakistan 'into China's arms, thus increasing India's predicament'.[69] However, Sarabhai allowed theoretical and design work to produce weapon-grade plutonium to continue.

India took a leading role in the extensive international debate on the NPT. In 1967–68, the question shifted from whether India should produce nuclear weapons to whether it should sign a treaty relinquishing the right to do so.[70] Unlike earlier decisions to develop a nuclear programme, there were careful (though secret) high-level government deliberations before the decision was taken. That said, not signing the NPT in June 1968 followed policies of least political risk and preserving the greatest strategic manoeuvrability.

The international community did almost nothing to help India sign a treaty that it saw as a form of nuclear apartheid. The greatest pressure came from the strongest capitalist power, the US, and from India's former colonial master, the UK – and both proved counterproductive. In addition, China denounced the treaty and stated that it refused to be bound by it in any way.[71] Far from making a security case for acquiring nuclear weapons, India strove to make a moral and political case as leader of the Non-Aligned Movement against those states with nuclear weapons and which refused to disarm. With tragic irony in light of subsequent developments, in April 1968 Indira Gandhi declared in the Lok Sabha, India's Parliament:

> ...events of the last twenty years clearly show that the possession of nuclear weapons has not given any military advantage... between nations possessing nuclear weapons and those who do not... The choice before us involves not only the question of making a few atom bombs, but of engaging in an arms race with sophisticated nuclear warheads and an effective missile delivery system. Such a course I do not think would strengthen national security. On the other hand, it may well endanger our internal security by imposing a very heavy economic burden which would be in addition to the present expenditure on defence. Nothing would better serve the interests of those who are hostile to us than for us to lose our sense of perspective and to undertake measures which would undermine the basic progress of the country.[72]

Following entry into force of the NPT in 1970, Sarabhai unveiled his ten-year plan for the development of nuclear energy and space capabilities, which became known as the Sarabhai Profile. The Atomic Energy Commission had fallen short of its target to have 600 megawatts of power on line by 1970–71, as the voracious demands of a nuclear programme had become apparent.[73] Even to achieve the Sarabhai Profile's scaled-down targets, some 3,000 more trained engineers and scientists were required; road and rail systems needed upgrading; the steel and electronics industries had to be significantly improved, and major investments in supporting industries and infrastructure were needed. These pressures, with massive budgetary implications, exposed the major flaw in Bhabha's plan: greater development was a precondition for the nuclear programme, not its outcome.

By then Sarabhai's opposition to nuclear weapons had weakened: allegedly, he had been swayed by the professed reliance on nuclear deterrence expressed by leading scientists and security specialists from the five recognised nuclear weapon states.[74] Nevertheless, both he and his political leaders recoiled at the technological, economic and moral barriers to building nuclear weapons, despite strong pressure led by 'realist' strategist K. Subrahmanyam, Dutt's pro-nuclear successor at the Institute for Defence Studies and Analyses.[75] Subrahmanyam argued that, far from losing moral stature, India's acquisition of nuclear weapons would serve its moral purpose by ensuring peace through deterrence. In so doing, he showed comparable speculative faith that deploying nuclear weapons entailed little risk.

The Sarabhai Profile made no mention of peaceful nuclear explosions. In Indira Gandhi's statements relating to India's position on the NPT, she had carefully distinguished between them and nuclear weapons. However, in July 1970 Sarabhai publicly asserted that India was capable of conducting underground nuclear explosions, and was entitled to do so having not signed the NPT. He told the Fourth International Conference on the Peaceful Uses of Atomic Energy in September 1971 that his scientists were developing nuclear explosive engineering for peaceful purposes as a top priority.[76] When he suddenly died that December, his successor was Homi Sethna, a chemical engineer who had played a leading role in developing India's plutonium-reprocessing and metallurgical capacities. Sethna came from the team pressing fervently to demonstrate Indian prowess and power through the nuclear programme, and he saw the cover of a 'peaceful nuclear explosion' as the quickest and politically feasible way to do it.[77]

War between India and Pakistan had intervened in November 1971.[78] Pakistan's first democratic election a year earlier had effectively been a referendum for autonomy for East Pakistan. With most of the military, bureaucratic and economic elite in West Pakistan and most of the population in the east, President Yahya Khan had attempted to negotiate greater autonomy for the east, but had failed. Violent conflict had ensued, with 10 million refugees from East Pakistan pouring into India. Among these had been Bangladeshi 'freedom fighters' who had launched attacks against Pakistani forces under cover of Indian artillery fire. In reprisal, on 3 December 1971 Pakistan attacked air bases in western India. India counter-attacked on both fronts.

Kissinger and Nixon took the view that the war had been instigated by India. In the midst of the crisis they ordered a battle group led by the nuclear-powered aircraft-carrier *USS Enterprise* into the Bay of Bengal as a none-too-subtle signal to Indira Gandhi that the Nixon administration was tilting towards Pakistan. This was linked to US alarm over a recently signed Treaty of Peace, Friendship and Co-operation between India and the Soviet Union, and Kissinger's unsubstantiated fear that China was preparing to assist Pakistan militarily which could cause the Soviets to intervene. Perhaps more significant was the fact that Kissinger's secret diplomacy with China had been coordinated through Islamabad which maintained close relations with Beijing. At the height of Pakistan's crackdown in its eastern province, Kissinger flew from the Pakistan capital to Beijing for his first meetings in China with Chou En-Lai and Mao Tse Tung. Throughout the war Kissinger exploited the Pakistan channel, while keeping the South Asia division of the State Department completely in the dark. From Kissinger's perspective Bangladesh was a 'sideshow', whereas opening the door to China represented the cutting edge of his diplomacy. US intervention, however, did not alter the outcome of the war, which came to a swift end on 16 December with the surrender of the Pakistani forces in East Pakistan and the emergence of the independent state of Bangladesh.

India had proved it could defeat Pakistan militarily. One consequence of this was that Pakistan became even more determined to build nuclear weapons. However, China had not militarily threatened India; and the new relationship with the Soviets enhanced India's sense of security. Thus the 1971 war provided no security imperative for India to develop nuclear weapons. On the other hand, US deployment of the carrier battle group rankled, with its enduring message that India was merely a pawn in the superpower game. This fed India's desire for major power status and a means to resist such 'blackmail' through acquisition of nuclear weapons.[79]

In 1972, Bhutto began to organise a nuclear weapon programme at a secret meeting of Pakistan's top nuclear scientists and bureaucrats in the northern city of Multan. Abdul Qadir Khan, the self-styled 'father of the Pakistan bomb', was not present: a metallurgist by training, he was held in low regard by most of the scientists. However, A.Q. Khan became prominent in 1974 when he informed Bhutto that he had stolen design drawings for constructing centrifuges from the URENCO uranium enrichment plant in the Netherlands, where he had gained the necessary expertise while working there. Over the next decade, Khan led a massive clandestine international procurement effort to assemble a gas centrifuge uranium enrichment plant at Kahuta, which became central to Pakistan's nuclear weapon programme.[80]

By 1974, a 40-megawatt Canadian-designed reactor, Canada-India Reactor-US (CIRUS), built at the Bhabha Atomic Research Centre at

Trombay with heavy water supplied by the US, together with a US-designed reprocessing plant had produced enough weapon-grade plutonium for India's first nuclear test. On 18 May 1974, Indira Gandhi authorised what was described as a 'peaceful nuclear explosion' at the Pokhran test site in Rajasthan.[81] The motivation lay in a combination of deepening domestic political crisis for the Congress Party from a rising tide of popular turmoil and protest at economic policy, corruption and misgovernance, and the nuclear scientists' lobby urgently needing to shore up their reputation as failure of the nuclear electricity generation programme became apparent. The foreign affairs establishment was not asked to assess likely international repercussions; and the military were not consulted about the implications for them.

After the underground test, Mrs Gandhi wrote to Pakistan's Prime Minister Bhutto to try to reassure him, but failed. The predictable response was to redouble Pakistan's nuclear ambitions. The international backlash prompted a public shift to ambiguity while still rejecting nuclear deterrence.[82] Mrs Gandhi felt misled by the scientists: her doubts about the morality and worth of nuclear weapons intensified, and she refused requests for more tests.

Morarji Desai defeated her in the 1977 election. Desai was firmly opposed to both nuclear weapons and peaceful nuclear explosions.[83] In 1976 Canada had withdrawn its support for the nuclear energy programme, following the 1974 test. This led Desai to negotiate with US President Jimmy Carter, who agreed in 1977 to re-supply reactor fuel for two nuclear electricity generating reactors at Tarapur on condition that India stopped all fuel reprocessing and any further peaceful nuclear explosions.[84]

In July 1977, Bhutto was overthrown by General Zia-ul-Haq. Under martial law, the military took full control of Pakistan's nuclear programme, which Bhutto had initiated and personally overseen in part to counterbalance the army's position as the dominant institution. From now on nuclear weapons would become central to military planning, unlike in India where the Prime Minister retained control.[85] Partly because of this, the US suspended military and economic aid to Pakistan and imposed sanctions after Bhutto was hanged in 1979.[86] US intelligence tipped off India that Pakistan's centrifuge plant was complete, which meant that weapon-grade uranium would soon be available.[87] Carter visited India in January 1978, when he and Desai issued the Delhi Declaration, which included their reaffirmed commitment to the reduction and eventual elimination of nuclear weapons.[88]

On Christmas Day 1979, the Soviets invaded Afghanistan.

Suddenly, Pakistan became strategically important to the US as a conduit for military aid to the Afghan *mujahideen*. Within months, Carter lifted sanctions and began supplying huge quantities of some of the latest US conventional arms, including F-16 strike aircraft.[89] Indira Gandhi, who returned to power in 1980, responded by ordering arms from the Soviet Union. India also revived its nuclear weapon programme as opinion-formers openly called for a nuclear capability to counter Pakistan and China. This period also saw the formation of the Hindu nationalist and pro-nuclear Bharatiya Janata Party (BJP), led by Atal Behari Vajpayee.[90] However, Mrs Gandhi continued to disavow 'belief in the deterrent theory'.[91] Indeed, India went so far as to table a UN resolution in the 1982 General Assembly disarmament session calling for a 'Convention on the Prohibition of the Use of Nuclear Weapons', and continued to do so annually thereafter.

Following the successful Israeli strike against the Osirak reactor in Iraq in 1981, the Indian air force had considered, but rejected, a similar pre-emptive attack on Pakistan's uranium enrichment plant at Kahuta. They concluded that, though feasible, it would provoke war, in which India stood to lose more from Pakistani counter-strikes on its much larger and more vulnerable nuclear facilities at Trombay, close to huge population centres such as Bombay. Two years later, India and Pakistan drew up an agreement not to attack each other's nuclear facilities.[92] For any of the current forty-four countries in the world possessing nuclear power plants and associated storage for intensely radioactive spent fuel, such facilities are vulnerable to attack with conventional weapons by military forces or extremist groups, with a potential risk of severe and long-term environmental damage.

Pressure from the Indian nuclear establishment was revived for another test. Sometime early in 1983, Mrs Gandhi gave her approval, only to withdraw it within twenty-four hours after being advised of the likely adverse world reaction.[93] Instead, she authorised a major project to produce ballistic missiles, following a successful launch of a satellite in 1983. This saw the emergence of Abdul Kalam, India's President from 2002–2007, who had been closely involved in India's space programme. The Prithvi tactical missile was flight-tested in 1988, followed by the longer range Agni missile in 1989; both were capable of carrying a nuclear warhead.[94]

Meanwhile, in May 1984 Mrs Gandhi had joined the leaders of Argentina, Greece, Mexico, Sweden and Tanzania in issuing an appeal for a freeze in the development and testing of nuclear weapons. Known as the Six-Nation Initiative, its effect was to inhibit India further from conducting another test.[95] In October, Mrs Gandhi was assassinated by her Sikh bodyguards in revenge for the Indian Army's assault on one of the holiest Sikh shrines, the Golden Temple in Amritsar. The temple had been occupied by Sikh militants with only marginal support in the Sikh community. Nevertheless, their defiance of New Delhi brought down the wrath of the central government, which many argued at the time was an unwarranted over-reaction by the federal authorities. Casualties were heavy on both sides.[96]

Her son Rajiv took over responsibility for India's nuclear policy for the next five years. More interested in technology than his predecessors, he was sceptical about the value of nuclear weapons for India, tried to foster reconciliation with Pakistan, and preferred his role as a leader in nuclear disarmament through the Six-Nation Initiative. He resented the Indian nuclear establishment's patronising attitude towards him, and was unimpressed by its failure to deliver nuclear-generated electricity, which was still only about 2 per cent of the national total. However, he did not prevent research continuing into the nuclear weapon option.[97]

In March 1985, media reports indicated further progress by Pakistan in its clandestine efforts to enrich uranium. India announced that Pakistan possessed this capability in November 1986. Rajiv Gandhi showed his concern in an interview with a leading Pakistani newspaper by rejecting the notion that nuclear weapons would stabilise South Asia, stating: 'I have never subscribed to the view that "terror", balanced or otherwise, would stabilise anything. A nuclear arms race in the sub-continent would only subject both our peoples to the worst possible fate on earth.' This cut no ice with Pakistan's leaders, who saw nuclear deterrence as compensating for their military inferiority to India. In both countries the motor of 'nuclear nationalism' was driving the quest for nuclear weapons: pro-nuclear Pakistanis and Indians perceived their own nuclear programmes as a way of standing up to the West and playing the nuclear weapon states at their own game. Thus US pressure on Pakistan not to proliferate would be ineffective.

US Pakistan policy had been compromised by the Carter administration's decision in 1979, in the aftermath of the Soviet invasion of Afghanistan, to back away from pressurising Pakistan to relinquish its nuclear programme. At the time, Pakistan's collaboration in orchestrating the *mujahideen* resistance to the Soviets had greater priority. This strategic shift, first initiated by Carter's National Security Adviser, Zbigniew Brzezinski, was built into a major political alliance with the Pakistan Army under Reagan's new CIA Director, William Casey. As a result, the Pakistani military served as a conduit for the largest US covert effort since the Vietnam War. Despite this, the Reagan administration initiated what became known as the Pressler

Amendment, which allowed military aid to Pakistan as long as it certified that it did not 'possess a nuclear explosive device'.[98] In so doing, the US essentially turned a blind eye to each successive Pakistani breach of constraints on its nuclear programme. Again, the explanation for this was the absolute US priority of opposing the Soviets in Afghanistan through the vast array of facilities Pakistan was pleased to provide.

Meanwhile, Mikhail Gorbachev had become Soviet leader in March 1985. In November 1986 he visited India and signed the Delhi Declaration with Rajiv Gandhi, which included steps on eliminating nuclear weapons worldwide. However, any reconciliation with Pakistan was dashed by an ill-judged, massive Indian military exercise near the Indo-Pakistan border, which was not explained to the Pakistani leadership and which led to a major crisis.[99] Tension also flared again between India and China over their border dispute, during which allegations were made that China had deployed nuclear weapons in Tibet targeted against India.

All this resulted in renewed political and media clamour for India to go nuclear, despite the crippling financial cost and the fact that, unlike Pakistan, China had never made nuclear threats against India. Moreover, no Indian strategist had demonstrated how India could develop and deploy a survivable arsenal capable of credible use against China without undermining India's security. Rajiv Gandhi himself commented in December 1987: 'We have lived with the Chinese bomb for several years without feeling that we must produce our own.'[100]

The end of the 1980s witnessed several political and security shocks in the region. In March 1987, an interview by Indian journalist Kuldip Nayar with A.Q. Khan was published in which Khan declared that Pakistan had enriched uranium to weapon grade and could test a nuclear weapon through laboratory simulations.[101] Early in 1988, the Soviets announced their withdrawal from Afghanistan. On 17 August that year, Pakistan's President Zia-ul-Haq died in a plane crash.[102] This led to elections, which brought Zulfikar Ali Bhutto's daughter Benazir to power. Reagan, keen to encourage tenuously restored democracy in Pakistan, sidestepped the Pressler Amendment strictures by certifying non-possession of a nuclear explosive device. This was despite plausible reports that Pakistan now had enough enriched uranium for 4-6 nuclear weapons, and China had provided a design of an advanced, miniaturised weapon.[103] Nevertheless, in December 1988 Rajiv Gandhi visited China and then, for the first time, Pakistan where he and Benazir Bhutto signed confidence-building agreements, including the one negotiated in 1985 not to attack each other's nuclear facilities.

Back in May 1988 at the third UN Special Session on Disarmament, Rajiv Gandhi had launched an 'Action Plan' to eliminate all nuclear weapons by 2010.[104] He took the opportunity to express his rejection of nuclear deterrence in surprisingly forthright terms:

> The doctrine is based on the assumption that international relations are frozen on a permanently hostile basis. Deterrence needs an enemy, even if one has to be invented. Nuclear deterrence is the ultimate expression of the philosophy of terrorism: holding humanity hostage to the presumed security needs of a few.

The plan proposed a new international convention to outlaw the threat or use of nuclear weapons, negotiations for which were to be completed in time to replace the NPT when it came up for renewal in 1995. The new treaty would include a binding commitment by nuclear weapon states to eliminate all nuclear weapons by the year 2010, and non-nuclear weapon states 'not to cross the threshold into the acquisition of nuclear weapons'. However, it had no impact on the nuclear states, and did not reflect the position of India's Foreign Ministry, Ministry of Defence or nuclear establishment.[105]

In February 1989, Pakistan conducted the first tests of its Hatf-1 and Hatf-2 short-range ballistic missiles, about a year after India had tested its Prithvi missile. In May, India tested its medium-range Agni missile.[106] Benazir Bhutto visited Washington in June, where she was secretly shown a mock-up of a Pakistani nuclear weapon and was warned that the US could no longer prevent the Pressler Amendment being invoked, unless Pakistan agreed not to enrich uranium above 5 per cent and not to manufacture cores for weapons. Bhutto agreed; but Pakistan continued design work and retained at least one unassembled weapon.[107] In July, India's Defence Minister K.C. Pant visited the US, where he said:

> India does not subscribe to the doctrine of nuclear deterrence. However, India cannot afford to overlook the fact that three major nuclear powers operate in its neighbourhood and Pakistan is engaged in a nuclear weapons programme. If we are to influence these major powers, then it becomes inescapably necessary for us to reckon with their nuclear deterrence belief concepts.[108]

In November 1989 Rajiv Gandhi, increasingly beleaguered politically and by a huge corruption scandal involving the Swedish Bofors arms company, lost an election to an awkward coalition of secular and Hindu nationalist parties led by V.P. Singh. Then early in 1990, violent discontent in Kashmir escalated into another serious Indo-Pak confrontation.[109] Escalating rhetoric and troop movements raised fears in the US Embassies in New Delhi and Islamabad that the blunders of the 1987 'Brasstacks' exercise would be repeated, with the added problem that weak governments on both sides would not back down.

This time, however, US intelligence learned that Pakistan was assembling at least one nuclear weapon.[110] President George Bush Sr sent a high-level team to the region to try to prevent the governments from blundering into war: with Soviet and Chinese support, this was achieved. Visiting Islamabad first, team leader Robert Gates told President Ishaq Khan and General Aslam Beg that the US had 'war-gamed every conceivable scenario between you and the Indians. There isn't a single way you win. The only question is how much territory and how many military forces you will lose' (quite apart from massive civilian casualties and an environmental catastrophe).[111] The US team found that India, far from being influenced by nuclear deterrence thinking, was not aware of the seriousness of the Pakistani nuclear threat; but they did not report this to the Indians. The US had taken the initiative because they perceived an alarming carelessness among both the Indian and Pakistani governments about the risks of escalation possibly to nuclear level. There were also indications that Pakistan's leaders were emboldened by their new nuclear capability, wrongly assuming that India had detected it. Evidence for this emerged in a 1992 interview by Beg:

> The balance of terror starts the moment the adversary realizes there is a threat from the other direction... The strategy of terror starts working from the first notion that there is retaliation. The fear of retaliation lessens the likelihood of war between India and Pakistan. I can assure you that if there were no such fear, we would probably have gone to war in 1990.[112]

As Perkovich pointed out, this belief may explain why Pakistani leaders ordered the assembly of at least one nuclear weapon in 1990; but it also reveals the danger of Beg's lack of awareness that India had not been deterred.

In October 1990, the Bush administration invoked the Pressler Amendment, cutting off both military and economic aid to Pakistan. Paradoxically, the associated signal that Pakistan now had a nuclear weapon served to unleash the nuclear hawks in India, and to generate an illusion that nuclear deterrence had begun to operate. A debate among a small group of Indian strategists on the rationale of nuclear deterrence ensued in the press. Those in favour, led by former army chief of staff General K. Sundarji, invoked Western thinking, making specious claims that a 'minimum nuclear deterrent' would not incur comprehensive targeting or launch control plans, or the excessive costs of an arms race. Yet he argued that India had to be capable of causing China unacceptable damage. No consideration was given to the effect that an overt Indian nuclear weapon programme would have on its international relations.[113] However, the Indian government held to its morally ambivalent line, restrained by its record and a desire not to lose US support. Meanwhile, Hindu-Muslim sectarian violence toppled V.P. Singh along with two more weak administrations by June 1991. Worse, on 21 May Rajiv Gandhi was assassinated by a female Sri Lankan Tamil suicide bomber. The resulting sympathy vote enabled his Congress Party to form a coalition government led by Narasimha Rao.

The 1991 Gulf War, followed by Gorbachev's fall from power, finally convinced India's leaders that the post-Cold War era had arrived. Pakistan's importance to the US had therefore declined, while India needed to draw closer to the sole remaining superpower. Economic strains meant a standstill in the Indian nuclear energy sector until 1996. The US continued to urge restraint on both sides, but tacitly acknowledged that neither would now give up its nuclear weapon programme. In December 1991, Li Peng became the first Chinese leader to visit India since 1962. China had at last signed the NPT in August: this signalled new restraint in assisting Pakistan's nuclear plans. However, suspicions flared again early in 1992 when China announced it would sell a 300-megawatt nuclear power plant to Pakistan.

In August 1992, Rao appointed Abdul Kalam as the new leader of India's Defence Research and Development Organisation. Kalam was destined to become the driving force for taking India across the nuclear threshold, for which he was rewarded with India's Presidency in July 2002. The essence of the motivation was first publicly admitted by a BJP spokesman in January 1993: 'Nuclear weapons will give us prestige, power, standing.'[114] Underlying this was a determination to resist the colonialism of the nuclear age. Meanwhile, political instability returned in Pakistan, and the administration of the newly inaugurated US President Bill Clinton decided to try exhortation rather than punishment by indicating that it might withdraw the Pressler Amendment in exchange for ending unsafeguarded fissile material production. This angered India and eased any pressure for it to show restraint.

Indo-Pak relations deteriorated again, punctuated by missile tests and new reports that both sides had enough fissile material for over twenty nuclear weapons. The US made its proposal to Pakistan, which included the delivery of 28 F-16 strike aircraft held back by the Pressler Amendment. India was then approached for a similar undertaking to ban unsafeguarded production of fissile materials plus a regional ban on deployment of nuclear-capable systems, with unspecified other inducements.[115] However, the initiative was doomed from the start when Senator Pressler went public with his objections and fuelled Indian resentment towards the US. India responded by hinting that, if Pakistan received the F-16s, it would deploy Prithvi missiles. Kalam added that India's missile programme would proceed in order to counter the 'racial prejudice where one group of people believes only they can do it'. Meanwhile, Pakistan complained that '[the enrichment plant at] Kahuta is the only symbol of sovereignty we have left.'[116]

The US did not give up. In May 1994, Rao made the first state visit to Washington by an Indian leader for nine years. He was invited to address a joint session of Congress, but many members snubbed him by giving their tickets to relations and interns. Clinton and Rao addressed nuclear issues in a summit meeting: this produced a joint statement in which, despite apparent objections from administration officials, both states expressed a commitment to the progressive reduction of weapons of mass destruction with the goal of eliminating such weapons. This was ignored by the US media. India also issued a statement at the Conference on Disarmament in Geneva that it supported the prospective Comprehensive Test Ban Treaty (CTBT) and negotiations to stop production of weapons-usable fissile materials.[117]

An indicator of India's public position appeared a month later when it surprisingly released to the UN its submission to the International Court of Justice following a request from the World Health Organisation for an advisory opinion on the health and environmental effects of the use of nuclear weapons. Though brief, it included the following statements:

> It is... imperative that nuclear weapons be eliminated. A first step in this direction would be to outlaw the use of such weapons... In 1978, India called for the total prohibition of the use of nuclear weapons. Since 1982, we have tabled a [UN] resolution calling for a Convention on the Prohibition of the Use of Nuclear Weapons... The devastation that would be caused by the use of nuclear weapons is totally out of proportion to the role claimed for it in the defence of the national security of a handful of States... The International Court of Justice is invited to confirm the generally accepted view among nations that the use of nuclear weapons is illegal.[118]

A year later, in nineteen pages of more detailed legal argument to the Court, India made the following statement on nuclear Deterrence:

> The use of nuclear weapons in response to attack by a conventional weapon would patently violate the principle of proportionality but also a nuclear response to nuclear attack... would violate the principle of discrimination, humanity, environmental security and probably the principle of neutrality as such an attack would not distinguish between combatants, ravaging the natural environment and contaminating the territory of neighbouring and distant neutral countries. Nuclear deterrence had been considered to be abhorrent to human sentiment since it implies that a state if required to defend its own existence will act with pitiless disregard for the consequences to its own and adversary's people.
>
> Another question which arises in relation to the theory of deterrence is whether the keeping of peace or the prevention of war is to be made dependent on the threat of horrific indiscriminate destruction which justifies the stockpiling of such weapons at enormous expense, in the hope that they will merely act as a deterrent but will not in fact be used. However, those who do not have such weapons would all the time be racing to build them and those who already have nuclear weapons would continue to develop even more destructive weapons to maintain the superiority necessary for deterrence and this would keep humanity in the perpetual fear of total destruction. A better and saner way to secure everlasting peace would be to ensure that [not] only are such weapons never used but also not made. The security of all nations would best be safeguarded by a nuclear weapon free world. If peace is the ultimate objective there can be no doubt that disarmament must be given priority and has to take precedence over deterrence.[119]

There were people in the Indian government who believed in these words. However, in light of what is now known about India's secret nuclear weapons programme at that time, the hypocrisy of this statement demonstrates how nuclear deterrence dogma can be so corrosive of a nation's integrity.

The Clinton administration did not help by releasing a 'new' nuclear posture which showed that it was sustaining the same level of nuclear warheads and alert status as the Bush Sr administration. The new element was an indication that the US would widen the role of nuclear weapons by threatening their use in response to WMD attacks against its interests. Moreover, the US lifted sanctions against China in exchange for stopping supply of missile equipment and technology to Pakistan and other states. These moves hardened Indian resolve to resist constraints on its nuclear programme.[120]

Meanwhile, Pakistan shifted the source for its missile components to North Korea in a deal negotiated by A.Q. Khan with the discreet sanction of the Pakistan military. China continued its long-standing role, dating back to the 1970s, of providing technical advice to Pakistan's nuclear programme in strategic areas of design development and construction. In all probability Chinese missile technology continued to be shared with Pakistan, while Pakistan traded its centrifuge uranium enrichment technology with the Koreans for their assistance in missile delivery systems.

In May 1995, the NPT was extended indefinitely amid controversy, following intense lobbying by the Western nuclear states and their allies. India opposed this because it signalled eternal 'nuclear apartheid'.[121] Within days of NPT extension, China conducted a nuclear test, and a month later the French announced a series of eight tests. In September, the US Senate passed an amendment to the Pressler sanctions releasing the F-16s to Pakistan.[122] Rao, under pressure from nuclear hawks, indicated that India no longer supported the CTBT, and secretly approved preparations for nuclear weapon tests. These were detected in December by US intelligence, and reported in the *New York Times* despite pressure from the US government because it was engaged in quiet diplomacy to press India not to test. The resulting media uproar in India forced Rao to deny that India was about to test.[123] Meanwhile, in November 1995 at the oral proceedings in the International Court of Justice on the case requesting an advisory opinion on the legal status of the threat or use of nuclear weapons (see Chapter 5), India withdrew its scheduled submission at the last moment.

In May 1996, the BJP won power for the first time. At once Prime Minister Vajpayee secretly authorised nuclear tests, which went as far as one device being placed in a test shaft, but he withdrew authorisation when his government fell after only twelve days.[124] In June, India formally rejected the CTBT as reaffirming nuclear apartheid, but also because its entry into force was made contingent on ratification by India, Israel and Pakistan among forty-four nuclear-capable states.

Although subjected to massive international pressure to sign, the domestic political imperative not to prevailed. India, seeing the CTBT as a symbol of the P5's hypocrisy and colonial coercion, blocked consensus on it in Geneva. However, Australia then proposed that the treaty be taken away from the Conference on Disarmament and put to a vote in the UN General Assembly. It was adopted on 10 September 1996 by 158 votes to 3: India, Bhutan and Libya comprised the 'No' votes (Pakistan abstained).[125] The following month, India lost out to Japan in a vote for rotating membership of the UN Security Council. Yet Foreign Minister Inder Gujral rashly said in the Indian Parliament that if they permitted him to sign the CTBT, he would promise that India would achieve permanent membership of the Security Council.[126] Gujral went on to demonstrate some skilful regional diplomacy by what became known as the 'Gujral Doctrine' of non-interference among India's smaller neighbours while resolving longstanding disputes. For example, India and Bangladesh signed an agreement on sharing the water of the Ganges.[127]

Pakistan was not so easy to placate, though initially progress was made. In February 1997 Nawaz Sharif convincingly defeated Benazir Bhutto in elections, and decided to use his mandate to ease tensions with India. The two Foreign Ministers had a positive meeting in April. Soon after, a crisis within the ruling Indian coalition resulted in Gujral becoming Prime Minister. He took the chance to raise contact to the highest level of Pakistan's leadership, and met Sharif in the Maldives, where they agreed to re-establish a hotline which had been shut down after a fruitless meeting between Benazir Bhutto and Rajiv Gandhi in 1989.[128]

Any optimism was short-lived. Pakistan tested a longer range Hatf-3 missile which was widely assessed to use Chinese technology. The Indian nuclear energy programme faltered again as the CIRUS plutonium-producing reactor had to be shut down for a major overhaul. Gujral came under pressure to allow nuclear weapon tests. In September the second round of Indo-Pak meetings at Foreign Minister level hit deadlock over Kashmir.[129] Both Gujral and Sharif attended the 1997 UN disarmament session in New York, and had separate meetings with Clinton. Gujral later revealed he had told Clinton that India perceived that only those with economic wealth or nuclear weapons achieve permanent membership of the Security Council. He had added: 'It is very difficult to achieve economic wealth.'[130] He returned to India to be told that the nuclear weapon scientists were ready to test, while Kalam wanted to deploy Prithvi missiles and test a redesigned Agni missile. Further political infighting resulted in Gujral's resignation at the end of November. Then news broke of a new Pakistani missile called Ghauri, allegedly capable of reaching most major Indian cities, which had been developed with North Korea's help.

In the ensuing election early in 1998, the BJP openly campaigned that it would exercise the nuclear option, and would 'take back that part of Kashmir that is under Pakistani occupation'.[131] The BJP was able to form a 14-party coalition government, and Vajpayee again became Prime Minister on 20 March. Having no doubt learnt from his previous bad experience in 1996, at first he took a moderate public line on nuclear policy. On 6 April, Pakistan tested the Ghauri missile, catching India by surprise: it surpassed India's capability, and threatened New Delhi and Mumbai. Reliable reports suggested that Pakistan, fearing the BJP's rhetoric over going nuclear and seizing part of Kashmir, saw its nuclear and missile programmes as the great equalisers and essential to its survival.[132]

Apparently India's decision to go ahead with nuclear tests had been taken by the end of March, so was not in reaction to Pakistan's missile test – but Vajpayee felt vindicated by it. He did not consult his government about the strategic or economic implications. This time, Kalam's team of scientists succeeded in concealing preparations from US intelligence; and Vajpayee gave no hint to a US delegation who visited New Delhi in mid-April, or to the Chinese army chief at the end of the month.[133] On 11 May, India duly tested three devices simultaneously at Pokhran: a fission device with a yield of about 12 kilotons, a claimed 43-kiloton thermonuclear device and a 0.2-kiloton device, probably using reactor-grade plutonium. Two days later, two more sub-kiloton tests were conducted. The reactor-grade plutonium was important, reflecting a contingency plan in the event of weapon-grade fissile materials being capped by a treaty.[134]

The Clinton administration, having first learned of the tests from the media, spent the next two weeks trying to isolate India and persuade Pakistan not to test too.[135] However, the US rejected the implication that it should practise the behaviour it urged on others. Vajpayee wrote to Clinton stating that the primary motivation for the tests, dubbed 'Pokhran II', had been the threat from China: 'We have an overt nuclear weapon state on our borders… a state which committed armed aggression against India in 1962.' To this he added Sino-Pakistani 'strategic level' nuclear and missile collaboration. When the letter was leaked to the *New York Times*, China condemned the tests, which showed 'outrageous contempt' for the international community. India backpedalled, reassuring China that it valued the ten-year-old process of constructive dialogue and meant no harm.[136]

Meanwhile, the Indian government was goading Pakistan into responding with its own tests as *ex post facto* justification for its own. Indeed, this was probably the first example of a nuclear weapon state inciting its main rival to go nuclear. According to Bidwai and Vanaik, the BJP 'had already decided that the road to Chagai (Pakistan's nuclear test site in the Baluchistan mountain ranges) must traverse through Kashmir'. Beginning on 18 May, Indian Home Minister L.K. Advani declared that 'Islamabad should realize the change in the geo-strategic situation in the region' and 'roll back its anti-India policy, especially with regard to Kashmir'.[137] A week later, Advani said that India would undertake 'hot pursuit' to chase insurgents from Kashmir into Pakistan.[138]

Sharif paused for over two weeks to assess how the US would punish India and offer inducements to Pakistan to show restraint, and to balance these against the inevitable domestic pressure to reciprocate.[139] This was despite the fact that A.Q. Khan informed him that it would take only three days for Pakistan to prepare for its own tests.[140] Benazir Bhutto, in opposition, called for a pre-emptive strike to take out India's capability. While testing would incur US sanctions when Pakistan was effectively in default over its balance of payments with foreign debt exceeding US$30 billion, restraint would help to overcome the stigma of involvement with the Taliban and support for Kashmiri secessionists in India. The US offered a US$5 billion package of economic aid and military assistance in special negotiations opened by the Deputy Secretary of State, Strobe Talbott.[141] However, it was not enough to overcome powerful internal pressure, including from the armed forces. Sharif was also disappointed by what was seen as relatively muted international condemnation of India, with Russia and France refusing to impose sanctions. Nor did the US offer to provide extended nuclear deterrence. On 28 May, therefore, Pakistan claimed to have conducted five tests of its own at Chagai, citing as justification an alleged Israel plot to destroy Pakistan's nuclear facilities in collusion with India. Then, to 'get even' with India's Pokhran test in 1974, two days later it claimed to have exploded one more device.[142]

On learning that Pakistan had followed India, Clinton may not have realised the irony of his reported response:

> I cannot believe that we are about to start the 21st century by having the Indian sub-continent repeat the worst mistakes of the 20th century, when we know that it is not necessary to peace, to security, to prosperity, to national greatness or to personal fulfilment.[143]

The US had already imposed economic sanctions on India, and India's international status was damaged, its dream of permanent membership of the UN Security Council at an end. The Security Council adopted a resolution condemning the tests, but took no further action.[144] On 18 June, the Clinton administration announced additional sanctions on both India and Pakistan.[145] However, these were undermined by the hypocritical US position on nuclear policy as shown by its failure to ratify the CTBT, and were insufficient to deflect either nuclear rival. Besides, they were gradually withdrawn over the next few months.

India's vague objective of achieving a 'minimum deterrent' – particularly against China when the border dispute had subsided as an issue – begged endless questions, as it became clear that it had no coherent nuclear strategy. Aside from the need to pre-empt entry into force of the CTBT, its decision to go overtly nuclear seemed largely driven by a visceral need to defy colonialism, racism and a sense of impotence in world affairs.[146] Allied to this was an illusion that primarily symbolic demonstrations of proficiency in nuclear and missile technology offered a short cut to scientific and technological greatness.[147] The world's most populous democracy had ignored the reality that economic power, not nuclear belligerence, was the key to international respect. Worse, the nuclear tests jolted India's creditworthiness, and its defence budget soared.[148]

On the other hand, India could be forgiven for having simply tried to ape the example of the five recognised nuclear states, and especially the UK, France and Russia whose political establishments saw in their nuclear arsenals evidence of great power status. Yet the rest of the international community now viewed this as a problem, not a source of respect. Moreover, now that both India and Pakistan had become *de facto* nuclear states, the nuclear postures of the P5 worked as a strong disincentive for either to relinquish their hard-won nuclear capability. Thus both South Asian rivals demonstrated a massive failure of the non-proliferation regime.

Pakistan's tests had brought US sanctions, which deepened its financial crisis. Even after the Clinton administration eased them following Pakistan's inability to make a major debt repayment to the International Monetary Fund, it was clear that the Pakistan economy was in no position to carry the massive burden of building a genuine nuclear weapons capability. Moreover, in no way could it be argued that its security had been enhanced. Quite apart from the lack of warning of an Indian first strike with a missile flight time of only three to five minutes, a central consequence was that Pakistan would come under pressure to consider pre-emptive use of nuclear weapons in order to counter its inherent disadvantage in conventional military forces.[149]

Aware of the new dangers of a regional nuclear war, Clinton continued to send delegations to urge both sides to step back. This diplomacy appeared to bear fruit in February 1999, when Vajpayee and Sharif met in Lahore and agreed on a new era of improved relations.[150] Sharif apparently thanked Vajpayee for conducting India's tests, as it had provided the pretext for Pakistan to follow suit! Nuclear hawks on both sides trumpeted the meeting as evidence of nuclear deterrence in action. Tragically, within months Pakistan had disregarded it by ordering some Islamic militants, supported by troops, to occupy an unguarded outpost on the Indian side of the disputed Line of Control in Kashmir. It seems that nuclearisation had made India complacent, while Pakistan had become emboldened in the false belief that its nuclear capability would deter India from a major military response.[151]

Just one year after the nuclear tests, bitter fighting broke out near the Kashmiri town of Kargil. During the two-month conflict, India deployed its air force for the first time since 1971. In response,

Pakistani fighter planes were scrambled for fear they might be hit on the ground, and air-raid sirens sounded in the capital city of Islamabad. Senior officials in both countries issued at least a dozen nuclear threats. The peace and stability that nuclear deterrence theorists have ascribed to nuclear possessor states were nowhere in sight. In retrospect, it could be argued that this, the fourth war between India and Pakistan, was the first to have been caused by the delusions of nuclear deterrence.

The US was forced to intervene. Sharif, fearful that any climb-down would jeopardise his hold on power, demanded a face-to-face meeting with Clinton in Washington on 4 July 1999. Clinton assented, but firmly gave Sharif an ultimatum to withdraw, in exchange for which Clinton would urge Vajpayee to accept a ceasefire. He asked Sharif if he knew that his military was preparing nuclear-armed missiles. Sharif seemed taken aback and said only that India was probably doing the same. After some more blustering, Sharif knew he was isolated even from Pakistan's most powerful ally and agreed on withdrawal.[152] After failing to remove the architect of the Kargil misadventure, Army Chief of Staff General Pervez Musharraf, Sharif was himself overthrown on 12 October 1999, by elements of the Army loyal to Musharraf. It later emerged that India had activated all its nuclear delivery vehicles, with at least four Prithvi missiles deployed and readied for a nuclear strike.[153]

South Asia had become the most likely flashpoint for a nuclear war. On 17 August 1999, the National Security Advisor to the Indian government released a *Draft Report of National Security Advisory Board on Indian Nuclear Doctrine*, signalling the end of any pretence about India leading the global struggle for a nuclear weapon-free world.[154] Instead it baldly stated: 'In the absence of global nuclear disarmament India's strategic interests require effective, credible nuclear deterrence and adequate retaliatory capacity should deterrence fail.' It went on to specify that deterrence required India to maintain:

* Sufficient, survivable and operationally prepared nuclear forces
* Robust command and control systems
* Effective intelligence and early warning capabilities
* Comprehensive planning and training for nuclear operations
* The will to use nuclear forces and weapons

The sense of unreality deepened with a statement that India's nuclear forces 'will be based on a triad of aircraft, mobile land-based missiles and sea-based assets'. These 'shall be designed and deployed to ensure survival against a first strike... The survivability of the nuclear arsenal and effective command, control, communications, computing, intelligence and information systems shall be assured... The Indian defence forces shall be in a position to execute operations in an NBC environment with minimal degradation... Space based and other assets shall be created to provide early warning, communications [and] damage/detonation assessment.' Hinting at defiance of anticipated shortfalls in resources for such a mammoth undertaking, it added: 'While India is committed to maintain the deployment of a deterrent which is both minimum and credible, it will not accept any restraints on building its R & D capability.' Its only gesture towards restraint was its undertaking that 'India will not be the first to initiate a nuclear strike', and that it 'will not resort to the use or threat of use of nuclear weapons against States which do not possess nuclear weapons, or are not aligned with nuclear weapon powers.'

Among many critiques by Indian scientists and former military leaders, the following conclusions by Dr T. Jayaraman, a theoretical physicist at the Institute of Mathematical Sciences in Chennai, merit citing:

> In a deeper sense, the country and society most threatened by Indian nuclear weaponisation is India and Indian society itself. The far-reaching programme of nuclear weaponisation prescribed by the dIND [draft Indian Nuclear Doctrine] would engender a serious negative shift in the priorities of Indian science and technology, away from development issues that need urgent attention, towards an inevitable militarisation of science and technology. The pursuit of the mad-cap vision of India's hawks would consume substantial resources, even if the goals set are never reached.
>
> This is hardly the vision of free India that inspired its freedom struggle. India's Strangeloves are well aware of this fact. In demanding that India possess 'the will to employ nuclear weapons', the dIND in fact unequivocally advocates that India abandon any moral values in its politics and discard any peace-orientated value systems underlying its foreign and nuclear policies.[155]

The US reaction was to warn India that developing a nuclear deterrent was 'unwise', while China urged New Delhi to renounce its nuclear weapons.[156] India responded by proposing bilateral talks with the US on its draft nuclear doctrine, which it then extended to Pakistan, with no result. In February 2000, Pakistan announced that it had established a command and control structure for its nuclear forces.[157]

It so happened that, soon after fighting broke out in Kashmir, General Lee Butler USAF (Ret) made his first visit to India since speaking out against nuclear deterrence. Now he was concerned to give India's leaders a reality check about this. During talks with a large

Indian delegation led by Subrahmanyam, Butler stunned his hosts by spelling out the utter impracticalities of implementing nuclear deterrence against Pakistan. Following further meetings, it was arranged for him to give a top adviser to Vajpayee a tutorial in New York on managing a nuclear war machine. This gave added purpose to a discreet gathering he orchestrated in Omaha of three top retired military officers from India with three from Pakistan, which resulted in 'a mutual recognition of how poorly the two sides understood each other professionally, the frightening misperceptions they had harbored throughout their careers about each other's actions and intentions and, most importantly, the dangerous path they were on with respect to their nuclear planning and force postures.'[158]

Then came the 11 September 2001 terror attacks in the US. The links to Osama bin Laden's al Qaeda network, with its bases in Afghanistan, led to a major US military operation to oust the Taliban regime and attack al Qaeda, especially in facilities tunnelled deep into the mountains near the border with Pakistan. Pakistan suddenly resumed its strategic importance to the US. The Bush administration lost no time in lifting sanctions, and offered inducements to General Musharraf that he could not refuse, with Pakistan's economy near collapse. Concern arose that Islamic extremists, aided by Pakistan's powerful pro-Taliban Inter-Services Intelligence (ISI) agency, might try to exact retribution against Musharraf and even seize Pakistan's nuclear arsenal.[159] Musharraf headed this off by sacking his ISI chief, detaining several suspected retired scientists, and redeploying the arsenal, estimated to be between twenty-four and forty-eight warheads (possibly more than India's thirty to thirty-five), to at least six new secret locations.[160] In any event, the Taliban regime was overthrown and a pro-US government installed without such concerns materialising.

However, on 13 December 2001 terrorists attacked the Indian Parliament, killing several guards. India, desperate to regain the initiative with the US, immediately accused Pakistan of being behind the attack and linked it to Islamist resistance to Indian armed forces in Kashmir.[161] Demanding that such attacks be equated with those on 11 September, India deployed its armed forces along the border with Pakistan. Pakistan followed suit, as it came under US pressure to crack down on extremist organisations. The mobilisation, totalling about a million troops, was the largest in the sub-continent's history.

On 12 January 2002, Musharraf made a radical break with Pakistan's 20-year policy of Islamisation, when he announced a plan to sever the links between political Islam and the state, between the military and the mullahs, and between Kashmir and terrorist violence.

Ten days later he offered to work towards de-nuclearising South Asia. Ever suspicious of Pakistani motives, on 25 January India rejected Musharraf's offer, punctuating its decision with a test of its nuclear-capable medium range Agni-II ballistic missile.[162] Meanwhile a report, published in January 2002 by the Italian arms control institution, the Landau Network, stated that Pakistan had established scenarios under which it would use nuclear weapons.[163] These include if India:

* attacks Pakistan and conquers a large part of its territory
* destroys a large part of Pakistan's land or air forces
* pursues the economic strangulation of Pakistan
* pushes Pakistan into 'political destabilisation or creates large scale internal subversion'

The crisis continued until October 2002. On 8 May a suicide car bomb attack in Karachi killed eleven French naval technicians. After an attack by terrorists on a bus in an Indian army base at Kaluchak near Jammu six days later, which left thirty-two dead, India blamed the Pakistani ISI and threatened 'limited war' and nuclear annihilation if Pakistan used nuclear weapons first.[164] However, with Musharraf allowing US troops to pursue al Qaeda suspects within Pakistan, it was far more likely that such atrocities were the work of anti-Musharraf Kashmiri extremists aiming to provoke war and weaken the state. Unlike in the Kargil clash in 1999, this time Pakistan was not isolated, and India was threatening escalation. There were reports of both sides deploying nuclear weapons.[165]

At the end of May the US and UK governments were sufficiently alarmed by the possibility of a nuclear confrontation to issue warnings to their citizens to leave the region.[166] These also served to dramatise the situation in the hope of reminding New Delhi and Islamabad of the special nature of nuclear weapons. In addition, the US leaked a Pentagon assessment of casualties in the event of a full-scale nuclear exchange. This estimated that up to 12 million immediate deaths plus 7 million injuries could result, and that radioactive contamination of the Himalayas could cause famine and disease across South Asia. After US Deputy Secretary of State Richard Armitage had persuaded both sides to step back during visits in early June, Vajpayee was reported to have said: 'India was prepared for an atomic war, but we were confident that our neighbour would not commit such an act of madness.'[167] Not to be outdone, Musharraf asserted that Pakistan's nuclear capabilities had deterred India from launching a full-scale war.[168] On 16 October, both sides agreed on a gradual, limited troop withdrawal, and the crisis subsided.

India's BJP-led government, beset by communal violence in Gujarat and political scandals, had seemed determined to 'call Pakistan's nuclear bluff'. This exposed a fundamental contradiction relating to its application of nuclear deterrence dogma. On the one hand, the risk of a nuclear holocaust had to be taken because otherwise Indian pride would always be tormented by an evil Pakistan regime obsessed with an irrational and unbalanced hostility to India. Yet this same regime could be relied upon to be rational and sufficiently balanced never to launch nuclear weapons whatever the military provocation from India, or even in the face of Pakistan's total defeat.[169] Completely absent from such simplistic posturing was any concern about the consequent risk of accidental nuclear war through over-reaction or other miscalculation.

Further evidence of the naïvety of both Indian and Pakistani nuclear hawks was their condemnation of travel warnings by other governments as unwarranted and 'excessive', or as tantamount to 'capitulating' to the other side's 'nuclear blackmail' and 'scaremongering'. Leading Indian expert K. Subrahmanyam agreed, adding that 'we can all sleep in peace'. General Aslam Beg, one of the 'fathers' of Pakistan's nuclear arsenal, swung to the opposite extreme: 'We can make a first strike, and a second strike or even a third.' Indian strategists calmly discussed how India could 'absorb' a nuclear strike by Pakistan and then wipe out the entire population of Pakistan in retaliation. Another Pakistani expert, Javed Ashraf Qazi, was more realistic as he echoed Israel's 'Samson Option': 'What is this damned nuclear option for? We will use it against India... [I]f I am going down the ditch I might as well take the enemy with me.'[170] On 30 December 2002, Musharraf publicly claimed that, during the Kargil clash in 1999, Pakistan had been on the verge of using 'non-conventional weapons', but had been dissuaded by the US and the UK. Both countries rebutted this suggestion.[171]

On 4 January 2003, the Indian government announced that its draft nuclear doctrine of August 1999 had become official policy, almost three years after Pakistan had led the way.[172] A Nuclear Command Authority (NCA) was now responsible for the management of nuclear weapons and the ultimate decision to use them. However, no further details were given about the composition of the NCA at its political and executive levels. The government also approved the appointment of a Commander-in-Chief, Strategic Forces Command responsible for the administration of the nuclear forces. A 'credible minimum deterrent' would be maintained, and nuclear weapons would only be used in retaliation against a WMD attack. While sustaining a no-first-use policy against nuclear attack, the only significant change from the draft doctrine was that India had followed US and UK policy by warning that it reserved the right to respond with nuclear weapons to a chemical or biological attack. Finally, the government had 'reviewed and approved the arrangements for alternate chains of command for retaliatory nuclear strikes in all eventualities.'

Back in July 2002, Abdul Kalam, recently retired architect of India's nuclear arsenal, had been elected India's new President. In an interview he had asserted: 'Nuclear deterrents on both sides have helped avert a war.'[173] He had added that his election would send 'the right signal' to the world. He had defended India's decision to go nuclear, saying that the subcontinent had been repeatedly invaded by foreign powers for centuries because of its weak military. With this mindset expressed by the President of India, concern was widespread in South Asia that some kind of nuclear exchange between India and Pakistan was inevitable – because where India led, Pakistan was sure to follow.

In March 2003, the US imposed sanctions on a nuclear research and uranium enrichment facility in Pakistan, and a missile export company in North Korea.[174] Accusations were made, hotly denied by Pakistan, that North Korea had provided ten Scud-B ballistic missiles in exchange for uranium enrichment technology assistance. Experts had long been convinced that the Ghauri missile was a version of North Korea's Nodong missile. Then, on 19 December, Libyan leader Muammar Qaddafi's sudden announcement that Libya would abandon pursuit of its WMD programmes was accompanied by revelations that it had received assistance from Pakistan's scientists.[175] Central to all these accusations was A.Q. Khan. He had made a number of visits to Pyongyang in the mid- to late 1990s, when Pakistan had been keen to match India's missile capability. Following questioning by US and European officials, strong links were also found with Iran's purchase of uranium enrichment centrifuge designs from Pakistan in 1988.

On 4 February 2004, in the presence of Musharraf, A.Q. Khan confessed on state-run television in Islamabad that he had been solely responsible for operating an international black market in nuclear weapon materials, components and production technology.[176] The next day, Musharraf publicly pardoned him, paying tribute to Khan's national hero status. With this and the need for Pakistan's cooperation in the 'war on terrorism', and specifically the hunt for Osama bin Laden in northwest Pakistan, the Bush administration chose not to press harder against the world's worst nuclear weapon proliferator, publicly accepting the Pakistan government's unconvincing line that all clandestine transactions took place before Musharraf seized power in 1999. Meanwhile, Israeli intelligence apparently had reliable information that Iran's nuclear weapon programme was based on a design obtained from A.Q. Khan via Libya. Evidence of a pan-Islamic link emerged with reports that Libya had bankrolled Pakistan and may even have supplied raw uranium. After Pakistan tested nuclear weapons in 1998, the Saudi government allegedly donated US$4 billion worth of oil over five years to help Pakistan survive sanctions.[177]

While the furore over A.Q. Khan gradually subsided, in India the BJP-led government surprisingly fell from power in May 2004. A Congress Party-led United Progressive Alliance, with Manmohan Singh replacing Vajpayee as Prime Minister, opted for caution regarding nuclear policy. Implicitly recognising that nuclear weapons had made the region a much more dangerous place, the first of a series of Indo-Pak talks on nuclear confidence-building measures was held in New Delhi. However, apart from reiterating their test moratoriums and upgrading the 'nuclear hotline', little was achieved. Indeed, the joint statement's assertion that 'the nuclear capabilities of each other… constitute a factor for stability', and that both countries would seek 'parity of status' with the P5, showed that little had been learned from the 1999 and 2002 crises.[178]

A revealing episode occurred six months later. India's Foreign Minister K. Natwar Singh, visiting Seoul, distanced himself from the previous Indian government's decision to test before saying: 'Even though we are ourselves a nuclear power, we support complete nuclear disarmament for Korea.'[179] This was consistent with his government's stated (but profoundly hypocritical) commitment to work for global nuclear disarmament and to update Rajiv Gandhi's 1988 action plan to achieve this. However, his remarks exposed a lack of political consensus, which reflected polls showing that more than two-thirds of Indians polled now opposed the manufacture or use of nuclear weapons by India. Reasons for this shift included the realisation that nuclear weapons had not made India more secure, and that nuclearisation had failed to impart stability or maturity to the India-Pakistan strategic relationship. On the contrary, it had encouraged adventurism, and nuclear weapons had become an enormously complicating factor in South Asia. Recognition of these realities was perhaps reflected in the lack of enthusiasm to celebrate the seventh anniversary of the Indo-Pak tests in May 2005. In India, there was almost no official media coverage, while in Pakistan, no doubt linked to the fall from grace of A.Q. Khan, replicas of the Chagai mountain and Ghauri missile had been quietly removed from display.[180]

Less than a month after the five-yearly NPT Review Conference ended in failure, on 28 June 2005 the US and Indian governments signed a *New Framework for the US-India Defence Relationship*.[181] Trumpeting that the two countries 'have entered a new era' building a 'strategic partnership', it charted their course for the next ten years, and paved the way for co-production in India of advanced combat aircraft and other weapons systems, cooperation on BMD (including the possible sale of the US Patriot short-range system, with implications for Pakistan's nuclear deterrence posture) and lifting of US export controls on other sensitive military technologies. Three weeks later, on 18 July a major new agreement was signed by Manmohan Singh and George W. Bush in Washington, establishing a 'global partnership' aimed at enhancing their ability to 'work together to provide global leadership in areas of mutual concern and interest'.[182] Central to the latter was US recognition of India as a 'responsible state with advanced nuclear technology', which should 'acquire the same benefits and advantages as other such states'. The US therefore undertook to 'adjust international regimes to enable full civil nuclear energy cooperation and trade with India'. While stopping just short of acknowledging India as a fully-fledged nuclear weapon state, the US had conferred on it the benefits of a non-nuclear signatory of the NPT.

Presumably this unilateral lurch away from the Bush administration's drive to tighten international controls on nuclear commerce was aimed at strengthening US efforts to oppose Islamic extremism, and build a regional counterweight to China.[183] However, such special treatment for one of only four nuclear-capable states refusing to sign the NPT dealt a body blow to this already severely weakened treaty, as the agreement breached the guidelines of both the Nuclear Suppliers' Group and Missile Technology Control Regime. Pakistan reacted with consternation. After the agreement was announced, US Secretary of State Condoleezza Rice telephoned Foreign Minister Khurshid Kasuri to reassure him that the US 'will remain responsive to Pakistan's security concerns', but that was not enough to prevent Prime Minister Shaukat Aziz cancelling a visit to the US.[184] Following the A.Q. Khan saga, there was no possibility that the US would extend the same benefits to Pakistan. Yet Pakistan was justified in arguing that India was the first nuclear proliferator in South Asia. The inevitable consequence of both bilateral agreements was to intensify the arms race between India and Pakistan, and weaken an already faltering peace process.

Indeed, after Bush endorsed the agreement with Manmohan Singh during his visit to New Delhi on 2 March 2006, Pakistan's Foreign Minister Khurshid Kasuri warned it would encourage Pakistan to seek a similar relationship with China: 'The US should be conscious of sentiments of this country. Public opinion sees things in black and white. They compare the US to China and feel that it has not been a constant friend the way China has.'[185] Foreign ministry officials said that Pakistan was looking actively for nuclear reactors and that the most likely supplier was China, which had already supplied one and started construction of a second at the Chashma site in Punjab province. Mr Kasuri added: 'We demand equality of treatment and we'll continue to pursue it. We have a large population and a fast-growing economy. If the Indian deal goes through there are some things we will do.'

Sure enough, on 24 July 2006 the *Washington Post* reported that satellite photographs of Pakistan's Khushab nuclear site showed what appeared to be a partially-completed 1,000 megawatt heavy water reactor capable of producing enough plutonium for forty to fifty nuclear weapons a year, a 20-fold increase from Pakistan's existing 50-megawatt plutonium production reactor.[186]

In 2018, the Arms Control Association estimates that India has 120-130 nuclear warheads, and Pakistan 130-140.[187]

Summary

France, shut out of the Manhattan Project and the post-World War II US drive for nuclear supremacy, depended upon Israeli technical assistance to develop its nuclear weapon programme in the early 1950s. This gave Israel leverage in obtaining French technical and engineering support to build a secret nuclear weapon plant at Dimona. Successive US administrations, influenced by a powerful domestic lobby of uncritical supporters of Israel, allowed a ruthless and highly competent Israeli politico-scientific-military nexus to pursue a unique form of existential nuclear deterrence, in which acquisition of a nuclear arsenal of some 80 warheads, with enough fissile material for up to 200, was denied. Israel proceeded to blackmail the US into supporting this and its aggressive foreign and defence policies, and providing massive military aid. Such a policy offered a clear pretext and incitement for Iraq and Iran to acquire their own nuclear arsenals.

In South Asia, bitter rivals India and Pakistan naively attempted to apply nuclear deterrence dogma to their security problems. In so doing, they were also motivated by perceived echoes of colonialism and racism, particularly from the UK and the US. For India, one penalty was the loss of moral high ground as any pretence of sustaining Nehru's Gandhian stance and leadership of the Non-Aligned Movement was jettisoned and Western nuclear assistance obtained. In

Pakistan's case this developed into A.Q. Khan's extensive black market, which might have remained undetected had it not been for Libyan leader Muammar Gaddafi's decision to expose it. The July 2005 nuclear cooperation agreement between the US and India signalled that the incestuous links between nuclear energy and weapons could not be effectively policed, and that the nuclear non-proliferation regime was collapsing under the weight of its hypocrisy and discriminatory rules.

In all three cases, regional insecurity and consequent arms races have been intensified by relying on nuclear deterrence. Periodic inevitable flare-ups of armed conflict have involved attempts to play the nuclear card, leading to US intervention amid intense anxiety about loss of crisis control as the contradictions of nuclear deterrence became manifest. Throughout each one, a disturbing theme has been the way in which pursuit of the nuclear deterrence delusion has involved such deep duplicity that the reputation and integrity of some of each country's most respected political, military and scientific leaders, and with them their nation's founding ideals, have suffered irreparable damage.

Notes

1 Ban Ki-moon address to the EastWest Institute, 24 October 2008, http://www.un.org/News/Press/docs/2008/sgsm11881.doc.htm.
2 Yossi Melman, 'Exclusive: Israel's rash behavior blew operation to sabotage Iran's computers, US officials say', (*The Jerusalem Post*, 16 February 2016), http://www.jpost.com/Middle-East/Iran/Israels-rash-behavior-blew-operation-to-sabotage-Irans-computers-US-officials-say-444970. For more on the JCPOA, see https://en.wikipedia.org/wiki/Joint_Comprehensive_Plan_of_Action.
3 Avner Cohen, *Israel and the Bomb* (New York: Columbia University Press, 1998). During the period from the mid-1950s to 1970, Israel's nuclear security strategy evolved through four stages: from secrecy, denial, and ambiguity to opacity. In the introduction Cohen explained the difference between opacity and ambiguity. Essentially, opacity is about deliberate obfuscation and concealment – though ambiguity can also be calculated.
4 Seymour M. Hersh, *The Samson Option* (London: Faber and Faber Limited, 1993), p. 321 and p. 326, paperback edition. Avner Cohen broadly endorsed Hersh's findings. Hersh and Cohen are the primary sources for the Israel section of this chapter.
5 Hersh (1993), pp. 8–16.
6 Ibid, p. 22. See also Cohen (1998), p. 13, for evidence that Ben-Gurion linked Arab enmity to Israel with Hitler's hatred of the Jews: 'We do not want the Arab Nazis to come and slaughter us.'
7 See also Cohen (1998), pp. 25–26 and 35–36. In 1949 Ernst Bergmann, a refugee from Nazi Germany and protégé of Chaim Weizmann before becoming Ben-Gurion's top scientific adviser, recommended that six promising physics graduates be sent to leading nuclear physics laboratories in the US and Europe as the nucleus of a national cadre of accomplished nuclear scientists.
8 Hersh (1993), p. 30.
9 Hersh (1993), p. 40.
10 Interestingly, Cohen (1998), pp. 244-245 quoted Nasser as discovering the limitations of nuclear deterrence applied to non-nuclear states when he defied the British ultimatum. Nasser apparently concluded that nuclear weapons were irrelevant to the Arab-Israeli conflict, which helps to explain Egypt's subsequent muted responses to revelations about Dimona. Egypt was not ready to oppose Israel militarily; also, Nasser believed that the US would not allow Israel to acquire nuclear weapons (Cohen, p. 255). On the other hand, he felt the need to react belligerently when the first revelations about Dimona appeared in December 1960. When asked in 1963 by Egypt's US ambassador what he would do if he learned that Israel was using the reactor to manufacture weapon-grade nuclear materials, he replied: 'Protective war. We would have no other choice.' (Cohen, p. 249).
11 Hersh (1993), pp. 41–43. Hersh, who is an American of Jewish descent, provided an interesting commentary on the growth of political influence of the US pro-Israeli Jewish community, starting with their $400,000 contribution to Truman's 1948 presidential campaign. By 1960, their support had become a major factor for John F. Kennedy and the Democratic Party – see Chapter 8, 'A Presidential Struggle', pp. 93–100, and Cohen at endnote 18. Hersh devoted the whole of Chapter 7 (pp. 83–92) to what he described as the problem of 'dual loyalty' for American Jews towards the US and Israel, concluding that its primary effect has been a form of self-censorship that has kept successive US governments from dealing rationally and coherently with the strategic and political issues raised by a nuclear-armed Israel.
12 Ibid, p. 43. French Prime Minister Guy Mollet, mortified by France's failure to support Israel, apparently told an aide: 'I owe the bomb to them.' See also Cohen (1998), pp. 57–59.
13 David Leigh, 'US kept in the dark as secret nuclear deal was struck', UK

Guardian, 4 August 2005. This extraordinary story, first revealed in the UK in a BBCTV *Newsnight* documentary on 3 August, ironically emerged from a declassified Foreign Office counter-proliferation file. However, Cohen (1998), p. 62, covered the story briefly. Apparently the decision was based simply on recouping losses from a deal with Norway, when it was decided after the £1.5million contract had been signed to pursue graphite as a reactor moderator rather than heavy water. Norway refused to cancel the contract so, in September 1958, Israel offered to buy the twenty-five tons of heavy water surplus to British requirements via the Norwegians. David Peirson, secretary of the UK Atomic Energy Authority, argued that it should be sold without safeguards because the British had obtained it for their own military purposes without them. Douglas Cape, the first secretary at the Foreign and Commonwealth Office in charge of nuclear security, agreed, stipulating that the US should not be informed as it could jeopardise the sale by insisting on safeguards. The agreed cover story was that the heavy water was 'understood to be required by Israel for peaceful use in a reactor connected with desert irrigation'. In June 1959, two shipments of ten tons of heavy water each were put on board Israeli ships in UK ports, and sent to Dimona. Israel never received the final five tons, because by 1960 US intelligence had become suspicious of the true nature of the reactor, culminating in a story being planted in the UK press via Chapman Pincher (see endnote 18).

14   Meirion Jones, 'Secret sale of UK plutonium to Israel', BBCTV *Newsnight*, 10 March 2006, . In a follow-up to the 3 August 2005 documentary above, *Newsnight* revealed that it had obtained top secret papers through the Freedom of Information Act showing that officials within the UK nuclear weapons industry went behind the backs of their political masters and defied Foreign Office orders against such a sale. Tony Benn, Minister of Technology at the time, was incredulous when told the details: 'I learned by bitter experience that the nuclear industry lied to me again and again.' The atomic files detail hundreds of nuclear deals with Israel flagged up as sensitive.

15   Cohen (1998), p. 20 and pp. 63–64. Peres faced criticism from experienced senior military officers, who had reservations about investing the nation's limited defence resources in the nuclear project, which many regarded as a fantasy.

16   Hersh (1993), pp. 67–68. Officials who worked at Dimona in those years proudly admitted that they 'raided every place in the country… [W]e depleted Israel's industrial system.' At its height, some 1500 Israeli scientists, many with doctorates, worked there. See also Cohen, pp. 18–20, who pointed out that Peres 'concluded early on that Israel's own nuclear physics "establishment", in the main, would not be a source of support. Most of the top men simply did not believe that Israel had the ability to build its own nuclear option, and they gave frank voice to their opinion.' He bypassed them for the younger generation.

17   Ibid, pp. 66–67. Peres formed a special group of trusted and discreet donors who became known as the Committee of Thirty. They included Baron Edmond de Rothschild in Paris and Abraham Feinberg in New York. Years later Peres bragged (inaccurately) to an interviewer: 'The project was financed from contributions I raised from Jewish millionaires who understood the importance of the issue.'

18   Ibid, p. 136.
19   Ibid, pp. 68–70. See also Cohen, pp. 73–75.
20   Ibid, pp. 74–79. Hersh provided a colourful account of developments that triggered the announcement. Central to this was a determined effort by the outgoing Eisenhower administration, in conjunction with the UK government, to make Israel acknowledge what it was doing at Dimona, following a major feature article by John Finney in *The New York Times* on 19 December 1960, and anticipated by Chapman Pincher in the UK *Daily Express* three days before. See also Cohen, pp. 85–95. Cohen, pp. 143–147 chronicled a period in 1962 when a small but vociferous group, the Committee for the Denuclearization of the Middle East, openly questioned the wisdom of Israel developing nuclear

21 Cohen (1998), pp. 99–134 covered in more detail than Hersh Kennedy's efforts to restrain Israel's nuclear plans and bring them under scrutiny. Kennedy always cited Israel as his example of the danger of proliferation. He was also well aware of the unique domestic US support enjoyed by Israel, and that he would not have been elected without the support of about 80 percent of Jewish voters. It was no coincidence that he was the first US President to have a close political aide, Myer (Mike) Feldman, who also liaised with the Jewish community and, as an unofficial adviser on Israel, handled his contacts with the Israeli government.

weapons – but its arguments did not make any impact and were ignored. That said, there was some internal discussion among Knesset members, but nobody was prepared to challenge Ben-Gurion.

22 Ibid, p. 115. The Cuban missile crisis in October 1962 strengthened Kennedy's commitment to prevent the spread of nuclear weapons.
23 Ibid, pp. 148–151.
24 Ibid, pp. 236–238. Peres apparently preferred to call it an 'option for a rainy day', the usual role of nuclear weapons as a tool of last resort in extreme military and political contingencies. However, it was soon realised that use of such weapons when, say, an Arab army had invaded Israel might be too late – but pre-emption would be too early. Furthermore, deterrence would only work if the enemy knew that nuclear weapons were deployed. From this came the need to develop a process of controlled leaks and rumours about Israel's nuclear capability, combined with a readiness to move quickly into demonstrating its ability to implement nuclear deterrence.
25 Hersh (1993), p. 137.
26 Cohen (1998), p. 3. He then devoted Chapter 9 to how Eshkol struck a deal with Kennedy in 1963, which preserved the Dimona project.
27 Ibid, pp. 195–217 covered the relationship between Johnson and Eshkol in detail.
28 Hersh (1993), pp. 138–139.
29 Cohen (1998), pp. 206–207.
30 Ibid, pp. 255–257.
31 Ibid, pp. 259–276. Cohen devoted a chapter to the run-up to the Six-Day War. Ever since Nasser had first threatened preventive war to destroy Dimona in December 1960, Israel had been concerned to protect it against air attack. The first Israeli Hawk air defence missile battery had been deployed around Dimona in 1965.
32 Hersh (1993), p. 162. This major breakthrough was achieved by staff in the US Embassy in Tel Aviv led by Ambassador Walworth Barbour, who became a close associate of the Israeli director of military intelligence, Major General Aharon Yariv. See also Cohen, p. 214.
33 Cohen (1998), p. 1 and pp. 273–274.
34 Hersh (1993), pp. 174 and 179. The cost of Israel's nuclear-armed missile programme, the final step to making the Samson Option operational, was estimated in 1967 to be US$850 million. This was more than the rest of the entire Israeli defence budget that year. One Israeli official recalled seeing estimates indicating that by the early 1970s a full-scale nuclear weapons programme would take up more than ten per cent of Israel's overall budget – nearly US$1 billion.
35 Ibid, p. 175.
36 Cohen (1998), p. 276.
37 Ibid, p.3 and p. 284.
38 Hersh (1993), pp183–184.
39 Cohen (1998), pp. 293–321 devoted a chapter to 'The Battle over the NPT'. The Soviet invasion of Czechoslovakia on 20 August 1968 allowed Israel to stall over signing, after which the US Presidential election campaign provided the next pretext. Following an abrasive meeting between Paul Warnke and Yitzak Rabin on 8 November, Israeli representatives petitioned the White House, and Rabin

contacted Abe Feinberg, a friend and strong supporter of President Johnson. Within days Warnke was told that Johnson wished to finalise the aircraft deal swiftly and without conditions.

40 A secret US study, which led to what was known as the 1965 'Gilpatric Report' (since declassified), showed how the decision was taken to negotiate the NPT, and to make non-proliferation, not disarmament, a goal of US policy. It remains relevant and topical. See .

41 Hersh (1993), pp. 209–211. Citing evidence from Morton Halperin, Kissinger's closest aide at the time, Hersh recounts that Nixon and Kissinger were convinced that Israel's nuclear ambitions were justified and understandable. They also shared a contempt for the NPT. In a major US policy change, they issued a secret presidential order to the bureaucracy undercutting their public endorsement of the treaty. National Security Decision Memorandum No.6 stated that 'there should be no efforts by the United States government to pressure other nations, particularly the Federal Government of Germany, to follow suit [and ratify the NPT].' See also Cohen, pp. 324–337.

42 Cohen (1998), pp. 287–289.

43 Hersh (1993), pp. 215–216.

44 Cohen (1998), pp. 277–291 covered the shift from ambiguity to opacity in Chapter 15, and in Chapter 17 how opacity became entrenched with Eshkol's successor Golda Meir and Nixon.

45 Hersh (1993), pp. 221–222.

46 Ibid, pp. 225–237. Hersh included a detailed account of the nuclear aspects of the Yom Kippur War, derived from the many published analyses plus his interviews with key participants or observers at the time.

47 Ibid, p. 232.

48 Ibid, p. 239.

49 Ibid, pp. 263–266 for more details on the collaboration between Israel and South Africa. Hersh devoted Chapter 20 (pp. 271–283) to the saga of the joint nuclear test. Also, as reported in an Israeli newspaper a US document released at the request of the Security Studies Centre at Georgetown University stated that the test was carried out on an offshore platform in the northern Antarctic. AFX News, Jerusalem, 20 May 2006. .

50 Ibid, pp. 286–288.

51 Ibid, pp. 289–290.

52 Ibid, pp. 290-291. This was five years before the whistleblower Mordechai Vanunu openly provided similar information to the UK *Sunday Times.*

53 Ibid, pp. 288-289. Hersh recorded that, a few weeks after Sharon's return from Washington, he called together the senior officers of the Israeli Defence Force and told them about his plan to invade Lebanon to "destroy the 'capital of terrorism'." Apparently he discussed the proposed operation with US Secretary of State Alexander Haig, but the plan authorised by the Israeli Cabinet was to go only 12 miles into Lebanon. In the event, Sharon went all the way to the outskirts of Beirut.

54 Robert S. Norris, William M. Arkin, Hans M. Kristensen and Joshua Handler, 'Israeli nuclear forces, 2002', Nuclear Notebook, *Bulletin of the Atomic Scientists,* September/October 2002, p. 75.

55 For Makhoul's full speech, see 'Knesset Debate on Israel's Nuclear Weapons', *Disarmament Diplomacy* No. 43, January-February 2000, under Documents and Sources, http://www.acronym.org.uk/dd/dd43/43kness.htm. See also Merav Datan, 'Relaxing the Taboo: Israel Debates Nuclear Weapons', op. cit., http://www.acronym.org.uk/dd/dd43/43israel.htm.

56 Uzi Mahnaimi and Matthew Campbell, 'Israel Makes Nuclear Waves With Submarine Missile Test', *The Sunday Times,* 18 June 2000.

57 Peter Beaumont and Conal Urquhart, 'Israel fits nuclear arms in submarines', *The Observer,* 12 October 2003.

58 Stephen Farrell, 'Israel admits bombing suspected Syrian nuclear reactor in

	2007, warns Iran', Reuters, https://www.reuters.com/article/us-israel-syria-nuclear/israel-admits-bombing-suspected-syrian-nuclear-reactor-in-2007-warns-iran-idUSKBN1GX09K.
59	'Nuclear Weapons: Who Has What at a Glance', Arms Control Association, January 2018, https://www.armscontrol.org/factsheets/Nuclearweaponswhohaswhat.
60	The account that follows again relies significantly on the research and scholarship of others. Among the most important contributions in this regard have been the work of George Perkovich in *India's Nuclear Bomb: The Impact on Global Proliferation* (Berkeley and Los Angeles: University of California Press, 1999), and of Praful Bidwai and Achin Vanaik in *South Asia on a Short Fuse: Nuclear Politics & The Future of Global Disarmament* (Oxford University Press, New Delhi, 2001).
61	See Perkovich (1999), pp16-17 for more on Bhabha's background and how he convinced Nehru soon after their first meeting in 1937.
62	Ibid, pp. 13-15 and 17-20.
63	Ibid, p. 29 and pp. 33-35. Nehru successfully lobbied for Bhabha to be the president of the first UN Conference on the Peaceful Uses of Atomic Energy, held in Geneva in 1955. Nehru's charisma and high moral standing meant that he was taken at his word when he professed that India would not build atomic bombs. However, in 1958 he warned: "We have the technical know-how for manufacturing the atom bomb. We can do it in three or four years if we divert sufficient resources in that direction. But we have given the world an assurance that we shall never do so. We shall never use our knowledge of nuclear science for purposes of war." This could be interpreted as an early, exaggerated attempt at nuclear deterrence by India.
64	Ibid, pp. 52-53.
65	Ibid, pp. 60-61.
66	Ibid, p. 108. Khan and Bhutto had noted that Bhabha had claimed that India could build a nuclear weapon within 12 to 18 months. A recently declassified US government cable indicated that in November 1964 Khan "expressed his deep concern at prospect of rapidly developing Indian nuclear capability which could be readily converted from peaceful to war-like purposes." Perkovich added that more research is needed on the influence of the nuclear weapon factor in this episode: "Unaddressed in the existing literature, this would constitute the first case of nuclear proliferation in one country (India) prompting an adversary to undertake military action to 'beat' the anticipated effects of nuclear deterrence." Patrick Keatley quoted Bhutto's remark in "The Brown Bomb", *Guardian*, 11 March 1965, p. 10.
67	Ibid, pp. 196-197.
68	Ibid, pp. 112-114.
69	Ibid, pp. 128-130.
70	Ibid, p. 134.
71	Ibid, p. 142.
72	Ibid, pp. 142-143. Statement by Prime Minister Indira Gandhi, Lok Sabha, 24 April 1968, in Jain, *Nuclear India*, 2, pp. 201-202.
73	Ibid, pp. 152-155.
74	Ibid, pp. 148-149. Subrahmanyam claimed this in an interview with Perkovich.
75	Ibid, pp. 156-158.
76	Ibid, p. 159.
77	Ibid, p. 160. Perkovich devoted a chapter to events leading up to the Pokhran test, its nature and the ramifications (pp. 161-189).
78	Ibid, pp. 161-166.
79	Ibid, pp. 166-170. Perkovich described how, despite the clear conventional military dominance demonstrated by India over Pakistan, pressure for a nuclear weapon capability resurfaced in 1972.
80	Ibid, pp. 195-196 and 204-205, and Bidwai and Vanaik (2000), pp. 94-95. See

	also Zahid Malik, *Dr A.Q. Khan and the Islamic Bomb* (Islamabad: Hurmat, 1992). A. Q. Khan cultivated the mythology that he was its father and guiding spirit, understating the role played by Munir Ahmad Khan in coordinating production of the first nuclear weapon.
81	Perkovich (1999), pp. 170-183, and Bidwai and Vanaik (2000), pp. 196-198. The decision seemed based on intuition, bureaucratic and technological momentum, and the personal, enigmatic calculations of a politically beleaguered prime minister under the influence of trusted nuclear scientists. In terms of enhancing domestic and international status, the demonstration of a nuclear explosive capacity was rational, even if it proved ineffective.
82	Ibid, pp. 185-186.
83	Ibid, pp. 200-201. Desai became still more averse to an Indian bomb as he became familiar with the Atomic Energy Commission. In an exchange in the Lok Sabha on 13 July 1977, he expressed contempt for those who had conducted the Pokhran test: "[T]he explosion that was made here for peaceful purposes – as it was claimed – has been misunderstood. And, therefore, it created all these difficulties. There is no question of any other explosion now for peaceful purposes."
84	Ibid, pp. 201-202.
85	Ibid, pp. 204-205, and Bidwai and Vanaik (2000), pp. 94-95.
86	Lawrence Lifschultz (personal communication with the author) recounted how Bhutto publicly claimed that the US had organised the coup precisely because he was pursuing a nuclear option. According to Lifschultz, close associates of Bhutto, plus several of his opponents and US sources, have alleged in interviews that the 1977 agitation led by the Pakistan National Alliance was covertly sustained by US efforts to bring down Bhutto and replace him with General Zia-ul Huq, who, elements in the Carter Administration believed, would halt progress on Pakistan's nuclear programme. However, Zia would ultimately pour vast resources into the nuclear programme once both the Carter and Reagan Administration made a strategic choice in 1979 to ignore it while accepting Zia's close cooperation in sustaining the US-backed 'jihad' against Soviet forces in Afghanistan. Imprisoned and awaiting execution, Bhutto wrote a fiery polemic, ultimately published under the title 'If I Am Assassinated', in which he described his confrontation with the US because of his determination to acquire a nuclear capability and alleged the US had played a key role in his overthrow.
87	Perkovich (1999), p. 217.
88	Ibid, pp. 209-210.
89	Ibid, p. 221. Lawrence Lifschultz (personal communication with the author) added that US military and financial support for the *mujahideen* began six months before the Soviet invasion and was intended to destabilise the pro-Soviet regime that had taken power in April 1978. The *mujahideen* were a group of Islamists whom Bhutto had trained as Pakistani assets in a complicated gambit he was playing with Daud, the then Afghan leader. See also Lifschultz, 'Afghanistan: The Not So New Rebellion', *Far Eastern Economic Review*, December/January 1980/81.
90	Ibid, pp. 237-238. The BJP had been formed in April 1980 essentially as the renamed Jana Sangh party, which had constituted the right-wing faction of the Desai coalition government. Vajpayee's deputy was the strongly pro-nuclear L.K. Advani, a former president of Jana Sangh.
91	Ibid, p. 232. Indira Gandhi, quoted in 10 July 1981 Indian Press, cited in US Embassy (New Delhi) to Secretary of State, June 1982, cable no. 11254, p16, in FOIA files, India, National Security Archive, Washington, D.C.
92	Ibid, pp. 240-241. Pakistani leaders were concerned by the possibility of Indian-Israeli collaboration.
93	Ibid, pp. 242-244. In the absence of any Pakistani provocation in the form of a nuclear test, her bad experience of the 1974 test when scientists misled her probably played a significant part.

94	Ibid, pp. 244-249. Sarabhai, India's leading space scientist, had seen the space programme as an entirely peaceful means to leapfrog India into modernity by stimulating the growth of technology in the fields of electronics, communications, cybernetics and material engineering. Under his leadership work had begun on India's first satellite launch vehicle, the SLV-3. Success meant that India had gained the capacity to produce a medium-range ballistic missile.
95	Ibid, p. 255. Parliamentarians for Global Action, a New York-based NGO, initiated the idea and coordinated the approach to governments. The aim was to revive negotiations on a Comprehensive Test Ban Treaty at a particularly dangerous moment in the Cold War. Indira Gandhi was the first leader to join. Led by Swedish Prime Minister Olof Palme until his assassination in 1986, it resulted in the Stockholm Declaration. At the Third UN Special Session on Disarmament in 1988, Palme's successor Ingvar Carlsson said that this '... stressed that all states have the responsibility to uphold the rule of law in international relations. Those who possess nuclear weapons have a crucial role... One important step would be to prohibit the use of nuclear weapons. And I believe that the time has come to explore the possibility of such a step...' The primary value of the initiative was that it raised the level of political awareness and action around the world; and it awakened the realisation among non-nuclear states that they could influence the nuclear weapon states.
96	Ibid, pp. 255-259.
97	Ibid, pp. 262-263.
98	Ibid, p. 297.
99	Ibid, pp. 278-279. Codenamed 'Exercise Brasstacks', it was predicated on a scenario in which an insurgency in Kashmir had become unmanageable and Sikh militants in Indian Punjab were declaring an independent state. These developments were scripted to have encouraged Pakistan to intervene to detach Kashmir and the independent state from India, prompting an Indian counteroffensive into Pakistan. Indian planners failed to realise that Pakistan was conducting its own annual exercises on their side of the border in the same region at the same time. When Pakistan detected the massive Indian troop deployments, it moved forces to counter them. Rajiv Gandhi returned from holiday to be briefed belatedly on the rapidly escalating crisis. He ordered a massive airlift of troops into the Punjab, triggering further mutual misunderstandings and consideration of pre-emptive attacks. Finally, the dormant telephone hotline was activated, and both sides agreed to talks and withdrawals.
100	Ibid, pp. 289-290.
101	Ibid, pp. 280-281. A.Q. Khan gave the interview on 28 January 1987, as the confrontation over Exercise Brasstacks reached its climax. However, as it was not published until well after the Indo-Pak crisis subsided, it did not achieve what some suspected was an attempt to inject an element of 'nuclear deterrence'. Had it been released immediately, Perkovich commented, such 'promiscuous nuclear saber rattling could exacerbate crisis instability rather than achieve deterrence.'
102	Lawrence Lifschultz (personal communication with the author) was informed by US officials who had access to the FBI report that Zia's aircraft exploded in what was widely believed to have been a successful assassination.
103	Perkovich (1999), pp. 297-298.
104	UN General Assembly, Document A/S-15/12, India letter, 20 May 1988 (New York, 1988).
105	Perkovich (1999), p. 298. Lawrence Lifschultz (personal communication with the author) was told by personal friends of Rajiv Gandhi that he was always sceptical about India becoming a nuclear weapon state. He grasped the essential point that possessing nuclear weapons could easily create greater insecurity and danger. Indeed, he was close to the view that the best defence against nuclear

106 Perkovich (1999), pp. 300-301. The Pakistan tests were announced by Army Chief of Staff General Mirza Aslam Beg, revealing how the military had taken control of the nuclear and missile programmes. As in 1974, the successful Indian missile test was trumpeted as part of its anti-colonial 'nuclear nationalism'.
107 Ibid, p. 303.
108 Ibid, p. 302. Quoted in Sidhu, 'The Development of an Indian Nuclear Doctrine', pp. 223-224.
109 Ibid, pp. 306-312. By some accounts, particularly Seymour Hersh, 'On the Nuclear Edge', *New Yorker* March 1993, the two states verged on nuclear war. Hersh quoted Richard Kerr, Deputy Director of the CIA at the time, as saying that this was 'a closer shave than the Cuban missile crisis.' Perkovich chronicled the events in some detail, and concluded that Hersh's assessment – that nuclear deterrence first began operating between India and Pakistan in the 1990 crisis and helped avert war – contained serious factual and interpretive flaws.
110 Ibid, pp. 308-309. Michael Krepon and Mishi Faruqee, eds, 'Conflict Prevention and Confidence-Building Measures in South Asia: The 1990 Crisis', Occasional Paper no. 17, Henry L. Stimson Center, Washington, D.C., 1994, pp. 30-31; Hersh, 'On the Nuclear Edge', p. 64; interviews by Perkovich with US officials, 1997 and 1998. From extensive interviews with senior Pakistani military officers in 1998-2001, Lawrence Lifschultz (personal communication with the author) came to believe that Hersh was wrong to claim that the Pakistanis loaded a nuclear weapon on an attack aircraft in plain view of US satellite surveillance, with orders to fly to its target if India crossed the Line of Control in Kashmir – meaning, in reprisal for a conventional Indian attack. However, it is true that Pakistan has refused to adopt a no-first-use doctrine.
111 Ibid, p. 309. As recalled by the then US Ambassador Robert Oakley to Perkovich, interview 14 January 1998.
112 Ibid, p. 312. Interview with Perkovich, Rawalpindi, 1992.
113 Ibid, pp. 314-316.
114 Ibid, p. 334. Also see Edward A. Gargan, 'Demands Growing for an India that's Truly Hindu', *The New York Times*, 24 January 1993, pA2.
115 Ibid, pp. 340-344.
116 Ibid, p. 343. Interview by Perkovich with a high-ranking Pakistani Foreign Ministry official, Islamabad, June 1994.
117 Ibid, pp. 345-348.
118 Annex to letter dated 17 June 1994 from Ambassador M.H. Ansari, India's Permanent Representative to the UN Secretary-General, published as UN General Assembly document A/49/181, 20 June 1994.
119 'WHO's Request for an Advisory Opinion of the International Court of Justice on Legality of Nuclear Weapons: Counter-Memorial of the Government of the Republic of India', pp. 17-18, in *Legality of the Use by a State of Nuclear Weapons in Armed Conflict (Request for Advisory Opinion Submitted by the World Health Organization), Written Comments on the Written Statements (Originals) (Article 66, Paragraph 4 of the Statute)*, International Court of Justice, June 1995.
Lawrence Lifschultz (personal communication with the author) about one of the drafters of both statements whom he knew: 'Every word of them was written with integrity. He is bitterly anti-Kalam and the way Kalam pushed forward his agenda from government to government, traitor-baiting and national security-baiting every politician who stood in his way. Occasionally, like with Rajiv Gandhi, India's nuclear fanatic couldn't win out and tapped his foot until his next chance.'
120 Perkovich (1999), p. 350.
121 Perkovich (1999), pp. 358-361. In the run-up to the NPT extension conference, the Indian government came under heavy pressure from the BJP, with their leader Vajpayee declaring for the first time that his party would build nuclear weapons if it came to power: 'The BJP is in favour of a nuclear-weapon-free

world, but not for a world in which a few countries possess nuclear weapons and the rest are subject to their hegemony.' Paradoxically, a package of steps towards nuclear disarmament agreed to by the P5 to secure indefinite NPT extension provided added stimulus to India's drive to test nuclear weapons – especially an undertaking to conclude a CTBT by 1996. In October 1995 Vajpayee, serving on India's delegation to the UN General Assembly's disarmament session, said that indefinite NPT extension had 'legitimised for all time... the division of the world into nuclear haves and have nots.' Statement by Atal Behari Vajpayee to the Fiftieth United Nations General Assembly, October 26, 1995, in Government of India, Ministry of External Affairs, *Statements by India on Comprehensive Nuclear Test Ban Treaty (1993-1996)*, p. 78.

122 Ibid, pp. 359, 363, 366 and 372. Republican Senator Hank Brown lobbied successfully for what became known as the Brown Amendment. When Clinton supported it, Rao warned him that such a clear tilt towards Pakistan would trigger an arms race. After the amendment was passed, the *Times of India* (18 December 1995) asserted that it was "the moment of truth" for Rao who until then had believed that the US was genuinely interested in non-proliferation.

123 Ibid, pp. 361-371. Rao innately disliked the notion of nuclear deterrence, and found the US position on non-proliferation so hypocritical as to be immoral.

124 Ibid, pp. 374-375. A 'United Front' coalition of 13 parties and backed by the Congress party took over, headed by the inexperienced H.D. Deve Gowda.

125 Ibid, pp. 383-384.

126 Ibid, p. 387. 'UN Council Seat for India Ruled Out', *Indian Express*, 18 December 1996, http://express.indiaworld.co.in/ie/daily/19961218/35350342.html.

127 Ibid, pp. 390-391.

128 Ibid, pp. 391-394.

129 Ibid, pp. 398-399.

130 Ibid, p. 400. Gujral interview with Perkovich, 9 March 1999. The transcript of the formal Clinton-Gujral meeting does not include this discussion (White House official interview with Perkovich, 1 April 1999.)

131 Ibid, p. 407. 'BJP Vows to Take Back Azad Kashmir', *Dawn*, 26 February 1998; Amit Baruah, 'BJP Statements Worry Pakistan', *Hindu*, 27 February 1998.

132 Ibid, pp. 409-411.

133 Ibid, pp. 411-415.

134 Ibid, pp. 415-420.

135 Ibid, pp. 417-419.

136 Ibid, p. 419. The Chinese nuclear threat was always implausible. See also Raj Chengappa and Manoj Joshi, 'Hawkish India', *India Today*, 1 June 1998, http://www.india-today.com/itoday/01061998/cover2.html; and Bidwai and Vanaik (2000), p. 66 and pp. 206-207.

137 Perkovich (1999), pp. 422-423. 'India Ratchets Up Rhetoric against Pakistan and China', *Agence France-Press*, New Delhi, 18 May 1998. See also Bidwai and Vanaik (2000), pp. 53-54 and p. 187.

138 Perkovich (1999), p. 423. See George Iype, 'Advani Wants Troops to Strike across LOC to Quell Proxy War in Kashmir', *Rediff on the Net*, 25 May 1998, http://www.rediff.com/news/1998/may/25geo.htm.

139 Ibid, pp. 418-419, and Bidwai and Vanaik (2000), p. 53.

140 Bidwai and Vanaik (2000), p. 97.

141 Ibid, pp. 186-187.

142 Perkovich (1999), pp. 424-435, and Bidwai and Vanaik (2000), p. 54 and pp. 98-106. There was confusion over the number and nature of both sides' tests. Neither the technical data released by each country nor evidence from international monitoring stations substantiated Pakistan's claim to have carried out six tests, and India's claim to have achieved a thermonuclear explosion.

143 Statement by Ambassador Robert Grey, US Representative to the Conference on Disarmament, Geneva, 2 June 1998, p. 4. He read for the record a statement by President Clinton on 28 May, which included this quote. See http://www.fas.org/news/pakistan/1998/06/98060201_npo.html.

144	See UN Security Council,Resolution 1172, 6 June 1998, http://www.un.org/Docs/scres/1998/scres98.htm.
145	Perkovich (1999), pp. 436-437.
146	Bidwai and Vanaik (2000), pp. 80-82 includes a stinging critique of India's hypocritical posturing over the CTBT: 'The very terms of the Indian debate on the CTBT were so shameful, dishonest and deceitful that they were even more dangerous than the Indian rejection of the treaty itself.' Two years later this played into the hands of the BJP, when it effectively carried out a sudden, undemocratic 'political coup', decisively shifting the direction of India on the nuclear question.
147	Perkovich (1999), pp. 441-442, and Bidwai and Vanaik (2000), pp. 76-80. In a section 'Nuclear Nationalism: the Sangh Factor', the latter describe how the tests were a key moment in a struggle for the 'soul of Indian nationalism'. See also Achin Vanaik, *The Furies of Indian Communalism: Religion, Modernity and Secularization* (London: Verso, 1997). Since the birth in 1925 of the Rashtria Swayamsevak Sangh (RSS), or National Volunteer Corps, their slogan has been 'Unite Hindus and Militarise Hinduism', encapsulating an aggressive, belligerent and exclusive nationalism. One of its members assassinated Mahatma Gandhi in 1948. With the political failure and historical decline of the Congress Party, the BJP (the parliamentary front for the Sangh) exploited the growing disarray and corruption, and made new converts among an increasingly hedonistic and insular urban elite. Having gained power, it mounted a concerted assault on Nehru's four founding principles for India: socialism, democracy, secularism and non-alignment. The result has been that a right-wing neo-liberalism holds sway over the economy; both secularism and democracy have been re-interpreted to favour Hindus; and India is now ruthlessly pursuing its ambition to become a Great Power, discarding the 'irrelevant moral posturing of non-alignment'. The joint statement issued by President George W. Bush and Indian Prime Minister Manmohan Singh in Washington on 18 July 2005 (see endnote 180) that the US would 'work with friends and allies to adjust international regimes to enable full civil nuclear energy and trade with India', with the implied acceptance of India as a nuclear weapon state, could be seen as a breakthrough for this strategy.
148	Tanvir Ahmad Khan, 'Defence Outlays in South Asia', *Dawn*, 10 March 2001. India's defence estimates for 2000-01 increased by an unprecedented 28 percent.
149	Bidwai and Vanaik (2000), pp. 106-107 and Perkovich (1999), pp. 436-437. See also a well-argued article 'Challenges to Nuclear Stability in South Asia' by retired Pakistani Brigadier General Feroz Hassan Khan published in the journal of the Center for Nonproliferation Studies at the Monterey Institute of International Studies, *The Nonproliferation Review*, 10, 1 (Spring 2003) abstract at http://cns.miis.edu/pubs/npr/vol10/101/abs101.htm#khan.
150	Lahore Summit 20-21 February 1999, The Henry L. Stimson Center, http://www.stimson.org/southasia/?sn=sa20020109215.
151	Bruce Riedel, 'American Diplomacy and the 1999 Kargil Summit at Blair House', *Policy Papers Series 2002*, Center for the Advanced Study of India, University of Pennsylvania, http://www.sas.upenn.edu/casi. Riedel was President Clinton's Special Assistant for Near Eastern and South Asia Affairs at the National Security Council at the time. He was a member of the US delegation led by Strobe Talbott sent to try to persuade Sharif not to retaliate with tests after India went overtly nuclear. As note-taker and the only official present during a face-to-face meeting between Clinton and Sharif at the height of the crisis, his account is authoritative and fascinating.
152	Ibid. However, Lawrence Lifschultz (personal communication with the author) argues that Sharif was already looking for a pretext to withdraw, and Washington provided it.
153	Raj Chengappa, *Weapons of Peace: The Secret Story of India's Quest to be a Nuclear power*, (New Delhi: Harper Collins, 2000), p. 437. Chengappa, a senior journalist with *India Today* with access to defence personnel, reported that India 'activated all its three types of nuclear delivery vehicles and kept them at what is known as

Readiness State 3 – meaning that some nuclear bombs would be ready to be mated with the delivery vehicles at short notice... Prithvi missiles were deployed and at least four of them were readied for a possible nuclear strike. Even an Agni missile capable of launching a nuclear warhead was moved to a western Indian state and kept in a state of readiness.' Cited in R. Rajaraman, M.V. Ramana, Zia Mian, 'Possession and Deployment of Nuclear Weapons in South Asia: An Assessment of Some Risks', *Economic and Political Weekly* (Bombay, India), 37, 25, (June 22-28, 2002).

154 See Indian Embassy, Washington D.C. website http://www.indianembassy.org/policy/CTBT/nuclear_doctrine_aug_17_1999.html.
A restrained but deeply sceptical critique by Air Marshal B.D. Jayal (Ret'd), 'Indian Nuclear Doctrine: A Discussion' appeared in the *Indian Defence Review*, 14, 3 (1999). For related commentary, see *Disarmament Diplomacy*, 39 (July-August 1999), http://www.acronym.org.uk/textonly/dd/dd39/39draft.htm.

155 T. Jayaraman, 'Questions about capabilities', Nuclear Issues, *Frontline*, 24 (September 1999), p. 93.

156 See http://nuclearweaponarchive.org/India/IndiaNPower.html.

157 'Pakistan Announces Nuclear Weapons Command-and-Control Mechanism', 3 February 2000, *The Acronym Institute*, http://www.acronym.org.uk/sasia/spmech.htm.

158 Lee Butler, *Uncommon Cause: A Life at Odds with Convention*, Vol II 'The Transformative Years', (Outskirts Press, 2016), pp. 300-313.

159 Seymour Hersh, 'Watching the Warheads: The risks to Pakistan's nuclear arsenal', *New Yorker*, 5 November 2001.

160 'Concern over Pakistan Nuclear Weapons', *Disarmament Diplomacy*, 61 (October-November 2001), http://www.acronym.org.uk/dd/dd61/61new03.htm.

161 'International Concern over Danger of Conflict in South Asia', *Disarmament Diplomacy*, 62 (January-February 2002), http://www.acronym.org.uk/dd/dd62/62nr01.htm.

162 Praful Bidwai, 'India Sharpens Its Nuclear Claws', Inter Press Service, 29 January 2002.

163 Paolo Cotta-Ramusino and Maurizio Martellini, 'Nuclear safety, nuclear stability and nuclear strategy in Pakistan: a concise report of a visit by Landau Network – Centro Volta', 21 January 2002, http://www.mi.infn.it/~landnet/Doc/pakistan.pdf. The authors interviewed Pakistan's Foreign Minister Abdul Sattar, and nearly 80 military and strategic planning experts including General Mizra Aslam Beg and the Director of the Army's Strategic Plan Division, General Khalid Kidwai. General Kidwai stated that 'for the time being' Pakistan did not intend to develop and publish a nuclear doctrine like India's.

164 See Achin Vanaik, 'Deterrence or a Deadly Game? Nuclear Propaganda and Reality in South Asia', *Disarmament Diplomacy*, 66 (September 2002). In this trenchant critique, he pointed out that the views of President Dr Abdul Kalam, Prime Minister Vajpayee, and a former Chief of Staff of the Indian Army, General V.P. Malik, on the efficacy of nuclear deterrence were contradictory. Vanaik then argued that Indian brinkmanship effectively made the prospect of war hostage to the actions of a small group of terrorists who were not fully controllable by either the Indian or Pakistani governments. Moreover, the only coercive diplomacy that really worked was neither India's nor Pakistan's, but that of the US.

165 Mayed Ali, 'Tactical N-Warheads Moved along Borders', *The News*, Islamabad, 28 May 2002. Cited in Rajaraman, 2002.

166 'India and Pakistan Camped on Brink of War over Kashmir', *Disarmament Diplomacy*, 65 (July-August 2002), http://www.acronym.org.uk/dd/dd65/65nr01.htm.

167 Interview with the *Dainik Jagran* newspaper, 14 June 2002. See News Review, *Disarmament Diplomacy*, 66 (September 2002), http://www.acronym.org.uk/dd/dd66/66nr02.htm.

168 Robert H. Reid, 'Musharraf: Nukes Deterred India War', Associated Press, 18 June 2002.

169 Achin Vanaik, 'False hope in deterrence," *The Hindustan Times*, 29 May 2002.

170 Praful Bidwai, 'Smug Nuclear South Asians', *The News International*, 13 June

2002.
171 Praful Bidwai, 'Chilling nuclear disclosure', *The News International*, 2 January 2003.
172 Indian Statement on 'Operationalisation' of Nuclear Doctrine, 4 January 2003, http://meadev.nic.in/news/official/20030104/official.htm. See Praful Bidwai, 'Creating The Nuclear Command', *rediff.com*, 13 January 2003.
173 Rajesh Mahapatra, 'India: Nuclear Deterrent Averted War', The Associated Press, 9 June 2002.
174 'Further Escalation of Political, Nuclear Tensions in South Asia', *Disarmament Diplomacy*, 70 (February-April 2003), http://www.acronym.org.uk/dd/dd70/70nr04.htm.
175 Praful Bidwai, 'Pakistan's nuclear dilemma', *Asia Times*, 6 January 2004.
176 Seymour M. Hersh, 'The Deal: Why is Washington going easy on Pakistan's nuclear black marketeers?', *The New Yorker*, 8 March 2004.
177 Pervez Hoodbhoy, 'For God and Profit', *Newsline*, February 2004.
178 J. Sri Raman, 'India-Pakistan Talks: Hotline to a Higher Nuclear Status?', *truthout*, 21 June 2004.
179 Praful Bidwai, 'A gaffe, or a historic choice?', *Frontline*, 22, 01 (1-14 January 2005), http://www.flonnet.com/fl2201/stories/2005-114007112400.htm.
180 Praful Bidwai, 'The Seven-Year N-Itch Hasn't Ended', *The News International*, 14 May 2005.
181 Press Release, Embassy of India, Washington, D.C., 28 June 2005, http://www.indianembassy.org/press_release/2005/June/31.htm.
182 Joint Statement Between President George W. Bush and Prime Minister Manmohan Singh, Washington, D.C., 18 July 2005, http://www.whitehouse.gov/news/releases/2005/07/print/20050718-6.html. During Bush's visit to India on 2 March 2006, he and Singh endorsed the agreement.
183 Michael Krepon, 'Is the U.S.-India nuclear cooperation agreement good or bad for proliferation?', *PacNet* 37A, Pacific Forum Center for Strategic and International Studies, (6 September 2005).
184 Anwar Iqbal, 'N-war in South Asia likely, warns US report', *Dawn*, 1 August 2005. A Congressional Research Services Issue Brief *Pakistan-U.S. Relations*, 26 July 2005, (see http://www.fas.org/sgp/crs/row/IB94041.pdf), considered that the arms race between India and Pakistan posed the most likely prospect for the future use of nuclear weapons by states.
185 Jo Johnson and Farhan Bokhari, 'Pakistan says Indian deal will hit arms treaty', *Financial Times*, 16 March 2006, http://news.ft.com/cms/s/674bb44c-b51f-11da-aa90-0000779e2340.html#.
186 Joby Warwick, 'Pakistan Expanding Nuclear Program: Plant Underway Could Generate Plutonium for 40 to 50 Bombs a Year, Analysts Say', *Washington Post*, 24 July 2006.
187 'Nuclear Weapons: Who Has What at a Glance', Arms Control Association, https://www.armscontrol.org/factsheets/Nuclearweaponswhohaswhat.

CHAPTER FIVE

MORALITY AND LEGALITY

Nuclear deterrence entails a fundamental moral deception: using the most immoral means imaginable to achieve what governments of nuclear states claim are their highest moral ends. The Cold War mindset required the creation of the morally bogus concept of a 'just deterrent' by those who believed they could save themselves by threatening to destroy potentially all civilisation and the entire ecosystem of the planet. Such a construct was necessary in order to mask the reality that nuclear weapons are the ultimate negation of the principle of proportionality between means and ends that used to characterise international politics.

Some pro-nuclear commentators contend that disproportionality is what makes nuclear deterrence credible. They complain that it is only since the military came under more pressure to be seen to use proportionate force for legal and moral reasons that questions have arisen about the credibility of nuclear deterrence.

Evidence of the lengths to which practitioners of nuclear deterrence are prepared to go in order to sustain credibility was revealed in a partly declassified 1995 assessment by US Strategic Command called *Essentials of Post-Cold War Deterrence*. This asserted that having US military or civilian leaders 'appear to be potentially "out of control" can be beneficial to creating and reinforcing fears and doubts within the minds of an adversary's decision makers.' It advocated that a perception that the US 'may become irrational and vindictive if its vital interests are attacked should be a part of the national persona we project to all adversaries.'[1]

Such irresponsible thinking risks provoking responses such as *Perimetr*, a Russian top-secret programme. According to *Jane's Intelligence Review*, if Moscow were to be attacked, or even if command links to key leaders were interrupted, *Perimetr* would automatically trigger a low-frequency radio signal. This would launch a communications missile transmitting the codes that would launch thousands of Russia's nuclear weapons against the US. The current status of *Perimetr* is unclear, though commentary in 1999 by a Russian analyst indicated that it remained operational.[2]

Acceptance of, and support for, disproportionality reinforces concern about the disregard for international law and morality shown by pro-nuclear deterrence advocates. Indeed, nuclear deterrence dogma should more accurately be called *state-sponsored nuclear terrorism*. Richard Falk is uncompromising: 'Nuclear weaponry and strategy represent terrorist logic on the grandest scale imaginable.'[3] It was appropriate, therefore, that the 2006 International WMD Commission chaired by Dr Hans Blix called their report *Weapons of Terror: Freeing the World of Nuclear, Biological and Chemical Arms*.[4]

The moral deception and associated hypocrisy deepened after President George W. Bush admitted that he no longer had any faith that nuclear deterrence would work against the greatest current threat to Americans: extremists armed with WMD. His administration's response was openly to plan to use nuclear weapons disproportionately, and even pre-emptively, in 'anticipatory self-defence' against attacks on US and allied 'vital interests'. The UK government, heavily dependent on the US for its nuclear capability, promptly parroted this blatantly unlawful posture, whereupon France followed suit. Possibly for the first time in the nuclear era, the fundamental immorality of threatening to use nuclear weapons was now plainly visible.

Another intrinsic, inescapable part of nuclear deterrence dogma is the generation of hostility and mistrust. By inhibiting cooperation in promoting true security, nuclear deterrence tends to be self-perpetuating. This adds another layer of deception, deepening the immorality further.

If nuclear deterrence fails or is considered unreliable, but nuclear weapons are seen as usable against undeterrable extremists armed with WMD, then the stage is set for new wars of unprecedented savagery. As already mentioned, nuclear weapons are terror devices that combine the poisoning horrors of chemical and biological weapons, plus inter-generational effects unique to radioactivity, with almost unimaginable explosive violence. New analyses reveal that even a regional conflict between India and Pakistan, for example, in which about a hundred Hiroshima-size nuclear devices were detonated on cities, would produce enough smoke to cripple global agriculture. Temperatures in the Northern Hemisphere would drop, leading to shortened growing seasons and loss of crops causing hundreds of millions of people to starve to death, even in countries far from the conflict.[5]

In 1985, even the Pentagon accepted the theory of 'nuclear winter' as valid. However, its response was reflected in the statement made by US Assistant Secretary of Defense Richard Perle while testifying to Congress a year before: 'Rather than eliminating nuclear weapons, the most realistic method of preventing nuclear winter is to build enough weapons to make sure that the Soviets will be deterred from attacking.'[6]

In 1984, New Zealand – the only Western-allied state to have rejected nuclear deterrence for its security – adopted a different approach, and discovered the consequences of committing such heresy. As the late David Lange, then Prime Minister of New Zealand, wrote:

> The test of membership of the ANZUS [Australia/New Zealand/US] alliance was belief in the doctrine of nuclear deterrence. As New Zealand found out, there wasn't any other test. Being a democracy wasn't enough; being well disposed towards NATO and the United States wasn't enough. You had to subscribe to deterrence to be in the alliance, and to prove it, you had to share in its risks. In face of the undoubted fact of New Zealand's rejection of deterrence, our diplomats struggled constantly to convince the United States and its allies that we had not abandoned the values of the West... [O]ur membership of ANZUS... led us too often into appeasement of deterrence and caused us too frequently to neglect our real interests. It offered nothing to New Zealand that was actually worth having. It was fool's gold.[7]

In a celebrated 1985 debate at the Oxford University Union against the US religious fundamentalist Jerry Falwell, Lange said:

> There is no moral case for nuclear weapons. The best defence which can be made of their existence and the threat of their use is that they are a necessary evil, an abhorrent means to a desirable end. I hold that their character is such that they have brought us to the greatest of all perversions, the belief that this evil is necessary when in fact it is not... It is a strange and dubious moral purpose which holds the whole world to ransom.[8]

Lange won the debate. The position adopted by New Zealand, and espoused with uncompromising clarity by him, is at the heart of the moral case against nuclear weapons. 'No nation,' he wrote, 'should carry the moral burden of having the capacity to devastate the planet.'[9]

The Nub of the Moral Argument

Nuclear deterrence doctrine entails an intention to explode nuclear terror devices over cities, and therefore the intention to commit multiple monstrous atrocities. The basis of deterrence is living by threats. The position is made clear to those states already branded as enemies: 'If you do anything to us we shall do the same and much worse to you.' In the real world, the laws that govern our conduct as citizens of civilised societies forbid the employment of threats and menaces in our interaction with one another. Therefore, if neighbours were found with loaded shotguns in their gardens with notices announcing their intention to use them if provoked, they would be indicted for an offence of 'issuing threats and menaces likely to lead to a breach of the peace'. A magistrate might well order confiscation of the guns and binding over both parties to keep the peace without weapons. For nuclear weapons, the analogy is that the neighbours have amassed enough high explosive laced with anthrax to blow up not only each other but the whole neighbourhood, making it uninhabitable for years.

The immorality of nuclear deterrence can be seen in the attempts to pretend that something so flagrantly wrong can be accepted as right. For example, it is outrageous that the following benediction was used in the religious ceremony to commission Britain's first Polaris ballistic missile submarine: 'Go forth into the world in peace: be of good courage; hold fast that which is good; render no man evil for evil; strengthen the fainthearted; support the weak; help the afflicted; honour all men; love and serve the Lord; rejoicing in the power of the Holy Spirit.'[10] Was it an ironic, veiled attempt to acknowledge this gross abuse by British political leaders in requiring the Royal Navy to operate such appalling terror devices when the last Polaris submarine was named *HMS Revenge*, and the last Trident submarine *HMS Vengeance*?

General Lee Butler USAF (Ret) had no doubt that nuclear deterrence is above all a moral question:

> By clinging to the extreme precepts of Cold War nuclear deterrence we erode the respect for life that anchors our sense of humanity, and the moral sensibilities that increasingly inspire us to contain the violence of war and the suffering of innocents.[11]

In 1997, Colonel Charles J. Dunlap, Staff Judge Advocate of US Strategic Command just three years after General Butler had been its Commander-in-Chief, warned that Butler's allegation that nuclear weapons are:

morally indefensible... if unanswered, it has the dangerous potential to undermine America's nuclear deterrent. While persons subject to the Uniform Code of Military Justice are obliged to obey lawful orders even if they conflict with their individual consciences, Butler's assertion questions the very legality of such orders. Even more troubling, his manifesto assaults the ethos of our armed forces – an ethos upon which America's future warfighting success depends... Obviously, when a military leader of General Butler's stature makes such a claim... moral uncertainty is introduced into the minds of thousands of conscientious and honorable men and women upon whom America's nuclear deterrent relies...[12]

This deeply disturbing statement exposes a warped perception of ethos, where the expedient need to sustain a policy of nuclear deterrence is the governing factor. He went on to warn potential adversaries 'not to miscalculate the resolve of the U.S. military. Should deterrence fail, our forces are – and must continue to be – ready to immediately execute orders of the national command authorities to employ nuclear weapons.'[13]

Nuclear Deterrence and the 'Just War' Doctrine

Insulation of the armed forces and citizenry of a nuclear weapon state from any moral or ethical concerns regarding the use of nuclear weapons is crucial if nuclear deterrence doctrine is to retain its influence. The concept of a 'just deterrent' deployed in the service of noble ends is therefore central to the argument.

In the debate on the morality of nuclear deterrence dogma, there is a tendency to argue from a Christian perspective. This is because the leading proponents are from the US and UK establishments, which have a long tradition of recruiting the most influential religious authorities in their causes as the professed guardians of the nations' moral values.

In 1997 Sir Michael Quinlan, a leading British champion of nuclear deterrence who had been Permanent Under-Secretary of State for Defence from 1988–92, published a booklet called *Thinking About Nuclear Weapons*.[14] As he explained in both this and an updated edition published shortly before his death in 2009, his natural starting point for an ethical appraisal of nuclear weapons was the body of concepts and criteria developed over a long period by Christian thinkers known as the 'Just War' doctrine. He added that people of other religions, including Islam, or other value-systems hold broadly similar concepts. The doctrine offers limiting principles for going to war (*jus ad bellum*) and its conduct (*jus in bello*).[15] While incurring some overlap with legal issues, this usefully illustrates how moral concerns have led and underpinned the evolution of good law.

Until World War II, states were considered free to go to war as an intrinsic right of sovereignty. However, *jus ad bellum* tempered this by requiring that:

* The cause is just
* There is a reasonable chance of victory
* The resulting good outweighs the harm inflicted, especially on the innocent

Following the horrors of total war culminating in the US nuclear strikes against Hiroshima and Nagasaki, even the victors found the political will to constrain their freedom of action thereafter, through binding international law in the form of the United Nations Charter. The Charter prohibits use of force except in self-defence against armed attack (Article 51), or as part of UN-approved enforcement action to maintain or restore international peace and security (Article 42).

By contrast, the principles of *jus in bello* invoke the entire body of what is known as the Law of Armed Conflict, drawn from international treaties and agreements such as the Hague Conventions, Geneva Conventions and Genocide Convention. The following three overarching principles govern the use, even in self-defence, of any weapon:

1) The right of belligerents to adopt means of injuring the enemy is not unlimited.

2) It is prohibited to launch attacks against civilian targets and the civilian population as such.

3) Distinctions must be made between combatants and non-combatants, so that non-combatants are spared as much as possible.

The US Naval/Marine Commander's Handbook accepts that these are part of customary international law.[16] Other more specific and interconnected principles are recognised, prohibiting the use of weapons which:

* Fail to discriminate between military and civilian personnel (*Principle of Discrimination*)
* Cause harm disproportionate to their preceding provocations and/or to legitimate objectives (*Principles of Proportionality and Necessity*)

* Cause unnecessary or superfluous suffering (*Principle of Humanity*)
* Affect neutral states (*Principle of Neutrality*)
* Cause widespread, long-lasting and severe damage to the environment (*Principle of Environmental Protection*)
* Use asphyxiating, poisonous or other gases, and all analogous liquids, materials or substances (*Principle of Toxicity*)

In light of the difficulties of reconciling use of nuclear weapons with these principles, it is simply unacceptable and deeply irresponsible for the government of a nation which prides itself on its democratic pedigree, championing of humanitarian values and respect for the law, to base its defence plans on nuclear deterrence. Any plea that such plans are designed to deter an 'evil force' is vitiated by the inescapable nature of nuclear weapons. As confirmed by Judge Mohammed Bedjaoui, President of the International Court of Justice when it gave its Advisory Opinion on the legal status of the threat or use of nuclear weapons in July 1996, nuclear weapons are the 'ultimate evil'.[17] This brings us back to the initial, inexorable reality: nuclear deterrence dogma is about using the most immoral means imaginable to achieve allegedly moral ends.

On 1 September 1998, no less than ninety-two Roman Catholic Bishops, members of Pax Christi USA, issued a statement entitled *The Morality of Nuclear Deterrence – An Evaluation*, which reviewed their position on the issue.[18] Their first concern was that, despite the end of the Cold War nearly ten years before, nuclear deterrence had become institutionalised. Also it had been expanded to include new potential aggressors, proliferators and so-called 'rogue nations', as well as protection of vital interests anywhere in the world. Thirdly, it had become clear that the US intended to retain its nuclear arsenal indefinitely. In calling, therefore, on the nuclear weapon states to eliminate 'these morally offensive weapons', they highlighted the following extract from a 1997 statement by the Vatican's Permanent Observer at the UN:

> The gravest consequences for humankind lie ahead if the world is to be ruled by the militarism represented by nuclear weapons rather than the humanitarian law espoused by the International Court of Justice. Nuclear weapons are incompatible with the peace we seek for the 21st century. They cannot be justified. They deserve condemnation. The preservation of the Non-Proliferation Treaty demands an unequivocal commitment to their abolition. This is a moral challenge, a legal challenge and a political challenge. That multi-based challenge must be met by the application of our humanity.[19]

The US Pax Christi bishops were unequivocal in their conclusion:

> Nuclear deterrence as a national policy must be condemned as morally abhorrent because it is the excuse and justification for the continued possession and further development of these horrendous weapons.[20]

In November 2017, Pope Francis went further than any of his predecessors by personally endorsing these positions.[21]

On 14 February 2008, I attended a lecture by Sir Michael Quinlan in which he presented his latest thinking on the morality of nuclear deterrence.[22] Nearly twenty years after the end of the Cold War, he argued that a position of unconditional rejection of any threatened use of nuclear weapons amounted to 'full-blown pacifism'. Thereby he ignored the range of formidable conventional deterrence and defence options now available, and other forms of asymmetric warfare which could be extremely potent – especially if conducted by a coalition of like-minded non-nuclear states whose populations were motivated by an aggressor sufficiently unprincipled to try nuclear blackmail.

Quinlan's persisting need for the UK to cling to possession of a nuclear arsenal overrode the implications of his commendable opening admission that nuclear weapons 'take the potential of all-out war between advanced states over a cliff-edge, into lunacy…' He swept aside any objections that nuclear deterrence has a credibility problem and incites nuclear arms racing and the spread of nuclear weapons; that nuclear weapons cannot be used discriminately or proportionately; and that nuclear weapon use would inevitably risk escalation. He failed to take into account the uniquely unacceptable long-term environmental and health consequences of even a limited nuclear exchange, avoiding any mention of the word 'radioactivity'. Instead, he retreated to a vague, inadequate conclusion that 'the right near-term course must be to do the best we can, *short of destroying deterrence*, in the spirit of the moral criteria.' (emphasis added)

Nevertheless, he then paid lip service to the need to study seriously the feasibility of abolishing nuclear weapons – only to dismiss this as unrealistic. Finally, he implicitly admonished Pope Benedict for asserting in his 2006 New Year message that 'the idea that nuclear weapons contribute to security was "completely fallacious".' When asked for an example of a morally and legally acceptable use of nuclear weapons in extreme circumstances, he gave as a target the Russian naval base at Murmansk. This disturbingly illustrated his Cold War mindset as a leading adviser to the UK government on this issue, which must be challenged.

Nuclear Weapons and Slavery

It is instructive to note that when the campaign to abolish slavery began in Britain in 1785, slavery was accepted in much the same way as nuclear weapons now are – by the establishments of a small group of predominantly Western/Northern nations and their allies. Three of the leading slaving nations were the US, the UK and France, whose governments today – regardless of who is in power – are the leading guardians of nuclear deterrence dogma. Pro-nuclear advocates, like Quinlan, argue that nuclear weapons are a 'necessary evil', 'cost-effective', 'not against the law', and anyway 'there is no alternative'. These were the slavers' arguments, condoned by the main churches.

They were outmanoeuvred by a small group of committed campaigners, who surprisingly focused on the *illegality* of slavery – not just its immorality and cruelty. For the first time, the law and public opinion were harnessed on a moral issue centred on human rights. This was what forced British politicians, who included most of the leading clerics in the House of Lords, to vote against a system that underpinned their wealth.[23]

The parallels do not end there. In their ruthless drive for nuclear weapons, the three Western powers imposed a new form of colonialism on the indigenous peoples of the Pacific by nuclear testing, and caused catastrophic health problems and environmental damage. Furthermore, they also diverted gigantic resources, without parliamentary approval, which otherwise would have been available for peaceful purposes.

Stigmatising Nuclear Weapons

It became possible for the overwhelming majority of states to prohibit chemical and biological weapons and to discard them as unusable because they came to be seen not only as inhumane, but as unethical, even cowardly, devices which moral and responsible military leaders would never order their forces to use. This was an important step in preparing the ground for the treaties banning such 'dirty', 'poisonous', and indiscriminate devices unworthy of being considered weapons. Similar stigmatisation by civil society of anti-personnel landmines and cluster munitions underpinned the successful campaign for treaties banning them.[24]

The far more repulsive and devastating characteristics of nuclear weapons, including genetic effects, need to be brought home to political leaders in particular, for whom possession of a nuclear arsenal has become imbued with fetishistic power.[25] Morton Halperin argued that nuclear weapons should be 'stigmatised', which they would be once they were recognised not to be instruments for fighting wars.[26] General Lee Butler agreed:

> Nuclear weapons are the enemy of humanity. Indeed, they're not weapons at all. They're some species of biological time bombs whose effects transcend time and space, poisoning the earth and its inhabitants for generations to come.[27]

The stigmatisation of nuclear deterrence received powerful reinforcement in 2017, when a citizen-led campaign focusing on the humanitarian implications of nuclear weapon use culminated in 122 states adopting a Treaty on the Prohibition of Nuclear Weapons – which is covered in more detail at the end of this chapter.

Legal Challenges to Nuclear Deterrence

Since the nuclear age began, there have been serious initiatives to outlaw nuclear weapons by a variety of states and citizen groups within the UN, beginning with the very first UN resolution, adopted unanimously, which called for the elimination of nuclear weapons and all other weapons of mass destruction. These continued, such as UN resolutions declaring the threat or use of nuclear weapons illegal, and attempts to include nuclear, chemical and biological weapons as subject to the 1949 Geneva Conventions. More recently, resolutions have called for a Nuclear Weapons Convention, an enforceable global treaty like the one banning chemical weapons.

Throughout the Cold War, all these initiatives were blocked or resisted by the nuclear weapon states using their political and economic power, including their Security Council veto. A massive anomaly now exists where they accept the illegality of chemical and biological weapons, but insist on their exclusive right to maintain their nuclear arsenals, thereby sustaining a discriminatory, immoral and destabilising position. This remains the case, despite the fact that the capacity for mass destruction of nuclear weapons puts them in a league of their own.

As the pre-eminent nuclear power in the world, the US has demonstrated that it will not accept any legal challenges to its position. Even before the emergence of a more aggressive nuclear posture under the administration of George W. Bush, the US Ambassador to the UN made the following surprisingly candid 1998 statement on the US position on the legal issue: 'Let me be clear: you will not make nuclear disarmament occur faster by suggesting that a fundamental basis of our national security for more than fifty years is illegitimate.'[28]

Figure 3. WORLD COURT ADVISORY OPINION ON LEGAL STATUS OF NUCLEAR WEAPONS – DISPOSITIF

THE COURT

(1) By thirteen votes to one,
Decides to comply with the request for an advisory opinion;

(2) Replies in the following manner to the question put by the General Assembly:

A. Unanimously,
There is in neither customary nor conventional international law any specific authorization of the threat or use of nuclear weapons;

B. By eleven votes to three,
There is in neither customary nor conventional law any comprehensive and universal prohibition of the threat or use of nuclear weapons as such:

C. Unanimously,
A threat or use of force by means of nuclear weapons that is contrary to Article 2, paragraph 4, of the United Nations Charter and that fails to meet all the requirements of Article 51, is unlawful;

D. Unanimously,
A threat or use of nuclear weapons should also be compatible with the requirements of the international law applicable in armed conflict particularly those of the principles and rules of international humanitarian law, as well as with specific obligations under treaties and other undertakings which expressly deal with nuclear weapons;

E. By seven votes to seven, (by the President's casting vote),
It follows from the above-mentioned requirements that the threat or use of nuclear weapons would generally be contrary to the rules of international law applicable in armed conflict, and in particular the principles and rules of humanitarian law;
However, in view of the current state of international law, and of the elements of fact at its disposal, the Court cannot conclude definitively whether the threat or use of nuclear weapons would be lawful or unlawful in an extreme circumstance of self-defence, in which the very survival of a State would be at stake;

F. Unanimously,
There exists an obligations to pursue in good faith and bring to a conclusion negotiations leading to nuclear disarmament in all its aspects under strict and effective nuclear control.

The track record of the Bush Administration demonstrated disregard, amounting to contempt, for international law. For example, its strategy to combat WMD undermined negative security assurances given to non-nuclear NPT signatory states. These comprise undertakings by nuclear weapon states not to use nuclear weapons against non-nuclear weapon states, including signatory states such as Iran and Iraq. The nuclear posture of the Bush Administration clearly signalled that it had no intention of honouring the unequivocal undertaking, given by all nuclear signatory states in the final document emerging from the May 2000 NPT Review Conference, to get rid of their nuclear arsenals.

Following President Obama's well-intentioned but ineffectual contribution to the debate, the Trump Administration's Nuclear Posture Review raises the prospect of replacing nuclear deterrence with pre-emptive use of nuclear weapons, courting escalation to nuclear war while brazenly flouting international humanitarian law.

The 1996 World Court Advisory Opinion

With the end of the Cold War, the first concerted effort to challenge the legality of nuclear deterrence was launched in 1992 by a coalition of international citizen organisations. Co-sponsored by the International Peace Bureau, International Physicians for the Prevention of Nuclear War, and the International Association of Lawyers Against Nuclear Arms, in 1994 the World Court Project helped to persuade the UN General Assembly to adopt a resolution requesting an Advisory Opinion from the International Court of Justice (ICJ), commonly known as the World Court, on the question: 'Is the threat or use of nuclear weapons in any circumstance permitted under international law?'[29] I participated as Chair of the project's UK affiliate.

The ICJ received twenty-eight written submissions from governments. It also held Oral Proceedings for two weeks in late 1995, at which twenty-two governments made statements, of which sixteen argued for illegality. The US, the UK, France and Russia – China took no part – were supported only by Germany and Italy in arguing for the Court to use its discretion not to answer the question. In all, over forty states plus the World Health Organisation gave evidence: this was more than twice the participation in any previous case in the Court's history. In addition, nearly 4 million individual Declarations of Public Conscience were presented to the ICJ in support of the case: this was the first time it had accepted 'citizens' evidence'.

After six months' deliberation, the Court gave its decision on 8 July

1996. It accepted the UN General Assembly's question, and gave a 34-page main Advisory Opinion, plus over 200 pages of separate statements and dissenting opinions by each of the fourteen judges. See Figure 3 for the final paragraph of the main Opinion, known as the *Dispositif.*[30]

Individual Judges' Positions. Five of the fourteen judges (one, from Venezuela, had died just before the case was heard) were from each of the recognised nuclear weapon states – also the permanent members of the UN Security Council. It was therefore encouraging that a verdict of general illegality was handed down. Analysis of each judge's position on use in the extreme case of self-defence revealed that seven were uncertain (including the Russian and Chinese), four thought it would be lawful (from the US, the UK, France and close US ally Japan), and the remaining three concluded that the question did not arise because any use was already unlawful under the existing rules of international law applicable in armed conflict. Thus ten judges were for illegality or uncertain, and only four in favour of legality. Moreover, the ICJ unanimously agreed that, even in such an extreme case, any use of nuclear weapons still must comply with international law.

Unique Characteristics of Nuclear Weapons. The ICJ cited the uniquely appalling characteristics of nuclear weapons: 'in particular their destructive capacity, their capacity to cause untold human suffering, and their ability to cause damage to generations to come.' Indeed, it added that only nuclear weapons 'have the potential to destroy all civilisation and the entire ecosystem of the planet.'[31] This effectively confirmed that nuclear weapons are in the same stigmatised category as chemical and biological weapons, which are banned regardless of size – only in most respects nuclear weapons are far worse.

Nuclear Deterrence Implicitly Condemned. The ICJ, wishing to avoid a direct conflict with the nuclear weapon states, did not specifically pronounce on the legal status of nuclear deterrence. This could have been linked to pressure from nuclear weapon state representatives at the Oral Proceedings on the case. For example, the French delegate warned 'against any pronouncement which, directly or indirectly, might imply judgment being passed on a defence policy based on deterrence.'[32] The UK echoed the US when it said that 'to call in question now the legal basis of the system of deterrence on which so many states have relied for so long for the protection of their peoples could have a profoundly destabilising effect.'[33]

Despite such pressures, the Court did discuss the relationship between the threat and use of force, and thus implicitly nuclear deterrence:

> Whether a signalled intention to use force if certain events occur is or is not a 'threat' within Article 2, paragraph 4 of the [UN] Charter depends upon several factors. *If the envisaged use of force is itself unlawful, the stated readiness to use it would be a threat prohibited under Article 2, paragraph 4.* Thus it would be illegal for a State to threaten force to secure territory from another State, *or to cause it to follow or not follow certain political or economic paths.* The notions of 'threat' and 'use' of force under Article 2, paragraph 4 of the Charter stand together in the sense that *if the use of force itself in a given case is illegal – for whatever reason – the threat to use such force will likewise be illegal.* In short, if it is to be lawful, the declared readiness of a State to use force must be a use of force that is in conformity with the Charter. For the rest, *no State – whether or not it defended the policy of deterrence – suggested to the Court that it would be lawful to threaten to use force if the use of force contemplated would be illegal.*[34] (emphasis added)

As already mentioned, the ICJ determined unanimously that any threat or use of nuclear weapons must conform to international humanitarian law. Thereby, it confirmed that the principles of the law of armed conflict apply to nuclear weapons. Then in paragraph 95 it concluded: 'In view of the unique characteristics of nuclear weapons... the use of such weapons in fact seems scarcely reconcilable with such requirements.' There is no scenario where the use of even a single 100-kiloton UK Trident warhead – six times the explosive power of the Hiroshima bomb – could meet these requirements. Thus the Court adroitly affirmed the general illegality of the fundamental practice that constitutes nuclear deterrence.

Military Implications. The ICJ confirmed that the Nuremberg Principles form a part of international humanitarian law.[35] This has serious implications for all those involved in planning and deploying nuclear forces. In particular, what is at stake here is a crucial difference between military professionals and hired killers or terrorists: *military professionals need to be seen to be acting within the law* – military, international and domestic law. That is why they are constrained from using prohibited weapons of mass destruction such as chemical and biological weapons. They need to know that, through the ICJ Opinion, nuclear weapons are now effectively in the same category.

Self-Defence Caveat No Loophole. The ICJ had one caveat. It stated: '(I)n view of the current state of international law, and of the elements of fact at its disposal, the Court cannot conclude definitively whether the threat or use of nuclear weapons would be lawful or unlawful in an extreme circumstance of self-defence, in which the very survival of a State would be at stake.'[36] The nuclear weapon states argued that the use of small, precisely targeted nuclear weapons in self-defence would not be unlawful. However, the ICJ's caveat left no loophole. On the contrary, it placed the burden of proof as to legality on the nuclear weapon states, because they had neither specified any legal circumstance for use, nor convinced it that 'limited use would not tend to escalate into the all-out use of high-yield nuclear weapons.'[37]

First Use Against Non-Nuclear Threats Illegal. Of immediate relevance was the US *National Strategy to Combat Weapons of Mass Destruction* released on 11 December 2002. Echoed by the British government, this deliberately implied possible use of nuclear weapons against regimes or extremists armed with chemical or biological weapons. This was corroborated on 26 January 2003 in the *Los Angeles Times*, when William Arkin revealed that Pentagon documents leaked to him showed that plans had been made for the possible use of nuclear weapons in Iraq.

The ICJ Opinion strongly suggested that the Principle of Proportionality renders illegal the use of nuclear weapons in response to an attack with non-nuclear weapons. Even if the very survival of the state is threatened, use of nuclear weapons – like any weapon – must not kill civilians indiscriminately, permanently endanger the environment or seriously affect neutral states.

Again, the explosive power of even one Trident warhead, for example, means that there is no scenario where its use could be lawful. The US version carries up to eight independently targetable warheads, each with a yield of 475 kilotons, which amounts to almost 240 times the power of the 16-kiloton Hiroshima bomb per missile – but does not imply, of course, that the Hiroshima nuclear strike was lawful. Following the 1998 UK Strategic Defence Review, each UK Trident missile carried only three warheads each of about 100 kilotons – but that was still the explosive power of eighteen Hiroshima bombs.

Judge Weeramantry's Dissenting Opinion. All fourteen judges made separate written statements, known as dissenting opinions. In his 87-page opinion, Judge Christopher Weeramantry (Sri Lanka) analysed the legal status of nuclear deterrence in the greatest depth:

> The deterrence principle rests on the threat of *massive* retaliation, and as Professor Brownlie has observed: 'If put into practice this principle would lead to a lack of proportion between the actual threat and the reaction to it. Such disproportionate reaction does not constitute self-defence as permitted by Article 51 of the United Nations Charter.' In the words of the same author, 'the prime object of deterrent nuclear weapons is ruthless and unpleasant retaliation – they are instruments of terror rather than weapons of war.'[38]
>
> [D]eterrence becomes not the storage of weapons with intent to terrify, but a stockpiling with *intent to use*. If one intends to use them, all the consequences arise which attach to *intention* in law, whether domestic or international. One *intends* to cause the damage or

devastation that will result. The intention to cause damage or devastation which results in total destruction of one's enemy or which might indeed wipe it out completely clearly goes beyond the purposes of war. Such intention provides the mental element implicit in the concept of a threat...

Deterrence is not deterrence if there is no communication, whether by words or implication, of the serious intention to *use* nuclear weapons. It is therefore nothing short of a *threat* to use. If an act is wrongful, the threat to commit it and, more particularly, a publicly announced threat, must also be wrongful.[39] (emphasis in original)

NATO's Nuclear Trio Respond

In a press statement on 8 July 1996, the US Department of State asserted that the ICJ had declined to pass judgment on nuclear deterrence. It added:

> Its opinion indicates that the use of nuclear weapons in some circumstances would be legal. The position of the United States supporting the legality of use of nuclear weapons is as we told the Court. We believe that the use of such weapons would be legal when they are used in compliance with the law of armed conflict applicable to all weapons. Nuclear deterrence has played a vital role in maintaining our common security and defending the United States and its allies over the past 50 years. Nuclear deterrence continues to make an essential contribution to preserving peace, security, and stability. We do not believe that the Court's opinions provide reason to alter the common defense policy of the United States and its allies. These are advisory opinions of the Court. Advisory opinions state the Court's views on legal questions asked by international organizations. They are not binding on governments.[40]

This misinterpreted subparagraph 2E (see Figure 3), which if anything lent weight to illegality when the Main Opinion is considered in its entirety. Also, the US position left no doubt about the central importance of nuclear deterrence, overriding any considerations regarding international law or morality. Finally, although advisory opinions are not binding on governments, it was incorrect to allege that the legal questions were only asked by international organisations, when the question in the UN resolution was clearly asked by those governments that voted for it.

The British government's response to the Court's judgment, by foreign affairs spokesman Lord Howe, was predictably similar:

> The opinion of the Court has no implications at all for our defence policy. We see no reason to change the fundamental elements of UK and NATO defence policy. Like the Court, we believe that the use of

nuclear weapons would be considered only in self-defence in extreme circumstances. For the UK, self-defence must include collective defence. I believe that it is right for me to emphasize that... nuclear forces continue to have an essential role within our defence posture and that of NATO and that we shall retain them as long as they are necessary for our security.[41]

Apart from echoing the US in its total denial of the Court's findings, and implying that the law is irrelevant if it challenges an essential plank of defence policy, the UK seemed intent on extending cover for its position to include NATO.

France's response was as follows:

France takes note of the opinion given by the International Court of Justice on the question of the legality of the use or threat of nuclear weapons. These opinions, which are not acts of jurisprudence, have no compulsory force. [The opinion] recognizes that the use or threat of nuclear weapons may be legal in exceptional circumstances of legitimate self-defence as defined in Article 51 of the United Nations Charter. That is also France's position. Nuclear deterrence is aimed at prohibiting any threat to our vital interests, as defined in the last resort by the head of state.[42]

As with the US statement, subparagraph 2E had been misinterpreted as implicit legality for use of nuclear weapons in extreme self-defence. Not content with that, France further claimed that nuclear deterrence was directed at protecting French vital interests, with the clear implication that these extended beyond defence of the French homeland.

These statements from the three NATO nuclear powers ignored the facts that the ICJ confirmed that self-defence is subject to international humanitarian law and that, if a weapon's effects inevitably render its use unlawful, then using it even in extreme self-defence does not make it lawful. A US Military Tribunal in the 1948 Krupp trial noted the applicability of the rules of the Law of Armed Conflict to extreme circumstances:

To claim that they can be wantonly – and at the sole discretion of any one belligerent – disregarded when he considers his own situation to be critical, means nothing more or less than to abrogate the laws and customs of war entirely.[43]

In its oral argument to the ICJ, the US was at least refreshingly candid about the impact of a finding that nuclear deterrence might be unlawful:

[E]ach of the Permanent Members of the Security Council has made an immense commitment of human and material resources to acquire and maintain stocks of nuclear weapons and their delivery systems, and many other States have decided to rely for their security on these nuclear capabilities. If these weapons could not lawfully be used in individual or collective self-defense under any circumstances, there would be no credible threat of such use in response to aggression and deterrent policies would be futile and meaningless. In this sense, it is impossible to separate the policy of deterrence from the legality of the use of the means of deterrence. Accordingly, any affirmation of a general prohibition on the use of nuclear weapons would be directly contrary to one of the fundamental premises of the national security policy of each of these many states.[44]

US Military Legal Assessments

Two Judge Advocates from the US Air Force assessed the ICJ Opinion. First, Lieutenant Colonel Michael Schmitt commented on its influence: 'Though non-binding, advisory opinions have enormous authority, for they represent articulations of what the world's most senior jurists believe the law to be.'[45] Colonel Charles Dunlap, Judge Advocate of US Strategic Command in 1997, wrote that 'it is influential in the court of world opinion and, indeed, may be accepted by a considerable number of countries as an expression of customary international law.' He added:

> The most important implication of the ICJ case for U.S. legal advisors and planners is its reflection of the international community's widely differing views as to the propriety of nuclear weapons. *Some allies or coalition partners in a given campaign might, for example, decline to support a nuclear mission under some or any circumstances* despite the fact that they are full, cooperative partners in conventional operations.[46]
> (emphasis added)

He went on to reveal a recent US decision to enhance the level of legal advice on the 'special issues that arise in the nuclear operations area'. Colonel Schmitt made the following additional comments:

> [A]ll the judges agreed that it would be difficult to employ nuclear weapons in a fashion consistent with international law... [I]f the threat to its survival derives from chemical or biological weapons, or even conventional weapons, may the state mount a nuclear response?... Perhaps more importantly, given the various security guarantees that have been made by the nuclear powers, does the non-decision on self-defense embrace *collective* defense?... in its substantive discussion, the Court [refers to] 'an extreme circumstance of self-defense, in which *its* very survival would be at stake.'[47] (emphasis in original)

The last point has serious implications for all non-nuclear states relying on extended deterrence. If, as is normally understood, the substantive discussion is taken to be more authoritative, then this means that the uncertainty is confined to individual self-defence by a nuclear weapon state, not to collective self-defence on behalf of non-nuclear states. It would follow, therefore, that *extended nuclear deterrence is unlawful under any circumstances.*

In his closing remarks, Colonel Schmitt observed that the ICJ had demonstrated institutional courage in taking on a highly politicised and extremely difficult issue, one from which it could easily, and within its discretion, have turned away. Therefore, in the long term the ICJ had enhanced its credibility by hearing the case. He concluded:

> The Court's opinion also makes it quite clear that the use of nuclear weapons is of questionable legality, that they are a suspect class. Those attempting to justify their employment in legal terms will henceforth bear a heavy burden indeed.[48]

UK Trident, Nuremberg and Prime Minister Blair

In October 1997, exactly fifty-one years after the Nuremberg War Crimes Tribunal delivered its judgment, as Chair of World Court Project UK, I wrote an Open Letter entitled *Trident and Nuremberg* to Prime Minister Tony Blair, the Royal Navy's First Sea Lord, Admiral Sir Jock Slater, and others involved in planning and executing deployment of Britain's Trident submarine force.

My letter drew their attention to the fact that, in light of the ICJ Opinion, the legality of Trident 'deterrent' patrols was in doubt, and that all those involved were flouting the Nuremberg Charter. In particular, it pointed out that the Nuremberg Tribunal firmly rejected the doctrine that in extreme circumstances the principles of humanitarian law could be abandoned. Principle IV of the Charter states: 'The fact that a person acted pursuant to order of his government or of a superior does not relieve him from responsibility under international law, provided a moral choice was in fact possible for him.'[49]

In a disturbing memorandum by the Royal Navy's top legal adviser, written before the ICJ announced its decision, the following informal advice was given on the legal position of Trident submarine Commanding Officers:

> Much will depend on the rationale of the ICJ's interpretation of the law, but if the Court were to deliver an adverse opinion, it would be

> ignored by the nuclear powers and *the servants of the states concerned, including SSBN Commanding Officers, would not be acting illegally in obeying orders and carrying out the policies of the state of which they were citizens.*[50] (emphasis added)

This was the Nazi defence at Nuremberg, which failed precisely because of Principle IV. In these circumstances, the reply from the Prime Minister's Secretary was misguided:

> Mr Blair hopes you will understand that, as the matter you raise *is the responsibility of the Ministry of Defence,* he has asked that your letter be forwarded to that Department so that they may reply to you direct on his behalf.[51] (emphasis added)

My reply stressed that the whole point of the Nuremberg Charter is that individuals, and especially leaders in war, should not be able to hide behind the State when taking decisions that might breach the principles and rules of international humanitarian law. That was why I sent individual copies to the First Sea Lord, the Secretary of State for Defence and others in the chain of command including the Commanding Officers of the operational Trident submarines, each having a specific individual responsibility. Then I reminded the Prime Minister of Nuremberg Principle III:

> The fact that a person who committed an act which constitutes a crime under international law acted as Head of State or responsible government official does not relieve him from responsibility under international law.

I warned him that, as the political leader given custody of the release codes, and ultimately responsible for authorising their release to allow the launching of Britain's nuclear arsenal, 'it is for you, Prime Minister, and no-one else to state your position on this matter. I look forward to your reply.'[52] This time, the response was more careful:

> There is no question of the Prime Minister seeking to avoid his responsibilities, as you seem to be concerned… [T]he Government is confident that the United Kingdom's nuclear deterrent is consistent with international law. It follows that those who are engaged in the operation and support of Trident, at whatever level within the Government, are acting legally under the Nuremberg Principles.[53]

It subsequently became clear that the UK government was reformulating its position on the legal challenges to the use or threat of use of nuclear weapons. A revised UK Joint Service *Manual of the Law of Armed Conflict* was published in 2004. The relevant section on nuclear weapons, which took into account the ICJ Opinion, read:

> 6.17. There is no specific rule of international law, express or implied, which prohibits the use of nuclear weapons. The legality of their use depends upon the application of the general rules of international law, including those regulating the use of forces and the conduct of hostilities. Those rules cannot be applied in isolation from any factual context to imply a prohibition of a general nature. Whether the use, or threatened use, of nuclear weapons in a particular case is lawful depends on all the circumstances. Nuclear weapons fall [sic] to be dealt with by reference to the same general principles as apply to other weapons. However, the new rules introduced in Additional Protocol I [to the Geneva Conventions] apply exclusively to conventional weapons without prejudice to any other rules of international law applicable to other types of weapons. In particular, the rules so introduced do not have any effect on and do not regulate or prohibit the use of nuclear weapons.
>
> 6.17.1. The threshold for the legitimate use of nuclear weapons is clearly a high one. The United Kingdom would only consider using nuclear weapons in self-defence, including the defence of its NATO allies, and even then only in extreme circumstances.[54]

This contradicted the Court's express ruling that 'the threat or use of nuclear weapons would generally be contrary to the rules of international law applicable in armed conflict, and in particular the principles and rules of humanitarian law.' Also, the assertion in the first sentence of this extract has been seriously challenged by the adoption of the Treaty on the Prohibition of Nuclear Weapons in July 2017. On 23 February 2017, following a 2016 challenge in the ICJ from the Marshall Islands over its lack of compliance with NPT Article VI requiring progress on nuclear disarmament, the UK Government further abrogated its legal responsibilities when it announced that it no longer accepted compulsory ICJ jurisdiction over cases relating to nuclear weapons policies unless all the other four nuclear weapon states recognised under the NPT accept such jurisdiction.[55]

Sir Michael Quinlan's Critique of the ICJ Opinion

Hostility to the ICJ opinion was intense among advocates of nuclear deterrence. In 1998, a British supporter of the World Court Project wrote to Sir Michael Quinlan, enquiring why he had made so little mention of the law in his book *Thinking About Nuclear Weapons*. His reply, which constituted a dismissive critique not just of the ICJ Opinion but also of international law in general, merits some discussion.[56] It offered a rare insight into the attitude of a leading

British exponent of nuclear deterrence to the legal dimension, and helps to explain how successive UK Governments have resisted efforts to outlaw nuclear weapons. His main points may be summarised as follows:

1) The Court did not state anything new about the issue
2) It was only an advisory opinion, which is non-binding
3) The judges found the task difficult and uncomfortable
4) No state would use nuclear weapons except in extreme circumstances
5) The final subparagraph 2F merely repeated Article VI of the NPT
6) International law is ineffective without enforcement
7) Would Israel be influenced by the Court's opinion?

In response, I have the following comments:

1) He misunderstood the ICJ's role, which is to draw together all the arguments relating to existing international law, and comment upon submissions from governments. On probably the world's most important and divisive issue in terms of its impact on security and politics, the world's highest legal authority had at last been given the opportunity to present its opinion.

2) While it is true that the ICJ opinion was only advisory, two US military assessments acknowledged its 'enormous authority', representing 'articulations of what the world's most senior jurists believe the law to be'. Moreover, '...it is influential in the court of world opinion and, indeed, may be accepted by a considerable number of countries as an expression of customary international law.'

3) As this was the first time that the ICJ had been asked a question that implicitly challenged the legality of nuclear deterrence, it was only to be expected that the judges – especially those from the recognised nuclear weapon states – would find the task difficult. It was also probably the first occasion on which any government of a nuclear-armed state had been obliged to make a legal case for its nuclear arsenal in a court with the jurisdiction to consider the question.

4) The argument that no state would use nuclear weapons except in extreme circumstances was disproved by US and UK statements over Iraq, in which use of nuclear weapons was threatened in response to, or even pre-emptively against, chemical or biological attacks on coalition forces.

5) The assertion that the final subparagraph 2F of the Court's opinion 'merely repeated Article VI of the NPT' is not true. Article VI states:

> Each of the Parties to the Treaty undertakes to pursue negotiations in good faith on effective measures relating to cessation of the nuclear arms race at an early date and to nuclear disarmament, and on a Treaty on general and complete disarmament under strict and effective international control.

The ICJ omitted the qualifying clause, '...and on a Treaty on general and complete disarmament...', by which the nuclear states have always tried to argue that the elimination of nuclear weapons must await the utopian achievement of comprehensive global disarmament. What is more, the Court seemed to express its frustration at the inadequate response by the nuclear weapon states by unanimously strengthening their Article VI obligation as follows: 'There exists an obligation to pursue in good faith *and bring to a conclusion* negotiations leading to nuclear disarmament in all its aspects under strict and effective international control.' (emphasis added) In what could well be the most important part of the ICJ Opinion, this also serves to rebut Sir Michael Quinlan's claim that it stated nothing new.

He cited Stephen Schwebel, the US judge, in support of this point. Immediately preceding Judge Schwebel's comments on subparagraph 2F was a long, detailed account of how Iraq was allegedly deterred by a US threat of nuclear weapon use from using chemical or biological weapons in the 1991 Gulf War. Aside from whether this was in fact the case, Schwebel's main argument was that, because the threat apparently worked, it was justified in law. He reinforced this by warning that as long as 'rogue' states or terrorists 'menace the world... it would be imprudent to set policy on the basis that the threat or use of nuclear weapons is unlawful "in any circumstance".'[57] This revealed an unacceptable attitude for a supposedly impartial judge, whereby he had allowed his evidently pro-nuclear views to take precedence over the law. No doubt for this reason his was not a majority ICJ view.

6) For a former top official in the UK Ministry of Defence to state that 'international law is ineffective without enforcement' is to denigrate, and reveal a serious misunderstanding of, the role of international law. Where does it leave the British military professional, whose prime distinguishing characteristic from a hired killer or terrorist is being seen to act within the law? Are the Hague and Geneva Conventions ineffective just because they are not backed by force? By such a simplistic dismissal, the whole edifice of compliance through example and respect for international law and institutions, patiently constructed over years of diplomacy and negotiations, is debased and diminished.

Finally, Quinlan cited Israel's non-compliance with international law as an argument against the validity of the Court's opinion. Israel was a disturbing choice, as it is an egregious offender against international humanitarian law. For example, terrorist attacks do not justify terror attacks in reprisal, let alone the brutal invasion of Lebanon in 1982 and 2006, and 2014 offensive against Gaza. Israel has also flouted UN resolutions on Palestine for almost fifty years. The implication was that Israel's behaviour might set the standard by which others are judged. On the other hand, Quinlan accurately reflected how the recognised nuclear weapon states have often behaved with respect to international law, especially when nuclear weapons are involved.

Trident Ploughshares v Scottish High Court

In 1999, the UK government came under pressure from Trident Ploughshares, a non-violent direct action campaign to symbolically 'disarm' the British Trident submarine force by disrupting activities at the submarine bases and nuclear weapon storage and refurbishment establishments.[58] Inspired by US actions invoking the Old Testament prophecies of Isaiah (2:4) and Micah (4:3) to 'beat swords into ploughshares', the leading Trident Ploughshares spokeswoman Angie Zelter decided to act after seeing that the UK government had rejected the ICJ Opinion. Almost twenty years on, the campaign continues, having lost none of its vigour or relevance.

The campaign's central thesis is simply that nuclear weapons six times as destructive as the one which devastated Hiroshima could never be used lawfully, so their threatened use must also be illegal. Campaigners have courted arrest in order to argue in court that they are upholding the law, and they are prepared to be imprisoned for doing so. They have steadily gained support among legislators and church leaders, particularly in Scotland, where the Faslane naval base on the River Clyde is home to the Trident submarine force. As with the campaigns to ban slavery and landmines, to gain votes for women, and to establish an International Criminal Court, they are tapping into a deep and growing awareness that they are on the right side of morality, commonsense, the law and public opinion. Also, the Nuremberg Principles are again being brought to bear on the Royal Navy.

Trident Ploughshares has achieved several acquittals in jury trials of activists in both Scotland and England. The most important of these so far was at Greenock Sheriff's Court on 21 October 1999, when the Sheriff instructed the jury to acquit three activists indicted for causing damage to equipment on a barge moored in Loch Goil used for minimising the underwater noise signatures of Trident submarines.

Because of this serious legal challenge to UK nuclear policy, the top Scottish law official, the Lord Advocate, requested the Scottish High Court in Edinburgh to rule on various points of law arising in the case, in a clear attempt to prevent other judges from following this dangerous precedent. During nine days of hearings, Zelter was able to make detailed submissions on the specifics of UK Trident and international law – which the UK government and courts would rather have avoided. In so doing, she became the first ordinary citizen to address the Scottish Law Lords directly in such a hearing.[59]

On 30 March 2001, under what is called a Lord Advocate's Reference, the Scottish High Court issued its judgment.[60] It found that the Sheriff had been wrong on the law: the deployment of UK Trident under the policy of nuclear deterrence was not unlawful, and that the defendants' actions were not justified under the doctrine of necessity or under international law. However, the High Court surprisingly assumed the following facts about UK Trident nuclear warheads:

* The warheads are '100 to 120 kilotons each, approximately eight or ten times larger than the weapons used at Hiroshima and Nagasaki.'
* The blast, heat and radioactive effects of detonation of such a warhead would be extreme, with 'inevitably uncontainable radioactive effects, in terms of both space and time.'
* '[T]he damage done, and the suffering caused, could not be other than indiscriminate.'
* It was not possible to use the weapons 'in restricted ways, defensively or tactically' or to direct them 'only against specific types of targets'.
* It was not possible to use the weapons in such a way as 'to remove this element of being indiscriminate in the suffering and damage which they would cause'.
* The weapons would be 'inevitably indiscriminate as between military personnel and civilians who could not be excluded from the uncontainable effects'.
* Even if much smaller warheads were used (and the possibility of this was not accepted in the context of the UK's deployment of Trident) 'one was still dealing with weapons of mass destruction, with uncontainable consequences'.

As to UK nuclear policy and intentions, the Court assumed the following:

- '[T]he familiar facts of deterrence and also statements in various forms from high Government sources indicating a willingness and intention to use these weapons in response not only to nuclear attack but in certain other circumstances.'
- If certain circumstances were to emerge, there would be a risk of threat and actual use.
- The continuing, and continuous, risk of actual use and indiscriminate consequences that are inherent in deployment of Trident nuclear weapons.

The High Court stated that its role was to reach 'its own conclusions as to the rules of customary international law, taking full account of, but not being bound by, the conclusions reached by the International Court of Justice.' It concluded that there were two 'fundamental flaws' in the contention that UK deployment of Trident is in breach of customary international law:

1) International humanitarian law is not concerned with regulating the conduct of States in time of peace. It specifically relates to armed conflict, and regulates the conduct of belligerents.

2) The current deployment posture does not amount to 'threat of use'.

Errors in the Scottish High Court's Findings

The High Court's conclusions were insupportable under international law and controverted by the very authorities upon which it relied.[61] It was wrong to claim that there are no restrictions on the use of force in time of peace. It also misinterpreted the ICJ Opinion as to the circumstances in which nuclear deterrence constitutes an unlawful threat under international law. Moreover, the High Court ignored the facts it had assumed on the effects of nuclear weapons.

As discussed earlier, the ICJ held that it is unlawful under international law for a state even to signal its readiness to use force which would be unlawful. It can be argued, therefore, that even deployment of a UK Trident-armed submarine on so-called 'deterrent' patrol in peacetime is unlawful. The basic argument follows:

1) Use of nuclear weapons would be unlawful, because the explosive power of each warhead and the radioactive effects

make them incapable of use without violating international humanitarian law.

2) In paragraph 47 of its Opinion the ICJ stated: 'If the envisaged use of force is itself unlawful, the stated readiness to use it would be a threat prohibited under Article 2, paragraph 4 [of the UN Charter].' The UN Charter is *applicable at all times.*

3) UK Trident is deployed under a policy of 'stated readiness to use', in order that nuclear deterrence is credible.

4) Nuremberg Principle VI states: 'The crimes hereinafter set out are punishable as crimes under international law:
   (a) Crimes against peace:
      (i) Planning, preparation... of a war... in violation of international treaties, agreements or assurances;
      (ii) Participation in a common plan or conspiracy for the accomplishment of any of the acts mentioned under (i);
   (b) War crimes...
   (c) Crimes against humanity...'

Besides, the Scottish High Court could not have it both ways. An attack on the UK which warranted a nuclear response under extreme self-defence at least implies a state of war, making humanitarian law applicable even under the High Court's disingenuous view of the matter.

The notion that nuclear deterrence may be unthreatening because nuclear delivery systems are deployed at low alert status is illusory. Only if the warheads were verifiably separated from delivery systems and stored ashore could such a claim be made. The reality from a potential target's point of view is that UK Trident warheads can be directed against specific targets within about a minute, and delivered from up to 5,000 miles in less than thirty minutes.

The threatening nature of the UK policy of nuclear deterrence is also evident from its substantial integration into US policy, including leasing Trident missiles and announcements echoing US threats to use nuclear weapons in, for example, Iraq. Indeed, it would appear that the US/UK invasion of Iraq qualified as a more immediate and specific level of threat which even the High Court recognised possibly would be 'equivalent to use', and therefore would be unlawful.

The High Court's principal error lay in following UK government policy on a central issue that it had been called upon to decide.

Whatever UK or US government policies on nuclear deterrence might be, the requirements of the law, at least as defined by the ICJ, are beyond reasonable dispute. Yet the Scottish High Court, purporting to apply the ICJ Opinion, emasculated it. The High Court made a serious mistake, therefore, in trying to find ways around the law in order to neutralise a fundamentally sound challenge to the UK government's nuclear deterrence policy.

In May 2007, the strongly anti-nuclear Scottish Nationalist Party (SNP) won enough seats in Scottish elections to gain power in Scotland. On 22 October 2007 the SNP-led Scottish government held a special summit, 'A National Conversation: Scotland's Future Without Nuclear Weapons', to discuss the implications for Scotland of the UK Government's decision to replace the Trident system.[62] An expert working group was appointed to explore, inter alia, options for Scottish planning, environmental and transport agencies to constrain the basing of UK nuclear weapons, with a view to forcing them to be removed from Scotland. Their report, published in 2009, drew attention to the fact that, in conformity with the NPT, the UK Government has given a commitment to multilateral nuclear disarmament.[63] It continued: 'It is therefore a question of *when* and not *whether* nuclear weapons will leave Scotland...' (emphasis in original).

A Treaty on the Prohibition of Nuclear Weapons

In 2007, the International Campaign to Abolish Nuclear Weapons (ICAN), a vigorous new civil society movement drawing upon the experience of the World Court Project and campaigns to ban anti-personnel landmines and cluster munitions, was launched in Australia. Six years later it had mobilised enough international public support and political will for the Norwegian government to host an unprecedented conference in Oslo in March 2013 to address the humanitarian consequences of nuclear weapon use, attended by 127 government delegations with key participation by the International Committee of the Red Cross.[64] Two follow-up conferences in 2014, in Mexico and Austria, resulted in adoption of a 2016 UN General Assembly resolution calling for urgent negotiations on a ban treaty.

A week of preliminary negotiations in the UN General Assembly in March 2017 set the scene for three more intensive weeks in June-July, where negotiations raced along in an unusually co-operative spirit after the nuclear weapon states and all but one of their allies boycotted the negotiations, bitterly protesting at the irresponsibility and naivety of the 130 participating states. On 7 July, a Treaty on the Prohibition of Nuclear Weapons (TPNW) was adopted by 122 votes to one – the sole objector being the Netherlands, which had been forced to participate after a citizen petition had resulted in a Parliamentary vote to do so. The hapless Dutch ambassador explained that his country had to vote 'No' because the TPNW was incompatible with NATO policy. The TPNW text includes specific prohibition of any threat to use nuclear weapons.

ICAN's successful campaign earned it the 2017 Nobel Peace Prize. However, the TPNW's lack of universality and comprehensiveness and weak clauses regarding withdrawal means that the struggle for a nuclear equivalent to the Chemical Weapons Convention must continue.[65] Trident Ploughshares are therefore intensifying their campaign, re-energised and inspired by ICAN's achievement.

Legal Impact of Trump's Interventions on North Korea

One significant consequence of US President Trump's recent intemperate rhetoric in response to North Korean leader Kim Jong-un's escalation of their trading of nuclear threats has been to raise alarm regarding the chain of command to authorise use of US nuclear weapons.

At a hearing of the Senate Foreign Relations Committee on 14 November 2017, General Robert Kehler USAF (Ret), Commander of US Strategic Command 2011-13, revealed that he would have refused an order to carry out a nuclear first strike if it did not satisfy the laws of war regarding necessity, proportionality and discrimination.[66] What he did not add was that, given their horrific effects, an order to use these weapons in any circumstances would fail those tests. Also, unsurprisingly there was no discussion at the hearing of the illegality under the UN Charter of attacking North Korea.

Summary

The uncontrollably indiscriminate nature of nuclear weapons and their long-lasting effects of radioactive contamination place the immorality of their threatened use in a unique, absolute category. Once the facts about them are understood, they stand condemned as the ultimate negation of the principle of proportionality between means and ends. Threatening to use them, therefore, entails a fundamental moral deception, and amounts to state-sponsored nuclear terrorism. Nevertheless, ever since the atrocities perpetrated on Hiroshima and Nagasaki, the US – with willing accomplices in successive UK and French governments – have gone to any lengths to deny this reality and justify their obeisance to nuclear deterrence dogma as 'practical moral commonsense'.

The refusal by the US, UK and France to concede the illegality of nuclear deterrence is understandable, but unacceptable. It is consistent with the hypocritical resistance of the most powerful states to outlawing previous unjust practices such as slavery.

The World Court Project harnessed the law and the public conscience to achieve the first serious legal challenge to nuclear deterrence. It exploited the end of the Cold War, when the international climate became more conducive to radical legal initiatives. It also developed a close partnership with a strong group of like-minded governments, and presented 'citizens' evidence' to the World Court for the first time.

In its historic 1996 Advisory Opinion, the Court determined unanimously that any threat or use of nuclear weapons should comply with international humanitarian law, of which the Nuremberg Principles form a part. It also decided that, because of their uniquely destructive characteristics and genetic effects from radioactivity, the threat or use of nuclear weapons would generally be illegal. This has serious implications for all those involved in planning and deploying nuclear forces. In particular, military professionals need to be seen to act within the law: this is the crucial difference between them and hired killers or terrorists.

Concerned and courageous citizens, such as those involved in the UK Trident Ploughshares non-violent direct action campaign, are aware that political will must be generated to persuade the governments of the NATO nuclear powers to comply with the law, morality and common sense. Inspired by former campaigns to abolish slavery, to gain votes for women, the World Court Project and adoption of the 2017 Treaty on the Prohibition of Nuclear Weapons, they are inviting arrest in order to educate public opinion and legislators through publicity from their trials, where their defence is that they, not the government, who are upholding the law. Acknowledgement of the US military's need to respect the law regarding nuclear weapon use has been one welcome consequence of alarm over US President Trump's unstable responses to the North Korean crisis.

Notes

1 *Nuclear Futures: Proliferation of Weapons of Mass Destruction and US Nuclear Strategy*, Appendix 2 (British American Security Information Council Research Report 98.2, March 1998), p. 25.
2 Kevin Sanders, 'The 'Nightmare Scenario', *The Nation*, 15 March 1999, p. 12. See also Steven J. Zaloga, 'Russia's "Doomsday" Machine', *Jane's Intelligence Review*, February 1996, pp. 54-56. See also Chapter 3, endnote 80.
3 Richard Falk, 'Nuclear Weapons and the End of Democracy', *Praxis International* 2:1 (April 1982), p. 7.
4 See http://www.wmdcommission.org.
5 Alan Robock and Owen Brian Toon, 'Local Nuclear War, Global Suffering,' *Scientific American*, January 2010, pp. 74–81. See also Steven Starr, http://www.nucleardarkness.org.
6 US Assistant Secretary of Defense, Richard Perle, testifying to Congress, cited by Kennedy Graham, *The Planetary Interest* (University College London Press, 1999), p. 40.
7 David Lange, *Nuclear Free – The New Zealand Way* (Auckland, NZ: Penguin Books, 1990), pp. 194–195.
8 David Lange, 'Nuclear Weapons Are Immoral', Oxford Union Debate, 1 March 1985. For an abridged transcript, see 'David Lange v the bomb', *Waikato Times*, 20 August 2005. For a full transcript see 'Nuclear Weapons are Morally Indefensible', (Argument for the affirmative, Oxford Union Debate, 1 March 1985), Rt Hon David Lange, Prime Minister, http://www.publicaddress.net/default,1578.sm;jsessionid=0B1F0867F79A5C8CF06EE892839C958B?ppid=1578&start=1#post1578.
9 David Lange, 'Nuclear disarmament: New Zealand', *The Planetary Interest*, Kennedy Graham ed. (University College London Press, 1999), p. 51.
10 'Form and Order of Service used in asking The Blessing of Almighty God upon Her Majesty's Ship Resolution in the presence of Her Majesty Queen Elizabeth the Queen Mother, Rosyth, 10 July 1971' (copy in author's possession).
11 General Lee Butler, 'Ending the Nuclear Madness', Nuclear Age Peace Foundation, *Waging Peace Series* Booklet 40 (September 1999), p. 4.
12 Colonel Charles J. Dunlap, Jr., USAF, 'Taming Shiva: Applying International Law to Nuclear Operations', *The Air Force Law Review*, 1997, p. 158.
13 Ibid, p. 171.
14 Michael Quinlan, *Thinking About Nuclear Weapons* (London: Royal United Services Institute for Defence Studies, 1997). Superseded by *Thinking About Nuclear Weapons: Principles, Problems, Prospects* (Oxford University Press, 2009).
15 Quinlan (2009), pp. 46–48.
16 United States Department of the Navy Annotated Supplement to the Commander's Handbook on the Law of Naval Operations (Naval Warfare Publication 9, 1987) (with Revision A, 5 October 1989) at 8-1 n.1.
17 *Legality of the Threat or Use of Nuclear Weapons* (Advisory Opinion of July 8), UN Document A/51/218 (1996), reprinted in 35 I.L.M. 809 & 1343 (1996). Also available at: http://www.lcnp.org/wcourt/opinion.htm.
18 See http://www.ccnr.org/pax_christi.html.
19 Archbishop Renato Martino, UN Permanent Observer of the Holy See, Statement to the UN First Committee, 15 October 1997.
20 Ibid.
21 Philip Pullella, 'Pope, in change from predecessors, condemns nuclear arsenals for deterrence' Reuters, 10 November 2017, https://www.reuters.com/article/us-vatican-nuclear/pope-in-change-from-predecessors-condemns-nuclear-arsenals-for-deterrence-idUSKBN1DA161.
22 Michael Quinlan, 'The Morality of Nuclear Deterrence', Farm Street Talk, delivered in the Church Hall of the Jesuit Church of the Immaculate Conception, Farm Street, London, 14 February 2008.

23 James Pope-Hennessy, *Sins of the Fathers: A Study of the Atlantic Slave Traders 1441–1807* (London: Weidenfeld and Nicholson, 1968). Also Ellen Gibson Wilson, *Thomas Clarkson: A Biography* (London: Macmillan, 1989) on the little-known British architect of the campaign to abolish slavery.

24 For a powerful commentary on these aspects, see Rebecca Johnson, 'Integrated Disarmament: a Prerequisite for Sustainable Nonproliferation', *Disarmament Diplomacy*, 82 (Spring 2006), http://www.acronym.org.uk/dd/dd82/82rej.htm.

25 See also Anne Harrington de Souza, 'Nuclear Weapons as the Currency of Power: Deconstructing the Fetishism of Force', *The Nonproliferation Review*, vol. 16, issue 3, November 2009, pp. 325–345, http://pdfserve.informaworld.com/567797__915796878.pdf.

26 Morton Halperin, *Nuclear Fallacy* (Cambridge, MA: Ballinger, 1987), pp. 49 & 138.

27 General Lee Butler, 'Ending the Nuclear Madness', (*Waging Peace Series* Booklet 40, September 1999), p. 10.

28 US Ambassador to the UN, Explanation of Vote on New Agenda Resolution,13 November 1998.

29 UN General Assembly Resolution 49/75K, adopted 15 December 1994. The author was Chair of the World Court Project's UK affiliate. The project is chronicled in: Catherine F. (Kate) Dewes, *The World Court Project: The Evolution and Impact of an Effective Citizens' Movement*, Doctoral Dissertation (unpublished), University of Canterbury Library, Christchurch, New Zealand, 1998. For a copy, and further commentary, see http://www.disarmsecure.org.

30 *Legality of the Threat or Use of Nuclear Weapons* (Advisory Opinion of July 8), UN Document A/51/218 (1996), reprinted in 35 I.L.M. 809 & 1343 (1996). Also available at: http://www.lcnp.org/wcourt/opinion.htm. See also John Burroughs, *The (Il)legality of Threat or Use of Nuclear Weapons: A Guide to the Historic Opinion of the International Court of Justice* (Munster: Lit Verlag, 1997).

31 ICJ Main Opinion, paragraph 36.

32 French Government Statement, Verbatim Record, ICJ Oral Proceedings, 1 November 1995, p. 36.

33 UK Government Statement, Verbatim Record, ICJ Oral Proceedings, 15 November 1995, pp. 86–87.

34 ICJ Main Opinion, paragraph 47.

35 Ibid, paragraphs 80–86.

36 Ibid, *Dispositif*, subparagraph 2E.

37 Ibid, Main Opinion, paragraph 94.

38 Ian Brownlie, 'Some Legal Aspects of the Use of Nuclear Weapons', *International and Comparative Law Quarterly* 14, (1965), pp. 446–447.

39 Dissenting Opinion of Judge Christopher Weeramantry, ICJ Reports, 1996, pp. 429–555.

40 Burroughs (1997), p. 153.

41 Lord Howe, UK Parliament House of Lords Defence Estimates Debate, 12 July 1996, *Hansard* Column 591. See also .

42 'France Says World Court Upholds Its Nuclear Stance', Reuters news despatch, 8 July 1996.

43 The industrialist Gustav Krupp was indicted at Nuremberg as representative of German heavy industry's role in armament production, but was too ill to appear. His son Alfred was tried in his place and convicted. See 'Trial of Alfred Felix Alwyn Krupp Von Bohlen und Halbach and Eleven Others', 10 LRTWC 139 (1949), quoted in United States Department of the Navy Annotated Supplement to the Commander's Handbook on the Law of Naval Operations 5-6 n.5 (Naval Warfare Publication 9, 1987) (With Revision A, 5 October 1989), known as the Naval/Marine Commander's Handbook.

44 ICJ Oral Proceedings, 15 November 1995, at 62, available at http://www.icj-cij.org/.

45 Lieutenant Colonel Michael N. Schmitt, USAF, 'The International Court of Justice and the Use of Nuclear Weapons', *Naval War College Review*, Spring 1998, vol. LI, no. 2), p. 93, http://www.nwc.navy.mil/press/Review/1998/spring/art6-sp8.htm.

46 Dunlap (1997), p. 160.

47	Schmitt (1998), p. 107.
48	Ibid, p. 110.
49	For definitions, see http://www.icrc.org/ihl.nsf/full/390.
50	Captain D.R. Humphrey, Royal Navy, Chief Naval Judge Advocate, 'Opinion' (undated 1996) (copy in the author's possession).
51	Letter from Mr G. Buckley, Prime Minister's Correspondence Secretary, to George Farebrother, Secretary of World Court Project UK, 24 October 1997.
52	Letter from the author to the Prime Minister, 29 October 1997.
53	Letter from Philip Barton, Prime Minister's Private Secretary, to the author, 24 December 1997.
54	*The Manual of the Law of Armed Conflict* (UK Ministry of Defence, Oxford 2004), pp. 117–118, paras 6.17-6.17.1.
55	Amendments to the UK's Optional Clause Declaration to the International Court of Justice: Written statement HCWS489, 23 February 2017, https://www.parliament.uk/business/publications/written-questions-answers-statements/written-statements/Commons/2017-02-23/HCWS489/. For more on the ICJ case submitted by the Marshall Islands, see http://www.theguardian.com/world/2016/jan/30/marshall-islands-sue-britain-india-and-pakistan-over-nuclear-weapons.
56	Letter from Sir Michael Quinlan to Christine Soane, 22 January 1998 (copy in the author's possession).
57	Dissenting Opinion of Judge Schwebel, pp. 10–14.
58	See http://www.tridentploughshares.org. Also Angie Zelter, *Trident on Trial: the case for people's disarmament* (Luath Press, Edinburgh, 2001).
59	See 'LAR Submissions and Court Records', Legal Section of *Trident Ploughshares* website, http://www.tridentploughshares.org/article963.
60	Lord Advocate's Reference No1 of 2000, Misc 11/00 H.C.J. (Scot.), also available at http://www.gn.apc.org/tp2000/lar/laropin.html.
61	For several of my arguments, I am indebted to Charles J. Moxley, Jr., a US attorney practicing in New York and author of *Nuclear Weapons and International Law in the Post Cold War World* (Austin & Winfield, Lanham, MD, 2000). Also see Moxley, 'The Unlawfulness of the United Kingdom's Policy of Nuclear Deterrence: The Invalidity of the Scottish High Court's Decision', in *Disarmament Diplomacy*, June 2001, pp. 7–14, available at http://www.acronym.org.uk/dd/dd58/58moxle.htm.
62	See http://www.acronym.org.uk/textonly/dd/dd86/86scot.htm.
63	*Working Group Report on Scotland Without Nuclear Weapons*, Report to Scottish Ministers, August 2009, http://www.scotland.gov.uk/Resource/Doc/288148/0088043.pdf.
64	Rebecca Johnson, 'Ukraine and Nayarit: The humanitarian case for nuclear disarmament', *Bulletin of the Atomic Scientists*, 14 March 2014, http://thebulletin.org/ukraine-and-nayarit-humanitarian-case-nuclear-disarmament. Also see International Campaign to Abolish Nuclear Weapons, http://www.icanw.org.
65	http://www.reachingcriticalwill.org/images/documents/Disarmament-fora/nuclear-weapon-ban/documents/TPNW.pdf. For an authoritative commentary, see Richard Falk, 'Challenging Nuclearism: the Nuclear Ban Treaty Assessed', http://apjjf.org/2017/14/Falk.html.
66	See https://www.theguardian.com/us-news/2017/nov/14/us-military-nuclear-weapons-strike-senate-trump .

CHAPTER SIX

SAFER SECURITY STRATEGIES

The current strategy of countering nuclear proliferation has failed. Led by the US and imposed on NATO, this strategy – underpinned by nuclear deterrence dogma – seeks by military means to prevent other states from acquiring nuclear weapons. Yet the entry of Israel, India, Pakistan, and North Korea into the closely guarded sanctum of nuclear weapon states provides striking evidence of its failure. What is worse, blind acceptance of nuclear deterrence by these proliferating states is encouraging reckless posturing on their part.

Nuclear deterrence is neither 'reliable' nor 'stable', as claimed by proponents. It has not prevented non-nuclear states from invading countries allied to nuclear weapon states. Examples include China entering the Korean War when the US had a nuclear monopoly in 1950; Argentina invading the British Falkland Islands in 1982, and Iraq invading close US ally Kuwait in 1990. Nor have nuclear-armed states been constrained from mobilizing for war with each other, as did India and Pakistan in 1999 and again in 2002, when US intervention was required to restore temporary stability.

In sum, nuclear deterrence, both as a security strategy to prevent the spread of nuclear weapons and as an instrument for averting war, has shown itself to be ineffective; and the risk of actual nuclear weapon use is growing. There is an urgent need, therefore, to find alternative safer security strategies that work.

Incentives to Find Alternatives

New Risk of Nuclear War. Until the Bush Administration's 2002 Nuclear Posture Review, the principal risk attached to nuclear weapons was one of inadvertent use driven by nuclear deterrence dogma. Since then, and now reinforced by the Trump Administration's 2018 Nuclear Posture Review, the world has to contend with a scenario whereby the US could decide upon deliberate use, even pre-emptively. This significantly raises the probability not only that nuclear weapons would be used, with unpredictable consequences, but also that their pre-emptive use would provoke reprisals which, in turn, could escalate to a major nuclear exchange.[1]

Furthermore, in any scenario involving either state-sponsored or non-state extremists, the US offers many targets for WMD attack. Alternatively, terrorists could achieve the equivalent effect of a nuclear strike by attacking a nuclear power plant with a hijacked airliner. Besides, a 'rogue' state is extremely unlikely to attack first with WMD, because it knows it would invite massive conventional retribution. However, if the US used nuclear weapons pre-emptively, this could provoke a WMD response – precisely the reverse of the intention. It would also incite proliferation as a way to reap revenge.

Even if the US does not initiate nuclear war, the inevitable dynamics of nuclear deterrence dictate revived nuclear arms racing, which this time will be multi-polar as China and India become increasingly powerful rivals, Israel and Iran face off in the Middle East, and North Korea feels increasingly cornered. Then there is the ongoing risk of accidental nuclear war as long as the US and Russia maintain their high alert postures.

New Global Security Problems. The sudden end of the Cold War in 1989, followed by disbanding of the Warsaw Pact, dissolution of the Soviet Union and reunification of Germany, were not predicted by anyone, including the 'realist' school of international strategic thinking. The consequent dangers of nuclear proliferation from an insecure former Soviet Union prompted some leading US think-tanks and legislators to consider the implications.[2]

During discussions, awareness grew that proliferation could not be treated in isolation from wider issues of security. Central to these was the realisation – since placed in doubt by Russia's annexation of Crimea and NATO's response – that the Cold War confrontation between the two superpowers was over. Instead, the primary risk would come from diffuse violence linked to formerly suppressed ethnic conflicts (e.g., in Chechnya, former Yugoslavia, and Ukraine), political uncertainty and the explosion of information technology. In addition, global pressures were intensifying from depleting resources (especially oil and water), population growth and migration, the expansion of market forces and concerns about climate change triggered by industrialisation. Whereas attention tended to be focused on problems in the US and its closest allies, the strains of globalisation were being most acutely felt in Russia, China and India. Meanwhile, the Middle East remains chronically insecure.

The deeply entrenched military establishments in the US and Russia, inured to maintaining strategic nuclear forces on high alert, have done little to respond to these new global security problems. For example, the Strategic Offensive Reductions Treaty signed by Bush and Putin in Moscow in May 2002 did not address the need for a mindset shift from deterrence to reassurance.

The incentives to do this are in line with 'realist' thinking. Increased ethnic conflict in Europe was quick to emerge in former Yugoslavia, and resulted in NATO's first armed intervention in 1999. This caused a temporary crisis between the US and Russia. Then came the terror attacks in the US on 11 September 2001. As in Northern Ireland, history shows that effective responses range far wider than military force, and ultimately require political solutions. Both Russia and the US have discovered the limits of a unilateral approach heavily weighted towards military punitive operations, in Chechnya, Iraq, Afghanistan and now Syria.

The Greatest Threat Remains Nuclear. Despite the trauma inflicted on the US by 9/11, the persisting deployment of nuclear weapons by the five recognised nuclear states remains the greatest threat to international security. This is because of the potential for accidental, and now pre-emptive, nuclear war and its massive consequences, extending long-term health and environmental effects far beyond the territories of the nuclear-armed states. To this must be added the potential for nuclear weapon use by Israel, India, Pakistan and North Korea, all of which are entangled in chronic security crises. Meanwhile, the 2003 US/UK invasion and occupation of Iraq sent a powerful, if misleading, signal to putative nuclear states such as North Korea that their security lies with rapid acquisition of nuclear weapons. When combined with new nuclear arms races as countries like Russia respond to the deployment of US BMD systems, this points to an exponential increase in the probability of nuclear weapon use, where nuclear deterrence acts as both engine and justification.

BMD Offers No Solution. The Bush administration's withdrawal from the ABM Treaty as it drove ahead with plans for a BMD system was presented as morally superior and less threatening than MAD. This was simply not credible to potential opponents: indeed, it was interpreted as disingenuous by such perceptive leaders as Gorbachev, and now Putin. The projected systems are too easily penetrated or sidestepped to be seen as purely defensive. Much more plausible is their potential role as cover for offensive operations, where they would strengthen conventional deterrence against limited regional WMD-armed ballistic missile threats.[3] This is in conformity with the Bush doctrine of pre-emptive strikes, reinforced by President Trump, as ruthlessly demonstrated in Iraq. China, with its smaller strategic nuclear forces, and Russia, to an increasing extent, are understandably concerned that their ability to deter the US would be seriously threatened.

Closely linked to this is the likelihood that BMD will draw both countries into a debilitating arms race that the US military-industrial complex reckons it will win, as it did against the USSR. Evidence of this emerged in November 2004 when Putin announced that Russia would 'soon deploy new nuclear missile systems that would surpass those of any other nuclear power', adding that Russia would continue to emphasise its nuclear deterrent.[4] The Russian military claim to have perfected ICBMs with manoeuvrable warheads in a 'hypersonic flying vehicle' capable of eluding a BMD system.

In an interesting Russian assessment by Alexei Arbatov and Vladimir Dvorkin *Beyond Nuclear Deterrence: Transforming the U.S.-Russian Equation*, the authors concluded:

> The end of the Cold War, in a sense, played a bad joke on the antinuclear aspirations of humankind: No longer terrified by the prospect of the escalation of certain conflicts to nuclear holocaust, the leading nuclear powers now emphasize actual nuclear warfare instead of deterrence. They plan for pre-emptive nuclear strikes and combined operations of nuclear and conventional systems in both offensive and defensive missions. In response to this, or using this as a convenient pretext, some third [sic] nuclear weapon states and threshold regimes treat nuclear weapons as the only means of deterring the great powers. Meanwhile, these aspirations open more channels for terrorists to gain access to nuclear explosives.[5]

They therefore recommended that mutual nuclear deterrence be removed as the foundation of the operational strategic relationship between Russia and the US and thus as the material embodiment of the two states' confrontational military relations. They argued that it is an impediment to the two countries' security and political cooperation against new threats, as well as a huge drain on their financial resources and scientific-technical innovations. They went on to propose plans for follow-up treaties to SORT cutting both strategic and tactical nuclear weapons, abandoning launch on warning and de-alerting most strategic nuclear forces by 2020. Unfortunately, however, they then advocated integrating the BMD systems of Russia and the US with a view to extending it to all signatory states of the NPT, CTBT and other agreements designed to limit the spread of nuclear weapon and missile technologies.

China and North Korea Need Reassurance. China's strategic arsenal, almost all of it land-based, is not continuously poised for rapid use, let alone for a first strike against the US. Moreover, after a scare about China's designs on Taiwan in 1999, a Chinese Foreign Ministry spokesman stated:

> We will not be the first to use nuclear weapons and will not use nuclear weapons against non-nuclear weapons countries and regions, let alone against our Taiwan compatriots.[6]

Any attempt by China to threaten Taiwan with conventional forces would trigger US backing for Taiwan, deploying vastly superior air power. While China is undoubtedly modernising its nuclear weapons and may be provoked by BMD to expand its arsenal more rapidly, a conventional arms race would be disastrous for China's economic development. There is every incentive, therefore, for China to respond constructively to a US policy shift from confrontation to reassurance. The corollary is that, as long as the US-China relationship is based on confrontation and nuclear deterrence, it will remain hostage to Taiwan's internal politics, which constitute a major strategic accident waiting to happen.

Indeed, Keith Payne warned that in this situation nuclear deterrence is inherently unreliable. The stakes involved are far higher for China, which is more able and prepared to absorb the costs and run risks to subdue Taiwan than is the US to prevent China from doing so. To put this in perspective, it is generally agreed that losing Taiwan would bring down the government in Beijing. Conversely, especially in light of other US military commitments, the Chinese leadership would probably judge that a majority of members of the US Congress and public would not see the future of Taiwan as a vital national interest worth war with China.[7]

North Korea is in desperate need of a similar shift in relationship with the US and regional allies South Korea and Japan. After the fall of the Berlin Wall in 1989, the fortified border between the two Koreas is the most obvious example of confrontation in the world, especially as it involves US forces. There is clearly substantial political will in South Korea for reassurance initiatives, linked to powerful aspirations for the eventual peaceful reunification of the Korean Peninsula.

Shifting the Mindset

On 11 September 1990, US President George H.W. Bush addressed a joint session of Congress about how Iraqi invaders would be ejected from Kuwait. Echoing a broader theme from a memorandum by Henry Stimson to President Truman on the same day forty-five years earlier, he said:

> A new world order is struggling to be born, a world quite different from the one we've known. A world where the rule of law supplants the rule of the jungle. A world in which nations recognize the shared responsibility for freedom and justice. A world where the strong respect the rights of the weak.[8]

He never elaborated, and intended it to apply only to what became known as the Persian Gulf War. However, his words were widely noted and discussed, if only to be dismissed by some as disingenuous rhetoric – not least because a serious attempt to implement it would inevitably jettison nuclear deterrence dogma as a central impediment. After a painful wake-up call on yet another 11 September, his son's approach was in almost total antithesis. Yet, with no end to the 'war on terror' in sight, perhaps the moment has come to revisit his vision.

New Zealand Led The Way. In making the shift away from nuclear deterrence, nations have discovered that *nuclear disarmament is a security-building process*. This was experienced by David Lange, Prime Minister of New Zealand when it rejected nuclear deterrence in 1984:

> Far from developing an irresponsible national policy on the subject, as most of our Western allies found it expedient to insinuate, New Zealand was in fact acting in a rational and calculated way, in the name of the traditional concept of strengthening national security. *We were, simply, safer without nuclear weapons in our defence than with them...* [T]he policy as expressed in law stands as a statement of the political will to eliminate nuclear weapons and a rejection of the doctrine of nuclear deterrence.[9] (emphasis added)

New Zealand adopted nuclear-free legislation in 1987.[10] Uniquely, it prohibits both nuclear weapons from New Zealand and its territorial waters and airspace and visits by nuclear-powered ships. In 1984, the newly elected Lange government announced the nuclear-free policy, and that it would promote a South Pacific Nuclear Weapon Free Zone and renegotiate the ANZUS Treaty to accommodate this. With the US fearing that the 'Kiwi disease' might spread to other allies such as Japan, Australia, the Philippines and Denmark, New Zealand was demoted from US ally to 'friend'; military co-operation under ANZUS was curtailed; the US and UK threatened trade; and New Zealand officials were ostracised from the Western group in the UN. Yet the government held firm, bolstered by a massive mobilisation of public support by the peace movement in New Zealand and the US. The French government's terrorist bombing of Greenpeace's anti-nuclear flagship, *Rainbow Warrior,* in Auckland coincided in 1985 with the creation of a South Pacific Nuclear Weapon Free Zone. When the Chernobyl nuclear power plant exploded in 1986, the combination of these events ensured the passage into law of the Nuclear Free Act.

In September 1999, President Clinton made the first state visit to New Zealand by a US President since 1965, during which he made no public mention of nuclear weapons. Two years before, General Lee Butler had thanked New Zealand for 'staying the course' against nuclear weapons:

> I know as well as anyone the courage it took for New Zealand to make that decision 10 years ago… If I had been here 10 years ago, I might have had a different message – but now I'm saying you got it right.[11]

Meanwhile, despite the rift on nuclear policy in ANZUS, New Zealand and Australian military forces continued to work harmoniously together on peacekeeping missions in their region, most recently in Bougainville, East Timor and the Solomon Islands. New Zealand was a leading member of the New Agenda Coalition, which broke out of the divisive Cold War negotiating blocs in the UN and injected new urgency into the nuclear disarmament process. In 2017 it was a leading negotiator of the Treaty on the Prohibition of Nuclear Weapons (TPNW).

New Zealand's experience of providing professional peacekeepers for UN tasks, and mediating among South Pacific island states, has won it far more international respect and true security than by trying to sustain a range of sophisticated military equipment which it cannot afford. After all, its total population of 4.5 million and US$185 billion GDP are roughly equivalent to those of the Australian state of Queensland. Its posture is evolving as a more independent small state practising minimal non-provocative defence, relying on enforcement of international law through the United Nations, and transferring resources from military procurement to training in peacekeeping and mediation skills. The principles of non-provocative defence revolve around war prevention by having a capacity to deny an aggressor the prospect of a cheap victory, but only a limited capacity to mount offensive operations in an opponent's territory.[12]

What Replaced Slavery? At this point it may be useful to re-introduce my analogy between slavery and nuclear deterrence. Critics dismiss it as lacking equivalence because, whereas abolition of slavery affected only the wealth of slaving nations, eliminating nuclear weapons would remove an allegedly irreplaceable fundamental guarantee of the possessor state's security. However, when the anti-slavery campaign began to gain traction, the governments of the leading slaving nations, the US, the UK and France, argued that their way of life depended on this 'necessary evil', for which there was no alternative.

While noting that all but about thirty states currently see their security as not requiring the current 'necessary evil' of dependence upon nuclear deterrence, my response to critics is: what replaced slavery? My answer is: more humane, lawful and effective means of creating wealth that did not incur denial of freedom of choice as to how some of humanity wished to live. Moreover, nuclear deterrence can be replaced with more humane, lawful and effective security strategies that do not enslave the whole of humanity with the risk of unprecedented suffering and damage to generations to come, and the potential destruction of the entire ecosystem of the planet.

Towards Common, Co-operative Global Security. The concept of common or co-operative security was coined in 1980 by Swedish Prime Minister Olof Palme as a replacement for nuclear deterrence:

> The doctrine of nuclear deterrence offers very fragile protection against the horrors of nuclear war. It is therefore of paramount importance to replace the doctrine of mutual deterrence. Our alternative is common security... International security must rest on a commitment to joint survival rather than on a threat of mutual destruction.[13]

Placing common security somewhere in the middle ground between 'realists' and idealists, the report on disarmament and security of the Palme Commission made an important contribution to tackling what is known as the 'security dilemma'. Simply put, this is the process whereby unilateral pursuit of security leads to more insecurity in others who take measures to defend themselves, thereby creating an arms race. In an increasingly interdependent world, *there is no such thing as national security*, as security problems transcend national borders. True security is about meeting human needs and tackling the root causes of peoples' insecurity. It is about seeing security as a safety-net for all, not a 'win/lose' military game. The emphasis on military spending and arms sales diverts resources from basic needs like clean water, food, shelter, health care, employment and education. Unprincipled arms sales cause or fan regional conflicts, sucking in adjacent nations and creating refugees.

When Mikhail Gorbachev embraced the concept of common security shortly before the Cold War ended, there was an upsurge of interest and consequent research into alternative security strategies.

However, with Gorbachev's fall from power the pro-nuclear fundamentalists closed ranks and reasserted control. The unreformed UN system means that national sovereignty persists as the arbiter of progress, with the five declared nuclear powers able to frustrate the will of the overwhelming majority of member states through their control of the Security Council.

As in the 1980s, initiatives in new security thinking, therefore, will need to come from civil society – but this time acting in close partnership with like-minded governments and local government representatives, such as Mayors for Peace.[14] This has already achieved encouraging results, including the World Court Project and the campaigns to ban anti-personnel landmines and cluster munitions, to establish an International Criminal Court, and to negotiate the TPNW.

Meanwhile, alternative safer strategies are needed to deal with the immediate threats.

Terrorists and Nuclear Blackmail

If the worst happens, and terrorists try nuclear blackmail, the first rule must be: *on no account try to oppose them with a threat of nuclear retaliation.* The bluff will be called, because targeting them with even a small modern nuclear weapon would be impossible without incurring unacceptable collateral damage and provoking global outrage. Indeed, some extremists could even provoke a nuclear state to do this, and hope to 'take as many others with them' as they could. So nuclear weapons are worse than useless.

Terence O'Brien, an experienced commentator on nuclear strategy and former New Zealand Ambassador to the UN, put it this way in a debate with Sir Michael Quinlan:

> The actual ability to employ nuclear weapons against terrorists, small break-away states or others must contend with the fact that *there are likely to be no targets as such*; and the spectre anyway of such weapons being directed against civilian populations in smaller states in our CNN-dominated world defies credibility. In these circumstances other methods, military and non-military, of pre-emption and deterrence must be resorted to. The emergence of a new generation of high-tech, precision-guided conventional munitions as well as sophisticated methods to disrupt communications and command and control, reduces the case for and indeed the appropriateness of nuclear weapons.[15] (emphasis added)

The only way to deal with nuclear blackmail is by negotiation while trying to neutralise the blackmailers using exhaustion, disorientation, etc, and if necessary, Special Forces armed with sophisticated and precise conventional weapons. An example of this was how the French authorities dealt with a man with explosives wrapped around his chest who hijacked a class of schoolchildren and threatened to blow them up with him if his demands were not met. They exhausted him by lengthy negotiations while installing surveillance devices to determine his condition and location. At an optimum moment Special Forces moved in and killed him with a silenced handgun. However, by *shifting the image of nuclear weapons from asset to stigmatised liability*, the risk of a regime or terrorists even wanting to get one is minimized, because it would destroy any support for their cause.

Security Does Not Need Nuclear Deterrence

In a speech in 1994 at the Minsk Academy of Sciences, US President Clinton told the Belarusians:

> As a new nation, one of your first decisions was to give up your nuclear weapons... It would have been easier to say these... weapons make us a great nation, they make us stronger, we will use them, we will rattle them around as threats, but you made a better choice – to live nuclear-free.

The reality is that an overwhelming majority of nations do not have nuclear weapons, and are not in nuclear alliances. New Zealand's status has been mentioned. Moreover, several countries which once had nuclear arsenals have eliminated them: South Africa is the supreme example. The Ukraine, which inherited the third largest nuclear arsenal in the world following the dissolution of the Soviet Union, as well as Belarus and Kazakhstan decided that their security would be enhanced by returning the warheads to Russia in exchange for security guarantees from both the US and Russia. In South America in the early 1990s, Argentina and Brazil mutually agreed to abandon their nuclear weapon research programmes, preferring to rely on the Tlatelolco Treaty that had established a nuclear weapon free zone throughout Latin America and the Caribbean in 1967.

Meanwhile, Australian Foreign Minister Alexander Downer echoed the words of President Clinton to the Belarusians in 1994 when he summoned the North Korean Ambassador in Canberra to protest about his country's nuclear test on 9 October 2006: 'I told him that this wouldn't improve North Korea's security, on the contrary this action has led to a deterioration in the security of north Asia.'[16]

Of the 188 countries signatory to the Nuclear Non-Proliferation Treaty as non-nuclear weapon states, all but the twenty-three NATO members, as well as Australia, Japan, South Korea and some former Soviet Union members, reject extended nuclear deterrence. Instead, they have opted to rely on modest conventional defence forces backed up by recourse to a mix of diplomatic, legal and economic forms of deterrence. These include nuclear weapon free zones and UN bodies like the International Court of Justice, as well as initiatives to strengthen international law such as through the establishment of an International Criminal Court.

Strengthening Self-Deterrence

A significant factor contributing to this rejection of nuclear deterrence is that the potential user of nuclear weapons is *self-deterred*, especially from using nuclear weapons against a non-nuclear state. Prime examples are the decisions by the US not to use nuclear weapons to try to avert defeat in Vietnam, and by the Soviets in Afghanistan. Reasons for this include:

* Pressure to respect Negative Security Assurances, whereby all nuclear weapon states have undertaken not to use nuclear weapons against non-nuclear states not allied to nuclear states.
* The growing likelihood that the potentially threatened state is covered by a nuclear weapon free zone.
* The worldwide outrage and consequent political and economic backlash that would engulf the user, especially if the victim state is much weaker.

Legally binding security assurances that stigmatize and, in effect, outlaw the use of nuclear weapons for everyone would significantly restrain nuclear weapon states from using their nuclear arsenals.[17]

An immediate, unacknowledged consequence of the World Court's Advisory Opinion in 1996 was that it made the world safer by strengthening self-deterrence. Though not binding on states, it provided a new, legal stop to help keep open the window of opportunity for nuclear disarmament created by the end of the Cold War. The 2017 TPNW has helped to reinforce this.

Linked to this is the need to raise awareness – particularly among the military – that, through the Court's decision and the TPNW, nuclear weapons are now implicitly in the same stigmatised category as chemical and biological weapons, which military professionals shunned even before they were banned by specific conventions.

Stand Down Nuclear Forces from High Alert

As described in Chapter 3, almost thirty years after the end of the Cold War, the US and Russia each still have over 1,000 strategic nuclear weapons at immediate readiness.[18] In 1996, the Canberra Commission made the following criticisms of this posture:

* It is a highly regrettable perpetuation of Cold War attitudes and assumptions.
* It needlessly sustains the risk of hair-trigger postures.
* It retards the critical process of normalizing US-Russian relations.
* It sends the unmistakable and, from an arms control perspective, severely damaging message that nuclear weapons serve a vital security role.
* It is entirely inappropriate to the extraordinary transformation in the international security environment.

Standing down all strategic nuclear forces from high alert would reduce the chance of an accidental or unauthorised nuclear weapon launch. It would also positively influence the political climate among the nuclear weapon states, and help set the stage for intensified co-operation. Taking nuclear forces off high alert could be verified by national technical means and nuclear weapon state inspection arrangements. In the first instance, reductions in alert status could be adopted by the nuclear weapon states unilaterally.[19] In its 1998 Strategic Defence Review, the UK government showed leadership by announcing that it had taken the British Trident force off high alert, relaxing the notice to fire for the single deployed submarine from 'minutes' to 'days'. However, this is unverifiable.

On the need for verification, in 1999 the US and Russian military were sufficiently concerned, despite de-targeting arrangements, about the risk of inadvertent nuclear war from the Year 2000 computer problem to establish a temporary joint Center for Y2K Strategic Stability at Peterson Air Force Base in Colorado, where they monitored information from their respective early warning systems. It proved so successful that Presidents Clinton and Putin signed an agreement in June 2000 to establish a permanent Joint Data Exchange Center in Moscow.[20] This ridiculously ironic arrangement was probably driven by the overriding imperative to sustain nuclear deterrence dogma, even at the expense of risking catastrophic damage to all humanity and the planet. With such mutual verification achieved between former implacable foes, it should be possible to extend this to monitoring reductions from high alert status.

The report of the Weapons of Mass Destruction Commission chaired by Hans Blix stated that eliminating launch on warning is the most urgent task facing the US and Russia.[21] The report suggested some bilateral verification measures such as participation by inspectors from both states in military exercises of strategic forces. It also recommended that the US and Russia should create a joint commission to facilitate a controlled, parallel decrease in operational readiness of a large part of their strategic forces through: reducing the number of strategic submarines at sea, and lowering their readiness to launch in port; storing nuclear bombs and air-launched cruise missiles separately from relevant airfields; and storing separately nose cones and/or warheads of most ICBMs.

An obvious follow-up would be the Canberra Commission's second recommended step: *mutually verified removal of warheads from delivery vehicles*. Advantages cited by the Commission include:

* Nuclear forces can be reconstituted to an alert posture only within known or agreed timeframes, much as is the case with bomber forces.
* Adequate response to nuclear threats would remain certain, but the risk of large-scale pre-emptive or surprise nuclear attack and the imperative for instantaneous retaliation would be avoided.
* The barriers against inadvertent or accidental use would be greatly strengthened.[22]

At the 2007 UN General Assembly Disarmament Session, New Zealand introduced a resolution 'Decreasing the operational readiness of nuclear weapons systems' calling for all nuclear weapons to be removed from high alert status.[23] The US responded by trying to claim that none of its nuclear forces were on 'hair-trigger alert'; but this was refuted by Bruce Blair. The resolution was adopted by 139 votes to 3, with 36 abstentions: the three NATO nuclear states voted against, but China abstained and Russia did not vote; Japan voted for it, while all the other non-nuclear US allies abstained.

In June 2009, a seminar in Switzerland co-sponsored by the EastWest Institute and the governments of Switzerland and New Zealand found that institutional resistance on both sides remains strong, demonstrating the pernicious influence of nuclear deterrence dogma.[24] In 2016, support for the UN de-alerting resolution grew to 174 states; but US pressure caused the resolution to be withdrawn from the 2017 UN General Assembly Disarmament Session.

Start Negotiating a Nuclear Weapons Convention

A favourite catch-cry of the pro-nuclear lobby is 'nuclear weapons cannot be disinvented'. Neither can chemical weapons. However, far from despairing about them, the international community has agreed on a Chemical Weapons Convention, an enforceable treaty banning every aspect of chemical weapons; and determined efforts, despite US moves to undermine them, are proceeding to strengthen a similar one against biological weapons. An immediate result of such a treaty is that military professionals refuse to operate them. To claim that 'this approach won't work for nuclear weapons' amounts to a limp mix of appeasement and fatalism. The world can, and must, do better than that.

Chemical and biological weapons are prohibited, despite verification problems from the large number of chemicals and biological agents capable of use in such weapons. Many of these agents have dual uses, and thus are readily available and easy to convert to weapon use.

Nuclear weapons, on the other hand, require fissile materials – plutonium or highly enriched uranium – which are extremely difficult and dangerous to make, not generally used for other purposes, and thus much easier to monitor. This means that verification of a Nuclear Weapons Convention would be significantly easier than for other weapons of mass destruction.

Placing nuclear weapons in the same stigmatised, outlawed status as chemical and biological weapons will mean that they are no longer perceived as assets. Instead, they become a security problem; and numbers held lose much of their significance other than as a dismantling burden.

In June 1999, China's President Jiang Zemin showed the way when he wrote:

> A convention on the comprehensive ban of nuclear weapons should be negotiated. Since biological and chemical weapons have been prohibited, there is no reason why nuclear weapons, which are more destructive, should not be comprehensively banned and thoroughly destroyed. All it takes to reach this objective is strong political will.[25]

With world population and other trends indicating a hegemonic shift towards Asia, Michael MccGwire argued that while the 'Euro-Westerners' are still strong they should expand, follow and enforce the rule of law in the international system.[26] They would then have hope of looking to its protection as they become relatively weaker in the decades ahead: 'For the West, the prospect of such a shift could serve as a powerful impulse to change its ways while there is still time.' He went on to point out that the Western powers are uniquely placed to establish such a political and legal regime, which would be of immediate help to control the spread of WMD. However, it would require them to moderate their emphasis on military force as an instrument of overseas policy. This would conform to global trends during the last 100 years: except as an instrument of punishment, resort to war has proved increasingly dysfunctional; the cost of projecting coercive force has risen exponentially, while its political utility has steadily declined.

A Model Nuclear Weapons Convention. In November 1997, at the request of Costa Rica, the UN circulated a Model Nuclear Weapons Convention as a discussion draft.[27] The model, drawn up by an international team of lawyers, scientists and disarmament experts, offered a plan for the prohibition and elimination of nuclear weapons in a series of graduated, verifiable steps. It was drafted on the same lines as the widely acclaimed Chemical Weapons Convention, which entered into force on 29 April 1997. The purposes of the model include:

* Demonstrating the feasibility of the elimination of nuclear weapons.
* Encouraging governments to resume nuclear disarmament negotiations.
* Identifying policies that are inconsistent with the goal of nuclear disarmament.
* Overcoming some of the barriers that make nuclear abolition appear utopian.
* Preparing for the day when the political will to begin negotiations emerges.

A recurrent objection by the Western nuclear weapon states to the demand for a model Nuclear Weapons Convention is that in today's political environment it is 'premature' or 'unrealistic idealism' to consider and discuss a framework for the prohibition and elimination of nuclear weapons. It is neither premature to begin devising a plan, nor unrealistic idealism for states to begin developing the verification mechanisms.

The debate was carried forward further by an important book, *Security and Survival: The Case for a Nuclear Weapons Convention.*[28] Published in 1999 by International Physicians for the Prevention of Nuclear War, it set out to fill a fundamental gap in the plans and policies of the nuclear weapon states: namely, a vision of what the goal of a nuclear weapon free world should look like, and a rough plan of how to get there. After demonstrating the necessity of achieving such a convention, it described what it would encompass, and explained the process by which it could be achieved. Then the reader was taken through an updated version of a model convention text, before discussing the latest concerns from the nuclear weapon states about it and offering practical solutions.

Nuclear Weapon-Free Areas

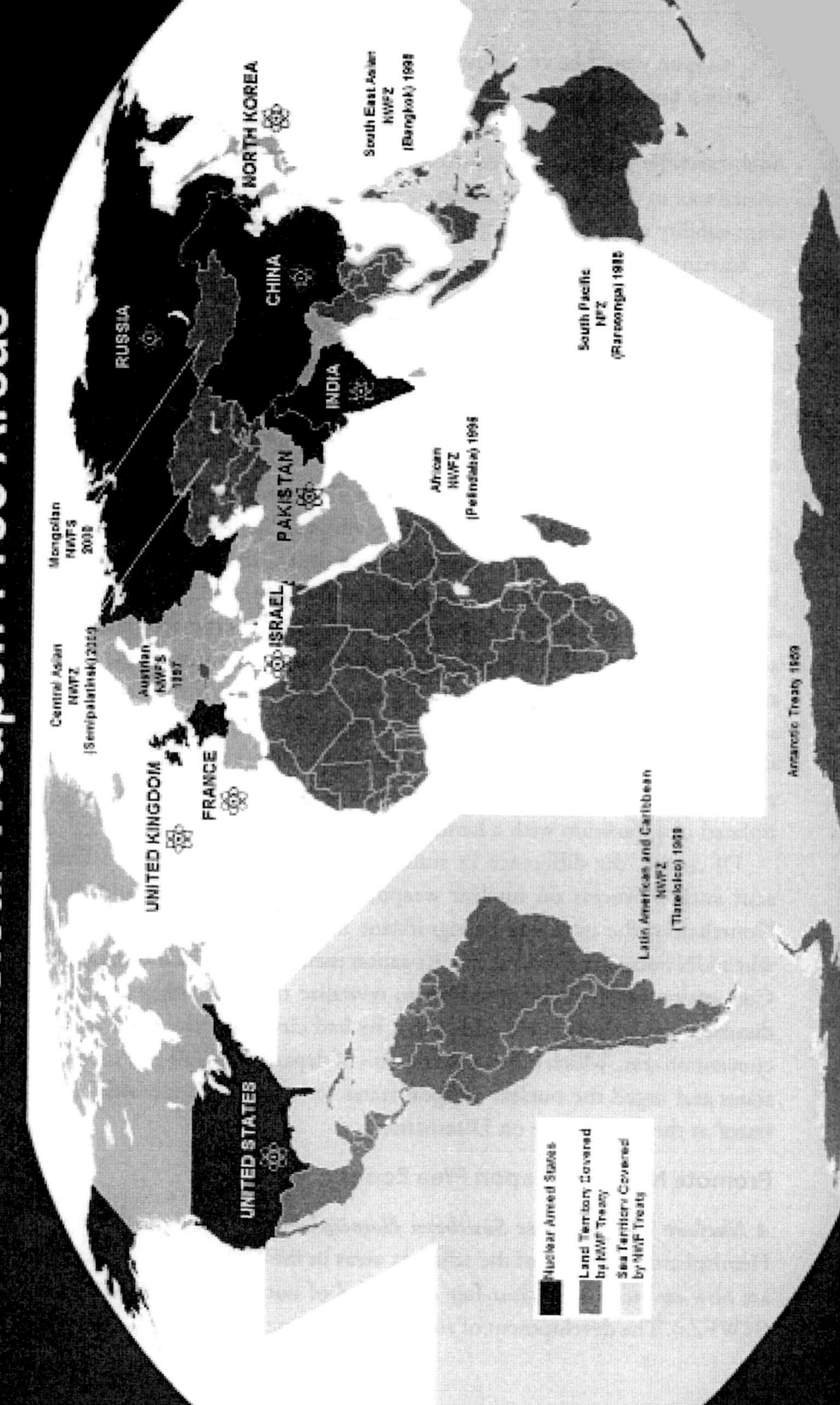

For example, in response to a question challenging the relevance of a Nuclear Weapons Convention in preventing nuclear terrorism, it first explained why nuclear weapons would not only be useless in responding to such a threat, but could stimulate terrorists to use them. It then added:

> A nuclear weapons convention, on the other hand, would make it much more difficult for a terrorist organization to acquire or build a nuclear weapon... The verification systems established under a nuclear weapons convention would make it easier to discover a potential terrorist threat from diversion of fissile material or technical expertise in time to prevent the building of a bomb. In addition, a nuclear weapons convention would reduce or remove the political power of nuclear weapons for a terrorist organization. Terrorists commit terrorist acts either to retaliate against perceived aggression, or to generate support for their cause through maximizing publicity. Once nuclear weapons have been prohibited, there could be no perceived aggression requiring a nuclear response, and any threat or use of such a weapon would be condemned universally and eliminate support for a terrorist's cause.[29]

Such carefully argued, non-confrontational work by citizen experts is a crucial tool in the struggle to achieve a paradigm shift of thinking from the impossibility to the practicality of nuclear weapons abolition.

Starting multilateral negotiations with this aim would be how the nuclear weapon states could best demonstrate a commitment to their obligations to achieve nuclear disarmament. The *very act of starting*, regardless of how long the negotiations last, would restore the political impetus towards nuclear disarmament. Nuclear weapon-capable states could no longer justify acquiring nuclear weapons by pointing to the lack of progress towards abolition, as did India.

Promote Nuclear Weapon Free Zones

A Nuclear Weapon Free Southern Hemisphere. Most of the Southern Hemisphere, and some of the adjacent areas in the Northern Hemisphere, are now covered by 'nuclear-free umbrellas' of nuclear weapon free zones (NWFZs). The development of zones in Latin America and the Caribbean, the South Pacific, Africa and Southeast Asia, coupled with the longstanding demilitarisation of Antarctica, makes it timely to consolidate the Southern Hemisphere as a zone free of nuclear weapons.

Every year since 1996 the UN General Assembly has adopted a resolution introduced by Brazil calling upon the states parties and signatories to the regional NWFZ treaties 'to promote the nuclear weapon free status of the Southern Hemisphere and adjacent areas', and to explore and implement further cooperation among themselves.[30] This involves consideration of complex issues, including possible linkages between the existing NWFZs. Any formal arrangements will need to be consistent with international law, including the UN Convention on the Law of the Sea.

The first Conference of States Parties to Nuclear Weapon Free Zones was held in Mexico in April 2005. This brought together delegates from nearly 110 states within NWFZs, as well as observer states and civil society, to establish a new and powerful forum for the delegitimisation and abolition of nuclear weapons.[31] The Conference adopted a declaration concerning the consolidation, strengthening and expansion of NWFZs, the prevention of nuclear proliferation and the achievement of a nuclear weapon free world.[32] A process was established for continuing communication and co-operation through which more ambitious proposals could be developed. These include, for example:

* Adopting a declaration on non-transit of nuclear weapons through the oceans included in the zones.
* Undertaking studies or preparing reports on the development of elements required for the abolition of nuclear weapons using the experience of the NWFZs.
* Hosting deliberations and negotiations for nuclear weapon abolition measures culminating in a Nuclear Weapons Convention.[33]

Progress in the Northern Hemisphere. Establishment of the 1995 Bangkok Southeast Asian Nuclear Weapon Free Zone Treaty showed that it is possible to develop such zones in the Northern Hemisphere despite the proximity of nuclear weapon states. Also, following the example of New Zealand, Austria adopted nuclear-free legislation in 1999, and Mongolia became a NWFZ in 2000.

Further progress was made when the five ex-Soviet republics of Kazakhstan, Uzbekistan, Kyrgyzstan, Tajikistan and Turkmenistan signed a Central Asian Nuclear Weapon Free Zone, although the NATO nuclear weapon states declined to support it.[34] Known as the Semipalatinsk Treaty (it was signed at the ex-Soviet nuclear test site on 8 September 2006), this is the first NWFZ located entirely in the Northern Hemisphere. It showcases a commitment to nuclear disarmament by a group of states which previously had Soviet nuclear weapons on their territory and continue to be surrounded by Russian, Chinese, Pakistani, Indian and Israeli nuclear weapons. Under its terms, the Central Asian states will be the first in the world legally bound to adhere to enhanced IAEA safeguards (known as the

Additional Protocol) on their civilian nuclear assets. The treaty also requires them to meet international standards for the physical protection of nuclear material. Considering the danger that Central Asia could become a source or transit corridor for terrorist smuggling of nuclear materials, this is an important counterterrorism measure.[35]

Since 1992, discussions have been conducted among interested parties on creating a Northeast Asia NWFZ covering the Korean Peninsula and Japan.[36] Associated with this would be the establishment of a Northeast Asia Co-operative Security Organisation, modelled on the Organisation for Security and Co-operation in Europe (OSCE). The US, Russia and China would be invited to sign protocols which provide for Negative Security Assurances in which the nuclear states agree not even to threaten to use their nuclear weapons against the states within the zone under any circumstances. In exchange, the non-nuclear states would reaffirm several undertakings they have made not to become nuclear weapon states. The most important objectives of such an initiative would be to:

* Prevent a nuclear arms race between Japan, South Korea and North Korea, or between Japan and a reunified Korea.
* Establish a mechanism for verifying implementation of the zone, as the first step towards further confidence-building in the region.
* Contribute to global nuclear disarmament.

A Northeast Asia Nuclear Weapon Free Zone Treaty is an example of how to provide an alternative to the current invidious choice, as perceived by each non-nuclear state, of either staying under US or Russian extended nuclear deterrence or pursuing a nuclear arsenal. It would also be in the interests of both nuclear superpowers, which should be encouraged to propose such an initiative as a powerful way to ease tension in the area, and enhance their security by hastening the peaceful reunification of the two Koreas and promoting co-operative security in Northeast Asia. Moreover, such an initiative would send a much-needed signal to India, Israel and Pakistan, reducing the salience of nuclear weapons in international politics.

This takes on added urgency in light of the reality that, if conflict is to occur among the nuclear weapon states, it is most likely to take place in Northeast Asia. The US, Russia and China all have substantial military forces as well as major stakes in the region. In addition, there are many sources of conflict among the three and their allies within the region, including the future of the Korean Peninsula and Taiwan, and control of natural resources and territory in local seas. The other region urgently in need of a 'nuclear-free umbrella' is the Middle East;

but progress there is stymied by Israel, with Western complicity.

One encouraging initiative that could be developed further has been Japan's key role in hosting and funding UN negotiations on a Central Asian Nuclear Weapon Free Zone, with the city of Sapporo providing a venue for several negotiating sessions. In the case of the Northeast Asian zone, there could be scope for other more impartial but interested Pacific littoral states with a good track record on disarmament, like New Zealand, to host and mediate further negotiations.

In 2008, Australia and Japan established a joint International Commission on Nuclear Non-proliferation and Disarmament, co-chaired by ex-Australian Foreign Minister Gareth Evans and ex-Japanese Foreign Minister Yoriko Kawaguchi. However, their report, *Eliminating Nuclear Threats: A Practical Agenda for Global Policymakers*, published in December 2009, failed to mention the extensive work undertaken to prepare the ground for a Northeast Asian NWFZ.[37]

In the South Asian sub-continent, the stand-off between India and Pakistan has stunted initiatives for a NWFZ. Nevertheless, and precisely because of the tense rivalry between the two nascent nuclear powers, there have been initial soundings for Nepal to establish national nuclear-free legislation following the examples of New Zealand, Mongolia and Austria; and for Bangladesh and Sri Lanka to join the Southeast Asian NWFZ.[38]

A Central European zone has been proposed by Belarus. It would extend from Sweden and Finland through the Baltic states, Poland, Belarus, the Czech Republic, Slovakia, Hungary, Austria, the Balkan states, the Ukraine, Romania, Bulgaria and Greece to Turkey.[39] This would be an important confidence-building measure both for Russia and the other former members of the Warsaw Pact which are either now in NATO or along Russia's western flank, and have long feared that they would be a nuclear battlefield. Such a zone could reassure Russia about further NATO expansion eastwards, and would prevent Moscow from deploying nuclear weapons in Belarus or Kaliningrad.

With climate change opening up the Arctic region, informal exploratory talks have begun to consider the feasibility of a zone there.[40] This would free both poles from deployment of nuclear weapons, and help build a more co-operative security environment in the North as the littoral states begin to jostle for transit rights and access to mineral resources on the seabed.

De-Couple Nuclear Weapons from Permanent UN Security Council Membership

If either the UK or France, or both together, were to give up their nuclear weapons, all indications are that this would be a way to *secure their continuing permanent membership of the UN Security Council.* This is because of the urgent need, following the South Asian nuclear tests, to break the perceived link between a permanent seat and possession of nuclear weapons. To date, their obvious intention to retain their nuclear arsenals is undermining the respect in which they are seen by the world, and hence their status.

The idea that non-nuclear countries such as Germany or Japan deserve a permanent Security Council seat is already widespread. If the suggestion that India should give up its nuclear weapons in order to gain a similar privilege were to be widely supported, the link would be strained further. This would affect thinking in France and the UK, both about their position and that of Europe in the world.[41]

There is an associated need in the International Court of Justice to challenge the semi-permanent status of each nuclear weapon state having a judge on the 15-strong panel.[42] As explained in the previous chapter, in the Court's 1996 nuclear weapon advisory opinion the US judge allowed his government's nuclear policy to take precedence over the law in his dissenting opinion.

From Nuclear Deterrence to Non-Provocative Defence

New Zealand is the role model on how to break free from obeisance to nuclear deterrence dogma, as the Lange government demonstrated at the height of the Cold War. Sooner or later NATO will have to bite the nuclear bullet if it is to maintain its cohesion and effectiveness – and *NATO holds the key to achieving a nuclear weapon-free world.* An encouraging indicator came in February 2010, when the governments of Belgium, Germany, Luxembourg, the Netherlands and Norway jointly pressed for the removal of US tactical nuclear weapons from Europe. Though unsuccessful, this issue has been re-ignited by the Trump administration's Nuclear Posture Review.[43]

The first step would be for US and Russian nuclear forces to be stood down from high alert. This would create the necessary relaxation of international relationships to allow the opening of negotiations for a Nuclear Weapons Convention. Such negotiations will require new levels of co-operation between former adversaries. They could, and should, be exploited to build confidence and trust to the point where the principles of non-provocative defence could be introduced. Currently, NATO claims that its posture is 'defensive', but it is intimidating to Russia – especially after NATO's enlargement through the entry of several East European states and with its evolving doctrine of 'humanitarian intervention', as first demonstrated in former Yugoslavia.

On 28 May 2002 in Rome, the heads of state/government of NATO and Russia issued a declaration 'opening a new page in our relations', and pledging a 'new quality' of co-operation and coordination on a range of security issues. Henceforth, the structural centrepiece of the relationship became a new NATO-Russia Council, replacing the Permanent Joint Council.[44] This opened up new opportunities for a review of NATO's nuclear posture. However, a communique three days later from NATO Defence Ministers avoided any mention of nuclear issues.

A Non-Nuclear Strategy for NATO

It is beyond the scope of this book to attempt to prescribe a comprehensive blueprint for a non-nuclear security strategy. Nevertheless, the following arguments and ideas are offered to help stimulate a debate on how NATO could devise a safer, more credible strategy in which nuclear weapons would play no part.

Even if NATO unilaterally gave up its nuclear weapons now, Russia would be deterred from a decision to attack a member state by NATO's proven ability to respond to any conventional attack or nuclear threat with massive conventional firepower. Thus a Western Europe robust in conventional military capability, self-confident politically, and resolved in the defence of core interests, has little to fear from nuclear blackmail.

Because of its prowess in conventional weaponry, the US has least need of nuclear weapons. Thus *it is in its direct security interest to encourage a major shift to a non-provocative, non-nuclear NATO defence strategy*. Those who think NATO could not survive such a change should ponder whether it can maintain its cohesion indefinitely with its current nuclear strategy. The case for this follows.

The Need to Reassure Russia. After the Berlin Wall came down so unexpectedly, both the Soviet Union and the Warsaw Pact were disbanded. Moreover, instead of a buffer zone being created between NATO and Russia of neutral former Central European Warsaw Pact members, NATO jurisdiction has extended to the territory and armed forces of almost all those states, of which only Belarus and the Ukraine are not NATO members. Even Georgia, firmly within Russia's historic sphere of influence, was courted to join, despite – or possibly triggering – the 2008 crisis related to unrest in the separatist Caucasus enclaves of Abkhazia and South Ossetia. NATO's confrontational response to the 2014 Ukraine/Crimea crisis has revived Russian sensitivities and resentment.

Meanwhile, economic and political disruptions, quite apart from a major intra-state war in Chechnya, have sapped the strength and morale of what is left of Russia's conventional military might. By contrast, NATO's intervention in the former Yugoslavia followed by the US-led replacement of the Afghanistan and Iraq regimes demonstrated not only the technological prowess of the US conventional military machine, but also US willingness to undertake offensive operations outside NATO's borders. In addition, NATO's Strategy Concept omits the political assurances given to Russia in 1997 that NATO would not deploy nuclear weapons in the Alliance's new member states during peacetime. US determination to deploy parts of its BMD system in Central Europe has plunged relations between the two nuclear superpowers back into a new Cold War.[45] The Trump administration's Nuclear Posture Review looks set to exacerbate this dangerous slide further, especially with the plans to replace the 200 B61 freefall tactical nuclear bombs based in Belgium, Germany, Italy, the Netherlands, and Turkey with the new, more accurate, ground-penetrating B61-12 version.[46]

In light of all these factors as well as NATO's huge conventional preponderance over Russia, there is an overriding need to provide Russia with incentives to become less dependent on its nuclear arsenal for its security. It also needs maximum reassurance that NATO has no offensive intentions. This especially means removing nuclear weapons from any potential conflict, thereby making them irrelevant to resolving the security problem instead of a primary cause.

The details of a non-nuclear security strategy for NATO will need to be worked out over several years. However, the following changes merit immediate and careful consideration:

Stand Down US and Russian Strategic Nuclear Forces. The overriding need for NATO to reassure Russia that it has no intention of exploiting Russia's military inferiority dictates that the US should immediately stand down its strategic nuclear forces from high alert status, and invite Russia to do likewise under mutual verification through the NATO-Russia Council. This would implement most of the agreed steps from the 2010 NPT Review Action Plan associated with promoting stability and security for all, taking further unilateral nuclear disarmament initiatives, increasing transparency and verification, reducing the operational status of systems and diminishing the role of nuclear weapons in security policies.

Reconsider Nuclear Deterrence Doctrine. The key to achieving these major shifts is to reconsider the claimed merits of nuclear deterrence doctrine. Specifically, the counterproductive aspects of extended nuclear deterrence must be addressed.

Withdraw NATO's Tactical Nuclear Arsenal. The B61s should be repatriated to the US into verifiable storage; the US and UK nuclear arsenals should no longer be assigned to NATO; and NATO's nuclear war plan should be withdrawn.

Negotiate a Tactical Nuclear Weapon Treaty. The withdrawal of NATO's tactical arsenal would constitute NATO's side of a major confidence-building process, and would be a powerful way to encourage Russia to negotiate a Tactical Nuclear Weapon Treaty, through which a plan could be pursued for their elimination. An immediate start on this could be made by formalising, and making irreversible (through transparency and mutual verification), the 1991–92 reciprocal unilateral withdrawals by the NATO nuclear states and Russia of all tactical nuclear weapons from ships and aircraft.[47]

The next stage would be to establish a tactical/non-strategic nuclear weapon register, in order to remedy the unacceptable absence of official figures, especially in Russia and the UK. Again, this could be achieved through the NATO-Russia Council. Given the renewed reliance on tactical nuclear weapons in Russia and the US, other states must take the initiative in devising and promoting ways to kick-start disarmament of tactical nuclear weapons. As the European NATO members have most to gain, they should provide the lead.[48]

Establish a Central Europe Nuclear Weapon Free Zone. Linked to the foregoing should be the simultaneous initiation of negotiations to establish a NWFZ in Central Europe. Although there is understandably little political will for this at present, especially among new NATO members, the evolution of a *de facto* NWFZ within European NATO would be achieved if more NATO member states emulated the Norwegian, Danish and Spanish precedents of refusing deployment of nuclear weapons on their territory in peacetime.[49]

These proposed changes should be considered with the following advice in mind from one of the foremost Western experts on Russia, George Kennan, on how to deal with the Russians:

> Above all, one must recognize, as I believe they do in their hearts, that war among advanced industrial powers is no longer an acceptable option for anybody in this age of high technology and vast destructive potential, and that other means will simply have to be found for the adjustment of those conflicts of philosophy and interest that inevitably affect the relations among great sovereign powers.[50]

With appropriate modifications, the changes are clearly applicable to the US/Japan, US/South Korea and US/Australia security treaties, all of which have at their core allegiance to extended nuclear deterrence. Such a shift is not only in the security interests of the nuclear weapon states and their allies, it is also a vote-winner, because it would bring their security policies into line with morality, international law and public opinion.

SAFER SECURITY STRATEGIES

Safeguards Against Cheating

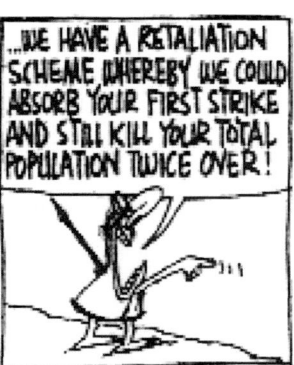

Because nuclear weapons are mainly possessed by nations with great power status, a decision by them to join the overwhelming majority of other nations in removing this threat to humanity will inevitably usher in a new approach to global security. The status of nuclear weapons, like chemical or biological weapons, will have shifted from asset to stigmatised, but far more dangerous, liability. In such a transformed situation, the process of nuclear disarmament will no longer be conducted on the basis of trying to ensure that no-one 'hides a few just in case'. Instead, possessor states will be negotiating to *enhance* their security – rather like a rescue team after an earthquake removing rubble carefully to avoid it collapsing on trapped survivors. Above all, there will be a clear understanding that nuclear blackmail cannot be dealt with by threatened retaliation with nuclear weapons.

The Crucial Role of Verification. Another significant part of the process will be its verification. The act of checking compliance not only provides information, but also creates interaction between military personnel of previously hostile countries. There will be opportunities to assess capabilities with much greater confidence, building trust between states as they move to a situation where they can no longer annihilate each other. Indeed, Dr Patricia Lewis, Research Director for International Security at Chatham House, predicts that the confidence-building aspects could eventually be verification's single and most important role: 'We could move from a position of the threat of nuclear war as security to one of verification as security.'[51]

World outrage against breakout from a nuclear weapon-free world would be so massive – including probable conventional military intervention on the scale of the 2003 invasion of Iraq, plus economic isolation – that there would be no political or military incentive to do so. The risk will diminish as the verification and enforcement arrangements are set in place. Moreover, that risk is minimal compared to the near inevitability of nuclear blackmail under the current policy, or nuclear war by over-reaction to provocation including cyber attack, accident, miscalculation or technical malfunction.

Securing a Durable Nuclear Weapon-Free World

The above proposals constitute a vital precursor and catalyst to advancing to the next step, which would provide the engine for achieving a durable nuclear weapon-free world: opening negotiations on a Nuclear Weapons Convention.

MccGwire contended that this could be seen as the real end of the Cold War, as it would feature an unprecedented confluence of interest where the most powerful states would be making the greatest concessions. Such negotiations would be free from the 'nuclear apartheid' aspects of the Non-Proliferation Treaty, thus removing the main stumbling block around agreeing to controls on fissile materials. This in turn would have positive spin-offs, such as facilitating policing the Chemical and Biological Weapons Conventions, because CB weapons could no longer be justified as the 'poor man's deterrent'.

Most importantly, it would also free up negotiations on how to prevent an arms race in outer space.[52]

From NATO to OSCENANA? As an integral part of breaking free from Cold War thinking, NATO's denuclearisation would also facilitate a resolution of the currently overlapping and competing security organisations in Europe and North America. This is because rejection of the confidence trick of nuclear deterrence would reassure Russia and those states remaining within its sphere of influence to the extent that negotiations could also begin for NATO to be merged into the Organisation for Security and Co-operation in Europe (OSCE).[53]

The OSCE is the world's largest security organisation whose fifty-six participating states encompass continental Europe, the Caucasus, Central Asia and North America. It grew out of the 'Helsinki process' in 1973, when for the first time in the Cold War experts from thirty-five states in both the East and West came together for a pan-European security conference. This resulted in the signing of the Helsinki Final Act by all thirty-five heads of state in 1975, which established an ongoing Conference on Security and Co-operation in Europe (CSCE).

The CSCE proved itself by offering a permanent channel of communication and a normative code of conduct for co-operation. As a result, it introduced real improvements in East-West relations when most contacts were characterised by alternating phases of tension and ambiguous *détente*. Also, it brought neutral and non-aligned states – Austria, Sweden and Switzerland – into the European security system on an equal basis with members of the two military alliances.

After the collapse of the Warsaw Pact, the CSCE was institutionalised through the Charter of Paris, signed on 21 November 1990, with small decentralised headquarters in Prague, Vienna and Warsaw. A CSCE Parliamentary Assembly was formed the following year; and in 1992 a Secretary General was appointed as it became Europe's regional security arrangement in the sense of Article VIII of the UN Charter. By then it was deploying missions to new conflicts in former Yugoslavia. In recognition of its growing status and roles, it was renamed the OSCE on 1 January 1995.

Within its coverage, the OSCE is the primary instrument for early warning, conflict prevention, crisis management and post-conflict rehabilitation. Its approach to security is comprehensive and co-operative, dealing with arms control, preventive diplomacy, confidence and security-building measures, human rights, election monitoring and economic and environmental security. High-profile operations in Bosnia and Herzegovina, Albania, Croatia, Chechnya and Kosovo have meant that it is now judged as much for its operational effectiveness as for its political role and commitments. This particularly applies in its largest and most challenging mission in Kosovo, where it took over from NATO in 1999.

Another benefit of merging NATO into the OSCE would derive from a release of the current tensions between NATO and the European Union over security, as the latter struggles to evolve a common foreign and security policy bedevilled by irreconcilable differences over how to deal with British and French nuclear forces. Although implementing the necessary paradigm shift in NATO's approach to security would require vision, strong leadership and perseverance, NATO would be transformed into a common safety net for all fifty-six states 'from Vancouver to Vladivostok'. This would merit a new name: perhaps the Organisation for Security and Co-operation in Europe, North Asia and North America (OSCENANA)? Of course, such a fundamental realignment of security structures would only be feasible in close consultation with other related regional initiatives like the Shanghai Cooperation Organisation, and negotiating further nuclear weapon free zones.[54]

The US is the Main Obstacle. The most formidable obstacle to starting negotiations for a Nuclear Weapons Convention is a deep-rooted US preference for autonomy in international affairs. Historically, US support for multilateral institutions has been directly proportionate to their acquiescence in endorsing US global interests and policies. This explains growing US frustration with the UN as new members, and more effective use of the UN system by NGOs, made it increasingly difficult to manipulate.

US disenchantment with both the UN and NATO intensified during the 1999 Kosovo intervention, where it could not prevent disputes about military operations in NATO, and the UN became involved despite US efforts to deny it any role. The next intervention, to remove the Taliban regime in Afghanistan and gain control over this key region for access to Central Asia's oil and gas resources, showed that the Bush administration had learned to avoid the Kosovo pitfalls. It took the process a stage further in Iraq in 2003, but over-reached itself by openly defying the UN and international law.

The consequences, still reverberating through Iraq and Afghanistan, spurred President Barack Obama to revive US public awareness that its vital interests can only be secured by co-operating with the global community and upholding international law. However, he found he could not face down the vested interests of the US nuclear military-industrial complex; and President Trump has wasted no time in courting it, and disregarding international law.

Exploiting the US-UK Special Relationship. Meanwhile, despite membership of most of the world's most influential clubs (P5, G8, OECD, NATO, EU), the UK has struggled to find a role since losing its empire. The UK government could be pivotal by exploiting its special relationship with the US, initiating a virtuous spiral. It is best placed to be the first P5 member to break out from dependence on nuclear deterrence. As the first medium-sized power to decide that it had to have nuclear weapons, the UK was the role model for France, Israel, India and Pakistan. The UK nuclear arsenal is the smallest of the P5, and is deployed in only one system, Trident, on relaxed alert of several days' notice for use.

If the UK were to announce that it had decided to reject nuclear deterrence, the US and UK anti-nuclear movements, and an overwhelming majority of world opinion, would erupt in support. One immediate domestic advantage, in light of the need for deep defence budget cuts, would be the opportunity cost of not replacing the four UK Trident submarines. The positive spin-off would extend far beyond nuclear policy. As initiator, organiser and energiser of a process that would start to shift Western attitudes from the current adversarial national security paradigm to one embracing co-operative security, the UK would gain a global role it has not enjoyed since the British Empire was at its zenith. This time, however, its influence would be welcomed overwhelmingly as truly a 'force for good'.

The first anti-nuclear 'breakout' by one of the P5 would be sensational, and would transform the nuclear disarmament debate overnight. In NATO, the UK would wield unprecedented influence in leading the drive for a non-nuclear strategy – which must happen if NATO is to sustain its cohesion. It would create new openings for shifting the mindset particularly in the US and France, and heavily influencing India, Israel and Pakistan, and others feeling the need to obtain nuclear weapons. Moreover, it would open the way for a major reassessment by Russia and China of their nuclear strategies, for all nuclear forces to be de-alerted, and for multilateral negotiations to start on a Nuclear Weapons Convention.

Blair's decision to replace the UK Trident force, announced on 4 December 2006 and eventually implemented by Parliament on 18 July 2016, means that the prospects for such British leadership are bleak. As suggested in Chapter 2, what drives uncritical UK government support for US nuclear and foreign policy is the UK's dependence on the US for a range of nuclear weapon-related military capabilities, from Trident missiles to satellite intelligence and communications, and warhead design and testing facilities.

Never has there been a more pressing need for the UK government to reconsider the consequences for Britain's true security interests. Indeed, one high-ranking US official has privately suggested that the UK government should consider abandoning Trident replacement, because 'either they can be a nuclear power and nothing else, or a real military partner'.[55] Trident replacement was an important issue in the referendum on Scottish independence in September 2014, because UK

Trident submarines can only be based in Scotland. With public opinion divided and a significant anti-nuclear citizen movement, the issue is being complicated by 'Brexit', the decision to leave the European Union.

The British should lead the French. Some political and military diehards argue that it is critical for the UK to retain its nuclear weapons because 'France must never be allowed to be the sole European nuclear power.'[56] However, for all the reasons laid out in this book, the security needs of the British and all fellow Europeans demand that both the UK and France move on at last from the Napoleonic Wars and loss of Empire and address the real security threats confronting them in the 21st century. As the first medium-sized power to acquire nuclear weapons, Britain now has the opportunity to set France a wiser and more responsible example. Central to this are the opportunity costs for both countries' defence policies. Finally, the ridiculous notion that France's greatness depends on possession of nuclear weapons should be exposed as demeaning to French citizens and culture. The reality is that threatening nuclear weapon use risks the annihilation of French culture within a devastated and poisoned land.

Summary

Finding a way back from the literal dead-end towards which the huge hoax of nuclear deterrence is driving us begins with the realisation that current nuclear strategies have failed. Incentives to shift the mindset include new risks of nuclear war, and the reality that nuclear weapons remain the greatest security threat, not only to those states relying on nuclear deterrence but to the overwhelming majority which feel more secure without it. In the same way as the abolition of slavery led to more humane, lawful and effective ways of creating wealth, the key is to see nuclear disarmament as part of a process of building confidence and moving from an adversarial to a co-operative security paradigm, where nuclear weapons are a liability.

It is in NATO's direct security interest to adopt a non-nuclear strategy as soon as possible. The steps to achieve this are proposed, which could be adapted for denuclearising the US security treaties with Japan, South Korea and Australia.

Once the leading nuclear weapon states have agreed to renounce their arsenals, the problem of 'breakout' will become less likely, and easier to prevent. Verification will be a central feature of a Nuclear Weapons Convention, helping to build confidence and trust in the process and minimising the risk of cheating. While the US remains the main obstacle to a durable nuclear weapon-free world, the UK could yet gain a new global role as a true 'force for good' if it reconsidered the decision to replace the Trident force and instead took the lead in rejecting nuclear deterrence.

Notes

1. In a disturbing major report published on 10 January 2008, five former defence chiefs from the US, UK, France, Germany and the Netherlands recommended reinforcing nuclear deterrence 'by proactive denial, in which pre-emption is a form of reaction when a threat is imminent'. See *Towards a Grand Strategy for an Uncertain World: Renewing Transatlantic Partnership*, http://csis.org/files/media/csis/events/080110_grand_strategy.pdf.
2. See John D. Steinbruner, *Principles of Global Security* (Brookings Institution Press, Washington, D.C., 2000).
3. See Karel Koster, 'The best defense…', *The Bulletin of the Atomic Scientists*, September/October 2004, pp. 26–28, for his interesting analogy with the Ancient Greek phalanx, where hoplite infantry attacked in a tight formation behind their shields.
4. Steven Lee Myers, 'Putin Says New Missile Systems Will Give Russia a Nuclear Edge', *New York Times*, 18 November 2004.
5. Alexei Arbatov and Vladimir Dvorkin, *Beyond Nuclear Deterrence: Transforming the U.S.-Russian Equation*, (Washington, D.C.: Carnegie Endowment for International Peace, 2006), pp. 164–170.
6. 'China Says It Will Not Use Nuclear Weapons against Taiwan', *The New York Times*, 3 September 1999.
7. Keith B. Payne, *The Fallacies of Cold War Deterrence and a New Direction* (The University Press of Kentucky, 2001), p. 170 et seq. His proposed response, however, was for the US to develop both a homeland and theatre BMD capability.
8. George H.W. Bush, 'Address before a Joint Session of the Congress on the Persian Gulf Crisis and the Federal Budget Deficit (September 11, 1990)', *Public Papers of the Presidents of the United States: George Bush*, book 2: *July 1 to December 3 1, 1990* (U.S. Government Printing Office), p. 1219.
9. David Lange, 'New Zealand' in *The Planetary Interest*, Kennedy Graham ed., (University College London Press, 1999), pp. 49–50.
10. The *New Zealand Nuclear Free Zone, Disarmament, and Arms Control Act* became law on 8 June 1987. See http://rangi.knowledge-basket.co.nz/gpacts/public/text/1987/an/086.html.
11. 'Anti-Nuke Stance', New Zealand *Dominion*, 1 October 1997.
12. For more details, see Bjorn Mueller, Dictionary of Alternative Defense (Boulder: Lynne Rienner Publishers, 1995); and for more discussion, see Ken Booth, 'Alternative Defence', in Ken Booth and John Baylis, *Britain, NATO and Nuclear Weapons*, (New York: St Martin's Press, 1989), p. 197.
13. Palme Commission, *The Report of the Independent Commission on Disarmament and Security Issues under the Chairmanship of Olof Palme, Common Security* (London: Pan Books, 1982).
14. Mayors for Peace, founded in 1982 by the Mayor of Hiroshima, has almost 3,800 affiliated cities in 143 countries and regions. Currently it is promoting its '2020 Vision' Campaign to eliminate all nuclear weapons by 2020, the 75th anniversary of the Hiroshima and Nagasaki atomic bombings. See http://www.2020visioncampaign.org/.
15. Terence O'Brien, Director of the Centre for Strategic Studies (CSS:NZ), address in debate with Sir Michael Quinlan, former Permanent Under Secretary of State, UK Ministry of Defence, Wellington, 3 July 1997.
16. Elaine Lies, 'Japan joins US push for harsh N Korea sanctions', Reuters, 11 October 2006.
17. Rebecca Johnson, 'Security Assurances for Everyone: A New Approach to Deterring the Use of Nuclear Weapons', *Disarmament Diplomacy 90*, Spring 2009, http://www.acronym.org.uk/dd/dd90/90sa.htm.
18. Bruce G. Blair, Harold A. Feiveson and Frank von Hippel, 'Taking Nuclear Weapons Off Hair-Trigger Alert', *Scientific American*, November 1997, http://www.cdi.org/aboutcdi/SciAmerBB.html.
19. Canberra Commission (1996), pp. 53–54, http://www.dfat.gov.au/cc/index.html.

20   See http://www.fas.org/nuke/control/jdec/index.html.
21   Weapons of Mass Destruction Commission final report, *Weapons of Terror: Freeing the World of Nuclear, Biological, and Chemical Arms*, Stockholm, Sweden, 1 June 2006. Electronic copy available at http://www.wmdcommission.org.
22   Canberra Commission (1996), p. 54.
23   See http://www.reachingcriticalwill.org/political/1com/1com07/res/L29.pdf.
24   *Reframing Nuclear De-Alert: Decreasing the operational readiness of U.S. and Russian arsenals*, EastWest Institute, Swiss Confederation, 2009, http://www.ewi.info/reframing-nuclear-de-alert-decreasing-operational-readiness-us-and-russian-nuclear-arsenals.
25   Jiang Zemin, 'How to Get On With Nuclear Disarmament', *International Herald Tribune*, 16 June 1999.
26   Michael MccGwire, 'Shifting the paradigm', *International Affairs*, 78, 1 (2002), pp. 11–12.
27   UN Document A/C.1/52/7.
28   Merav Datan and Alyn Ware, *Security and Survival: The Case for a Nuclear Weapons Convention* (International Physicians for the Prevention of Nuclear War, 1999).
29   Ibid, Comments and Critical Questions, Section 3-11.
30   'Nuclear-Weapon-Free Southern Hemisphere and Adjacent Areas', UNGA 54/54L. Revised versions have been adopted each year since then.
31   La Conferencia de Estados Partes y Signatarios de Tratados que Establecen Zonas Libres de Armas Nucleares, .
32   Declaration for the Conference of Nuclear-Weapon-Free Zones, adopted 28 April 2005, http://www.sre.gob.mx/eventos/zlan/declarzlaningl.htm.
33   See Alyn Ware, Kate Dewes and Michael Powles, 'Snaring the Sun: Opportunities to prevent nuclear weapons proliferation and advance nuclear disarmament through an abolition framework', Disarmament & Security Centre, Christchurch, New Zealand, January 2005, , pp. 24–26. See also the Report from the Civil Society Forum, Conference of States Parties and Signatories to the Treaties that establish Nuclear-Weapon-Free Zones, Annex IV to Working Paper of the NPT Review Conference NPT/CONF.2005/WP.46 submitted as a Note Verbale dated 10 May 2005 from the Permanent Mission of Mexico to the United Nations addressed to the President of the Conference, http://www.reachingcriticalwill.org/legal/npt/RevCon05/wp/index.html.
34   'Negotiations on Central Asian nuclear-weapon-free-zone treaty concluded', UN Press Release DC/2842, 30 September 2002. Michael Steen, 'Central Asia declares nuclear free zone', *The Scotsman*, 8 September 2006, http://news.scotsman.com/latest.cfm?id=1330112006. See also report by the Arms Control Association, http://us.oneworld.net/article/view/139136/1/7263.
35   For an authoritative commentary, see Scott Parrish and William Potter, *Central Asian States Establish Nuclear-Weapon-Free-Zone Despite U.S. Opposition*, Center for Nonproliferation Studies, Monterey Institute of International Studies, http://cns.miis.edu/pubs/week/060905.htm.
36   John E. Endicott, 'A Limited Nuclear-Weapons-Free Zone in Northeast Asia: A Track II Initiative', *Disarmament Diplomacy*, March 1999, pp. 19–22. For a recent discussion, see *The Future of the Peace Process and Prospects for a Nuclear Weapon Free Zone in Northeast Asia*, 2013 NPT Preparatory Committee NGO Workshop, Palais des Nations, Geneva, 25 April 2013, http://www.peacedepot.org/e-news/2013NPTWS.pdf.
37   See http://www.icnnd.org/reference/reports/ent/index.html.
38   See Achin Vanaik, 'Building a Nuclear Disarmament Movement in India, Pakistan and South Asia: Some Policy Perspectives', *Economic and Political Weekly*, 6 February 2005, http://www.tni.org/archives/archives_vanaik_building.
39   *Tactical Nuclear Weapons Preliminary Research Findings* (UNIDIR, April 2000), http://www.unig.ch/unidir.
40   Alexa McDonough and Alyn Ware, *Freeing the Poles of Nuclear Conflicts? Time for an Arctic Nuclear Weapon Free Zone*, Disarmament & Security Centre, 2009,

	http://www.disarmsecure.org/Freeing%20the%20poles%20of%20nuclear%20weapons.pdf.
41	Bruno Tertrais, 'Nuclear Policies in Europe', *Adelphi Paper* 327 (London: International Institute of Strategic Studies, March 1999), p. 33.
42	See Judge Nagendrea Singh (ICJ President 1986), *The Role and Record of the International Court of Justice* (Martinus Nijhoff, Dordrecht/Boston/London, 1989), p. 350.
43	Wilbert van der Zeijden, Susi Snyder and Peter Paul Ekker, *Exit Strategies: The case for redefining NATO consensus on U.S. TNW*, IKV Pax Christi, April 2012.
44	'NATO and Russia Confirm New Relationship, Stress Non-Proliferation Cooperation', *Disarmament Diplomacy*, July/August 2002, pp. 45–47.
45	On 9 February 2008, President Vladimir Putin used a major televised speech to accuse the US of unleashing a new arms race that left Moscow no choice but to retaliate in kind. He also renewed his objections to NATO's eastward expansion into the former Russian sphere of influence, symbolised by a meeting of NATO defence ministers in Vilnius, Lithuania as he was speaking. See Shaun Walker, '"A new phase in the arms race is unfolding," says Putin', *The Independent*, 9 February 2008, http://www.independent.co.uk/news/europe/a-new-phase-in-the-arms-race-is-unfolding-says-putin-780183.html.
46	In 2001, Greece withdrew from its nuclear sharing agreement with the US, with no severe consequences for NATO deterrence doctrine or unity. On 26 June 2008, the US secretly removed its 110 B-61 free-fall nuclear bombs from RAF Lakenheath, UK, . See Wilbert van der Zeijden, Susi Snyder and Peter Paul Ekker, *Exit Strategies: The case for redefining NATO consensus on U.S. TNW*, IKV Pax Christi, April 2012.
47	At the 2002 UN General Assembly Disarmament Session, the New Agenda Coalition introduced a new resolution, 'Reductions of Non-Strategic Nuclear Weapons', UNGA 57/58 (L.2/Rev.1*). It called upon the US and Russia to formalise their 1991 and 1992 Presidential Initiatives into legal instruments, and for additional measures to reduce the operational status of tactical nuclear weapons. It was adopted by 120 votes to 3 (the NATO nuclear trio) with 42 abstentions. At the 2003 Disarmament Session, a revised version of the resolution, A/C.1/58/L.39/Rev.1, was adopted by 128 votes to 4 (Russia joined the US, UK and France), with 42 abstentions.
48	*Tactical Nuclear Weapons Preliminary Research Findings* (UNIDIR, April 2000), .
49	Ibid, p. 27.
50	George F. Kennan, *At A Century's Ending: Reflections 1982–1995*, (New York: W.W.Norton, 1996), p. 106.
51	Patricia Lewis, 'Verification of Nuclear Weapon Elimination', in Regina Cowen Karp ed., *Security Without Nuclear Weapons? Different Perspectives on Non-Nuclear Security*, (Oxford University Press, 1992), p. 146.
52	MccGwire (2002), pp. 14–15.
53	See 'The OSCE at work', http://www.osce.org/resources/23463.html.
54	For more on the Shanghai Cooperation Organization, see http://www.cfr.org/publication/10883/.
55	'UK Must Balance Trident Renewal with Ability to Conduct Traditional Military Campaigns', Global Security Newswire, 1 May 2013, http://www.nti.org/gsn/article/uk-renewal-trident-will-impact-ability-conduct-traditional-military-campaigns-us/ .
56	For example, see the exchange between Sir Michael Quinlan and members of the Parliamentary Defence Select Committee, 'The Future of the UK's Strategic Nuclear Deterrent: The Strategic Context', Uncorrected Oral Evidence, 14 March 2006, Questions 44–45, http://www.publications.parliament.uk/pa/cm200506/cmselect/cmdfence/uc986-i/uc98602.htm.

CHAPTER SEVEN

CONCLUSIONS

My breakout from unquestioning acceptance of nuclear deterrence began in the early 1970s, when I discovered that my military leaders required me to be prepared to conduct a suicide mission with a nuclear depth-bomb. This was deemed necessary because a conventional weapon had yet to be developed to counter the speed and depth advantage of a nuclear-powered submarine. For me, that requirement epitomised the irrationality of an arms race where the balance between effectiveness and potential cost in collateral damage became completely lost. The gross 'overkill' and associated military incompetence shocked me into a less trusting, more questioning frame of mind. Looking back from my current vantage point, it is easier to understand how such irresponsible, foolish thinking led to British military professionals being ordered to practise using such a nuclear device.

There is a fundamental paradox about nuclear deterrence. Why is it that professed 'realists', who pride themselves on understanding the often unpredictable aspects of human nature and the history of conflict, have such faith in the rationality of leaders of nuclear-armed states and their ability to control events? 'Realists' speak of nuclear arsenal management techniques that make deterrence safe and provide security. Yet their arguments require no less of a leap of faith in the triumph of hope over experience than nuclear disarmament – especially after India and Pakistan shook the foundations of the 'realist' thesis in 1998. From this clash between ideologically driven dogma and commonsense reality, it would seem that the future comes down to choosing between living in perpetuity with the dangers of nuclear weapons, or risk trying to achieve security without them. My carefully considered conclusion is that abolition is safer, with the added attraction of being both morally sound and lawful. Furthermore, it would relieve military professionals, including Commanding Officers of Royal Navy Trident-armed submarines, of the dirty work of being poised to press the nuclear weapon launch button for their posturing political leaders, and restore funding to maintain conventional force levels.

Unlike the late Sir Michael Quinlan's unprovable assumption that nuclear weapons prevent major war, will history show that their one constructive purpose has been to frighten us into choosing less nihilistic ways to resolve conflict, more worthy of a species with the arrogance to name itself *homo sapiens*? The US, in denial over its atrocities in Hiroshima and Nagasaki, seized upon the bogus mantra of nuclear deterrence to play on people's fears, and justify sustaining the unaccountable, highly profitable scientific and military monster bequeathed by the Manhattan Project. Since then the guardians of nuclear deterrence have struggled to provide intellectual coherence as endless adjustments to the doctrine were made to accommodate the latest expansion of the nuclear arms race it had provoked. Uncritical repetition by political leaders, careerist 'experts' and mainstream media of simplistic soundbites gave it the intellectual and moral aura of a state religion, to the point where it echoes the fable of the emperor with no clothes.

The reality is that nuclear deterrence, highly vulnerable to failure because of its insoluble credibility problem, fosters international hostility and mistrust, and a paranoid, zero-sum approach to security. Threatening a greater evil than it sought to prevent, during the Cold War the dogma echoed the communist line that ends justified means. As nuclear arsenals grew, the explicit threat to the Soviet Union evolved into an implicit threat to the survival of the human race. Nuclear deterrence was imbued with a selective respectability that put the world at risk through state-sponsored nuclear terrorism, while the West pursued the chimera of total security for itself.

For British and French leaders, the traumas of Suez and their waning empires drove them to crave the counterfeit currency of power of nuclear deterrence to sustain their status and influence. In the case of France, this need was dire after the carnage of the First World War, followed by defeat and Nazi occupation less than a generation later. The French chose to develop, at massive cost, an indigenous nuclear weapon and delivery capability. The British, having decided they could not afford this, signed a Faustian bargain with the US by choosing dependence for submarine and warhead designs, missiles, nuclear weapon testing, and satellite targeting, intelligence and communications. Embarrassingly, the UK remains the only nuclear weapon state without its own space launch capability.

The pay-back involved uncritically supporting US demands that undermined British independence in foreign and domestic policy.

Examples include eviction of British citizens, its indigenous population, from Diego Garcia; allowing US interception of British communications on British territory; and being accomplices in illegal, counterproductive military punitive expeditions such as the 1986 US air strikes against Libya and the disastrous invasion and occupation of Iraq in 2003.

The world was fortunate that the West's opponent was the Soviet Union – which, with a staggering 20 million dead from World War II, was well-motivated not to risk another total war – and not a mirror image of the US. Unlike NATO, the Soviets did re-evaluate the threat as years passed. By 1959 they had decided that the danger was no longer a deliberate attack by a US-led capitalist coalition, but inadvertent war. By definition, inadvertent war could not be deterred – but it might be avoided, given the right mix of policies.

In 1985, the clear-thinking and innovative new Soviet leader Mikhail Gorbachev gained sufficient power to propose a feasible agenda for stepping back from the nuclear abyss. At Reykjavik in 1986 he called US President Ronald Reagan's bluff on the true intentions of the US military-industrial complex regarding its Strategic Defense Initiative, which had more to do with enhancing the insatiable vested interests of its military-industrial complex and exhausting the Soviet economy than strengthening US security. Tragically, Gorbachev was rebuffed by the pernicious US preference to maintain its disingenuous promise of extended nuclear deterrence, and associated control, over its allies. Then the 1991 coup attempt against Gorbachev marked the end of enlightened thinking from Russia's leaders. With its crumbling military forces and chaotic economy, Russia grasped at Western nuclear deterrence dogma to sustain its superpower status and assuage its sense of vulnerability as NATO expanded eastwards.

Meanwhile the nuclear weapon programmes in Israel, India and Pakistan (like those of the five recognised nuclear-armed states plus South Africa, Argentina, Brazil, Iraq and North Korea) demonstrated the incestuous links between nuclear energy and weapons, consequent failure of the nuclear non-proliferation regime, and the massive costs and risks of relying on nuclear deterrence for security. Moreover, no consideration was given to the potentially catastrophic consequences of exposing nuclear power plants and associated highly radioactive waste to attack in conventional war or by extremists, let alone nuclear war; nor of the 'inalienable right' of non-nuclear states to nuclear energy in the Non-Proliferation Treaty.

In Israel's case, support came first from France, and then from the US and UK. Shut out of the Manhattan Project and US drive for nuclear supremacy, France depended upon Israeli technical assistance in the early 1950s. This gave Israel leverage in obtaining French technical and engineering support. Then successive US administrations, appeasing a powerful Israeli lobby and convinced that a militarily dominant Israel served US strategic interests in the Middle East, allowed a ruthless and highly competent Israeli politico-scientific-military nexus to develop some 80 nuclear warheads. Israel persuaded the US and its allies to turn a blind eye to this, support its belligerent foreign and defence policies, and provide massive military aid.

In South Asia, Indian governments became convinced, in part by Britain's example, that nuclear deterrence held the key to guaranteed security and acceptance as a great power; and Pakistan followed India. Both were also motivated by perceived echoes of colonialism and racism, particularly from the UK and US. Apart from the hypocrisy of the UK/US 'do as we say, not as we do' line regarding possession of nuclear arsenals, over the years British and American governments and experts had insinuated that nuclear weapons were beyond the abilities and levels of political maturity of Indians or Pakistanis to build and operate responsibly. Then Western and Chinese greed and venality allowed export controls to be by-passed, as exemplified by the revelations of A.Q. Khan, one of the 'fathers' of Pakistan's nuclear programme. Now, India and Pakistan are locked into a nuclear arms race where nuclear deterrence doctrine is hopelessly impractical to implement – as General Lee Butler USAF (Ret) tried to explain to their governments.

After the Cold War ended, the massive effort expended by US pro-nuclear fundamentalists to find new roles for nuclear weapons betrayed their fear that nuclear deterrence dogma was in trouble. It should not be forgotten that the Clinton administration initiated the posture shift to threaten use of nuclear weapons in response to non-nuclear weapon of mass destruction attacks against US interests.

The 1996 Advisory Opinion on the legal status of the threat or use of nuclear weapons by the International Court of Justice constituted a historic breakthrough by implicitly confirming that nuclear deterrence is unlawful. This was the first time that any of the nuclear powers felt obliged to try to defend the legality of their nuclear policies in the world's most respected court of law. Despite clear warnings from the US, UK and France not to rule against nuclear deterrence, the Court adroitly affirmed the general illegality of the fundamental practice that constitutes nuclear deterrence. The three Western nuclear powers, having accepted the outlawing of chemical and biological weapons of mass destruction, were reduced to vague assertions that the legality of the threat or use of nuclear weapons depends on circumstances; yet they must know that there is no scenario where use of even one nuclear warhead would be legal. In 1998, they revealed lack of confidence in their own arguments by lodging reservations on ratifying the Geneva Conventions that they do not apply to nuclear weapons. The UK Government effectively gave up trying to defend the legality of its nuclear posture in 2017 by withdrawing its acceptance of compulsory ICJ jurisdiction for cases involving nuclear weapons. In so doing, it left the command team of the deployed Trident submarine in an unacceptable position of legal jeopardy.

The implications of the Court's legal challenge impinge on those involved in planning and deploying nuclear forces. To distinguish themselves from hired killers or terrorists, military professionals need to be seen to act within the law. They particularly, therefore, need to know that the Court confirmed that the Nuremberg Principles form a part of international humanitarian law, and that nuclear weapons, though not yet specifically prohibited, were now effectively in the same stigmatised category as chemical and biological weapons.

Then came President George W. Bush's administration. Initially, his public admission that nuclear deterrence was not credible against extremists was refreshingly candid. Confirmation followed in a statement from the 2002 US National Security Strategy: 'We know from history that deterrence can fail; and we know from experience that some enemies cannot be deterred.'

However, Bush's use of this acknowledgement to justify reviving ballistic missile defence, echoing Reagan's disingenuous line, was followed by the 'Bush doctrine', which postulated pre-emptive strikes against 'rogue' regimes suspected of acquiring weapons of mass destruction. The pro-nuclear advocates' strongest (but unprovable) claim, that nuclear deterrence prevents major war, had thereby been turned on its head by the Bush Administration's response: deliberate, pre-emptive war backed by ballistic missile defence. Unilateral US withdrawal in 2002 from the Anti-Ballistic Missile Treaty, while the US and Russia each persisted with about 2,000 strategic nuclear warheads on high-alert status, meant that the world was now at greater risk from the consequences of nuclear deterrence than during the Cold War.

NATO's acceptance of the new US nuclear strategy meant it could not harmonise its posture with the 2000 NPT Review final document, in which thirteen practical steps leading to a nuclear weapon-free world were agreed by consensus. NATO's current strategic concept, published ten years later, again ignored these contradictions with the 2010 NPT Review final document, which broadly reiterated those thirteen steps. Thus, as demonstrated on 7 July 2017 in the UN General Assembly when 122 states adopted a specific Treaty on the Prohibition of Nuclear Weapons, NATO stands condemned as the primary impediment to genuine nuclear disarmament. It has no answer to the argument that, because it places so much political value in its nuclear forces, it is providing a justification for proliferators. Instead, its current enforcer, the Trump Administration, makes clear in their 2018 Nuclear Posture Review that, effectively ignoring nuclear deterrence, they are planning for first use of low-yield nuclear weapons to deal with even non-nuclear 'rogue' regimes and strategic cyber attacks.

NATO claims to uphold democracy, human rights and the rule of law. Yet nuclear deterrence is about threatening the most indiscriminate violence possible, unrestrained by morality or the law. It is therefore a policy of gross irresponsibility and the antithesis of democracy. By contrast, almost thirty years after the end of the Cold War, the overwhelming majority of states understand that nuclear disarmament is a security-building process, where nuclear weapons are a liability and a security problem.

The most pressing priority, therefore, is to denuclearise the security strategies of the Western allies which, if they redirect some of the cost of modernising their nuclear arsenals to restoring credible conventional forces, will be strong enough in political, economic and military terms to do this before the non-proliferation regime unravels further. This will enable nuclear forces to be verifiably stood down, and Russia and China to be reassured enough for negotiations to begin on a Nuclear Weapons Convention, an enforceable comprehensive global treaty providing a plan to go to zero nuclear weapons. This book has offered some specific ideas for debate as part of a major review of NATO nuclear policy, which could be adapted for application to the US bilateral alliances with Japan, South Korea and Australia.

To consolidate the paradigm shift of rejecting nuclear deterrence and reassuring Russia and its former allies remaining in its sphere of influence, consideration should be given in the longer term to NATO merging with the Organisation for Security and Co-operation in Europe (OSCE). Most of the current tensions between NATO and the European Union would fall away, with NATO transformed into a common safety net for all states 'from Vancouver to Vladivostok' – perhaps to be renamed the Organisation for Security and Co-operation in Europe, North Asia and North America (OSCENANA)?

Extension of such co-operative security thinking to the rest of the world community, pioneered by Olof Palme and championed by Mikhail Gorbachev, will be vital to achieve a durable nuclear weapon-free world. New Zealand showed how to break free from obeisance to nuclear deterrence, and achieve real security through building confidence and trust with its neighbours in the Asia-Pacific region. It has evolved a strategy combining minimal non-provocative defence with peacekeeping, and strengthening international law and multilateral institutions under UN auspices. It has also applied its track record in nuclear disarmament through new coalitions that bridge the old Cold War negotiating blocs in the UN.

Probably no further significant progress will be made until one of the recognised nuclear weapon states breaks out. The US is the main obstacle; but Britain is by far the best-placed candidate for anti-nuclear 'breakout'. Tony Blair had the opportunity to heal the wounds over Iraq and reassert Britain's independence by simply deciding not to replace the four *Vanguard* class Trident-armed submarines. Instead, he passed on to his successors a divisive decision to maintain the status quo despite the need for deep defence budget cuts, prompting US officials to suggest that the UK must choose between being 'a nuclear power and nothing else, or a real military partner'. Making a virtue from necessity, a perhaps unlikely new world leadership role awaits the UK here by exploiting its special relationship with the US as truly a 'force for good'.

New Zealand's visionary Prime Minister, the late David Lange, argued powerfully in his famed 1985 Oxford Union debate that the true strength of the West, in the form of its democratic institutions, 'is threatened, not defended, by nuclear weapons. The appalling character of those weapons has robbed us of our right to determine our destiny, and subordinates our humanity to their manic logic.' He added that rejecting nuclear deterrence does not mean surrendering to evil, but instead asserts the moral force of humanity over evil.

Finding our way back from the nuclear abyss, on the edge of which nuclear deterrence has held us hypnotised and terrorised for over seventy years, will not be easy. As with all earlier major advances in human rights and justice, the engine for shifting the mindset has to come from among civil society. Within this, as epitomised by General Lee Butler USAF (Ret), there is a crucial role for former military leaders with experience of nuclear weapons, giving them unrivalled authority to speak truth to power. For Britain to become the first recognised nuclear weapon state to reject nuclear deterrence, these nuclear veterans will be needed to help explain this shameful abuse of the Royal Navy and misappropriation of British taxpayers' money.

It was Mahatma Gandhi, as he launched the final push towards evicting the British from India in 1938, who said: 'A small body of determined spirits fired by an unquenchable faith in their mission can alter the course of history.' The American anthropologist Margaret Mead's more famous adaptation of this added: 'Indeed, it's the only thing that ever has.' Determination on the part of a small group of individuals fuelled the campaign to abolish slavery. As with nuclear deterrence, three of the leading proponents of slavery were the power elites of the US, UK and France, who tried to sustain their immoral and unlawful assertion that slavery was a 'necessary evil' for which there was 'no alternative'. They failed, because courageous ordinary British, American and French citizens – some of whom had been involved in the slave trade – mobilised unstoppable public and political support for their campaign to replace slavery with more humane, lawful and effective ways to create wealth. The analogy holds for nuclear deterrence, which can and must be discarded for more humane, lawful and safer security strategies if civilisation and the Earth's ecosystems are to survive.

GLOSSARY

ABM. Anti-Ballistic Missile (Treaty). The US and Soviet Union signed this treaty in 1972, whereby both agreed to restrict the development and deployment of anti-ballistic missiles by allowing just a single ABM system on their territories, in an attempt to limit their nuclear arms race and preserve their deterrence relationship of Mutual Assured Destruction. However, in 2002 the US withdrew from the treaty in order to build and deploy a national ballistic missile defence system.

ANZUS Treaty. Australia, New Zealand and United States Treaty, signed in 1951. Following the re-establishment of peace between Japan and the United States, Australia and New Zealand asked for a defence treaty making it clear that an attack on any of the three signatory countries would be considered an attack upon all; and they accepted US extended nuclear deterrence. New Zealand's 1985 refusal to allow US nuclear-powered or nuclear-armed ships to enter its ports caused the US to downgrade its relationship from ally to friend in 1986; however, New Zealand has not formally withdrawn from the alliance.

Assured Destruction. A 'worst case' US strategy of nuclear deterrence by punishment, which replaced Controlled Response in 1962 following the continuous deployment of numbers of **second-strike** invulnerable Polaris submarines in addition to **first-strike** land-based ICBMs in hardened silos backed up by long-range bombers.

BMD. Ballistic Missile Defence. A generic description for all variants of missiles and their sensor systems designed to intercept and destroy ballistic missiles. These range from Patriot missile batteries first used by the US and Israel with mixed success against short (up to 600 km) range Iraqi Scud missiles in their terminal phase during the first Gulf War in 1991, through theatre missile defence such as the US Navy's ship-borne Aegis system to intercept short, medium (up to 1,300 km) and intermediate (up to 3,500 km) range ballistic missiles in their boost, mid-course and terminal phases, to US-based missile systems to intercept intercontinental (5,500-10,000 km) range missiles in mid-course and terminal phases. The US is developing a variety of land, air and space-based sensors and weapons, and ultimately plans to deploy interceptor weapons in outer space. This risks US space domination, as such weapons would have the capability to destroy satellites.

Canberra Commission. In November 1995 the Canberra Commission on the Elimination of Nuclear Weapons was established as an independent commission by the Australian Government, despite its nuclear alliance with the US, to propose practical steps towards a nuclear weapon-free world, including the related problem of maintaining stability and security during the transitional period and after this goal is achieved. Its 17 members included: former Manhattan Project scientist and Nobel Peace Prize-winner Joseph Rotblat; General Lee Butler USAF (Ret), former Commander-in-Chief US Strategic Command 1992-94 in charge of all US nuclear forces; Robert McNamara, US Secretary of Defense during the 1962 Cuban Missile Crisis; Field Marshal Lord Carver, UK Chief of Defence Staff 1973-76, and former French Prime Minister Michel Rocard. They published a report in August 1996 in which they warned: 'The risks of retaining nuclear arsenals in perpetuity far outweigh any possible benefit imputed to nuclear deterrence... The end of the Cold War has created a new climate for international action to eliminate nuclear weapons, a new opportunity. It must be exploited quickly or it will be lost.'

CB. Chemical and biological weapons.

CND. Campaign for Nuclear Disarmament. Founded in 1958, it is the UK's oldest and biggest grassroots citizen organization committed to ridding the world of nuclear weapons.

Controlled Response. A short-lived US nuclear deterrence strategy introduced by Kennedy's Defense Secretary Robert McNamara to replace Massive Retaliation from 1960-62. It attempted to offer graduated responses to correct the indiscriminate threats of Massive Retaliation, which was too inflexible and not credible in deterring aggression short of all-out war. However, it contained serious contradictions: with the Soviets not able to deploy their equivalent of Polaris for several years, they were forced to target US cities as the only remaining politically coercive choice. Worse, the combination of an invulnerable US second-strike capability with a US first-strike counterforce strategy placed the Soviets under pressure to strike first.

Counter-Force. A nuclear targeting policy focused on neutralizing the enemy's key military assets, including command centres and first strike nuclear delivery systems. Its weakness is that effectively it is inseparable from a first strike/use strategy. Also, it places the enemy in a 'use it or lose it' dilemma at the outset of the crisis. However, proponents argue that such an approach enables nuclear war to be limited, with the option of Escalation Dominance.

Counter-Value. A nuclear targeting policy focused on causing maximum damage to the enemy's population centres and social and economic infrastructure. Proponents argue that this is the only realistic approach to nuclear deterrence, because there is no military use for thermonuclear weapons, and a counter-force exchange would quickly escalate to counter-value targeting.

CTBT. Comprehensive (nuclear weapon) Test Ban Treaty. Opened for signature by states in 1996, it must be ratified by forty-four named states – those with nuclear energy programmes, and therefore theoretically capable of building nuclear weapons – before it can enter into force. The main stumbling block is the US, which is among the thirteen key states that have not ratified, raising the suspicion that the Bush administration might break a nuclear test moratorium agreed in 1993. Despite this, the CTBT Organisation Preparatory Commission has pressed ahead with an international monitoring system linked to a network of seismic stations worldwide to verify compliance.

Deterrence. This is a strategy to convince an opponent who is contemplating undesirable action that the costs will exceed any possible gain. Deterrence therefore lies midway between conflict avoidance and waging conflict. The two most common versions are:
(1) Deterrence by the prospect of **denial.** Primarily the traditional version, it means threatening physical interference with the opponent's military efforts, affecting the gains to be made from a war.
(2) Deterrence by the prospect of **punishment.** The primary role of nuclear deterrence, this is the threat to meet an attack in less direct but still unacceptably damaging ways, such as a retaliatory strike on the opponent's society, which will affect the losses it will suffer.

For deterrence to be predictably successful, it is essential that the opponent perceives that its action would result in unacceptable damage to its interests. The following distinct conditions need to be present:
- The two sides must share similar values so that the intended threat will be perceived as such.
- The threat must be inherently credible under these conditions.

- Communications between the parties must be reliable enough to transmit the threat message.

EMP. Electro-Magnetic Pulse. A high-altitude nuclear detonation produces an immediate flux of gamma rays, emitting high-energy free electrons, which are then trapped in the Earth's magnetic field giving rise to an oscillating electric current. This current causes a rapidly rising radiated electromagnetic field. The pulse can easily span continent-sized areas, and this radiation can affect electrical systems on land, sea, and air. The first recorded EMP incident accompanied a 1962 high-altitude nuclear test over the South Pacific and resulted in power system failures as far away as Hawaii.

Escalation Dominance. This is a concept where the deterrer deliberately escalates the conflict to show sufficient resolve to deter the opponent from continuing. That risks the opponent misperceiving deterrence as offensive and provocative. It also intensified the nuclear arms race.

EU. European Union. This comprises a group of democratic states committed to working together for peace and prosperity. Originally called the European Economic Community when it was founded in the early 1960s, it now covers most of Europe. Member states have delegated some of their sovereignty to common institutions, including a European Parliament. The Treaty of Maastricht (1992) created the EU, and introduced new forms of co-operation between the member-state governments, such as working towards common foreign and defence policies.

Existential Nuclear Deterrence. This is where a nuclear possessor does not deploy any weapons, but simply announces that its arsenal exists and demonstrates that it has the ability to deliver them. This would appeal to a state with insufficient resources to sustain deployed nuclear forces. Clearly the deterrent effect would be less immediate. India, Pakistan and North Korea could be said to practise this.

Extended Nuclear Deterrence. This is achieved by a nuclear weapon state extending its so-called 'nuclear umbrella' to cover the territories of its non-nuclear allies. It has been provided by the US to non-nuclear NATO member states, Japan, South Korea and Australia since the early 1950s.

First Strike. The initiation of strategic nuclear war. This would entail the launch of the most accurately guided warheads targeted to destroy military forces including the enemy's own first-strike systems.

First Use. Under a strategy of Flexible Response, this is the use of tactical or sub-strategic nuclear weapons to escalate the war from conventional to nuclear level. The problem here is that mutual first use threats tend to lead to actual first use, because of the pressure both to destroy the opponent's first-strike systems, and for the opponent to avert this.

Flexible Response. The US nuclear deterrence strategy from 1962-1989, it was a more complex version of Controlled Response. Adopted by NATO in 1967, it entailed initial deployment of some less destructive **tactical** or **sub-strategic** nuclear warheads posing deterrence by denial before escalating to deterrence by punishment with **strategic** nuclear warheads. The implied flexibility related not to whether to escalate, but when. However, this introduced three disadvantages:

(1) The notion that **nuclear weapons could be used for fighting a war.**
(2) The temptation to **lower the nuclear threshold,** meaning the moment in a war when the use of nuclear weapons would be considered essential or justified.
(3) The associated **difficulty in controlling escalation.**

This in turn encouraged Escalation Dominance. Because of these problems, after the Cold War ended in 1989, NATO announced that it had effectively abandoned Flexible Response, and that its nuclear posture was one of **last resort.** Nevertheless, NATO continues to deploy some sub-strategic nuclear weapons as 'an essential element in ensuring that no nuclear-armed aggressor could gamble on us being **self-deterred** by fear of an inevitable strategic exchange. In such extreme circumstances this capability would allow the limited use of nuclear weapons to send an aggressor a political message of the Alliance's resolve to defend itself.'

G8. The world's leading eight economic powers: the US, Japan, Russia, UK, France, Germany, Canada, Italy. Their heads of state meet annually to discuss macro-economic management, international trade, terrorism and relations with developing countries.

HDBTs. Hardened and deeply buried targets.

HMS. Her Majesty's Ship.

IAEA. International Atomic Energy Agency. Established in 1957 in Vienna, it is the UN's agency for helping to prevent the spread of nuclear weapons. It conducts safeguards inspections to verify a state's undertaking not to divert fissile materials from peaceful uses to weapons, and to ensure that it is complying with safety and security standards. However, it has a conflicting mission to promote the peaceful uses of nuclear energy.

ICBM. Inter-Continental Ballistic Missile (5,500-10,000 km range).

ICC. International Criminal Court. Established in 1998, it is the world's first permanent international judicial body capable of trying individuals for genocide, crimes against humanity and war crimes when national courts are unable or unwilling to do so. It is independent of the UN, and sits in The Hague in the Netherlands; its Statute entered into force on 1 July 2002. However, the US withdrew its signature in May 2002, in order that US military should not be liable for prosecution. Since then the US has pressured many states to sign bilateral agreements excluding US military from prosecution under each state's jurisdiction. The ICC has eighteen judges elected for nine years by the 139 states parties to the court's statute.

ICJ. International Court of Justice. Also known as the World Court, it sits in the Peace Palace at The Hague. It is the principal judicial organ of the UN and the supreme tribunal ruling on questions of international law. The Court comprises fifteen judges drawn from the different legal systems of the world. The UN Security Council and General Assembly elect them for nine years. They are under oath to act impartially and are paid by the General Assembly. As a general practice, however, there are nearly always judges from the five permanent members of the Security Council. The Court's two functions are to decide legal disputes between states (known as contentious cases) and to give advisory opinions. The Security Council and General Assembly may request an advisory opinion on any legal question. Other UN organs and specialized agencies, such as the World Health Organisation, may also request advisory opinions on legal questions arising within the scope of their responsibilities.

International Association of Lawyers Against Nuclear Arms. In 1989, lawyers from all over the world joined together to influence governmental policy toward the total abolition of nuclear weapons and keeping nuclear disarmament a fundamental issue on the international political agenda. They offer legal advice to governments on nuclear disarmament (see wwwdalana.org).

International Peace Bureau. Founded in 1892, the IPB is the world's oldest and most comprehensive peace federation. It was awarded the Nobel Peace Prize in 1910, and has its offices in Geneva, Switzerland (see www.ipb.org).

International Physicians for the Prevention of Nuclear War. Founded in 1982, IPPNW is a non-partisan global federation of medical organizations dedicated to research, education, and advocacy relevant to the prevention of nuclear war. To this end, IPPNW seeks to prevent all wars, to promote non-violent conflict resolution, and to minimize the effects of war and preparations for war on health, development, and the environment. It was awarded the Nobel Peace Prize in 1985 (see www.ippnw.org).

JCPOA. Joint Comprehensive Plan of Action successfully negotiated in 2015 by the P5 plus Germany and the EU, whereby Iran agreed to restrict its uranium enrichment programme under IAEA supervision, in exchange for relief from nuclear-related economic sanctions.

Kiloton. Explosive power equivalent to 1000 tons of TNT (Trinitrotoluene), a conventional chemical explosive.

Launch Under Attack. Also known as **launch-on-warning.** Because of the fear that a pre-emptive first strike could decapitate the centre of decision-making, both the US and Soviet Union still each keep over 1000 strategic nuclear warheads ready at minutes' notice to launch before the other side's first strike arrives.

Massive Retaliation. The first announced US nuclear deterrence strategy 1954-1960, threatening a 'tripwire' response of instant all-out strikes to destroy major Soviet cities and civilian (**counter-value**) targets as punishment for conventional aggression against NATO territory in Europe.

Minimum Deterrence. China, the UK and France claim that their much smaller nuclear arsenals would achieve enough assured destruction to be credible. This encompasses whatever level of capability that states consider necessary. Thus, the UK has defined its Trident submarine force as a 'minimum deterrent', despite the fact that it represents a major increase in firepower over the Polaris force it replaced, at a time when the Russian capability has markedly declined.

MAD. Mutual Assured Destruction. This phrase was coined by Robert McNamara. He stressed that this was not a nuclear deterrence strategy: rather, it was how he described the nuclear posture or relationship between the US and Soviet Union by the late 1960s, when both had the ability to launch a pre-emptive **first strike** using **counter-force** missiles against the other's nuclear forces and command centres, and had deployed a relatively invulnerable **second-strike** force based in submarines with **counter-value** targets of each other's cities and economic infrastructure.

NATO. North Atlantic Treaty Organisation, the biggest military alliance of Western states (see www.nato.int).

Negative Security Assurances. These are undertakings by possessor states not to use nuclear weapons against non-nuclear states that are signatories of the NPT. However, they are non-binding. Moreover, recently the US, UK and France have weakened them by stating that they reserve the right to use nuclear weapons in response to WMD attacks by non-nuclear states against their vital interests, which are unspecified.

No First Use. A nuclear deterrence strategy, currently only declared by China, where the possessor state announces that it will not initiate nuclear war, but will only retaliate to a first strike. NATO refuses to adopt this strategy, on the basis that it is only declaratory and that it wishes to strengthen the credibility of its nuclear deterrence posture by not ruling out first use, especially if attacked with other weapons of mass destruction such as chemical or biological weapons.

NPT. Nuclear Non-Proliferation Treaty. The most important treaty on nuclear weapons, it was opened for signature in 1968 and entered into force on 5 March 1970. Its objective is to prevent the spread of nuclear weapons and to further the goal of achieving general and complete disarmament. The NPT's duration was originally limited to twenty-five years, and Review Conferences have been held every five years since 1975. In 1995, the NPT was extended indefinitely, but with a strengthened review process. There are 189 signatory states, comprising five recognized nuclear weapon states and 184 non-nuclear states, with only India, Israel and Pakistan refusing to sign; but in January 2003 North Korea announced its withdrawal from the NPT, citing US hostility and a crisis over inspections of its nuclear facilities by the IAEA. The NPT is criticized as legitimizing the division of the world into nuclear 'haves' and 'have-nots', and it imposes stringent controls on the latter while the obligations on the former are not so strict or enforceable. Also, it ignores the insurmountable link between the military and peaceful uses of nuclear technology, highlighted by the double role of the IAEA as promoter and controller of nuclear energy.

Nuclear Deterrence. In comparison to conventional weapons, nuclear devices represent an almost unimaginable step change, both in intensity and extent of destructive power and poisonous, persisting after-effects. This means that nuclear deterrence threatens unacceptable damage extending beyond the opponent's territory with the potential to affect the entire planet through radioactive fallout and the 'nuclear winter' phenomenon.

Nuclear Sharing. The US introduced this concept to its European NATO allies in the late 1950s, in response to their fears that Europe was being detached for use as a nuclear battleground in exchange for the US restricting its nuclear targets to Soviet forces. The US provided free-fall nuclear bombs to seven NATO allies in Europe, six of them nonnuclear states (Belgium, Germany, Greece, Italy, Netherlands and Turkey – the UK was the seventh). Host states joined NATO's Nuclear Planning Group. These arrangements were designed to symbolize a US guarantee to sustain extended deterrence and the hosts' commitment to sharing its benefits and risks. Greece withdrew in 2001, and the US moved its free-fall arsenal from the UK to Germany in 2008.

Nuclear Winter. A hypothetical global climate condition predicted to be a possible outcome of a nuclear war. Cold weather would be caused by detonating large numbers of nuclear weapons, especially over flammable targets such as cities, where large amounts of smoke and soot would be injected into the Earth's stratosphere. These would be blown by strong west-to-east winds, forming a uniform belt of particles encircling the northern hemisphere from 30° to 60° latitude. Thick black clouds could block out much of the sun's light for a period as long as several weeks, causing surface temperatures to drop by as much as 20°C. The combination of darkness and low temperatures, combined with high doses of radioactive fallout, would severely damage plant life in the region. These effects, combined with the widespread destruction of industrial, medical, and transportation infrastructures plus food supplies, would trigger a massive death toll from starvation, exposure, and disease. (See www.nucleardarkness.org)

OECD. The Organisation for Economic Cooperation and Development has 30 member states, who share a commitment to democratic government and the market economy.

P5. The five permanent members of the UN Security Council: the US, Russia, China, France and the UK.

Pax Christi. An international Catholic movement for peace, founded in 1950.

Perimetr. The codename of a secret Russian command back-up system comprising a dedicated communications missile which, in the event of communications being lost between the President and the main nuclear command and control centre following a US first strike, would be automatically launched to transmit the codes to launch Russia's strategic nuclear forces.

Polaris. The first US second-strike submarine-launched nuclear-armed ballistic missile system, which became operational in 1960. The UK purchased the system in 1962, Fitting it in four *Resolution* class submarines, scaled-down versions of the *George Washington* class.

SDI. Strategic Defense Initiative. In 1983 President Ronald Reagan announced his vision of a national ballistic missile defence system that would obviate the need to maintain a nuclear arsenal, and spell the end of what he described as the immoral strategy of nuclear deterrence that had triggered the nuclear arms race and was leading humanity to the brink of destruction. Officially called SDI, it was quickly dubbed 'Star Wars', but despite expenditure of some US$70 billion, it could not be made to work. However, President George W Bush revived a more modest version of it in 2001.

Second Strike. The launch of relatively invulnerable submarine-based strategic nuclear warheads in retaliation for a first strike from those systems which survive a first strike, or are invulnerable to one.

SIOP. Single Integrated Operational Plan. First promulgated by the US in 1960, this coordinated the nuclear targeting of the three armed forces. This was then extended to NATO nuclear forces under the Nuclear Sharing arrangements. It has been regularly updated since then.

SORT. Strategic Offensive Reductions Treaty. Signed by the US and Russia in Moscow in May 2002, both sides agreed to reduce their strategic arsenals to 1,700-2,200 by 2012. However, there was no requirement for verification or irreversibility, allowing obsolete warheads to be placed in storage rather than being dismantled; and the treaty expires in 2012. In 2010, SORT was effectivley superseded by the New Strategic Arms Reduction Treaty (New START); and the US and Russia recently reached the missile launcher levels required by the treaty.

START I, II and III. Three Strategic Arms Reduction Treaties between the US and Russia. START I, signed in 1991, entered into force in 1994. START II was signed in 1993 by Presidents George Bush Sr and Boris Yeltsin, and ratified by both countries; however, it was overtaken by SORT before it could enter into force. In 1997, Presidents Clinton and Yeltsin agreed a negotiating framework for START III once START II entered into force, which would have resulted in verified, irreversible reductions of strategic nuclear warheads to equivalent levels to those in SORT.

Sub-Critical Testing. Following a self-imposed moratorium on underground nuclear testing in 1993, the US introduced a 'Stockpile Stewardship' programme covering nuclear weapons research, development, testing, production and disassembly. In exchange for banning full-scale tests, nuclear weapon design is being continued through simulations using super-fast computers. New diagnostic information is being obtained from inertial confinement, pulsed power and chemical explosive-driven fusion experiments in the National Ignition Facility, a huge laser fusion research device at Lawrence Livermore National Laboratory in California. Other experiments include above-ground hydrodynamic explosions at the Dual Axis Radiographic Hydrotest Facility, and sub-critical `zero yield' underground tests at the Nevada test site. The UK is collaborating closely with this US programme, while France has built similar test facilities.

TPNW. Treaty on Prohibition of Nuclear Weapons, adopted by the UN General Assembly on 7 July 2017.

Trident. The current US second-strike submarine-launched nuclear-armed ballistic missile system. The UK leases Trident II-D5 missiles from the US, deploying them in four *Vanguard* class submarines, scaled-down versions of the US *Ohio* class.

UK. United Kingdom.

UN. United Nations.

US. United States of America.

USS. United States Ship.

WMD. Weapons of Mass Destruction. These are currently understood to cover nuclear, radiological, chemical and biological weapons.

SELECTED BIBLIOGRAPHY

Baylis, John, *Ambiguity and Deterrence* (Oxford University Press, 1995).

Betts, Richard K., *Nuclear Blackmail and Nuclear Balance* (Brookings Institution Press, Washington, D.C., 1987).

Blake, Nigel & Pole, Kay eds, *Dangers of Deterrence: Philosophers on Nuclear Strategy* (Routledge & Keagan Paul, London, 1983).

Bobbitt, Philip, *Democracy and Deterrence – The History and Future of Nuclear Strategy* (Macmillan, London, 1988).

Booth, Ken and Baylis, John, *Britain, NATO and Nuclear Weapons* (St Martin's Press, New York, 1989).

Booth, Ken ed., *Statecraft and Security – The Cold War and Beyond* (Cambridge University Press, 1998).

Boyle, Francis A., *The Criminality of Nuclear Deterrence* (Clarity Press, Inc., Atlanta, 2002).

Burroughs, John, *The (Il)legality of Threat or Use of Nuclear Weapons: A Guide to the Historic Opinion of the International Court of Justice* (Lit Verlag, Munster, 1997).

Butler, George Lee, General United States Air Force, Retired, *Uncommon Cause: A Life at Odds with Convention* (Outskirts Press, Inc., 2016).

Cimbala, Stephen, *Nuclear Strategizing: Deterrence and Reality* (Praeger Publishers, New York, 1998). Also *Military Persuasion – Deterrence and Provocation in Crisis and War* (Pennsylvania State University Press, 1994).

Coker, Christopher, *British Defence Policy in the 1990s* (Brassey's, London, 1987).

Datan, Merav and Ware, Alyn, *Securing Our Survival (SOS): The Case for a Nuclear Weapons Convention* (International Physicians for the Prevention of Nuclear War, 2007).

Dauber, Cori Elizabeth, *Cold War Analytical Structures and the Post Post-War World* (Praeger Publishers, Westport, 1993).

Ellsberg, Daniel, *The Doomsday Machine: Confessions of a Nuclear War Planner* (Bloomsbury USA, 2017).

Freedman, Lawrence, *The Evolution of Nuclear Strategy* (St Martin's Press, NewYork, 1981; Macmillan, London, 1989).

Gorbachev, Mikhail, *Memoirs* (Doubleday, Transworld Publishers, London, 1996).

Halperin, Morton, *Nuclear Fallacy* (Ballinger, Cambridge, MA, 1987).

Hersh, Seymour M., *The Samson Option: Israel, America and the Bomb* (Random House, New York, Faber and Faber, London, 1991 and 1993).

Heuser, Beatrice, *Nuclear Mentalities? Strategies and Beliefs in Britain, France and the FRG* (Macmillan Press, London, 1998).

Jervis, Robert, *The Illogic of American Nuclear Strategy* (Cornell University Press, 1984).

Karp, Regina Cowen ed., (1991) *Security with Nuclear Weapons?* (Oxford University Press, 1991). Also *Security Without Nuclear Weapons? Different Perspectives on Non-Nuclear Security* (Oxford University Press, 1992).

Kenny, Anthony, *The Logic of Deterrence* (University of Chicago Press, 1985).

Lange, David, *Nuclear Free – The New Zealand Way* (Penguin Books, Auckland, 1991).

Lebow, R. Ned and Stein, Janice, *We All Lost the Cold War* (Princeton University Press, 1994).

Lee, Stephen R, *Morality, prudence and nuclear weapons* (Cambridge University Press, 1993).

Moeller, Bjorn, *Dictionary of Alternative Defense* (Lynne Rienner Publishers, Boulder, 1995).

Moxley, Charles J., *Nuclear Weapons and International Law in the Post Cold War World* (Austin & Winfield, Lanham, MD, 2000).

Mueller, John, *Retreat from Doomsday: The Obsolescence of Major War* (Basic Books, New York, 1989).

Paterson, Robert H., *Britain's Strategic Nuclear Deterrent* (Frank Cass & Co. Ltd, London, 1997).

Payne, Keith B., *The Fallacies of Cold War Deterrence and a New Direction* (The University of Kentucky Press, Lexington, 2001).

Perkovich, George, *India's Nuclear Bomb: The Impact on Global Proliferation* (University of California Press, 1999).

Perkovich, George and Acton, James M., Editors, *Abolishing Nuclear Weapons: A Debate* (Carnegie Endowment for International Peace, 2009).

Pope-Hennessy, James, *Sins of the Fathers: A Study of the Atlantic Slave Traders 1441-1807* (Weidenfeld and Nicholson, London, 1968).

Powell, Colin, *A Soldier's Way* (Hutchinson, London, 1995).

Quinlan, Michael, *Thinking About Nuclear Weapons* (Royal United Services Institute for Defence Studies, Whitehall, London, 1997). Also *Thinking About Nuclear Weapons: Principles, Prospects, Problems* (Oxford University Press, 2009).

Schell, Jonathan, *The Fate of the Earth* (Pan Books Ltd, London, 1982); *The Abolition* (Avon Books, New York, 1984); *The Gift of Time: The Case for Abolishing Nuclear Weapons Now* (Metropolitan Books, New York, 1998); and *The Seventh Decade: The New Shape of Nuclear Danger* (Metropolitan Books, New York, 2007).

Steinbruner, John D., *Principles of Global Security* (Brookings Institution Press, Washington, D.C., 2000).

Wilson, Ellen Gibson, *Thomas Clarkson: A Biography* (Macmillan, London, 1989).

Vanaik, Achin & Bidwai, Praful, *New Nukes* (Olive Branch Press, Interlink Publishing, 1999).

Zelter, Angie, *Trident on Trial: the case for people's disarmament* (Luath Press, Edinburgh, 2001).

Zuckerman, Solly, *Monkeys, Men, and Missiles – An Autobiography 1946-88* (WW Norton & Company, New York/London, 1988).

INDEX

A-4E Skyhawk 127, 128
Abkhazia 230
Acton, James 75, 264
Advani, L.K. 150
Advisory Opinion, 1996 9, 33, 55, 69, 181, 185-187, 204, 219, 229, 246
Afghanistan 29, 46, 97, 139, 141, 142, 154, 211, 219, 231, 236
Agni 140, 143, 149
Agni-II 156,
Ailleret, General 71
Alamagordo 37
Albania 235
Algeria 70
Allon, Yigal 126
Al Qaeda 155, 156
Anti-Ballistic Missile/ABM Treaty 17, 20, 60, 94, 211, 247
Arbatov, Alexei 212
Argentina 18, 30, 71, 121, 140, 209, 218, 245
Ark Royal, HMS 27
Arkin, William 60, 64, 104, 106, 189
Armitage, Richard 156
Assured Destruction 49-51, 54, 66, 88
Atlas 48
Atomic Weapons Establishment, Aldermaston 41, 43
Attlee, Clement 38, 39
Auschwitz 33
Australia 45, 46, 48, 55, 56, 101, 148, 202, 214, 218, 232, 238, 248
Australia/New Zealand/US (ANZUS) Alliance/Treaty 177, 214, 215, 228
Austria 202, 226, 228, 235
Axworthy, Lloyd 56
Aziz, Shaukat 160
Aziz, Tariq 106
B61-12 nuclear bomb 76, 231
B61 Mod 11 nuclear bomb 103
Baghdad 32, 33, 59, 123
Bahamas 41
Baker, James 106
Ball, Murray 10
Ballistic Missile Defence/BMD 19, 46, 47, 160
Ban Ki-moon 15, 121
Bangkok Southeast Asian Nuclear Weapon Free Zone 226, 228

Baylis, John 38, 262
Bedjaoui, Mohammed 181
Beg, Aslam, General 144, 157
Begin, Menachem 130, 131
Belarus 21, 52, 218, 228, 230
Belgium 49, 57, 229, 231
Benedict, Pope 182
Benghazi 45
Ben-Gurion, David 123-126
Bergmann, Ernst 124
Berlin Wall 32, 213, 230
Bertrand Russell Peace Foundation 10
Bhabha, Homi 134-136, 138
Bharatiya Janata Party/BJP 140, 145, 148-150, 157, 159
Bhutan 148
Bhutto, Benazir 142, 143, 149, 151
Bhutto, Zulfikar Ali 135, 138, 139
Bidwai, Praful 150, 264
Biological Weapons Convention 234
Blackham, Sir Jeremy, Vice Admiral (Ret'd) 10, 13, 262
Blair, Bruce 113-114, 221
Blair, Tony 43, 46, 193-194, 237, 249
Blix, Hans 176, 220
Blue Streak 40
Bobbit, Philip 101, 262
Booth, Ken 108, 262
Bosnia and Herzegovina 235, 265
Bougainville 215
Boyle, Francis 111, 262
Brazil 55, 71, 121, 218, 225, 245
Brown, Des 99
Brown, Gordon 46
Brownlie, Professor 189
Brzezinski, Zibigniew 141
Buccaneer 27, 266
Buenos Aires 30
Bulgaria 228
Bundy, McGeorge 101
Bush, George H, Sr 32, 33, 53, 54, 144, 147, 214
Bush, George W, Jr 20, 46, 58-60, 62-64, 66, 75, 77, 78, 98, 102-104, 106, 108, 115, 155, 158, 160, 176, 184, 186, 210-212, 236, 247
Butler, Lee, General USAF (Ret) 10, 52, 53, 87, 90, 102, 104, 107, 110-114, 154, 155, 178, 179, 183, 215, 246,

249, 262
Buzzard, Sir Anthony, Rear Admiral 39, 48, 88
Cameron, David 16, 18
Canada 37, 55, 56, 105
Canberra, Commission 87, 91, 218, 220, 221
Carter, Jimmy 130, 139-141
Carver, Field Marshal Lord 28
Casey, William 141
Castro 86
Central Europe Nuclear Weapon Free Zone 228, 232
Chagai 150, 159
Chagos Archipelago 43
Chashma 135, 161
Chechnya 210, 211, 230, 235
Chemical Weapons Convention 203, 222, 223, 234
Cheney, Dick 60, 63, 107
Chernobyl 31, 93, 215
Chirac, Jacques 47, 72, 73
Chou En-Lai 138
Christmas Island 39
Churchill 38, 97
Cimbala, Stephen 96, 101, 262
CIRUS 138, 149
Clinton, Bill 53, 64, 62, 145-153, 215, 218, 220, 246
Cohen, Avner 127
Collins, Robin 10
Comprehensive Nuclear Test Ban Treaty/CTBT 14, 22, 23, 146, 148, 151, 213
Conference on Disarmament 148
Conference on Security and Co-operation in Europe/CSCE 235
Controlled Response 47-49, 54, 66, 70
Conventional Forces in Europe Treaty 47
Corbyn, Jeremy 78
Cordoba 30
Costa Rica 223
Counter-force 51, 69
Counter-value 51
Crimea 76, 210, 230
Crimean War 28
Croatia 235
Cruise missiles 29
Cuba/Cuban missile crisis 40, 49, 85-88, 105, 110
Cyprus 46
Czech Republic, the 47, 228
Dassault 127
Datan, Merav 263
Dayan, Moshe, General 126, 128
De Gaulle, Charles, General 70, 71, 73, 123, 125, 128
Del Tredici, Robert 10

Deir al-Zor 132
Denmark 49, 214
Desai, Morarji 139
D'Estaing, Giscard 97, 98, 100
Dewes, Kate 10
Diego Garcia 43, 44, 46, 245
Dimona 123-126, 128, 129, 131, 161
Dolphin submarines 132
Doomsday Clock 76
Downer, Alexander 218
Dreadnought 43
Dresden 97
Dulles, John Foster 38
Dunkerton, Martin 10
Dunlap, Charles J., Colonel USAF 178, 192
Dutt, Som, Major General 135, 137
Dvorkin, Vladimir 212
Eagle, HMS 27
East Timor 215
EastWest Institute 221
ECHELON 44
Egypt 55, 123, 125, 127, 128, 130
Eisenhower, Dwight 97, 123-125
Ekeus, Rolf 106
Electro-Magnetic Pulse 102
Ellsberg, Daniel 263
Enewetak Atoll 38
Enterprise, USS 137
Escalation Dominance 51
Eshkol, Levi 126
European Court of Human Rights, Strasbourg 44
European Union/EU 46, 122, 133, 236, 238, 248
Evans, Gareth 228
Exocet 30
Extended nuclear deterrence 47, 66, 101
F-4 Phantom 128, 129
F-15 132
F-16 123, 132, 140, 145, 146, 148
F-111 45
Falk, Richard 176
Falkland Islands 18, 29, 30, 209
Falwell, Jerry 177
Faslane Naval Base 198
Finland 228
First Use 51
Fischer, Joschka 55
Fleet Air Arm 27
Flexible Response 16, 17, 50, 51, 54, 57, 58, 66, 88
Foreign & Commonwealth Office/FCO 44
Formosa Strait 91
Francis, Pope 182
Freedman, Sir Lawrence 87, 263
Fylingdales 46

Gaddafi, Muammar, Colonel 45, 158, 162
Galili, Israel 126
Galtieri, General 30
Gandhi, Indira 95, 135-137, 139, 140
Gandhi, Mahatma 133, 249
Gandhi, Rajiv 141-143, 145, 149, 159
Gates, Robert 144
Gaza 198
General Assembly, UN 21, 33, 55, 56, 140, 148, 186, 187, 202, 221, 225, 247
Geneva Conventions 64, 184, 195, 197, 247
Genocide Convention 180
Germany 48, 49, 55, 57, 71, 72, 90, 91, 97, 122, 132, 133, 186, 210, 229, 231
Georgia 230
Ghauri 149, 159
Gibraltar 45
Goldstein, Barukh 132
Gorbachev, Mikhail 53, 77, 92-94, 101, 142, 145, 212, 216, 217, 245, 248, 263
Government Communication Headquarters (GCHQ), Cheltenham 45
Gray, Colin 85
Greece 49, 140, 228
Green, Thomas 10
Grechko, Andre, Marshal 127
Gujral, Inder 148, 149
Gulf War, 1990-91 32, 33, 52, 63, 71, 77, 102, 106, 131, 145, 197, 214
Hague Conventions 180, 197
Halperin, Morton 183, 263
Hanly, Gil 10
Har-Even, Avi 131
Hatf-1 143
Hatf-2 143
Hatf-3 149
Hayes, Peter 108
Heikal, Mohammed 127
Helsinki, Final Act 235
Hersh, Seymour 32, 122, 131, 263
Heuser, Beatrice 73, 263
Hiroshima 14, 15, 28, 34, 37, 77, 90, 176, 180, 188, 189, 199, 203, 244
Hitler 37, 123
Hoon, Geoff 99, 103
House of Lords 28, 44, 183
Howe, Lord 190
Hungary 228
Hussein, Saddam 32, 33, 46, 59, 64, 76, 77, 107
Iceland 49, 93
Ikle, Fred 88
India 23, 47, 55, 58, 62, 66, 68, 71, 95, 96, 108, 110, 111, 115, 121, 122, 133-161, 209-211, 228, 237, 243, 245, 246, 249
Indochina 91, 111

Intermediate-Range Nuclear Forces Treaty 17, 20, 22, 47
International Atomic Energy Authority /IAEA 122, 125, 134, 226
International Campaign to Abolish Nuclear Weapons/ICAN 9, 202, 203
International Commission on Nuclear Non-proliferation and Disarmament 228
International Committee of the Red Cross 202
International Court of Justice/ICJ 9, 55, 69, 146, 148, 186, 187, 188, 190-193, 195-202, 219, 229, 246, 247
International Criminal Court 44, 198, 217, 219
International Physicians for the Prevention of Nuclear War/IPPNW 223
Iran 23, 53, 61, 63, 108, 122, 130, 133, 158, 159, 210
Iraq 32, 45, 46, 52, 53, 61, 63, 64, 71, 76, 102, 104, 106, 115, 121, 130, 132, 140, 189, 196, 200, 209, 211, 212, 230, 234, 236, 245
Ireland 55
Irish Republican Army 33
Iskander IRBM 20, 76
Israel 17, 23, 32, 33, 55, 59, 66, 68, 71, 108, 115, 121-133, 148, 157, 161, 196-198, 209-211, 228, 237, 245, 246
Italy 48, 49, 57, 91, 186, 231
Japan 13, 29, 48, 55, 56, 62, 90, 91, 101, 105, 110, 128, 148, 187, 213, 214, 218, 221, 227-229, 232, 238, 248
Jayaraman, Dr T. 154
Jericho I 127, 129
Jericho II 131
Jiang Zemin 222
Johnson, Lyndon 125, 126, 128
Johnson, Rebecca 10
Joint Comprehensive Plan of Action/JCPOA 122, 133
Joint Data Exchange Center 220
Jong-un, Kim 10, 76, 78, 203
Jupiter ICBM 86
Just War doctrine 179
Kahn, Herman 88
Kahuta 138, 140, 146
Kalam, Abdul 140, 145, 146, 149, 150, 158
Kaliningrad 20, 76, 228
Kaluchak 156
Kargil 66, 96, 115, 152, 153, 156, 157
Kashmir 95, 110, 133, 135, 143, 149, 150, 152, 154, 155
Kasuri, Khurshid 160, 161
Kawaguchi, Yoriko 228
Kazakhstan 21, 52, 218, 226
Kehler, Robert, General USAF (Ret) 203
Kelly, Tom 107
Kennan, George 90, 101, 108, 232

Kennedy, John F. 40, 41, 48, 70, 77, 85, 88, 105, 125, 126
KH-11 130
Khan, Abdul Qadir/A.Q. 138, 142, 147, 150, 158-160, 162, 246
Khan, Ayub 135
Khan, Ishaq 144
Khan, Yahya 137
Khomeini 130
Khushab 161
King's Bay, Georgia 41
Kiribati 40
Kissinger, Henry 74-76, 78, 101, 107, 128, 129, 137, 138
Korea/Korean War 38, 47, 91, 92, 97, 111
Kosovo 62, 235, 236
Krieger, David 10
Kristensen, Hans 64, 68, 69
Khrushchev 85, 86, 105
Kuwait 32, 209, 214
Kyrgyzstan 226
Lange, David 74, 177, 214, 229, 249, 263
Launch On Warning 112-114
Lebanon 198
Lebow and Stein 105, 263
Lewis, Patricia 234
Li Peng 145
Libya 45, 53, 61, 63, 102, 148, 158, 159, 245
Livermore, Lawrence 41
Lord Advocate 199
Los Alamos 41, 59
Luxembourg 49, 229
M4 ICBM 71
M45 ICBM 71
M51 ICBM 72
Macmillan, Harold 40, 41, 70, 77, 89
Magoudi, Ali 30
Major, John 72
Makhoul, Issam 131
Manhattan Project 33, 77, 123, 161, 244, 245
Mao Tse Tung 138
Marcoule 123
Massive Retaliation 38, 40, 47-49, 66
Mastny, Vojtech 90
MAUD Committee Report 37
Mauritius 44
Mayors for Peace 217
MccGwire, Michael, Commander RN (Ret'd) 10, 11, 91, 92, 96, 222, 234
McMahon Act 33, 38, 40
McNamara, Robert 40, 48-50, 70, 86, 87, 102
Mead, Margaret 249
Menwith Hill, RAF 44, 46
Mexico 55, 105, 140, 202, 226

Meyer, Sir Christopher 46
Ministry of Defence/MoD 29, 42, 44, 197, 266
Minuteman ICBM 86, 113
Mirage IV 71
Mitterrand, Francois 30, 70
Mongolia 226, 228
Monte Bello 38
Mountbatten, Earl, Admiral of the Fleet 98, 101
Moynihan, Daniel Patrick 95
Murrell, Hilda 31
Musharraf, Pervez, General 153, 155-158
Mutual Assured Destruction/MAD 17, 49, 50, 52, 58, 60, 63, 75, 112, 114, 211
Mutual Defence Agreement 40, 43
Nagasaki 15, 31, 37, 77, 90, 122, 180, 199, 203, 244
Nassau 41
Nasser, Gamal Abdel 123, 124, 128, 129
National Ignition Facility 43
National Security Agency/NSA 44, 45
NATO 16, 23, 27, 33, 47, 70, 73, 76, 91, 97, 98, 101, 110, 115, 177, 190, 191, 203, 204, 209-211, 213, 221, 226, 228-232, 235, 236, 238, 245, 247
Nayar, Kuldip 142
Negative Security Assurances 219, 227
Nehru, Jawaharlal 133-135, 161
Nepal 228
Netanyahu, Benjamin 132, 133
Netherlands, the 49, 57, 203, 229, 231
Nevada 41
New Agenda Coalition 55, 56, 215
New Zealand 11, 48, 55, 177, 214-215, 217, 218, 221, 226, 228, 229, 248, 249
Nixon, Richard 128, 129, 137
Norris, Robert S. 10, 68
North Korea 10, 22-24, 53, 61, 68, 108, 115, 122, 133, 147, 149, 158, 203, 209, 210, 211, 213, 218, 227, 245
Northeast Asia Co-operative Security Organisation 227
Northeast Asia Nuclear Weapon Free Zone 227, 228
Norway 49, 57, 229
NPT Review Conference 56, 57, 58, 159, 186
Nuclear Non-Proliferation Treaty/NPT 14, 17, 20-23, 48, 53, 57, 63, 71, 121, 128, 135-137, 148, 160, 181, 186, 196, 202, 213, 218, 231, 234, 245, 247
Nuclear Posture Review 60, 62, 76, 186, 210, 229, 231, 248
Nuclear sharing 49
Nuclear Weapon Free Southern Hemisphere 225

Nuclear Weapons Convention 146, 184, 221-225, 229, 234, 236, 237, 238, 248
Nunn, Sam 74-78
Nuremberg Principles 34, 188, 193, 198, 200, 204, 247
Obama, Barack 9, 75, 78, 186, 236
O'Brien, Terence 217
Observer 27
Ofek satellites 131
Omaha 42
Organisation for Security and Co-operation in Europe/OSCE 227, 235-236, 248
Organisation for Security and Co-operation in Europe, North Asia and North America/OSCENANA 235-236, 248
Osama bin Laden 154, 158
Osirak 123, 130, 132, 140
Owens, Bill, Admiral 58
P5 122, 133, 148, 152, 159, 237
Pakistan 23, 47, 55, 58, 62, 66, 68, 71, 95, 96, 108, 110, 111, 115, 121, 122, 133-161, 209, 211, 228, 237, 243-246
Palestine, Liberation Organisation 130, 198
Palme, Olof 216, 248
Pant, K.C. 143
Parliament, UK 43
Partial Nuclear Test Ban Treaty 22, 23
Patriot ABM system 32, 160
Payne, Keith 108, 213, 264
Pearl Harbor 37, 90
Pelindaba African Nuclear Weapon Free Zone Treaty 53
Pentagon 46, 47
Peres, Shimon 124-126
Perimetr 114, 175-176
Perkovich, George 75, 144, 264
Perle, Richard 177
Perrin, Francis 124
Perry, William 74-76, 78, 102
Persian Gulf 91, 111, 132
Philippines, the 214
Pincus, Walter 58, 65
Pluton 71
Plutonium 239 37
Pokhran 139, 150, 151
Poland 46, 228
Polaris 29, 30-32, 41, 43, 48, 49, 50, 70, 77
Portugal 49
Powell, Colin, General 60, 63, 100, 103, 107, 264
Prague speech 75
Pre-emption, Bush Doctrine of 63, 78
Presidential Decision Directive 54, 64
Pressler Amendment 141, 142, 144-146, 148
Prithvi 140, 143, 146, 149, 153

Putin, Vladimir 47, 62, 63, 211, 212, 220
Qasi, Javed Ashraf 157
Queensland 215
Quinlan, Sir Michael 10, 19, 91, 92, 95, 179, 182, 183, 195-198, 217, 244, 264
Rainbow Warrior, Greenpeace flagship 74, 215
Rao, Narasimha 145, 146, 148
Reagan, Ronald 20, 30, 41, 45, 54, 59, 60, 92, 93, 95, 101, 112, 130, 141, 245, 247
Reykjavik, Summit 92-95, 101, 245
Revenge, HMS, SSBN 178
Rice, Condoleezza 109, 160
Romania 228
Roosevelt 37
Rothschild, Emma 96
Royal Air Force/RAF 4
Royal Navy/RN 10, 27-29, 38, 41, 193, 244, 249, 265, 266
Rumsfeld 60, 61
Rydell, Randy 10
Sadat, Anwar 129, 130
Sagan, Scott 106
Samson Option 32, 122, 124, 126, 157
Sandia 41
Sarabhai, Vikram 135, 136, 137
Satan ICBM 62
Schell, Jonathan 34, 87, 93, 113, 114
Schmitt, Michael, Lt Col USAF 192-193
Schwebel, Stephen 197
Scotland 198, 202, 238
Scottish High Court 198-202
Scud-B 32, 33, 59, 131, 158
Sea King 27
Security Council, UN 23, 45, 46, 57, 72, 148, 149, 151, 184, 192, 217, 228-229
Self-Deterrence 97-98
Semipalatinsk Central Asian Nuclear Weapon Free Zone 226, 228
Sethna, Homi 137
Shamir 32, 33
Shanghai Co-operation Organisation 236
Sharif, Nawaz 149, 150-153
Sharon, Ariel 130, 131
Shavit 131
Sheffield, HMS 30
Short, Clare 45
Shultz, George 74-76, 78
Simpson, Tony 10
Singh, K. Natwar 159
Singh, Manmohan 159, 160
Singh, V.P. 143, 145
Single Integrated Operational Plan/SIOP 27, 48, 53
Six-Day War 127, 128
Six-Nation Initiative 140, 141

Sizewell 31
Skybolt 40
Skynet 4 42
Skynet 5 42
Slater, Sir Jock, Admiral 193
Slavery 183, 215-216
Slovakia 228
Slovenia 55
Smith, Gerard 102
Solidarnosc 29
Solomon Islands, the 215
South Africa 21, 55, 121, 130, 218, 245
South Korea 48, 101, 213, 218, 227, 232, 238, 248
South Ossetia 230
South Pacific, Nuclear Weapon Free Zone 214, 215
South Sudan 23
Special Forces 217
St Petersburg 27
Stalin, Josef 71, 90
Stimson, Henry 214
Strategic Arms Limitation Talks/SALT 17, 21
Strategic Arms Reduction Treaty/START 17, 21, 22, 54, 62, 112
Strategic Defence and Security Review/SDSR 16
Strategic Defence Initiative/SDI 20, 92, 94, 95, 245
Strategic Defence Review 43, 220
Strategic Offensive Reductions Treaty/SORT 17, 62, 63, 211, 212
Subrahmanyam, K. 137, 154, 157
Sub-Strategic Nuclear Deterrence 98-100
Suez, Canal 39, 69, 77, 124, 128, 129, 244
Sundarji, K., General 144
Super Etendard 30
Sweden 5, 140, 228, 235
Switzerland 221, 235
Syria 61, 63, 132, 133, 211
Tactical Nuclear Weapon Treaty 232
Taiwan 62, 213, 227
Tajikistan 26
Talbott, Strobe 151
Taliban 46, 155, 236
Tanzania 140
Tel Aviv 32, 59, 123
Tennyson 28
Thatcher, Margaret 29, 30, 41, 45
Theatre Ballistic Missile Defence/TBMD 20, 110
Three Mile Island 29
Tibet 142
Tlatelolco Treaty 218
Treaty on the Prohibition of Nuclear Weapons/TPNW 9, 22, 24, 184, 202-204, 215, 217, 219, 247
Treblinka 33
Trident 10, 16, 29, 30, 41-43, 54, 76, 98, 99, 188, 189, 193, 198-202, 220, 237-239, 244, 249
Trident Ploughshares 198, 203, 204
Triomphant, Le, SSBN 71, 74
Tripoli 45
Trombay 139, 140
Truman 38, 214
Trump, Donald 10, 75-78, 186, 203, 204, 210, 212, 229, 231, 236, 248
Turkey 49, 55, 105, 228, 231
Turkmenistan 226
UK Atomic Energy Authority 124
Ukraine, the 21, 52, 90, 210, 218, 228, 230
Uncommon Cause 10
UN Convention on the Law of the Sea 226
United Nations, UN 21, 23
Uranium 235 37
US Air Force/USAF 45
US Navy 42, 45, 48
US Nuclear Posture Review 53, 58
Uzbekistan 226
Vajpayee, Atal Behari 140, 148-150, 152, 153, 155, 156, 159
Vanaik, Achin 150, 264
Vanguard, HMS, SSBN 41-43, 74, 249
Vanunu, Mordechai 131
Vengeance, HMS, SSBN 178
Vietnam 97, 127, 141, 219
W76 42
Ware, Alyn 10, 263
Warsaw Pact 32, 52, 210, 228, 230, 235
WE177 27, 28, 43
Weapons of Mass Destruction Commission 220
Weeramantry, Christopher 189
Weinberger, Caspar 130
Weinstein, John 64
Wheeler, Nicholas 108
Wilson, Harold 43, 44
WMD Awareness Programme 42
World Court Project 9, 33, 186, 193, 195, 202, 204, 217
World Health Organisation 146, 186
Yeltsin, Boris 54, 62, 66, 113
Yom Kippur War 129
York, Herbert 89
Yost, David 97
Younger, Stephen 59
Yugoslavia 210, 229, 230, 235
Zelter, Angie 198, 199, 264
Zia-ul-Haq, General 139, 142
Zuckerman, Sir Solly 40, 264

ABOUT THE FOREWORD'S AUTHOR

VICE ADMIRAL SIR JEREMY BLACKHAM KCB MA AFRUSI

In a 41 year naval career from 1961 to 2002, Sir Jeremy had four sea commands: the minesweeper *HMS Beachampton,* the Tribal Class frigate *HMS Ashanti,* the Type 42 destroyer *HMS Nottingham,* and the Invincible Class aircraft-carrier *HMS Ark Royal* (when he commanded the first RN Task Group off Bosnia). Ashore he filled important staff appointments including Commandant of the Royal Navy Staff College, Director of Naval Plans, Director General Naval Personnel Strategy, Assistant Chief of Naval Staff, Deputy CINC Fleet and was the first Deputy Chief of Defence Staff (Capability), being a key player in the implementation of the Smart Acquisition Initiative, a major change programme.

On leaving the RN in 2002, he spent three years with EADS (European Aeronautic Defence and Space Company, now Airbus), as UK Country President, before becoming an independent consultant. He is Chairman of Sarnmere Consulting Ltd, of Atmaana plc, Deputy Chairman of CondorPM, and was Chair of the Blackheath Conservatoire of Music and the Arts from 2000-2007. He was a Non-Executive Director of Airbus Helicopters UK from 2007-2016, and has been an advisor to several medium and small companies.

He is a former member of the Chief of the Defence Staff's Strategic Advisory Panel. He was a Vice President, Trustee and Associate Fellow of RUSI (Royal United Services Institute) between 1996 and 2010, Editor of the prestigious in-house RN journal *The Naval Review* from 2002-2017, and is a frequent writer on defence, strategic issues and international affairs including acquisition, in many publications and newspapers. He has frequently given evidence to the House of Commons Defence Committee. He speaks and chairs regularly at conferences in UK and abroad, lectures in Public Management at King's College London, and is an external examiner at Kingston University. He holds a BA (Hons) degree in history and philosophy and a Masters degree in Classical Studies, and is an active member of the Association of Business Mentors. He is a Spanish interpreter and is currently learning Afrikaans. His leisure pursuits include music and opera, walking, travel, cricket, reading, theatre and general writing.

ABOUT THE AUTHOR

Photograph: Thomas Green

Commander Robert Green served for twenty years in the British Royal Navy from 1962-82. As a bombardier-navigator, he flew in Buccaneer nuclear strike aircraft and anti-submarine helicopters. On promotion to Commander in 1978, he worked in the Ministry of Defence before his final appointment as Staff Officer (Intelligence) to the Commander-in-Chief Fleet during the Falklands War.

Commander Green chaired the UK affiliate of the World Court Project (1991-2004), an international citizen campaign which led to the International Court of Justice judgment in 1996 that threat or use of nuclear weapons would generally be illegal. From 1998-2002 he was Chair of the Strategic Planning Committee of the Middle Powers Initiative.

Now Co-Director with his wife, Dr Kate Dewes ONZM, of the Disarmament & Security Centre in New Zealand, he is also the author of *The Naked Nuclear Emperor: Debunking Nuclear Deterrence*, and *Fast Track to Zero Nuclear Weapons: The Middle Powers Initiative*. The UK edition of his book, *A Thorn in Their Side: The Hilda Murrell Murder*, was published in 2013. On 28 October 2017, Commander Green gave the first TEDx talk on nuclear deterrence, in Christ's College Old Boys' Theatre, Christchurch – see https://www.youtube.com/watch?v=nH6xkjMNdnk.

His leisure pursuits include enjoying his step-grandchildren, gardening, theatre, music, delving into Maori history and language, and exploring the spectacular scenery of his adopted homeland.